# W. S. Gilbert

# W. S. Gilbert

## A CLASSIC VICTORIAN
## AND HIS THEATRE

JANE W. STEDMAN

OXFORD UNIVERSITY PRESS
1996

Oxford University Press, Walton Street, Oxford OX2 6DP

Oxford New York
Athens Auckland Bangkok Bombay
Calcutta Cape Town Dar es Salaam Delhi
Florence Hong Kong Istanbul Karachi
Kuala Lumpur Madras Madrid Melbourne
Mexico City Nairobi Paris Singapore
Taipei Tokyo Toronto

and associated companies in
Berlin Ibadan

Oxford is a trade mark of Oxford University Press

Published in the United States
by Oxford University Press Inc., New York

British Library Cataloguing in Publication Data
Data available

Library of Congress Cataloging in Publication Data
Stedman, Jane W.
W.S. Gilbert: a classic Victorian and his theatre /
Jane W. Stedman.
p. cm.
Includes bibliographical references (p.  ).
1. Gilbert, W. S. (William Schwenck), 1836–1911.
2. Great Britain—History—Victoria, 1837–1901—Biography.
3. Theater—Great Britain—History—19th century.
4. Dramatists, English—19th century—Biography.
5. Librettists—Great Britain—Biography. I. Title.
PR4714.S74 1996 822'.8—dc20 [B] 95–35533
ISBN 0–19–816174–3

1 3 5 7 9 10 8 6 4 2

Typeset by Hope Services (Abingdon) Ltd
Printed in Great Britain
on acid-free paper by
The Bath Press Ltd
Bath, Avon

*For George*

# CURTAIN-RAISER

WHEN in 1955 I wrote the doctoral dissertation of which this book is a too-long-gestated descendant, Victorian drama was a scarcely recognized field of scholarship. 'But, Jane,' a colleague once said pedantically to me, 'do you not agree that the glory of the nineteenth century is its poetry and fiction, not its drama?' Granting this point, however, does not mean that the Victorian theatre is beneath critical attention. Yet, in those days, scholars and general readers accepted at face value George Bernard Shaw's persuasive dismissal of the theatre from which he himself rose, kicking down the ladder behind him as he went. Fortunately, this point of view has altered, and I hope that in some small measure I have assisted in the welcome change.

In William Schwenck Gilbert's case, this former attitude has led not to neglect but to a proliferation of popular biographies and books, sometimes so-called 'coffee-table books', dealing with the Savoy Operas and their early casts. With few exceptions these biographies have tended to repeat and frequently distort data from one to another, often beginning with Hesketh Pearson's *Gilbert: His Life and Strife* (1957). Although Pearson was invited to use the Gilbert Papers before they were deposited in the British Library, he, like some of his successors, was more interested in Gilbert's temper than his plays, as the title indicates. Unhappily, Pearson's biography contains many errors, and paradoxically the best treatment of Gilbert's relations with Sullivan during their long collaboration is Arthur Jacobs's *Arthur Sullivan: A Victorian Musician* (1984). Luckily, Gilbert's works have been better treated by serious editors and bibliographers such as Reginald Allen, James Ellis, and George Rowell, among whom I should like to include myself as editor of Gilbert's German Reed Entertainments. Critical articles have also increased, although I have made little use of them in this book.

What I have attempted to do here is to reconstruct the life of a nineteenth-century man of the theatre, who began by being compared to Meilhac and Halévy and ended as a standard by which the young George Bernard Shaw was measured: a dramatist who was the most important author of stage comedy between Sheridan and Shaw; a dramatist produced and stimulated by the Victorian theatre, but transcending it; a man whose old age as a country gentleman the *New York Times* said was 'the most English thing that has happened since Shakespeare planted his mulberry tree and applied for a coat-of-arms'.

Gilbert wrote in every theatrical form of his day except that of the highest tragedy; he created an immensely popular body of comic verse and developed, although he did not originate, a satiric style of reviewing the prolific stage of the 1860s and 1870s. He wrote fiction and critical articles (although less well), illustrated his own works in a 'grinning Gothic' kind of fashion, controlled every aspect of theatre production from costume designing to directing, and was the forerunner of the new Drama of Ideas.

I have therefore by no means limited myself to a full discussion of Gilbert's some twenty years of collaboration with Sullivan, but have included in some detail his journalism, his other plays and librettos, and, to a necessarily smaller degree, his fiction, and have tried to see them as his contemporaries saw them or at least to take them seriously as important works in their day (and sometimes worthy of revival in ours). I have, however, tried to make synopses as brief as possible.

Readers familiar with earlier biographies than mine may look in vain for most of the familiar jokes repeated so often; many of them were foisted on Gilbert just as they had been on his comic predecessor H. J. Byron. Others, while funny as a quick retort, are less amusing in the reading than in the telling. I have also deleted or shortened some of Gilbert's speeches—in fact, I have given none at full length—assuming that what I have chosen will be sufficient indication of the threads of his discourse. Nor have I discussed the notorious 'Sod's Opera', allegedly written by Gilbert, because it does not exist. Gilbert's generosity, which *did* exist, is occasionally exemplified. As for his frequent recourse to law, I have felt no necessity to discuss all his injunctions and lawsuits in detail. He wrote for a theatre in which, when he began, the writer counted for very little and the actor or actress did what he or she wished with a play. Gilbert's refusal to accept such a position was important and contributed largely to turning the late Victorian stage from an actor-controlled theatre to an author- and director-controlled one. Finally, I have not felt it necessary to quote letters in full when a few sentences are sufficient. For the full letters of the carpet quarrel, one may, for example, consult Jacobs's biography of Sullivan (the first edition of which is the one I have at times cited).

The three great repositories of Gilbert material, both manuscript and printed are the Gilbert Papers in the British Library; the Gilbert and Sullivan Collection in the Pierpont Morgan Library, and the D'Oyly Carte Papers, formerly in the possession of the late Dame Bridget D'Oyly Carte and now largely deposited in the British Theatre Museum. The latter archive includes correspondence by Gilbert, Sullivan, Richard and Helen D'Oyly Carte, contracts and other business papers relating to the Savoy Theatre and its productions and management, and early prompt-books, including those for original runs and revivals (sometimes misdated by Rupert D'Oyly Carte).

I must here thank these libraries for permission to use and quote from their collections, as well as the Beinecke Library of Yale University, the possessor of Sullivan's holograph diaries, the Folger Shakespeare Library, the National Library of Scotland, the University of Virginia Library, King's College, University of London Archive, the Bodleian Library, the County Record Office of Gloucestershire, the Harvard Theatre Collection, the Henry E. Huntington Library, the Newberry Library, and the Harry Ransom Humanities Research Center, the University of Texas at Austin.

I am especially grateful to the Royal Theatrical Fund, which, as owner of the subsisting copyright in W. S. Gilbert's unpublished works, has kindly given me permission to quote extensively from Gilbert's letters and manuscripts still in copyright.

More thanks are due to the staffs of these libraries and of the former Enthoven Collection, now absorbed into the British Theatre Museum; to all those who in the late 1960s and 1970s willingly talked to me of their childhood memories of Gilbert and Kitty and of their parents' association with them, people, whom I fear, have for the most part gone 'to join the great majority', as the Victorians put it; to others who provided printed and manuscript material, pictures, and memories, and who searched records: Catherine Ashmore, the late George Baker, CBE, the late Jevon Brandon Thomas, Herbert Cahoon, Rosalie Crutchley, R. A. Flicker, J. C. G. George (Kintyre Pursuivant of Arms), Tristram Gilbert, Russell Jackson, Peter Joslin, Thomas O. Jones, Dr Harold Kanthor, Nancy LaBay, Anthony Latham, John Kennedy Melling, Tina Montrose, Suzanne O'Farrell, Fernley Pascoe, the late Emily Paxton, George Rowell, Mollie Sands, David Stone, Commander Talbot, Naomi Tarrant, the late Albert Truelove, Carol Kyros Walker, Brigadier E. T.

Weigall, Robert Whittaker, Timothy Wilson, John Wolfson, Mary Worthington,—all helpful in many ways. Special thanks are owing to Ralph MacPhail, Jr., who has been indefatigably encouraging and has read portions of this typescript. Other names are acknowledged in my footnotes.

I must also acknowledge the kindness of the late Lilian Gordon, who permitted me to read, copy, and make use of the unpublished papers of her father J. M. Gordon, who learned stagecraft under Gilbert and perpetuated his standards; and of the late Phyllis Bevan, who made George Grossmith's letters received available to me and agreed to my publishing excerpts from them.

I am especially grateful to the late Dame Bridget D'Oyly Carte for her generosity in giving me repeated access to her family papers and in giving me 'carte' blanche, so to speak, to publish hitherto unpublished letters, memoranda, and other documents. Her conversation was always an illumination and a great pleasure, and I miss her.

Without the late Reginald Allen, the doyen of Gilbert scholars, this book would be incomplete. I retain a great sense of my indebtedness to his collection, his conversation, and his willingness to share his great knowledge of both Gilbert and Sullivan. To his successor as curator, Fredric Woodbridge Wilson, I owe a debt of much gratitude, combined with a lively sense of pleasure in our many conversations, as well as thanks for reading portions of my typescript. I wish also to thank Arthur Jacobs for his help in making this book possible and for his encouragement and his knowledge.

Had I but footnotes enough and time, acknowledgements to Colin Prestige and Dr Terence Rees would appear on many a page in addition to those which already bear them. The pleasantest and wittiest companions in the quest for Gilbert, they have generously shared knowledge and ideas, and Mr Prestige has read portions of the present manuscript.

I also must express my gratitude for grants and fellowships given me by Roosevelt University, the American Council of Learned Societies, the Fulbright Commission, and the John Simon Guggenheim Memorial Foundation.

And above all, my greatest day-to-day, almost hour-by-hour, debt is to my husband, George C. McElroy, to whom this book is dedicated as a small recompense for his intellectual interest and support; his patient reading of successive drafts of my typescript; his soothing, comforting, and sustaining; and his constant throwing-out lifelines when I seemed to be drowning in a sea of notecards. True happiness for married scholars is adjoining desks in what we still call nostalgically the British Museum.

J.W.S.

*October 1995*

# CONTENTS

# LIST OF PLATES

*(between pages 172 and 173)*

1. One of Gilbert's many self-caricatures. *Reproduced by permission of the Bodleian Library, Oxford, MS Autogr. e.13, fo. 51ʳ.*

2. The rising dramatist of the early 1870s. *From the collection of David Stone.*

3. Herbertina Turner. *Author's collection.*

4. H. J. Byron. *Author's collection.*

5. Gilbert's sketches on a blank page in his bound volume of *Fun. From the collection of Peter Joslin.*

6. Hermann Vezin and Marion Terry in the first production of *Dan'l Druce, Blacksmith. From the collection of David Stone.*

7. Madge Robertson (Mrs Kendal) sees herself in a mirror as the animated statue in *Pygmalion and Galatea. Author's collection.*

8. The Princess Toto. *Author's collection.*

9. Dressed in a burlesque version of a brigand queen's costume, Kate Santley appears in Gilbert and Clay's Princess Toto. *Author's collection.*

10. Sullivan leads a procession. *Author's collection.*

11. Emma Howson, the first Josephine. *Author's collection.*

12. 'The beautiful Miss Fortescue post-Savoy'. *Author's collection.*

13. Sheet music cover for 'If you go in'. *Author's collection.*

14. A cartoonist's view of a Gilbertian first night. *Author's collection.*

15. One of Gilbert's letters to the artist Frank Holl. *Author's collection.*

16. Lucy Gilbert. *Author's collection.*

17. The assured dramatist in mid-life. *Author's collection.*

18. Bucks, blades, ancestors, and bridesmaids surround Durward Lely (Richard Dauntless) and Leonora Braham (Rose Maybud). *Author's collection.*

19. In spite of Carte's urging, *The Yeomen of the Guard* did not reach the stage of the Savoy Theatre until October 1888. (*The Entr'acte*, May 19, 1888.) *Author's collection.*

20. The audience came to admire, but laughed when she said, 'Let us pray.' (*Brantinghame Hall*). *Author's collection.*

# LIST OF FIGURES

# ABBREVIATIONS

| | |
|---|---|
| Bevan Coll | Letters to Grossmith in the collection of Dr James Bevan |
| BL | British Library |
| Bodleian | Bodleian Library, Oxford |
| B/Y | Beinecke Rare Book and MS Library, Yale University |
| DOYC/TM | D'Oyly Carte Papers, including letter copy books, formerly in the possession of the late Dame Bridget D'Oyly Carte, now in TM |
| Folger | Folger Shakespeare Library, Washington DC |
| Huntington | The Huntington Library, San Marino, California |
| JWS | Letters, MSS, and pictures in the collection of the author |
| LC/BL | Licence copy of plays deposited with the Lord Chamberlain, now in BL |
| LG | Material formerly in the possession of the late Lilian Gordon; present whereabouts not known to the author |
| NLS | National Library of Scotland, Edinburgh |
| PML | Material in the Gilbert and Sullivan Coll. in the Pierpont Morgan Library, New York |
| PRO | Public Record Office, London |
| Talbot Corr. | Letters from Gilbert to Mary Talbot, formerly in the possession of her son, Com. Talbot; now in the Pierpont Morgan Library, New York |
| TM | Theatre Museum, Covent Garden, London |
| WSG/BL | Gilbert Papers, British Library |

# NOTES

IN references to manuscript sources, all letters, diaries, drafts, and memoranda are holograph unless otherwise stated. 'Copy' indicates a holograph copy or a pressed copy of the original.

All quotations from Gilbert's works are taken from first editions, unless otherwise stated. For the librettos of the Savoy operas I have used the Oxford World's Classics two-volume edition (1962), this text having been supervised by Dame Bridget D'Oyly Carte. I have very occasionally and tacitly corrected what are obviously changes in performance pronunciation by the light of Reginald Allen's *The First Night Gilbert and Sullivan* (1958), which, as its title indicates, is also the source of librettos as they were performed on opening nights before cuts and other changes were made. For earlier versions of the librettos I have consulted the licence copies, prompt copies, etc.

In quoting from Gilbert's manuscripts and letters, I have, for the most part, preserved his punctuation or lack of it. I have, however, silently added an occasional apostrophe; generally I have not attempted to reproduce his varieties of length in dashes or crossings-out. I have preserved his use of 'don't', which was an acceptable contraction of 'does not' in the nineteenth century. When quoting material already published elsewhere, I have in almost every instance, gone back to the MS sources themselves and used them since earlier transcriptions are sometimes inaccurate in small ways.

I have made use of many press cuttings in Gilbert's own scrapbooks, in the D'Oyly Carte press-cuttings books, in the T. H. Lacy Scrapbooks, etc., and it has frequently proved impossible to discover the name and date of the newspaper from which the cutting comes. In many cases, I have omitted dates when they could be found in order to avoid a plethora of parentheses or footnotes. I have also omitted volume numbers, when they exist, from weekly periodicals.

What is to become of me? Am I destined to revolutionize the art of comic writing? Am I the man who is to write the burlesques and extravaganzas of the future? Are managers of theatres and editors of light literature doomed to fall prostrate at my feet in humble obeisance? Is it to me that society at large must look for its amusement for the next (say) forty years? To these questions I unhesitatingly reply, 'I am! They are! It is!'

W. S. Gilbert, writing as 'A TREMBLING BEGINNER', in 'The Art of Parody', *Fun* (9 Sept. 1865).

# 1

## A Miscellany of Beginnings

First you're born—
*Utopia (Limited)*

'I SUPPOSE you have heard that Mrs Gilbert has a little son and I can assure you she is not a little proud of him,' Catherine Gilbert wrote from Hammersmith to a friend, Mrs West, in Pangbourne.[1]

The little son was William Schwenck Gilbert, born in his maternal grandfather's house, 17 Southampton Street, Strand, on 18 November 1836, seven months before Victoria came to the throne.[2] He outlived her by ten years and made the world from California to the Antipodes, from Canada to India laugh—and very occasionally weep.

William was the only son and eldest child of Dr William Gilbert, a crotchety humanitarian, a naval surgeon, and, upon receiving a comfortable inheritance, a traveller *en famille* and man of letters. His mother was Anne Mary Bye Morris, daughter of a Scottish surgeon, who must have conceived her son on or shortly after her wedding night (12 February 1836) and who was Dr Gilbert's second wife.[3] The couple were then living with her father, Dr Thomas Morris, and on 11 January 1837 had their baby christened at the nearby church of St Paul, Covent Garden, an edifice which came to be called 'the actors' church'. David Garrick had lived nearby.

Gilberts appeared in the 'Domesday Book', according to Gilbert père's imperfect genealogical investigations late in life. They were originally Hampshire and Wiltshire yeomen, and it was a pleasant fancy of

---

[1] 26 Dec. 1836: WSG/BL Add. MS 49,345.

[2] Interestingly enough, the great-grandfather of the Gilbert and Sullivan scholar Colin G. Prestige lived at 9 Southampton Street as a small child. A month older than William Schwenck, George Prestige probably played with him.

[3] William Gilbert's first wife was a minor, Mary Ann Skelton, whom he married on 5 Sept. 1832 at St James's, Westminster. He himself lived at Clapham. The date of Mary Ann Gilbert's death is unknown. I am indebted for this information to Colin Prestige.

Gilbert fils that the Elizabethan Sir Humphrey Gilbert was his ancestor. But although an image of Sir Humphrey's squirrel crest adorned
one of his houses and his signet ring, as well as forming a diamond
brooch for his wife, the relationship remained a fancy.

The elder Gilbert had been born in 1804, the son of William Gilbert,
a grocer in Commercial Row, Blackfriars, who lived only until 1812. His
wife had died two years earlier, her tuberculosis perhaps intensified by
the birth of her youngest child Jane in 1809. Between William and
Jane, Joseph Mathers Gilbert had been born and named for his
mother's family. These children, now orphaned, were left to the care of
Mary and John Samuel Schwenck by their father's will. Mary was their
mother's sister, then 35 years old and childless, but she proved so affectionate a surrogate mother that both William and Joseph named their
sons after her: William Schwenck Gilbert and Francis Schwenck
Gilbert, who were also her godsons.

In 1830 when he was 26 William Gilbert became a member of the
Royal College of Surgeons, and six years later married Dr Morris's
daughter in the presence of her father, sister, and brother-in-law
(Harriet and J. W. Edwards), his brother and sister, and John Samuel
Schwenck. Family connections were maintained all round, and it was
Dr Morris whom W. S. Gilbert years later described as the last man in
London to wear a pigtail and Hessian boots.

When the youngest William was not yet 2, and only a few months
before his first sister, Jane Morris Gilbert, was born in October 1838, Dr
William and Anne were on their way to Florence from Naples. If we
believe his memory, their first-born had already had an adventure in
the city they were leaving. His foolish nurse had delivered him up to a
pair of brigands, who told her 'the English gentleman' wanted his baby.
Bab, as his parents called him, remembered riding in front of a
mounted man along a street, which he long after recognized as the Via
Posilippo, toward mountains, from where £25 and a small detachment
of *carabinieri* rescued him. The episode is appropriately Babish and
brigandish, and he told it to his first biographer when he was 70 years
old. It suggests, however, not so much an exact event as a tale often told
and embellished by his parents during his childhood, very likely arising from a much less serious predicament. For one thing, there is no
record of such a kidnapping,[4] while, for another, Gilbert's recognition

---

[4] Dr Leon E. A. Berman has made an extensive search without finding any reference to such
a kidnapping: 'The Kidnapping of W. S. Gilbert', *Journal of the American Psychoanalytic
Association* (May 1985), 133–48.

of the street would be explained as *déjà vu*. (Nor, as often alleged, is there any evidence that Sir David Wilkie, struck by Gilbert's childish beauty, asked to paint his portrait.)

The family continued to travel, sometimes returning to Hammersmith, but setting out again. By the time Bab was 9, he had three sisters and in 1845 his mother returned from France to wean Anne Maude, the youngest.[5] Meanwhile, both Dr Gilbert's sister and brother had died of tuberculosis in 1841. Joseph and his wife Catherine had come to stay with William and Anne, since Hammersmith air was reputedly salubrious[6]—but unfortunately it did not prove salubrious enough to keep him alive. His will and a codicil made his wife, John Samuel Schwenck, and later his brother co-guardians of his two little boys.

The Gilberts returned to France, in fact to that favourite haunt of English debtors, Boulogne, although the doctor made it clear they were not there because they lacked funds. Bab was enrolled in school and his father occasionally journeyed to London, being engaged in a guardianship battle with Catherine, culminating in a Chancery suit, drawing in the Schwencks as well.[7] 'If you have read anything of Mrs Cath Gilbert's law proceedings, in the papers,—against us—I must inform you,—it is *all incorrect*, & put in . . . I think, to annoy us,' Mary Schwenck wrote to Mrs West.[8] Not until March 1846 was it settled, and, although Catherine and her brother-in-law sometimes met thereafter over legal problems of Jane Gilbert's estate, any friendly connection between the two families was broken. Catherine did not trust his wish for money and control; he disapproved of what he believed was her immoral conduct with a man she now might marry.

When W. S. Gilbert was 10, he was sent to Western Grammar School at Brompton and after that to the prestigious Great Ealing School. Almost as good as Eton and Harrow, its faculty included Thomas Henry Huxley's father as mathematics master, and Thomas himself was a student in what, however, he described as 'a Pandemonium of a school'.[9] During his years there Gilbert was admittedly lazy with intervals of

---

[5] Mary Schwenck to Mrs West, 20 June 1845: WSG/BL Add. MS 49,345.

[6] Catherine Gilbert to Mrs West, [1841]: WSG/BL Add. MS 49,345.

[7] David Eden has published relevant letters and documents of the case in *A Tale of Two Kidnaps* (Coventry: Sir Arthur Sullivan Society, 1988), 5–21. These do not, however, include the BL letters quoted above.

[8] Mary Schwenck to Mrs West, 20 June 1845: WSG/BL Add MS 49,345.

[9] C. Bibby, *T. H. Huxley: Scientist, Humanist and Educator* (London: Watts, 1959), 3.

hard enough work to make him headboy and to win him prizes for verse translation. Early fascinated by the theatre, he enjoyed the picturesque delights of 'penny plain, tuppence coloured' prints, and at school wrote plays, acted in them, and painted sets, but, as he once told a friend, 'I was not a popular boy, I believe.'[10]

In his last year at Great Ealing, under the influence of Charles Kean's performance in Dion Boucicault's play *The Corsican Brothers*, Gilbert went to ask Kean if he might join his company at the Princess's Theatre. Since Kean knew Dr Gilbert, his son, no doubt, hoped to be welcomed. No such luck—or rather, no such ill luck, for the schoolboy was saved for more important things than carrying a Kean spear. The actor sent him back to Ealing.

At some time during his years there, Gilbert caught typhoid fever and had his head shaved as was then the medical habit. From this came his first known verses, written in Paris, where he had been taken to recuperate.

> When the horses, white with foam,
>   Drew the Empress to her home
> From the place whence she did roam,
>   The Empress she did see
>   The Gilbert Familee.
> To the Emperor she said:
>   'How beautiful the head
> Of that youth of gallant mien,
> Cropped so neat and close and clean—
>   Though I own he's rather lean.'
> Said the Emperor: 'It is!
> And I never saw a phiz
> More wonderful than 'is.'[11]

Pleasant moments such as watching Napoleon III and Eugénie drive by were to become rarer in the 'Gilbert Familee'.

From Great Ealing, Gilbert might have been expected to go to Oxford, but instead he registered in March 1853 as an Occasional Student at King's College, University of London (at a fee of 5 guineas). By the following September he was admitted to the Department of

---

[10] S. Dark and R. Grey, *W. S. Gilbert: His Life and Letters* (London: Methuen & Co. Ltd., 1923), 5.

[11] Mrs Francis Carter, W. S. Gilbert's niece, recited these lines to Leslie Baily; the pattern of indentation is no doubt his. *The Gilbert and Sullivan Book* (rev. edn. London: Spring Books, 1966), 38–9.

General Literature and Science as a regular student and frequented the Great Hall with its Corinthian columns, then the heart of the college. Gilbert attended academic sessions from 1853 to 1856[12] and left his mark, if only temporarily, on the Engineering Society, recently called the King's College Scientific Society. On 31 October 1854 a member named Geary moved to replace that group with a Shakespearean Reading Society, which, after an amendment by Gilbert was carried, became the Shakespearean Reading and Dramatic Society. He became secretary, taking part in discussions and giving a paper on 'The Theory of Apparitions',[13] perhaps with data gleaned from his father, who was also interested in 'hauntings'. After Gilbert took his degree in 1857, the society returned to the engineers, who passed a resolution forbidding literary papers.[14]

Very likely Gilbert completed his work for the bachelor's degree in 1856, since he did not attend the 1856–7 session and since the University of London granted degrees only once a year. What he did do in the autumn of 1856 was to read for the late December competitive examination for commissions in the Royal Artillery. The Crimean War was in progress; patriotism and adventure fired Gilbert's romantic breast, and he hoped to fling himself into the thick of it. He would be a few weeks over the age limit, but he had obtained a dispensation from the Secretary of War. Before he could take the examination, however, it was postponed indefinitely. The war had unexpectedly ended and left him with the alternatives of a line regiment or a competitive examination for a Civil Service clerkship, which required a series of certificates attesting to character and tests in English composition, précis-making, some law, and bookkeeping.[15] He chose the examination, became an assistant clerk in the Education Department of the Privy Council Office for four years, and hated it.

An often-repeated anecdote tells how Gilbert at a fellow clerk's request wrote him an order for a box at the theatre. When the discomfited clerk returned, saying the order had not been honoured, Gilbert replied that he had said he would write an order, but he had not said it would be of any use. It was a cruel joke, emphasizing verbal

---

[12] Published by permission of King's College, London.

[13] W. O. Skeat, *King's College London, Engineering Society 1847–1957* (London: University of London, n.d.), 17.

[14] D. North, 'Gilbert and the Engineers', *Gilbert & Sullivan Journal*, 6 (Jan. 1950), 173.

[15] 'Civil Service Examinations', *London University Magazine*, 2 (July 1857), 484–5.

accuracy of the sort which disappoints Rosamund in Maria Edgeworth's *Early Lessons*, but since another clerk is also credited with doing the same thing, Gilbert may not have been to blame.

He soon had the pleasure of appearing, although anonymously, in print. Euphrosyne Parepa, born the same year as himself and a play-mate for as long as he could remember, had become a singer at Promenade Concerts. Her most successful number was a laughing song from Scribe and Auber's *Manon Lescaut*, which she asked her friend to translate into English for the playbill. He did, changing the original fire-eating *commissaire* to 'A legal dignitary | Particularly wary', and going every night to watch promenaders reading his song as Euphrosyne sang. With these verses, he began his lifelong habit of reusing his materials, for he stored the song in his memory and took it out in 1870 for Cyril's laughing song in his burlesque *The Princess*, revising the words. By then there was a certain topicality in the 'Éclat de Rire', as it was called, for Adelina Patti had been using it as her les-son aria in *Il Barbiere di Siviglia*.

By 1859, Gilbert had responded to the call of the new Volunteers *faute de* Crimea. What seemed to be the danger of a French invasion found England with a depleted military force at home, to supplement which a large volunteer force would have to be raised. Recruits responded eagerly, and Gilbert rapidly rose to lieutenant in the Civil Service Rifles, later joining the West Yorkshire Militia. No invasion took place, but the non-professional soldiers became a permanent part of the country's defences, ultimately merging with the Territorials.

Gilbert suffered more from belt-swinging Guardsmen than from invading Frenchmen, for on 3 October 1860 he wrote to *The Times*, describing an unprovoked attack made on him, which he fought off with the help of a passer-by. Earlier in the year he had been instru-mental in the arrest of two Guardsmen, who nearly killed a policeman and wounded another with their belts. Since making a complaint to the barracks was futile, he now suggested that belts be firmly stitched to the backs of the tunics so they could not be used for weapons.

Even with the quasi-military pleasure of being a Volunteer, Gilbert disliked desk-work more and more. He had already entered himself as a student at the Inner Temple, and now a windfall of £300 enabled him to shake the Education Department's disorganized dust from his boots, pay for his call to the Bar, and leave home (21 Victoria Road) or the Pimlico boarding-house where he had probably been staying to set up chambers for himself.

William Schwenck Gilbert was now 25 years old; he was not particularly a success although he obviously had skills in writing and drawing waiting to be developed further and travel had perfected his French. His childhood had not interested him greatly, and he believed 'we advance in happiness as our intellectual powers expand'. He dismissed the 'poetic fashion to look back with sentimental regret upon the days of early childhood', for he considered that the happiness of infancy lay merely 'in its total irresponsibility, its incapacity to distinguish between right and wrong, its general helplessness, its inability to argue rationally, and its having nothing whatever upon its half-born little mind,—privileges which are equally the property of an idiot in a lunatic asylum.'[16] His mind was original, and he liked the play of logic, even if his decision to become a barrister seems to be almost as much a reaction against the Civil Service as a compelling interest in a legal career.

In spite of a strong, but hidden, sentimental streak which made him enjoy flirtation, he had not yet experienced passion as far as we know. He had rarely seen the love, but often witnessed the quarrels, of his parents in which his father's flaming temper met his mother's sullenness. He too had a temper which increased with the years, and from his mother came a voice sometimes audible in her few extant letters and his quarrels, a certain note of 'Why, you know you did,' spoken accusingly. His mother, however, remains for the most part enigmatic after we see her first with her new-born son. Her letters have disappeared, and the fact that none of the Gilberts kept personal letters[17] means that little of their feelings for or dealings with each other can be reconstructed. Schwenck, as he was called within the family, seems to have had no communication with his sisters Florence and Maude, but rather than cutting himself off from them, he may simply have destroyed their correspondence at the time or later in life when he burned many papers.

His closest relationship was with his father, for whom he illustrated books and stories. Although Gilbert told Edith Browne that his father began to write after he himself had achieved a certain success,[18] Dr Gilbert's first published work was a pamphlet, *On the Present System of Rating for the Relief of the Poor in the Metropolis*, in 1857, followed

---

[16] 'Thumbnail Studies: Getting Up a Pantomime', *London Society*, 13 (Jan. 1868), 50.

[17] Dark and Grey, *W. S. Gilbert*, 4. Gilbert kept business letters, however, 'both disagreeable & the reverse', as John Hare remarked in a letter to him, dated only 'Sunday Feb 3': WSG/BL Add. MS 49,332.

[18] *W. S. Gilbert* (London: John Lane, 1907), 9.

by *Dives and Lazarus* the next year. His greatest period of productivity was, however, the late 1860s and early 1870s. From first to last, two sorts of narrative or description preoccupied him, although he occasionally wrote on other subjects. The first of these was fiction and non-fiction dealing with 'the social deposits' (persons in abject poverty) and the often concomitant problems of drunkenness. The second involves abnormal psychological phenomena, monomanias, hallucinations, compulsions, and magic. They show that Dr Gilbert was, on the one hand, interested in French work in psychology and, on the other, delighted by the supernatural. He was an honorary secretary of the Society for Relief of Distress, where his work provided material for such stories as *The Washerwoman's Foundling* and *The Weaver's Family*. He also wrote for a number of periodicals, among them the *Cornhill*, the *Fortnightly Review, Good Words, St Paul's, Britannia*, and *Temple Bar*. He was anti-Catholic, anti-Church of England, anti-vivisection, and pro-Semitic. From his earliest days he believed poverty, not innate depravity, was the cause of crime.

Dr Gilbert's first novel, *Shirley Hall Asylum* (1863), is narrated by a 'sane' man, who has spent five years in a private madhouse. He accepts imprisonment as self-sacrifice, for 'Satan himself seemed to be incorporated in me, and told me how I could accomplish the destruction of the universe.'[19] In *The Wizard of the Mountain* and *The Magic Mirror*, both of which Schwenck illustrated, a series of interlocking tales are both magical and moral. The first depicts a benevolent astrologer, the Innominato, whose enchantments instruct the good and destroy the evil. In each story of the second, a Venetian mirror grants a wish which leads not to happiness but to trouble.

Although Dr Gilbert was by no means a novelist of the first order, his works did not lack publishers, and he was usually well reviewed, even at times compared to Defoe. As he said in the first chapter of *The Memoirs of a Cynic*, 'I have been haunted through my whole existence by the absurd.' This helped make him 'highly formidable to grown-ups', but 'a delightful companion' to a bookish child such as his great-nephew Gilbert Murray, to whom he talked about foreign coun-

---

[19] *Shirley Hall Asylum; or, The Memoirs of a Monomaniac* (London: William Freeman, 1863), 15. For a discussion of Dr Gilbert's works, see J. W. Stedman, '"A Peculiar Sharp Flavour": The Contributions of Dr William Gilbert', *Victorian Periodicals Review*, 19 (summer 1986), 43–50.

tries, Bismarck, and insanity.[20] The sense of absurdity and the consciousness of social injustices descended by association to W. S. Gilbert.

Injustice of a more trivial sort did not count at home. There was a legend in his niece's family that Dr Gilbert came home one evening to find preparations for a party under way. It had been talked of for weeks, but he insisted he had never heard of it; so, sending his wife and daughters to bed and turning out all but one light, he told guests who arrived that they had made a mistake. Then he moved to the club, and if he and Mrs Gilbert happened to call on any one thereafter, they were entertained in separate rooms.[21]

Eventually Dr Gilbert moved to Salisbury to live with his daughter Jane at No. 9, The Close. She had married Alfred Weigall, a miniature-painter, whose brother Henry painted a portrait of Schwenck as a young man.[22] More devout than her siblings, Jane Weigall visited Salisbury Cathedral daily for nearly forty years as her memorial tablet, placed there by her children, tells us.

Little is known about Maude, except that, like her sisters, she was tall and handsome; she lived till 1932, surrounded by bibelots, cabinets, etc.—the family detritus.[23] Florence Gilbert, however, became a pupil at the National Training School for Music, studying with Stainer and Prout. She began to compose songs in 1866, but not until the 1890s did she achieve a degree of concert popularity; unfortunately, she survived her brother by less than four months. One other woman was part of Gilbert's early life—his first cousin Agnes Ann Edwards, the daughter of Harriet Morris. Her elder brother Sutherland, a journalist, had gone to Australia in the 1840s, but returned to England to become the first editor of the *Graphic* and a dramatist of sorts. Agnes (or Annie) was more or less Schwenck's age, tall, a good linguist and musician, vivacious, and well dressed. Like him, she had a lively sense of humour and a quick perception of people,[24] although she was more sympathetic than he. They amused each other until she, too, left for Australia in 1860, not returning until 1877 as the widowed Lady Murray with her younger son Gilbert, named for his great uncle. This was the 11 year old

---

[20] *Gilbert Murray: An Unfinished Autobiography* (London: George Allen & Unwin Ltd., 1960), 79.

[21] Ibid. 78.          [22] Letter from Brigadier E. T. Weigall, 24 July 1974.

[23] Telephone conversation with Tristram Gilbert, July 1974.

[24] G. Wilson, *Murray of Yarralumla* (Melbourne: Oxford University Press, 1968), 271–2.

who so much enjoyed Dr Gilbert's conversation and who would in time adore the Savoy librettos.

But all that is far in the future; in 1861 Schwenck is only about to begin.

# 2

## The 1860s: First Pages

> The 'Bab Ballads' are in the manner of a riot.
>
> Max Beerbohm, 'A Classic in Humour' (1905)

I N the autumn of 1861, weary of clerkship and having had a manuscript returned from *Good Words* as promising but too long,[1]
Gilbert began 'the usual Bar, Newspaper, Theatre round of the better
Victorian journalists'.[2] He submitted a short article and a woodblock
drawing to H. J. Byron, whose new periodical *Fun* had begun publication on 21 September. A kind of burlesque James Joyce, whose almost-
fulfilled ambition was to write a play in which every word turned on a
pun, Byron was the most popular and prolific comic dramatist of the
day, with works such as *The Lady of Lyons; or, Twopenny Pride and
Pennytence*; *Bluebeard from a New Point of Hue*; and *Esmeralda; or,
The Sensation Goat*, all in rhymed couplets. Later, he would also write
prose comedies, among them *Our Boys*, the longest-running play of the
century (*Vaudeville Theatre*, 16 January 1875–18 April 1879).

Characteristically, the first number of *Fun* contained an introduction
in which Byron punned on 'Fun', 'Fun(d)s', 'funn'ell' ('Fun will'), and
described his new weekly as 'a penny-seer (small prophets and quick
returns)', since it sold for a penny an issue. In format and content,
Byron's intention was to imitate outwardly the threepenny *Punch*,
whose contributors alluded scornfully to their younger and livelier
competitor as '*Funch*' (Thackeray's coinage).[3]

Gilbert's first three-quarter column and half-page drawing (which
cannot now be identified)[4] were almost certainly imitative too. After

---

[1] E. A. Browne, *W. S. Gilbert* (London: John Lane, 1907), 18.

[2] R. G. G. Price, *A History of Punch* (London: Collins, 1957), 127.

[3] A. A. Adrian, *Mark Lemon: First Editor of Punch* (London: Oxford University Press,
1966), 106.

[4] Beginning in May 1865 the proprietor's copies of *Fun* in the Henry E. Huntington Library
are marked with contributor's name and remuneration. Although Gilbert's own copies are

all, he was teaching himself what would be his vocation for more than a decade. As an artist, he was then largely self-taught unless some school drawing-master had shown him how to square out his paper and set up a figure. Later, from March 1868 to September 1871, Gilbert subscribed to the Langham Sketching Club, a jokey offshoot of the well-established Artists' Society. There he drew from live models, nude or in costumes of which the Society had a great store.[5] In 1861, however, Gilbert knew enough to draw directly in pencil or ink on the prepared surface of a woodblock. When engraved, such a block produced the heavy black and white contrasts so important for grotesque effects.

Whatever Gilbert's initial offerings were, Byron liked them, accepted them, and asked for a weekly column and drawing from thenceforth. This editorial encouragement staggered the novice journalist, who believed he had poured his all into that first offering and was already, as he later signed himself, 'Our Used-Up Contributor'. It was a sensation which became very familiar to him, indeed, one which recurred throughout his creative life and had significant consequences in his collaboration with Arthur Sullivan. This bogy, as Gilbert called it in his 1883 scrap of autobiography, 'invariably haunts me . . . on the completion of every work involving a sustained effort. At first it used to scare me; but I have long learnt to recognise it as a mere bogey, and to treat it with the contempt it deserves.'[6] Yet he never really exorcized it, for a decade later he told an interviewer that upon finishing a play he felt 'absolutely incapable of further effort'.[7] This emptiness came from

marked for earlier work, they do not identify his first contributions. These copies are now in the possession of Peter Joslin, to whom I am indebted for pre-1865 dates in this chapter. Because Victorian comic journalists often had a style and a subject-range in common, attribution of anonymous or pseudonymous works on internal evidence alone is difficult at best and usually impossible. For 1861 drawings by Gilbert, see J. Cattermole, 'Gilbert's Bow in "Fun"', *Gilbert & Sullivan Journal*, 8 (Jan. 1962), 93. Gilbert's first *Fun* drawing signed 'Bab' (9 Nov. 1861) is reproduced by Harold Kanthor in *W. S. Gilbert: An Anniversary Exhibition* (Rochester, NY: University of Rochester Library [1986]), 5.

[5] The Artists' Society was founded in 1830. Members were elected by ballot, and subscribers who were not members could draw from the Society's models. The Society had its rooms in All Soul's Place, Langham Place, hence the name Langham Sketching Club. The Langham's general taste was evidently theatrical, although some of its members objected to the introduction of comic songs and recitations at meetings; J. L. Toole was a guest there. 'Proceedings of Societies', *Art-Student*, 2 (May 1865), 380. PML has three sketches by Gilbert, two female nudes and a male in what seems to be a theatrical pose and costume, endorsed: 'Left at School by W. S. Gilbert | (Bab) | Elected Subs! 19 March 1868. | Resigned Sept! 1871'.

[6] 'An Autobiography', *Theatre*, NS 1 (2 Apr. 1883), 218.

[7] H. How, *Illustrated Interviews* (London: George Newnes Ltd., 1893), 9. These interviews originally appeared in the *Strand Magazine*.

Gilbert's utter concentration on his work; he was 'absolutely engrossed by it. . . . It swamps every other consideration.'[8] Working on a play, he would 'eat that piece and drink that piece and exude that piece, and identify myself altogether with that piece'.[9] In time to come, this single-minded intensity helped to make Gilbert tenacious of his least successful plays and to throw him out of gear when Sullivan rejected a long-worked-over scenario.

But now in 1861, at the beginning of an increasingly close association with *Fun*, working to a weekly schedule, he had little time to indulge his bogy. If it grew too troublesome he wrote a column about it. For Gilbert found he did have something left—in fact, a decade's worth of squibs, fillers, puns, verses, drawings, social and dramatic criticism, suggestions for double acrostics (a special *Fun* feature), absurd letters, and, of course, the Bab Ballads, which out-laughed anything *Punch* had to offer. His pseudonyms, some with developed personalities of their own, came to include The Comic Physiognomist, The Comic Mythologist, A. Dapter, Desiderius Erasmus, A Trembling Widow, R. Ditty, A. Pittite, Animal Carraccio, R. Chimedes, and Snarler.

The staff that Byron and his editorial successor Tom Hood collected informally from friends and beginners was, for the most part, young and 'Bohemian', as one of them, Jeff Prowse, wrote in his often-quoted verses 'The City of Prague' (*Fun*, 16 March 1867):

> How we laughed as we laboured together!
>   How well I remember, to-day,
> Our 'outings' in Midsummer weather,
>   Our winter delights at the play!
> We were not over-nice in our dinners;
>   Our 'rooms' were up rickety stairs;
> But if Hope be the wealth of beginners,
>   By Jove, we were all millionaires!

The Bohemianism of the '*Fun* gang', as they called themselves, consisted, however, in frequenting cheap unconventional clubs where Dickens might drop in; in having ties with a stage not yet considered respectable, and in ebullitions of irreverence and independence both in private and in print.

---

[8] 'From Our Stall', *Fun* (3 June 1865).

[9] Letter to 'My Beloved B.', 13 Dec. 1878: PML. B. is one of Gilbert's child correspondents, Beatrice de Michels.

Most of them lacked money; one or two needed soap. Some drank too much, and some died too early. But many were young men from professional families, with university educations and legal training, who worked in government offices, but, like Gilbert, gravitated to journalism. Their bachelorhoods or marriages were generally respectable too. In short, their Bohemianism was essentially a sentimental, laughing, crusading camaraderie—or, at least, some of them, looking back, thought so.

To *Punch*, the *Fun* gang and their cheeky paper seemed racketty and coarse. The well-established, increasingly complacent Mr Punch prided himself on taking 'the gentlemanly view of things',[10] and his editor Mark Lemon won a modified immortality as the man who saved his readers' sensibilities by rejecting Gilbert's ballad 'The Yarn of the "Nancy Bell" ', in which an ancient mariner acquires multiple identities through cannibalism.

Nevertheless, *Punch* occasionally printed contributions by *Fun* writers, Gilbert among others. His comic poem 'The Return' appeared (21 October 1865) two weeks after he had used some of the same material for 'Back Again' and two other pieces in *Fun*. Whether this annoyed Mark Lemon is not clear, but he did refuse to accept further contributions unless Gilbert left *Fun* for ever.[11] Nor would Lemon promise a permanency if he did. Of course, Gilbert refused, but, interestingly enough, when Lemon died five years later, rumour named Gilbert as his successor. There was, however, no real question of his being offered or accepting the post. Shirley Brooks was almost immediately appointed and some time later found himself apologizing to Gilbert for *Punch*'s unintentional plagiarism of 'The Advent of Spring' which Gilbert had published during his first six months on *Fun*.[12]

The *Fun* gang with whom Gilbert remained might not boast a Thackeray, but its members were not inconsiderable in their day. Many, like Prowse and E. L. Blanchard, combined comic with serious journalism elsewhere. Blanchard was also a prolific dramatist as were William

[10] Price, *History of Punch*, 101.

[11] M. H. Spielmann, *The History of 'Punch'* (New York: Cassell Publishing Co., 1895), 528. I assume Gilbert's break with *Punch* came in the autumn of 1865 after 'The Yarn of the "Nancy Bell" had been submitted and refused. It was published in *Fun* on 3 Mar. 1866. According to R. G. G. Price, Gilbert submitted fifteen poems and illustrations to Lemon, who then uttered his ultimatum. This behaviour was not untypical; Lemon encouraged young writers, sometimes even persuading them to leave other papers, and 'when pressed with submissions became hostile'.

[12] G. S. Layard, *A Great 'Punch' Editor: Being the Life, Letters and Diaries of Shirley Brooks* (London: Sir Isaac Pitman & Sons Ltd., 1907), 42.

Brough, Tom Robertson, and F. C. Burnand, who joined the gang two months after Gilbert did, and who maintained a lifelong inimical 'friendship' with him. Very soon, however, Burnand moved to *Punch*, of which he eventually became editor; no doubt he suited Lemon's preference for 'a good sensible ready-handed man' rather than a genius.[13]

Like Byron, Burnand was also an occasional actor, as was Arthur Sketchley, who wrote few plays, but gave public readings in the person of his creation 'Mrs. Brown'. This redoubtable dialect character, Dickensian in appearance, became a regular figure of *Fun*. Tucked between book covers, she sold in her thousands, and for a short time in 1870–1 Gilbert joined Sketchley in a comic paper, *Mrs. Brown's Budget*, which ended in financial contretemps and coolness.[14] Sketchley had been a Church of England clergyman until he was attracted to lay Roman Catholicism. Nicknamed 'Rosey' by his colleagues (his real name was George Rose), he described himself as 'talented, though obese'.[15]

Perhaps the most conspicuous Bohemian on *Fun*'s staff was the dilatory Henry S. Leigh, a second-generation eccentric with an acid tongue. His father, called 'Dagger' Leigh because of his sharp wit, had known Dickens, Thackeray, and *Punch*'s radical Douglas Jerrold. Six months younger than Gilbert, Harry Leigh seemed older. An amateur musician, he provided numbers for the Moore and Burgess Minstrels, and in 1871 began translating the librettos of *opéras bouffes*. Leigh habitually carried tiny manuscripts about in his pockets, polishing his rhymes of which he was very proud.[16] His best-known book of verse was *Carols of Cockayne* (1869), while his *Strains from the Strand* (1882) indicates the physical boundaries of his life, which took place between Temple Bar and Charing Cross.

Leigh also wrote a good deal of prose for *Fun*, including a weekly theatre column to which Robertson, Gilbert, and others frequently contributed. A 'last leaf' indeed, Harry stayed with *Fun* after its old gang

[13] Price, *History of Punch*, 103, quoting Henry Silver's unpublished diary.

[14] Gilbert contributed both prose and Bab drawings, including the picture of Mrs Brown which appeared on the first page of the first number (1 Aug. 1870). The draft of a letter from Gilbert to George Rose, 22 Mar. 1871 (WSG/BL Add. MS 49,330) implies that for a time they may have been partners. There is also a receipt from Rose in a form Gilbert wrote out, dated 11 Mar. 1871, to the effect that Rose has received £30 from Gilbert 'in full satisfaction of all claims in the matter of "Mrs. Brown's Budget"' (WSG/BL Add. MS 49,330).

[15] E. Yates, *Edmund Yates: His Recollections and Experiences* (2nd edn.; London: Richard Bentley & Son, 1884), ii. 182.

[16] W. H. Morton and H. Chance Newton, *Sixty Years' Stage Service* (London: Gale & Polden Ltd., 1905), 142. Leigh boasted that he 'never wrote a cockney rhyme'.

had left the paper or the world. At his own too-early death, the *Athenaeum* (23 June 1883) described the distinctive qualities of his verse as 'humour and gaiety, but the gaiety is that of a pessimist, albeit a kindly pessimist'.

Another *Fun* reviewer, original staff member, and close friend of H. J. Byron was Tom Robertson—untidy, sensitive, sarcastic, the eldest of a large theatrical family, at one time Mme Vestris's stage-manager, and soon to be the author of a series of innovative plays which brought domestic realism to the English stage. In 1865 Byron recommended Robertson's *Society* to the actress Marie Wilton (later Mrs Bancroft) with whom he was managing the Prince of Wales's Theatre. A week before Gilbert's twenty-ninth birthday the gang went in a body to opening night, discovering delightedly that Tom had depicted their evenings in his 'Owl's Roost' scene. Gilbert immediately recognized Robertson's significance ('Stagecraft was an unknown art before his time'),[17] and the older dramatist allowed his junior to watch and learn from his Prince of Wales's rehearsals. Here, too, the foundations of Gilbert's friendship with the Bancrofts were laid.

Among the younger *Fun* contributors was Clement Scott, five years Gilbert's junior and nicknamed 'Kitten'. Scott was already a drama critic, working here, there, and everywhere, eventually succeeding Blanchard on the *Daily Telegraph*, and leading the rearguard reaction against Ibsen. Short on wit but long on sentiment, Scott's contributions to *Fun* were unremarkable. More important to the paper as a whole was its second and most successful editor. In May 1865 Charles Maclean, the toothy proprietor of the paper, sold it to Edward Wylam, and the Bauble, as the editorship was called, passed from Byron to Tom Hood— poor Tom Hood as old *Fun*sters tended to call him in their memoirs.

Tom's father was the more famous Thomas Hood, journalist, editor, master of light verse, and friend of Lamb and Hazlitt. His serious ballad 'Eugene Aram' and his punning 'Faithless Nelly Gray' were recited everywhere, while his social commentaries 'The Bridge of Sighs' ('One more Unfortunate | ... | Gone to her death') and 'The Song of a Shirt' ('Stitch! stitch! stitch! | In poverty, hunger, and dirt') were famous protests which younger writers still hoped to emulate. Published in *Punch*'s 1843 Christmas number, 'The Song of a Shirt' had increased its reputation and circulation, which may account for the slight

---

[17] Gilbert to William Archer, in Archer, *Real Conversations* (London: William Heinemann, 1904), 43.

decrease in *Punch*'s animosity when the younger Hood took over *Fun*.[18]

Certainly, young Tom did his best to live up to the father he adored. He wrote light verse, nonsense, and social satire for *Fun*:

> Nothing at all in the papers to-day!
>    Only a murder somewhere or other—
> A girl who has put her child away,
>    Not being a wife as well as a mother.

(13 March 1869)

Hood was a skilful caricaturist, published a book on metrics, and taught his protégé Clement Scott to write better verse.[19] He did not have to teach Gilbert.

These were the men with whom Gilbert was closely associated, professionally and socially, during the 1860s and beyond. He rose rapidly through their ranks, and from having been 'A Trembling Beginner' in 1861, he became an old hand who regularly climbed the stairs to *Fun*'s office, 'small and particularly hot and printing-inky'.[20] Within two years he was advising others. 'I have given your M.S. to the Editor', he wrote to an aspirant on 30 May 1863, 'but I am afraid that it is too long. Brevity is the great thing in articles for such a paper. I seldom have anything longer than ½ a column. Anything of that length is pretty sure to go in—but a longer article is very doubtful.'[21]

As a matter of fact, Gilbert was soon writing longer articles, but meanwhile he also contributed to Tom Hood's short-lived journal *Saturday Night* (1862) and to H. J. Byron's almost as ephemeral *Comic News*. He went to the Derby with E. L. Blanchard, getting some verses from the outing. He joined the *Fun* table at Evans's, now under the benign management of an old actor, Paddy Green, and much less rowdy than when it shocked Thackeray's Colonel Newcome. At Evans's one could enjoy music and a midnight supper of devilled kidneys or grilled bones with baked potatoes and stout.[22] From the mid-1860s on, Gilbert usually frequented the Arundel Club at 12 Salisbury Street, Strand, for

---

[18] Adrian, *Mark Lemon*, 107.

[19] E. S. Lauterbach, 'Fun and its Contributors: The Literary History of a Victorian Humor Magazine', Ph.D. thesis, Urbana, Ill.: University of Illinois, 1961, 52.

[20] 'The Comic Physiognomist', *Fun* (22 Oct. 1864), 58.

[21] To G. R. Gatti [Gattis?]: PML.

[22] This picture of Evans's is drawn from M. E. Perugini, *Victorian Days and Ways* (London: Jarrolds, 1932), 161–3, and A. W. à Beckett, *Green-Room Recollections* (Bristol: J. W. Arrowsmith [1896]), 201.

his 'devils' or tureens of tripe.[23] The Arundel was a bohemian club, whose members dined in shirt-sleeves in warm weather. It came to life only well after midnight, most of its habitués being 'theatricals' or journalists, who wrote their reviews and articles under its elaborately decorated ceiling. A copper kettle was always ready for hot grog, and a delicious smell of whiskey and lemon wafted through the tobacco smoke.[24]

Many of the *Fun* gang were on the rolls of the Arundel, and Blanchard was one of its founders. Gilbert appears in a contemporaneous description of its members as 'Jack Pungent . . . most entertaining of conversationalists, very cynical, very severe in his remarks, yet pronounced by everyone to be an excellent fellow at heart.'[25]

At the club Gilbert met Dante Gabriel Rossetti, who did not take to him;[26] the young Swinburne was there, too, a 'short, nervous little fellow, with bright fun', as Blanchard found him at first meeting.[27] Both Rossetti and Swinburne delighted in the Bab Ballads, Swinburne once sending his own obscene variation on 'The Bishop and the Busman' to Simeon Solomon, the painter.[28]

For four years Gilbert also attended a private social gathering: Hood's 'Friday Nights' in Thurloe Square, where Tom, his wife, sister, and an assortment of pets welcomed the gang and their friends to beef, pudding, drink, cigars, and music with James Molloy at the piano to sing his own songs. In time, he would set Gilbert's words, as in 'Corisande' and 'Eily's Reason' (both 1870), while the 1868 Gilbert–Molloy 'Thady O'Flinn' continued to be sung at annual Irish concerts for years.

[23] It is not possible to date exactly the year Gilbert joined the Arundel Club: his name is not on the 1863 list of members, but it is on the 1866 list. The BL does not have lists for 1864 or 1865.

[24] This description of the Arundel Club is drawn from E. L. Blanchard, *The Life and Reminiscences of E. L. Blanchard, with Notes from the Diary of Wm. Blanchard*, ed. C. Scott and C. Howard (London: Hutchinson & Co., 1891), i. 240 n; T. H. S. Escott, *Club Makers and Club Members* (London: T. Fisher Unwin, 1914), 264–9; C. Hay, *The Club and the Drawing-Room. Being Pictures of Modern Life: Social, Political, and Professional* (London: Robert Hardwicke, 1870), i. 255–70, and 'Theatre Gossip', *Era* (9 Sept. 1882), 5.

[25] Hay, *Club and Drawing-Room*, i. 267–8. Jack Pungent is the 'most accomplished and epigrammatic of nineteenth century playwrights'.

[26] *Dante Gabriel Rossetti: His Family Letters with a Memoir by William Michael Rossetti* (Boston: Roberts Brothers, 1895), i. 256. Nevertheless, Rossetti recited Bab Ballads 'in all sorts of companies'.

[27] Blanchard, *Life*, ii. 359. All following quotations from E. L. Blanchard come from this edition of his diary unless otherwise noted and will not be further documented.

[28] Swinburne to 'My dear Gabriel', 1 Mar. [1870], in *The Swinburne Letters*, ed. C. Y. Lang (New Haven: Yale University Press, 1959–62), ii. 106.

From these evenings came a Christmas book, *A Bunch of Keys* (1865), to which Robertson, Hood, Gilbert, Prowse, Scott, and Thomas Archer each contributed a story; Gilbert's was the Dickensian 'Key of the Strong Room', better known as 'Johnny Pounce'. Hood's preface described the collection as 'the growth of friendly communion, of pleasant chats of an evening, of fellowship of taste and feeling'.[29] If the public liked it, he promised an annual successor.

The public liked it indeed, so much so that four more collaborations were published in annuals between 1866 and 1869: 'Rates and Taxes', 'The Five Alls', 'On the Cards', and 'Two 'pon Ten'. The third of these appeared in *Routledge's Christmas Annual* for 1867, which also contained Gilbert's text and drawings for 'The Converted Clown', a swindler who exploits his prison term and repentance. The last picture shows a clown-preacher into whose hat coins are falling.[30]

Although Gilbert was only briefly a member of the Savage Club, he joined in its charity effort, *The Savage Club Papers*, in 1867. His pseudo-Germanic fairytale 'The Triumph of Vice' ends with a characteristically inverted but accurate moral: 'Cunning, malice, and imposture may not flourish immediately they are practised; but depend upon it, my dear children, that they will assert their own in the end.'[31]

Meanwhile Gilbert had begun a club himself—'The Serious Family'—of whom he was the *enfant terrible* and for whom he provided steaks and ale in his lodgings at 3 South Square, Gray's Inn. According to its attendance book, which he preserved, the Family began on 23 December 1865 and continued more or less weekly into the following May.[32] Hood, Sketchley, Prowse, and the illustrator Paul Gray were regulars. Clement Scott came frequently, and others dropped in and out. After the Serious Family broke up, Gilbert salvaged its name (taken from a farce by Morris Barnett) for a club in his short story 'Tom Poulton's Joke' (*Dark Blue* [March 1871]). There, Tom, a briefless barrister, presides over a sociable club; as a joke he pretends to die and attends his own funeral, only to find that his friends refuse to recognize his existence. Shorn of the club, elements of this plot reappear in

[29] (London: Groombridge & Sons, 1865), p. viii.

[30] 'The Converted Clown' may have been William Weaver, convicted several years before of bigamy but in 1869 a 'revivalist'. Other 'converted clowns' appeared in 1872 and 1883, the latter a swindler.

[31] (London: Tinsley Brothers, 1867), 195. Gilbert deleted this moral when he republished the story in his 1890 collection *Foggerty's Fairy and Other Tales*. In 1867 he also contributed two illustrations to stories by Sketchley and Edward Draper in *The Savage Club Papers*.

[32] WSG/BL Add. MS 49,303.

Gilbert's long farce *Tom Cobb* (1875), in *The Mikado* (1885), and in *The Grand Duke* (1896).

During these years Gilbert's copy for *Fun* itself ranged from 'Gossip of the Week' (short columns of one-liners such as 'The public lecturer who dwelt upon a topic has changed his residence' [1 August 1863]), through comic or ironic attacks on temperance excesses or sweated labour, to the page-long featured columns under a pseudonymous byline. His drawings went from Bodger exploding in lightning flashes because he wears the 'new steel collar and wristbands' in a thunderstorm (3 May 1862) to caricatures of the Royal Academy show (14 May 1864) and fantastic figures in a full-page drawing for the 1871 *Fun Almanack*, labelled 'OUR PICTORIAL CENTUPLE ACROSTICO-CHARADICAL PUZZLE' (see Fig. 1), for which Gilbert promised 'The solution will be given on the 31st of September next, by which time the Artist thinks he will have found out what it means, himself.'

Gilbert soon learned how to turn his personal life into prose, verse, and picture. He drew well-known barristers, and having been called to the Bar in November 1863, he described courtroom scenes and invented a breach of promise suit (11 April 1868), which reached the stage of the Royalty Theatre in 1875 as *Trial by Jury*. In 'The Student' (1 July 1865), a faint parody of Poe's 'The Raven', a Gilbert persona sits in his Gray's Inn window, 'Speculating vaguely, widely, | On my aunt's unopened will'. Mary Schwenck had died the preceding May, leaving Gilbert £500, two houses, and a number of stock shares; the 'Student' had not long to wait—her will was proved on 3 July.[33]

Having joined the militia, two of Gilbert's alter egos wrote and drew 'The Physiognomist in the Army' (25 January 1864) and 'Our Own Correspondent at the Sham Guildford Fight' (2 April 1864). When Gilbert then transferred to the Royal Aberdeenshire Militia as a lieutenant, he took the Physiognomist to a levee (30 March 1867) and depicted the military types there, including himself in full fig.

Gilbert coined his experience in other periodicals, too. In December 1863, shortly after he was called to the Bar, his story 'My Maiden Brief' was published in the *Cornhill Magazine*. In it, a young barrister loses his first case, the defence of a pickpocket, who throws her boot at his head. Although Gilbert, in a much later interview, spoke of this incident as really happening,[34] F. C. Burnand's reminiscences also contain

---

[33] This legacy is not that which Gilbert said allowed him to leave his clerkship; it came two years after his call to the Bar.

[34] How, *Illustrated Interviews*, 11–12.

*OUR PICTORIAL CENTUPLE ACROSTICO-CHARADICAL PUZZLE.*

(The solution will be given on the 31st of September next, by which time the Artist thinks he will have found out what it means, himself.)

1. Gilbert's drawing 'Our Pictorial Centuple Acrostico-Charadical Puzzle', *Fun Almanack* (1871)

21

an anecdote about a client throwing her shoe at *him* for *winning* her case.[35] Perhaps it was a habit among petty female criminals, or perhaps it was a floating anecdote available to any barrister turned journalist. Autobiographical or not, 'My Maiden Brief' was invested with a number of legal details which lent corroborative verisimilitude, and the *Cornhill* paid Gilbert 8 guineas, one more than it gave his father for an article the next April.[36] But it rejected the younger Gilbert's straightforward report on the Army Clothing Department ('Our War Paint') eventually published in *Temple Bar* (September 1866); the equally straightforward 'Honours of the Shrievalty' (a county sheriff's duties at assizes) had already appeared in *London Society* for May 1865.

Small personal and large social dislikes are apparent in Gilbert's work for *Fun*. He seems, for instance, to have been unusually sensitive to stale air, peppermint breath, bad odours, men who spat, and organ-grinders. (In the more affluent future he insisted on the best cigars, 5 inches long, and on large windows.) Like most of his colleagues he was against stuffiness in character, and, like them but more cuttingly, he satirized hypocrisy, exploitation, Sabbatarianism, and that peculiar Victorian purity which denounced the stage. As Snarler (14 April 1866), he attended a scruffy murder trial, death to the prisoner but amusement to the ladies in the gallery. In a more boisterous vein, his story 'The Astounding Adventure of Wheeler J. Calamity' (Christmas number, 1866) drops a sanctimonious hypocrite through a pond into the Region of Burlesque, where he is forced to speak in doggerel rhymes and to behave with pantomimic abandon.

Of all Gilbert's contributions to *Fun*, however, three groups stand out: 'The Comic Physiognomist' series, the burlesque dramatic reviews, and, of course, the Bab Ballads, which have continued in print for more than a century.

The Physiognomist, whose identity Gilbert established during his first four years on *Fun*, was essentially a comic journalist's version of Theophrastus under the influence of Boz's 'Sketches of Young Gentlemen', with Bab illustrations. He went from classifying chins and noses to characterizing types of actresses, clergymen, old schoolmates, 'social scum', etc. Gilbert even drew himself as a worried

---

[35] Sir F. C. Burnand, *Records and Reminiscences Personal and General* (London: Methuen & Co., 1904), i. 391–3.

[36] *Cornhill* Accounts, George Smith Papers, NLS MS 23,187. The senior Gilbert, however, was paid 13 guineas for a later article. W. S. Gilbert signed his manuscript (PML) as 'W. Schwenck Gilbert', probably to avoid confusion with his father.

Physiognomist, trying to write about Christmas 'when all the world give each other spontaneous and unregretted presents!' (19 December 1863; see Fig. 2).

In November 1864 he killed off this popular persona, replacing him with the much less amusing 'Comic Mythologist', a conventionally funny alter ego, who debunked the classics. The Mythologist had a short page life, probably because travesties of gods and heroes were too familiar. Disappearing, he left behind an illustration which became the frontispiece of Ambrose Bierce's *The Fiend's Delight* (1873). (Gilbert had drawn King Peleus extracting the infant Achilles from a kitchen fire; Bierce's title, however, has made people ever since erroneously suppose an old gentleman is toasting a baby at a grate.)[37] Fortunately, the Comic Physiognomist returned in February 1867 with a new series, entitled 'The Men We Meet'. Also in 1867 Gilbert did some comparable 'characters' for *London Society* under the heading of 'Thumbnail Studies in the London Streets'.

Gilbert's second important group of *Fun* contributions were the parody reviews in dialogue form, which ran almost weekly from 1865 to early 1871. His work had always contained strong theatrical elements, as witness his 1863 series 'The People of Pantomime' and his 1864 'On Pantomimic Absurdities'. But now he developed a style of reviewing that was simultaneously trenchant and hilarious, exaggerated but proceeding from strict critical principles. He wanted accuracy in all details, from the smoke of a fired gun to the proper numerals on a policeman's collar. He continually objected to scenes too long and too straggling. He abominated low comedians who depended on catchwords. He wanted everything made clear and credible to the audience. His page-long, illustrated travesties showed the clichés, illogicalities, inaccuracies, and absurdities, not only of plot and characterization, but of sets, stage business, acting, costumes, and enunciation.

In Gilbert's review of *The Yellow Passport* (21 November 1868), for instance, Inspector Javert announced:

I am the usual idiot inspector of the British Drama who never catches anybody by any chance, unless it is to allow them to escape immediately after. The bill says I 'would have arrested my own father had I found him escaping from justice.' But I should *not* have found him escaping from justice. I never yet

---

[37] Undoubtedly Bierce intended the frontispiece to suggest toasting rather than extricating. His first contribution to *Fun* (22 June 1872) was a letter asking people to take parcels away, among them a bundle of 'Our baby's wardrobe . . . I have eaten the child, and anybody can have the clothes. I care nothing for the chrysalis when the jewel is flown.'

2. Gilbert's 'The Comic Physiognomist', *Fun* (19 Dec. 1863)

detected anyone under those circumstances, and I never shall. As to arresting any one, I don't know how it's done.

(Thus anticipating Gripper, the incompetent detective of *A Sensation Novel* (1871) and Ko-Ko, the failed executioner.)

When an actress playing Lady Isabel in *East Lynne* proved unintelligible, Gilbert rewrote her lines as she spoke them (17 February 1866):

Though I am the wife of a mere country mumble, yet I am the daughter of an Earl. Mumble, mumble, mumble. My husband is wealthy and mumble, and I love him mumbly; but I am jealous of him. I fear he loves Barbara Hare. Mumble.

Clutching her child, she says wildly, 'Ha! ha! Mumble! It is my own Mumble!' In Act 4 she dies, crying, 'Oh, I am mumbling, I am mumbling!'

As one of the few who sat through Edmund Falconer's interminable Irish drama *Oonagh*, Gilbert repeatedly inserted editorial brackets in his review (8 December 1866) to the effect that '*A conversation, twenty minutes long . . . cut out for want of space. Apologies to* MR. FALCONER.' Opening night was further signalized by a deliberately mistimed stage-cloth which literally upset a row of actors and convulsed the already antagonistic audience.[38]

At first, Gilbert made no direct comment in these reviews, but later he added a paragraph labelled 'Ourselves' in which he pronounced summary justice. Here, however, he did not neglect to praise good acting; indeed, some of the actors he noticed, such as Hermann Vezin and Edgar Bruce, were later to appear in his own plays. He liked Vezin's intelligence and Bruce's 'gentlemanliness', by which he meant a quiet style.

Although Gilbert did not invent the burlesque review,[39] he made it peculiarly his own, and the Savoy librettos were to benefit from it. The intrusive music, for instance, which accompanied the hero of *Wait and Hope*, retitled by Gilbert 'The Builder's Private Band' (18 March 1871), would one day remind the Duke of Plaza-Toro that 'It is at such moments as these that one feels how necessary it is to travel with a full band.' The theatrical types hired to represent the Prince of Monte Carlo's suite in *The Grand Duke* are undoubtedly 'Adelphi guests', as

[38] R. Reece, 'Unrehearsed Effects', *Theatre*, NS 2 (Apr. 1879), 168.
[39] See T. R. Ellis III, 'Burlesque Dramas in the Victorian Comic Magazines', *Victorian Periodicals Review*, 15 (winter 1982), 138–43.

Gilbert christened the lacklustre supers of that theatre in the 1860s. '[D]on't stand like sticks,' the Prince adjures them, 'but appear to take an intelligent and sympathetic interest in what is going on.' In *The Mikado* Ko-Ko escapes execution for flirting by being made the executioner himself, the townspeople reasoning that 'who's next to be decapited | Cannot cut off another's head | Until he's cut his own off.' This reasoning seems to be a refinement of Christal's speech in Gilbert's review of *Jezebel* (24 December 1870): 'I am a bigamist. I was sentenced to death for the crime, and should have been hanged if it had not been that there was a difficulty in finding someone who wasn't a bigamist, to hang me.'

Concurrent with these reviews, *Fun* was publishing Gilbert's most durable contributions, the Bab Ballads. 'Bab' had begun as his signature for illustrations. Short for 'Baby', pronounced 'Babby', it was characteristic of an era of short *noms de plume* and *du crayon*: Phiz, Ape, Gilbert's favourite Boz, Spy, and so on.

In Bab's fantastic yet topical world, Captain Reece, the Bishop of Rum-ti-Foo, Sir Blennerhasset Portico, the Reverend Hopley Porter, and their ilk lead lives—or deaths—compounded of the grotesque and the impossibly logical. Cause and effect are dislocated; modifiers annul their nouns; things become their physical, behavioural, or moral opposites, especially in 'My Dream' (19 March 1870), Gilbert's first detailed enunciation of the laws of Topsyturvydom.

Tight metrical structures and rhymes give Bab's personages a frame to burst out of, and in this respect they are like figures in a farce. Their energy results in frequent, parodistic violence, which is regularized into laughter by the rules of etiquette, and by the ridiculous names of the characters involved. When, for example, Macphairson Clonglocketty Angus McClan finally elicits 'something resembling an air' from his bagpipes, the agonized Sassenach, Pattison Corby Torbay, draws his claymore and '(this was I think, in extremely bad taste), | Divided CLONGLOCKETTY close to the waist.' The Scottish maidens wail until Pattison touches his hat, addresses them as his dears, and points out his own superior charms. They vow that 'A pleasanter gentleman never was seen.' In the accompanying drawing, Clonglocketty's lower half sits upright on a hilltop while the prettiest maiden, Ellen McJones Aberdeen, goes off with Pattison Corby Torbay.

Other ballads, other satire. The eponymous Prince Il Baleine (28 August 1869), exhausted by the foolish adulation of British snobs, introduces his valet Brown, to them. Brown shines with reflected light, and

26

'The Snobs, with joy insane, | Kotoo'd to Brown unseemly;' Brown, however, does not complain, and snobs and valet reappear in Gilbert's *The Fortune Hunter* (1897). The subtler 'Bishop and the Busman' (17 August 1867) demonstrates the power that labels and stereotypes have over our view of reality. Here, a bearded Jewish bus-driver is daily badgered by an antisemitic bishop. Finally, to escape this persecution, the busman agrees to 'Become a Christian kid!' (the bishop's wording). Immediately his beard turns to blond whiskers, his nose shrinks, his name instantly becomes Adolphus Brown and he marries the bishop's pretty daughter.[40]

Often Bab tinkered with proportions or equations. When the Periwinkle Girl (1 February 1868) is offered only 'guilty splendour' by two dukes she thinks will marry her, she turns to 'A man of lowly station— | A miserable grov'ling Earl', whose 'soul was good and pure, | Although his rank was humble', and who has fortunately had 'A decent education'. Conversely for Gentle Alice Brown, the daughter of a robber (23 May 1868), marriage to a respectable young man would shock her parents and family priest, who lives by absolving family crimes at a very low figure.

Neither the army, the navy, the church, nor the stage escapes Bab's attention, and many a satiric figure remained 'Photographically lined | On the tablet of [his] mind' when he came to write librettos. But above all, Bab satirized human nature in its inconstancy, greed, egotism, self-interestedness, hypocrisy, credulity, and, ultimately, in its mortality. In 'The Pantomime "Super" to his Mask' (24 February 1866), an ugly 'big head' reproaches its wearer for himself being a mask which distorts and degrades his brain and soul. A cadaverous actor in 'At a Pantomime' plays Father Christmas in *Harlequin Life and Death* at the Theatre Royal, World (28 December 1867), which Gilbert believed was one of the best things he ever wrote.[41]

Other ballads are purely funny, however, as are Ferdinando's search for the writer of the bonbon mottoes that Elvira pulls at supper ('Ferdinando and Elvira', 17 February 1866) and Old Peter's difficulties when he becomes invisible, but his clothes do not ('The Perils of Invisibility', 20 August 1870).

---

[40] Sinclair Lewis used the same satiric device, of seeing stereotypes rather than reality, but very seriously, in his novel *Kingsblood Royal*, where a fair-skinned, red-haired young man discovers a trace of 'black blood' in his ancestry. Immediately in his former friends' eyes he assumes caricature negroid features.

[41] Browne, *W. S. Gilbert*, 16–17.

The wild originality of the Babs falls within the broad outlines of nineteenth century comic verse as practised by Thackeray, Calverly, the elder Hood, *et al.* Perhaps, however, they have most often been coupled with Richard Harris Barham's *Ingoldsby Legends*, the last series of which appeared when Gilbert was 11. He could scarcely not have read them, for not only were they very popular and often reprinted, but they were also just the sort of supernatural tales his father enjoyed. Yet, some shared motifs apart,[42] Barham's irregular headlong rhymes and gruesomely grinning Gothic are generally very different in effect from Gilbert's neat stanzas and contemporaneity. To take a characteristic example, instead of Barham's gibbeted murderers in the supernatural 'Hand of Glory', Gilbert's 'The Ghost, the Gallant, the Gael, and the Goblin' (14 March 1868) describes a contest between a tragedy ghost and a low-comedy goblin. For years they haunt 'a stalwart Englishman' and a 'hardy Hieland man' in vain, never realizing that one is a tailor's dummy and the other a tobacconist's wooden Scot.

Likewise, Bab's illustrations have been compared to John Tenniel's (not yet Sir John in the 1860s), but any resemblance arises not so much from influence (Bab and Alice are almost exact contemporaries) as from a tradition and engravers in common.[43] In fact, Gilbert's use of disproportion makes his style closer to that of William Brunton, another *Fun* artist. Tenniel's pictures, moreover, are far more detailed than Gilbert's, whose individuality lies in the kinetic vitality of his contorted figures, always in motion or about to be.

Nevertheless, when Tenniel and Noel Paton both declined to illustrate *Through the Looking Glass*, Dodgson, casting about, thought of Gilbert, whom he did not know, but whose drawings he had seen: 'his power in grotesque is extraordinary,' Dodgson wrote to a friend in June 1868, '—but I have seen no symptoms of his being able to draw anything pretty and graceful. . . . Some of his pictures are full of fun'.[44] Gilbert could, of course, draw delightful grown-up girls, but Tenniel returned to the fold and nothing came of it. Interestingly enough, when

---

[42] Gilbert's 'The Troubadour' and Ingoldsby's 'The Forlorn One' both use the same kind of reversal in which objects of sentimental pity turn out to be criminals. Other examples of shared motifs are wildly comic names, dismemberment, and decapitation, which Ingoldsby treats much more bloodily and frequently than does Gilbert.

[43] P. James, 'A Note on Gilbert as Illustrator', in *Selected Bab Ballads Written and Illustrated by W. S. Gilbert*, introd. H. Pearson (privately printed; Oxford: Oxford University Press, 1955), 117.

[44] P. Muir, *English Children's Books 1600 to 1900* (London: B. T. Batsford Ltd., 1954), 140–1.

*Through the Looking Glass* was published in 1872, Tom Hood, reviewing it enthusiastically (6 January 1872) was reminded of the Bab Ballads.

When Tom Hood became editor of *Fun*, his self-appointed task had been 'to secure "the greatest laughter of the greatest number" ' (20 May 1865) and to shoot follies with the double-barrels of wit and humour (a coincidental foreshadowing of Gilbert's epitaph forty-six years later). By the time that its second proprietor, Edward Wylam, sold the paper to the Dalziels in 1870, its copyright and good will were worth £6,000,[45] then a by no means inconsiderable sum. Hood had raised its circulation to rival *Punch*'s forty thousand, and there is no doubt that Gilbert was essential to this success.

He continued to be a journalist into the early 1870s, adding to his regular work for *Fun* any other posts he could contrive. He reviewed not only for the *Illustrated Times*, but briefly for the *Daily News*, for the *Sunday Times*, and the *Observer*. He and Clement Scott filled in for each other, and, according to Scott, Gilbert's forthright criticism as his stand-in lost Scott his job. Considering Scott's own reviews, this seems unlikely. Gilbert even wrote for the *Invalide Russe*, the organ of the Russian War Office. All these and his contributions to monthly magazines augmented *Fun*'s pay of £1 a column, or less than a column, less than £1.[46] He no longer had a Civil Service salary, and, as a barrister, he rarely had a chance of addressing a British jury. But at the same time, he had found another way of supplementing his income—he was embarking on his true *métier* and writing for the theatre.

---

[45] G. and E. Dalziel, *The Brothers Dalziel* (London: Methuen and Co., 1901), 273–4.

[46] C. E. Lauterbach, 'Taking Gilbert's Measure', *Huntington Library Quarterly*, 19 (Feb. 1956), 198. Gilbert sometimes received a few extra shillings.

# 3

## The 1860s: First Stages

let there be no huge red noses, nor extravagant monstrous wigs,
nor coarse men garbed as women

Gilbert, *Rosencrantz and Guildenstern*

THE theatrical milieu of the *Fun* gang alone might have fixed
Gilbert's interest on the playhouse, even had he not been a stage-
struck boy who once followed a famous clown down the Strand[1] and
who forced his schoolmates to act in dramas of his own composition.
Since then he had written enough unproduced plays to qualify as a
'Great Unacted', but by late 1865 he had gained some experience in the
lighter forms of his day, especially in farce and pantomime.

The early Victorian playbill with its curtain-raiser, serious drama,
musical play, and after-piece had dwindled, but short pieces were still
necessary. These were usually one-act farces and comediettas, the farces
heavily influenced by John Maddison Morton's archetypal *Box and
Cox*, completely 'Englished' from French originals as was the custom.
The dramatis personae of farce were both exaggerated and stereotypic,
often drawn from the small tradesman class (grocers were evidently
intrinsically funny). Their dialogue was repetitive, filled with catch-
phrases and distorted pronunciation, wordplay having replaced French
sexual innuendo. 'Screaming farces', a speciality of the Adelphi
Theatre, were so called because of their pace and because audiences
screamed with laughter and surprise at rapid alternations, alterations,
complications, and extrications which composed the plot, as characters
see-sawed through permutations of disguise and recognition or com-
peted for some desired person or object. Words were often mistaken for
things; characters snatched with incorrigible ingenuity at improbable
expedients, and timing was of the essence.

---

[1] E. A. Browne, *W. S. Gilbert* (London: John Lane, 1907), 11. The clown was Tom Barry,
who disillusioningly entered a pub before Gilbert could speak to him.

Such a farce may have been Gilbert's 'All in the Wrong', submitted unsuccessfully to the Strand Theatre in 1860, of which only the title remains, and was certainly Gilbert's *A Colossal Idea*, probably written in 1862 and intended for, but not achieving production.[2] The latter is a workmanlike manipulation of conventional materials, originally imported from France, to which Gilbert added the topicality of the Volunteer Movement. The colossal idea is an expedient of Mr Yellowboy, a retired, red-haired grocer in a check suit, who nightly shuts himself up, allegedly to write the 123rd edition of the *Encyclopedia Britannica*, but really to steal away to masquerades, costumed as Richard Cœur de Lion. His wife, in turn, conceals her purchase of a fashionable 'Rifleman' jacket. Of course, Yellowboy assumes the 'Rifleman' is a person, specifically a large Volunteer, who cut him out at the masquerade. Also, of course, the Volunteer is his brother-in-law, newly arrived and wearing a false moustache. At last all identities, including those of the jacket and the moustache, are sorted out, and Yellowboy gives up the *Encyclopedia* since his 'research' has led him into low places.

This farce, although neat, playable, and still funny, really differs little from many others of its day, such as the anonymous 'Carte de Visite' (1862), where the ambiguous garment is a borrowed shawl, the discussion of a photograph is mistaken for a threat of assassination, and the supposed lover is really a brother.[3] Nor was Gilbert's first staged play particularly individualized. This was a comedietta, *Uncle Baby*, performed as a curtain-raiser at the Lyceum Theatre, 31 October 1863.

Comediettas generally confined themselves to less extravagant plots than those of farce; they were amusing yet capable of sentiment, and

[2] A holograph letter from Gilbert to W. H. Swanborough of the Strand Theatre, on Education Department notepaper, 17 Oct. 1860, says he is sending Swanborough the MS of an original farce, 'All in the Wrong', which he thinks is 'adapted to the resources of your company': Harry Ransom Humanities Research Center, the University of Texas at Austin. In the case of *A Colossal Idea*, a MS partly in Gilbert's hand, partly in a copyist's, is extant in PML, together with letters showing that this is the text of *A Colossal Idea*, introd. T. Searle (London: G. P. Putnam's Sons Ltd., 1932) and misleadingly dated by Searle. The last page of the MS ends with '(Tag to follow)', indicating it was intended for performance since the 'tag' was spoken from the stage at the end of a play. This parenthesis has been crossed out, perhaps by Searle. On the first page 'Margate No. of "Fun" 1873' has been added, but I have been unable to find such a number. Although Gilbert was no longer a regular contributor to *Fun* in 1873, it would be very like him not to let *A Colossal Idea* go to waste, especially since it is set in Margate.

[3] LC/BL. This farce was licensed on 22 Dec. 1862 without any indication of author or theatre.

*Uncle Baby* is no exception. The title character, alcoholic Uncle John, is a financial burden to his orphan nieces, one of whom exclaims, 'drink is the devil's best servant on earth'.[4] Another line, later deleted, described drink as 'the parent of lust, theft, & murder',[5] a sentiment which Dr Gilbert would have approved. At the denouement, Uncle Baby shows he has grown up and secures a happy ending.

The Lyceum curtain rose half an hour late on opening night, which put the large audience in a bad mood. They wanted to get on to the main piece, *Bel Demonia*, with Charles Fechter and Kate Terry, and they audibly expressed their impatience. At least one reviewer misassumed that *Uncle Baby* was a farce, while its serious temperance talk annoyed spectators. Fortunately, the second night went better, and Gilbert's little play was applauded. Nevertheless, on 28 November *Punch* devoted a page-long parody review to demolishing the comedietta without naming its author (see Fig. 3). It managed to last until Christmas, but no manager asked Gilbert for another such piece. Intentionally or not, he dismissed *Uncle Baby* from his usually retentive memory and attempted the form no more.

Instead, after an interval, his next works to be staged were essays in pantomime and burlesque or extravaganza, popular forms so closely related that one might easily become the other by the addition or omission of a harlequinade. A burlesque might also be designated an extravaganza if it were more wittily written and less topical, more elegantly staged, more fairy- than folk-tale. Burlesque numbered Fielding's *Tragedy of Tragedies* among its antecedents, but J. R. Planché had introduced extravaganza in the 1830s, modelling it on the sparkling and spectacular French *féerie*, which gave the form elegance and wit. While Planché preferred tales from Madame D'Aulnoy and *Le Cabinet des fées*, burlesque subjects ranged from the Brothers Grimm to Dr Johnson's *Rasselas*, from Shakespeare to *Lady Audley's Secret*, although close parody was not required.

Pantomime, burlesque, and extravaganza were written in iambic pentameter couplets, ending in puns. Interpolated songs were set to traditional, popular, and operatic airs (the latter especially in extravaganza), and dances included breakdowns, cellar flaps, and pretty aerial

---

[4] *Uncle Baby* was not printed till 1968, when Terence Rees edited a privately printed text. In his introduction Dr Rees lists the portions of the play not in Gilbert's hand and suggests some collaboration and possible re-writing took place.

[5] LC/BL. These temperance sentiments, unfortunately, occur in a passage Dr Rees believes was written by Gilbert's collaborator.

## SHADOWS OF THE WEEK.

NTER now our Theatrical Shadows, and at once we take off our hat to MR. FECHTER, expressing a hope that his Theatrical Shadow may never be less! The Romantic Melodrama, *Bel Demonio*, has been preceded by a charming little piece, entitled *Uncle Baby*. Any one with the slightest pretension to taste in theatrical matters ought to go early and see *Uncle Baby*. For the benefit of those who, either by reason of a late dinner or dyspepsy, circumstances over which they have no control, may be prevented from witnessing this truly delightful Comedietta, we will attempt to give some slight notion of the plot, dialogue, and interesting situations.

The curtain rises and discovers MISS CARLOTTA LECLERCQ, dressed as *Mary* (shall we say *Mary?* very well), and seated at a desk. MISS LECLERCQ looks at the audience, and everybody cheers enthusiastically for about the space of two minutes, by MR. BARNETT's, the Acting Manager's, watch. When this has subsided the play begins in earnest.

*Mary (putting some money in a secret drawer).* Ah! for these many years——

(Goes on saying something which evidently affects her deeply, but which is totally inaudible in the gallery, and not heard in the other parts of the House, in consequence of there being some confusion in the Boxkeepers' minds as to the precise numbering of the seats.)

*Enter MR. SHORE, lightly.*

(He is supposed to be in love with *Mary*. Shall we call him *Arthur?* we never heard his name and it wasn't in the bills :—very good then, *Arthur* be it.)

*Arthur (aside).* Ah, she little knows who's down-stairs. *(Aloud.)* Mary!

*Mary (turns suddenly and almost crying).* Arthur! *(Pouts.)* How you frightened me.    [*Looks at the carpet and pouts again.*

*Arthur (who evidently has very limited ideas on any subject—aside).* She little knows who's down-stairs. *(Aloud.)* Mary!

    [MARY *pouts and locks up sixpence in a secret drawer.*

*Arthur (opening a door—aside).* She little knows who is down-stairs.

*Enter a Girlish Young Lady, whom we'll call ELLEN.*

*Ellen (with feeble passion).* Mary!

*Mary (emotionally affectionate).* Ellen! Sister!!

    [*They embrace three times.*

*Arthur (aside).* She knows who was down-stairs. *(Aloud and bashfully.)* As it's your birthday, Mary, I've brought you *this*.

("This" appeared from where we were sitting to be a small cabbage leaf, but as *Mary* called it violets on the spot, we suppose she was right.)

*Mary (rapturously).* Oh, Arthur!    [*Shakes his hands heartily.*

*Ellen.* And I've brought you this.    [*We forget what.*

*Mary (more rapturously and sobbing).* Oh, Ellen!

    [*Embraces her several times.*

*Enter a Little Boy about nine years old, whom we will call JIMMY.*

*Jimmy (squeaking).* I've brought you some Vi-lets, be-cos Sis-ter loves Vi-lets.    [*Finishes in a very high key.*

*Mary (ecstatically).* Real Violets. (*The others weren't then?*). Oh!

[*She embraces* JIMMY, *who stands with his hands in his pockets. Then crosses and embraces* ELLEN, *who embraces* MARY, *who shakes hands with* ARTHUR, *who pats* JIMMY'S *head.*

*Arthur (suddenly).* Let's hide! [*They all get behind tables and chairs.*

*Enter UNCLE BABY, played by MR. WIDDICOMB.*

*Uncle Baby (in a wandering manner).* I met a friend, and I said, there's my Mary at home.    [*They all come out of their hiding-places.*

*Mary.* Oh, you dear Uncle Baby.

[*Embraces him, he embraces* MARY, *she embraces* ELLEN, ELLEN *hugs* UNCLE BABY, UNCLE BABY *hugs* ELLEN *and* MARY, ARTHUR *shakes hands with* JIMMY, *and then the business of the scene continues.*

(*Ellen* begins telling her secret, supposed to be only intended for her sister's ear, either ear of course, probably the one farthest from the audience.)

*Gentleman in Pit.* Speak up!

*Gentleman in Boxes (angrily).* But I've got number 48, boxkeeper, and this is the third time that——

*Everybody (in every part).* Hssssssssssssh!

*Enter an aimless young man, played by MR. F. CHARLES, let us call him DUMPKINS.*

*Mary (politely).* Mr. Dumpkins—my sister—Ellen—my sister Ellen.

*Dumpkins (jumping a good two feet from MARY by way of indicating a start, aside).* Ha!

*Ellen (giving a little cry).* A—(*it doesn't get to "h."*)

*Mary (cleverly).* You've met before.

*Uncle Baby (who knows nothing about it).* They've met before.

*Arthur (who has not said anything for some time).* I know what's downstairs (*goes to fetch it whatever it is*).

*Mary (severely).* I understand it all.

*Gentlemen in Pit (loudly).* That's more than we do.

[*Exeunt everybody except* MARY *and* ELLEN, *who, being alone, embrace one another in the right hand corner of the stage.*

*Mary (sweetly).* Ellen!

(*Ellen* is supposed to say "Mary," as perhaps she does. Anyhow they walk to the left-hand corner and embrace again by way of novelty. *Ellen* tells her long and melancholy history, during which the following observations are made by the deeply interested audience.)

*Indignant Paterfamilias (in Dress Circle).* Look here, boxkeeper. Where's 48? I've been put into——

*A Voice (close at hand).* A passion.

[PATERFAMILIAS *turns, but owner of voice remains undiscovered.*

*Paterfamilias.* I've been in 97 and 84—

*Somebody.* '84! Good vintage.    [*Remains undiscovered.*

*Boxkeeper.* Let me see your tickets.

*Lovers of Order.* Hussssssssssssssh!

*Paterfamilias.* I've given you my tickets. I've got none *now*.

*Boxkeeper.* Well, S r, if you've got no tickets you must go out.

*Paterfamilias.* But I've paid, I tell you, and I've given you—

*Lover of Order.* Hush, Hush, Hush!

[*Exit* PATERFAMILIAS *with* BOXKEEPER, *and they are heard having it out in the lobby. In the meant me* ELLEN *has told her story, and* MARY *has embraced her and appealed to the picture of her mother over the door ;* UNCLE BABY *enters intoxicated.*

*Uncle Baby.* Mary, lendmertenpounds!

*Mary (opens desk).* My earnings——

*Ellen.* Oh, Uncle!    [*Embraces* MARY.

[*Exit* UNCLE BABY, *and enter aimless* DUMPKINS, JIMMY, *and* ARTHUR.

*Dumpkins.* Oh, Ellen!    [*Takes her hand.*

*Arthur (bashfully).* If she only knew what was down-stairs.

*Enter UNCLE BABY, sober.*

(*Uncle Baby.* I've seen him and sold the annuity, and got permission for you all to be married. Take her—bless you—be happy ;—and if our friends in front will only join, then there will not sit down a happier party to supper than *Uncle Baby*.)

*Curtain descends.*

This piece, turned into a very pretty ballet, with *costumes à la Watteau*, and sparkling music by MR. W. H. MONTGOMERY, would open the evening very well ; but who that knows how to give a good entertainment will dose his guests with a glass of sixth-rate Chablis with his oysters, simply because the remainder of the dinner is to be washed down with the very best sparkling Moet and Chaudon? No, no, MR. FECHTER, *Bel Demonio* will suffice for everybody, and begin at eight by all means ; but if there must be a comedietta, by way of first course, then let it be something better of its kind than *Uncle Baby*.

## LINCOLN AND SHAKSPEARE.

A SENTIMENTAL admirer of PRESIDENT LINCOLN, imitating the sycophantish watch which parasites keep on the gestures of kings in the Old World, tells us in print that MR. LINCOLN lately went to hear *Macbeth*, and that when the *Macduff* had uttered the following celebrated passage, the President "wore a sad, sober face, as if suddenly his thoughts had wandered far away."

> "New sorrows
> Strike on the face of heaven, that it resounds
> As if it felt with Scotland and yelled out
> Like syllables of DOLOUR."

We are not surprised that the last word struck the President. The syllables of Dol-lar well mouthed out, are just those which would arrest MR. LINCOLN'S attention. But we suspect that his thoughts did not wander farther than MR. CHASE's manufactory of Green Backs.

### Stupid Old Woman.

MRS. PARTINGTON wants to know why the Americans cannot imitate the French in this last move as in everything else. Why not submit the quarrel to arbitration? She is sure MR. LINCOLN is arbitrary enough for anything.

3. Parody review of Gilbert's *Uncle Baby, Punch* (28 Nov. 1863)

ballets in which girls were suspended near the flaming gaslights. In all three forms, actresses in more or less discreet tights played 'principal boys' and other youths while male low comedians appeared as knockabout middle-aged women or 'dames', continuing traditions.

Pantomimes consisted of an 'opening' in which Demon King and Fairy Queen harassed or protected young mortal lovers, whose tribulations formed the plot, which was followed by a transformation scene in which the Queen changed the characters into *commedia dell'arte* figures amid tinsel showers and special effects; and, finally a concluding harlequinade, finishing with a 'rally', or grand mêlée, of rushing about and throwing things. By Gilbert's day, processions had been introduced: long march-throughs of gorgeous costumes on some theme, which increasingly curtailed the harlequinade—to the dismay of E. L. Blanchard, who had written the Drury Lane pantos for many years.

Since pantomimes were holiday entertainments for children, authors such as Blanchard slipped moral or social lessons into their openings. Extravaganza and burlesque, on the other hand, were not primarily family treats: they substituted satiric comment for didacticism and added verbal slapstick to physical slapstick.

Gilbert's first attempt at these forms may have been some lyrics for Charles Millward's 1865 pantomimes 'King Salmon; or, Harlequin Prince Paragon and the Queen of the Valley of Perpetual Spring' at the Theatre Royal, Liverpool, and 'Cock-a-Doodle-Doo; or, Harlequin Prince Chanticleer and the Princess of the Golden Valley', performed before an unruly audience at Sadler's Wells. Both these Christmas pieces are essentially the same, a thrifty practice not unknown to seasonal entertainments. They had some songs and dialogue in common, as well as plot outlines, with fish changed to fowl, Princess Silvertongue to Princess Rosytint, and so on. They also shared a pestilentially demonic villain, Grinderpest. Several lyrics in the licence copy of 'Cock-a-Doodle-Doo' are in a hand resembling Gilbert's, although his name does not appear.[6]

Millward was not a member of Gilbert's immediate circle, but he knew the *Fun* staff, especially Tom Robertson, to whom he had once lent money. A journalist, a 'mural mason', a London correspondent for country papers, and the father of William Terriss's future leading lady, Millward was only an occasional playwright. Nevertheless, his pan-

---

[6] These pantomimes have consecutive licence copy numbers, which indicate they were sent in together. 'King Salmon' has been endorsed 'Rec'd Dec. 21. Licensed Dec. 22'; no dates are given for 'Cock-a-Doodle-Doo'.

tomimes were usually successful, and he was a generous, good-natured bohemian in spite of occasional depression. H. J. Byron once said of him that 'he looked as proud as a corpse with two tombstones'.[7] There may be a touch of Millward in Gilbert's 1866 short story 'Maxwell and I', in which two young journalist-dramatists write London letters for 'credulous country journals' and collaborate on a Christmas piece for a minor theatre.

Gilbert gained more experience than money by writing songs for fin and feather. Nevertheless, he joined Millward the next Christmas for Astley's 'Great *Nation*-al Pantomime', entitled 'Hush-a-Bye, Baby, on the Tree Top; or, Harlequin Fortunia, King Frog of Frog Island, and The Magic Toys of Lowther Arcade'.[8] '*Nation*-al' was a play on W. H. C. Nation, a wealthy eccentric, who was one of the short-term managers of Astley's during a 'legitimate' interval between hippodrames.

Although Gilbert's name was absent from the playbills, Millward told Nation that he had written 'a considerable part of it' and had taken part in rehearsals.[9] With a transformation scene in a Grove of Golden Palms, a Ladybird Ballet, a perspective of Arches fringed with crystal pendants, and other splendours too numerous to mention, 'Hush-a-Bye, Baby' was obviously staged with great éclat. Underneath all this, the plot was 'tolerably simple', according to *The Times* (27 December) and was well received by a crowded house. On the satiric side, there were hits at Reform agitation, advertising, and the popular taste for 'claptrap' music-hall songs. 'Hush-a-Bye, Baby' settled in for a run of ten weeks or more on 'the Surrey side'.

Meanwhile, a more important theatrical event was taking place in the West End—the opening of Gilbert's first acknowledged play, *Dulcamara! or, The Little Duck and the Great Quack*, a burlesque of Donizetti's opera *L'Elisir d'Amore*. For this opportunity, he was indebted to Tom Robertson, who recommended him to Miss Herbert, lessee, manageress, and beautiful leading actress of the St James's Theatre. Robertson jokingly introduced his protégé as 'a stage-struck

---

[7] H. Furniss, *My Bohemian Days* (London: Hurst & Blackett, 1919), 15–16.

[8] Alternatively, in the playbill, 'Lowther Arcade' became 'Lowther Arcadia'. For a discussion of Gilbert's probable contributions to this pantomime, see T. Rees, 'W. S. Gilbert and the Pantomime Season of 1866', in J. Helyar (ed.), *Gilbert and Sullivan: Papers Presented at the International Conference Held at the University of Kansas in May 1970* (Lawrence, Kan.: University of Kansas Publications, Library Series, 37, 1971), 149–73.

[9] W. H. C. Nation, letter to *Stage* (8 June 1911).

officer in a Highland Militia Regiment'.[10] Miss Herbert, who needed a Christmas piece, gave the officer a deadline, variously remembered as a week, ten days, or two weeks;[11] he responded with 'An Eccentricity', which he must have begun to write soon after 1 December, the day on which a well-publicized libel trial ended with an award of 1 farthing damages to the plaintiff, Dr Robert Hunter.

Hunter, whose degree was American and who was not licensed in England, had antagonized English doctors by denigrating their remedies for consumption (tuberculosis) and by touting his own. He advocated inhalation of oxygen and various drugs, including belladonna and chloric acid, which he advertised heavily. Inhalation was at least healthy for Dr Hunter's income, and, indeed, no worse than more conventional treatments. When the *Pall Mall Gazette* published 'Dupes and Imposters' and named Hunter, the Doctor sued for libel. After hours of complicated medical testimony, the jury 'vindicated' him, but its contemptuous award left him a charlatan still in public opinion.[12]

Here was Donizetti's quack Dr Dulcamara ready-made to Gilbert's hand; in fact, the trial very likely turned the playwright's attention to a scarcely explored operatic subject. Hence his burlesque doctor, entering with a bellows, announces:

> I am no *jalaping* snob of Savile Row!
> I cure all maladies, in every station,
> By my new process—simple inhalation[13]

Hunter had been accused of frightening healthy readers of his advertisements into consulting him; so Gilbert's quack diagnoses consumption in each robust patient: 'I amass my patients' wealth | By telling them that they're *in ailing* health!' He advises the love-sick Nemorino, 'You'd better far inhale, as you can see | If you *in hale* condition wish to be.' Beppo, Dulcamara's zany, refers to one trial and a penny profit.

[10] L. Irving, *Henry Irving: The Actor and His World* (New York: Macmillan Company, 1952), 132. As a matter of fact, Gilbert was such an officer, but Robertson must have been joking since Gilbert, as a reviewer, would have been known in theatrical circles.

[11] Browne, *W. S. Gilbert*, 35. In 1907 Gilbert remembered that he wrote *Dulcamara* in eight days and rehearsed for ten. In his 1883 biographical sketch in the *Theatre*, he remembered it as ten days' writing and a week's rehearsal. The licence copy was sent on 18 Dec. and approved 21 Dec. under the title *The Elixir of Love*.

[12] Dr Hunter had earlier been the defendant in a trial for rape and had been acquitted.

[13] 'Jalaping snob of Savile Row' is Gilbert's parody of Alfred Vance's popular song, 'The Galloping Snob of Rotten Row'; jalap, a purgative, alludes to Dr Hunter's low opinion of conventional medicine.

Aside from this topicality, Gilbert's travesty did not radically distort the plot of the original. He did, however, add a final multiple revelation of identity in which the dramatis personae are all each other's long-lost relations, regardless of age or sex. (Beppo admits he is really Dulcamara's mother!) This is just the sort of numerically extended, parodistic denouement which Gilbert enjoyed and continued to use. He also satirized the *données* of burlesque itself by describing the peculiarities of a village

> Where all the humblest peasants talk in rhyme,
> And sing about their pleasures and their cares
> In parodies on all the well-known airs.

Furthermore, 'Each speech should have a pun in it, with very foolish fun in it', and each ballad should finish 'With a flip-up in the Skidamalink, and a flip in the juben-jube!'

*Dulcamara* was splendidly mounted: 'I never saw anything to equal it,' the young Henry Irving wrote his father after the first month of the run.[14] It was also well cast, with Carlotta Addison as a delightful Adina, the little duck, and Frank Matthews as the great quack, winning a double encore with Gilbert's parody of the popular song 'Champagne Charley'.

Since the burlesque did not appear until the Saturday after Christmas, 29 December, reviewers probably saw it with eyes somewhat rested from the strain of Boxing Day premières. They welcomed the young author's 'smart' and 'carefully written' dialogue and referred to his journalistic reputation. The allusions to Dr Hunter were immediately recognized, although critics were careful not to mention his name. Almost alone, the *Athenaeum* questioned the taste of such personal references, but conceded that they were the error of a young writer. On the same date (12 January 1867), *Fun*, with a certain predisposition to praise, ranked Gilbert with H. J. Byron, an enviable position: 'many have striven for years to achieve what Mr. Gilbert has done with his first burlesque'.

Gilbert himself had never doubted his success. As he wrote later, he had no reputation to lose,[15] and he even invited a dozen friends to an after-theatre supper at the Arundel Club. In the future he 'would as soon invite friends to supper after a forthcoming amputation at the

---

[14] 28 Jan. 1867, quoted in L. Irving, *Henry Irving*, 134.

[15] 'An Autobiography', *Theatre*, NS 1 (2 Apr. 1883), 219.

hip-joint,'—a most dangerous operation, as his father put it.[16] But in December 1866 the new dramatist was happy, although his first success brought him less money than it was worth.

In the hurry of writing and rehearsing, Gilbert evidently left open the question of author's fees. After opening night W. S. Emden, Miss Herbert's acting manager, asked what sum he expected. Accustomed to *Fun*'s measure pay of £1 per column and totting up time spent, Gilbert modestly requested 30 guineas—20 for text and 10 for rehearsals.[17] It was a reasonable demand, playwrights not being well paid, but Emden immediately knocked the guineas down to pounds, thereby saving a pound and a half. Gilbert accepted, whereupon Emden advised him never again to take so little for a piece so good. He never did, and no doubt this episode contributed to his future determination always to have his just due.

Meanwhile, he had made a new friend, with whom he discussed stagecraft far into the night at his rooms in Gray's Inn. This was Henry Irving, late of the provinces, now actor and stage manager at the St James's. Gilbert invited Irving to his supper party and introduced him to the Arundel *habitués*.[18] After *Dulcamara* closed at Easter 1867, however, Gilbert and Irving were never again so closely associated, although some years later Irving evidently asked Gilbert to write a play for him. Gilbert suggested something based on Victor Hugo's *Le Roi s'amuse*, but nothing came of it.[19] He continued to have a strong personal regard for Irving and to admire his acting until he came to feel that the adulatory public had encouraged Irving to violate 'the plainest canons of his art'[20] and to adopt a style of 'wild caricature'.

---

[16] W. Gilbert, *Shirley Hall Asylum; or, The Memoirs of a Monomaniac* (London: William Freeman, 1863), 178. W. S. Gilbert's reference to amputation has sometimes been taken out of context as evidence that he feared symbolic castration, but it was a classic gruelling operation which a doctor's son might well use as a simile. See W. S. Cox, *A Memoir on Amputation of the Thigh, at the Hip-Joint* (London: [1843]).

[17] Browne, *W. S. Gilbert*, 35–6. Professional men were paid in guineas. By agreeing to Emden's terms, Gilbert lost approximately the pay for two Bab Ballads.

[18] L. Irving, *Henry Irving*, 33.

[19] Two letters to Irving, 29 May and 7 July [n. y.] These are among other Gilbert–Irving letters in TM, marked '1881, 1883', but content suggests a much earlier date, perhaps 1874.

[20] Gilbert to Edward Pinches, 7 May 1883: PML. Pinches had asked Gilbert to let his name appear on the list of stewards for a farewell dinner to Irving, who was leaving for America in autumn. In 1869 Gilbert praised Irving as 'the very king of fashionable villains' (*Illustrated Times*, 17 July), and later admired Irving's performance of Robert Macaire: 'the perfection of eccentric character-acting' (letter to Irving, 8 May 1888: TM). In 1889 Irving agreed to be a witness for Julia Neilson, who was being sued by a predatory agent (Gilbert to Irving, 3 Feb. 1889: TM).

Although Gilbert never became, like Byron and Burnand, an incessant writer of burlesques, he did not wait long to capitalize on the success of his first venture. His second, *La Vivandière; or, True to the Corps!* was produced on 15 June 1867 by Maria Simpson's Liverpool company. Advertised as 'The New, Original, and Brilliant Operatic Extravaganza . . . From the pen of W. S. Gilbert, Esq.', it was based on another Donizetti opera, *La Figlia del Reggimento*. The subtitle was a topical allusion to A. R. Slous's just-revived prize melodrama *True to the Core; A Story of the Armada.*

Artistically speaking, *La Vivandière* was not a notable advance over its predecessor; in reading, it lacks a little of Dulcamara's *élan*, but it contains an amusing parody of Lord Byron's Manfred as played by Samuel Phelps, the tragedian. There is also an attack on the ill-mannered chauvinistic British tourist who wears his hat in foreign churches, comments on Waterloo to the French, and so on—a stereotype which Gilbert had already used in *Fun*. The wordplay in *La Vivandière* is neat: for example, 'In my chilly chalet *shilly shallying*' and Maria's farewell to her drum, 'I bid a long *tata* to my *tattoo*.'[21]

Again the denouement consists of a welter of unlikely identities, including recognition by the absence of strawberry marks. Otherwise, *La Vivandière* is notable for containing Gilbert's first 'elderly, ugly' dame (really middle-aged and somewhat plain), written for a contralto rather than some low male comedian, whose petticoat vulgarity Gilbert always disliked. The padded, dyed, and rouged Marchioness of Birkenfeldt, adapted from the opera, was played by Harriet Everard, the future Dame Partlett and Little Buttercup. At her twenty-first birthday celebration the Marchioness is confronted by a long-lost 19-year-old daughter. 'You must have been a Ma at two years old', exclaims Lord Margate, anticipating Lord Mountararat's arithmetic in *Iolanthe*.

By now, Gilbert was sure enough of his stagecraft for the piece to be announced as under his 'immediate superintendence' prior to its London production. Yet he was aware of its imperfections, or perhaps was uttering a characteristic disclaimer when he thanked a sympathetic critic for 'being good enough to blind yourself to many defects which are only too apparent to me'.[22] Less kindly, the *Porcupine* (22 June)

[21] All quotations from *La Vivandière* come from the Liverpool edition, which is the text of the first production. When the burlesque was staged in London the next year, Gilbert made a number of changes.

[22] To J. Nightingale, 27 June 1867: PML. Gilbert also asked the reviewer for another copy, his servant at the barracks having torn up the paper, and for the *Porcupine*.

4. Sketch of the burlesque *Robinson Crusoe*, showing Gilbert as An Invisible Black:
*Illustrated Times* (13 July 1867)

found Gilbert's second burlesque no better and no worse than other burlesques popular with Liverpudlians. Attributing its warm reception to its cast of favourites, the critic at least admitted that *La Vivandière* had an attractive mediocrity of conception.

Its author had scarcely read his notices when he hurried off to Aberdeen for militia duty at the King Street Barracks, returning to London by 6 July. That afternoon he played the infinitesimal role of An Invisible Black in the *Fun* gang's benefit burlesque *Robinson Crusoe; or, The Injun Bride & the Injured Wife*, which he had helped to write (see Fig. 4). Performed at the Haymarket Theatre, it raised money for the mother of their comrade Paul Gray, dead at 20. Tom Hood appeared as Hunkey Dorum, King of the Cannibal Isles; Molloy as Crusoe; Sketchley as Mrs Brown (of course). Clement Scott was A Servile Courtier, and others were accommodated with equally small roles. A professional actress, Teresa Furtado, played Pocohantas.

A month later William Schwenck married Lucy Agnes Blois Turner at St Mary Abbot's Church, Kensington; went to Boulogne for his honeymoon; and wrote a Bab Ballad, 'Babette's Love', on the way.

# 4

## Love, Marriage, Farce, and Burlesque

When a wooer | Goes a-wooing!
Gilbert, *The Yeomen of the Guard*

L UCY Turner was not, after all, Gilbert's first choice; he married
her after his courtship of Annie Thomas proved unsuccessful.

Gilbert always enjoyed the company of women, particularly intelligent ones, and he was attractive to them. He talked well, with a certain
flirtatious ease of manner, and was an excellent dancer even in a
Highland reel. Writing as The Comic Physiognomist (2 March 1867),
he described his youthful 'crushes',[1] which he would use again in his little play *Sweethearts* in 1874, and at 22 he was interested in Caroline
Milliken, the future mother-in-law of Sir John Martin-Harvey. Neither
Carry nor William seems to have been seriously in love, however, for he
drew an amusing picture of her, sitting on a Boulogne dune with
another young man's arm about her waist (see Fig. 5). He labelled Carry
'L'INFIDELE CHIFFONETTE', and the interloper, 'LE MAUDIT COLLÉGIEN'. The
tone is scarcely heartbroken.[2]

In his early *Fun* days, Gilbert found time to attend parties, masquerades, impromptu theatricals, and balls. 'I appreciate the compliment,'
he wrote in answer to an invitation (28 November 1865); ' "A Comic

[1] References to Hammersmith and King's College make it likely that some of this piece is
autobiographical.
[2] PML. This unsigned sketch, watermarked '58', formerly belonged to Caroline's daughter,
whose husband, Sir John Martin-Harvey, identified the figures as Gilbert and Caroline. This
identification obviously took place long after the drawing was made and was probably based on
family tradition. It is unlikely that Gilbert depicted himself as 'le maudit collégien', however,
for, at 22 he had his B.A. and would not be a *collégien* in the French sense, i.e. a student in a
secondary school. Nor is there any reason for Gilbert to label himself 'cursed' since the *collégien*
seems to be on very friendly terms with the young lady. If Gilbert's arm were round Carry's
waist, he would hardly call her an 'unfaithful little rag-pickeress'. Finally, the uniform which
the young man wears looks more French than English, perhaps the uniform of a *collégien*.

5. Gilbert's unsigned sketch of the 'collégien' and Caroline Milliken: PML

Romeo!" Well I never did! But I will, if you like.' He ended his acceptance 'With tender (but comic) remembrances to the Comic Juliet
(whoever she may be)'.[5] No doubt, this was to be an amateur performance of a farce or burlesque. Another Gilbert letter (28 April 1866),
written from Liverpool asks a friend to procure an invitation to Mrs
Buckstone's ball for him.[4] More amateur theatricals found him enjoying a mild flirtation with Kate Terry, while her sister Ellen flirted with
Arthur Sullivan.[5] When Marie Wilton's company was playing in
Liverpool and Gilbert was practising law on the Northern Circuit, the
young players and young barristers spent evenings holding impromptu
mock trials in lodgings, Marie presiding as judge in pink dressing-gown
and cotton-wool wig. For variety they once gave an 'opera' extempore
in Italian gibberish with Marie as prima donna, Gilbert as lover, and
the actor John Hare, becloaked, behatted, and bedaggered as villain. In
the audience, Tom Robertson and H. J. Byron laughed their utmost; 'it
was a very happy time'.[6]

[5] To Miss Coyne: PML.  [4] To Stirling Coyne: PML.

[5] E. Terry, *The Story of My Life* (New York: Doubleday, Page & Co., 1909), 127.

[6] *Mr. & Mrs. Bancroft On and Off the Stage: Written by Themselves* (3rd edn.; London:
Richard Bentley and Son, 1888), i. 207–9.

It must have been an especially happy time for Gilbert since he was shortly to fall in love, if he had not already done so, with Annie Hall Thomas, a novelist two years younger than himself. The only daughter of Lieutenant George Thomas, RN, Annie published her first book when she was 24, and William Tinsley said of her thereafter that she could write a three-volume novel in six weeks.[7] Eventually she wrote more than a hundred, to say nothing of short stories, articles, and verses.

Always popular but never prestigious, Miss Thomas's work was soon grouped with that of her friend Florence Marryat, M. E. Braddon, and other writing women, who, as a male critic said, 'appeared to know everything that men knew', and whose readers could therefore 'attain an almost perfect knowledge of every vice that festers beneath the sun'.[8] He allowed Miss Thomas some cleverness and smartness, but little else, and his comments were characteristic of the next thirty years of reviewing. Even in the broader-minded 1890s, the *Illustrated London News* (10 April 1897) remarked that the hero of her *Four Women in the Case* would be the villain of a more wholesome story. This reviewer depicted the authoress as writing hand to mouth in headlong haste, and it is certainly true that Annie Thomas was never a dilettante 'lady novelist', but always a professional who wrote rapidly for money—and earned a comfortable sum. Her 'festering vices' would hardly count as a cold sore in today's fiction.

Although she was later attracted to spiritualism, Annie's mind was essentially modern: 'We love the modern time, | We prize the present day,' she exclaimed in *London Society* for January 1869. Her heroines are often impetuous, independent, and unconventional, sometimes vagabonds or actresses, but always attractive. Indeed, as Robinson Crusoe asked, in *Fun*'s benefit burlesque: who would be 'reluctant to forget his promises | For some fair heroine of Miss Annie Thomas's?' Evidently very few!

Annie's novels cast no stones at stage or sinner; like Gilbert, she preferred kindness to propriety. In her 1868 novel *False Colours*, for instance, her character Mrs Scorrier, a good woman with an illegitimate child, anticipates both Gilbert's Mrs Van Brugh (*Charity*, 1874) and Wilde's Mrs Arbuthnot (*A Woman of No Importance*, 1894) in being intrinsically kinder, more virtuous, and more truly charitable than the

---

[7] W. Tinsley, *Random Recollections of an Old Publisher* (London: Simpkin, Marshall, Hamilton, Kent & Co. Ltd., 1890), ii. 248–9.

[8] 'Women's Novels', *Broadway* (Mar. 1868), 505. By Sept. *Broadway* was publishing an Annie Thomas serial.

'unfallen' society around her. Annie's tone is mildly ironic, occasionally acerbic or satiric; she looked at her world with a wry smile, and she was very skilful at reproducing women's cut-and-thrust social fencing. Frequently she was epigrammatic: for example, the Pottingers are 'Ready, in fact, to be agreeable after their lights, which were dim';[9] or, Miss Barlow is 'one of those products of nature of which the supply is considerably in excess of the demand'.[10]

Miss Thomas also used the journalistic background she had so rapidly acquired. Stanley Villars, for instance, the disappointed clergyman–journalist of *On Guard* (1865), descends through the circles of authorship to slave for a pittance. His editor, Bacon, who pays more in politeness than in coin, seems to be Annie's view of James Hogg, editor of *London Society*, for whom both she and Gilbert wrote. Furthermore, the young journalist Bligh who does his best to save Stanley, suggests Gilbert.

A much fuller picture of Gilbert in his first professional decade, however, appears in the hero of Annie's 1866 novel *Played Out*. Roydon Fleming in his late twenties has somewhat better brains than most young men, a fact not immediately apparent, the novelist tells us, 'for though Roydon Fleming had a vein of humour, and a tolerable command of brilliant language in which to clothe it, he was apt to be reserved, almost brusque, to strangers and to those whom he did not like'.

Roydon is over 6 feet tall; unlike Gilbert he has had no military training, but possesses a lounging grace and can arrange a plaid picturesquely over his shoulders. (William had transferred from the West Yorkshire Militia to the Aberdeenshire Militia the year before.) Rather shy, Roy nevertheless has a dangerous knack of looking suddenly serious and a little hurt when he wants to appeal to a woman. Girls mistakenly think him 'German-looking' because he is fair, with tawny moustaches and blue eyes; although he is not handsome, he commands observation. Like Annie herself Roy loves horses, and she sees him as a thoroughbred, bearing the mark of the governing classes even though he is only a third-class clerk, making £200 a year at Somerset House.

Away from the office, Roydon belongs to journalistic Bohemia, where one of his highest ambitions at the moment is to have a burlesque produced. When Annie describes Roy as a writer, his identity is

---

[9] *False Colours* (London: Tinsley Brothers, 1869), ii. 53.
[10] *Played Out* (London: Chapman and Hall, 1866), ii. 198.

even more obvious, for he has 'the art of wording nonsense epigram-matically' and his phraseology is happy, tricky, and ear-catching. Although it is unlikely that Miss Thomas visited Mr Gilbert's bachelor chambers, her description of them is characteristic enough: bookcases full of standard modern novelists and his favourite Fielding, Smollett, Wycherly, Jonson, Bacon, Addison, and Ingoldsby, among others; a table heaped with rough sketches, drafts or notes for pieces for weekly papers, uncorrected proofs, rejected copy, and pen-and-ink caricatures of friends.

Roydon's resemblance to Gilbert is most developed in volume i of *Played Out*; after that the tides of plot bear him away from his original (although, prophetically, in the last volume he marries a beautiful, fresh blonde who appeals to his artist's soul). Yet it is clear that Annie Thomas modelled him on a man she knew well, and whom she found physically attractive and intellectually congenial. They must have appealed to each other's sense of fun. Of course, William read *Played Out* and drew a teasing sketch, after Millais's *Trust Me*, in which he holds out his hand for 'The Novel' which Annie is hiding behind her back (see Fig. 6).[11]

What happened next must be surmised and is impossible to date completely. Yet it would seem that sometime during 1866, Gilbert pro-posed marriage and was rebuffed by Annie's widowed mother, perhaps because of his bohemianism and increasing connection with the stage. This proposal and rejection may have taken place in late May, since on 9 June, Gilbert published 'To My Bride (Whoever She May Be)' in *Fun*. The speaker, someone very like Gilbert, offers himself to the marriage market as being

> Tall, gentlemanly, but extremely plain
> Neat—dresses well; his temper has been classified
> As hasty; but he's very quickly pacified.

He is working 'mildly' at the Bar, but is not affluent. He has already been broken to harness

> by a lady
> Who parts with him—perhaps a poor excuse for him—
> Because she hasn't any further use for him.

[11] PML. The drawing suggests Annie had intentionally used Gilbert as a model and perhaps told him so.

6. Gilbert's sketch, after Millais's *Trust Me*, showing himself with Annie Thomas: PML

The last lines taste bitter, for Gilbert did not take Annie's refusal lightly whenever it came. When she wrote him the next summer to say that she was about to marry a curate named Pender Cudlip, he answered:

My dear Annie—
I am heartily glad to [hear] of your approaching marriage—heartily glad—after a little qualm of irritation and unreasonable jealousy. I sincerely hope you will be quite happy—I'm sure the Rev Pen (I can't read the rest) will be—unless he hates horses. Please remember that I always prophesied a clergyman or a Marine—. . . . Is he Sensation, Ritualistic or Homely Domestic? Croziers, Crosses, Crucifixes, or Cabbages? I hope he hasn't got a Devonshire living, but that you will come to London to live. I can see you at work embroidering an Altar Cloth or a Pulpit Cushion for him. I suppose you have extemporized a taste for Charity Children & subscribe to the Religious Tract Society.

I don't know (joking apart) when I have heard anything that gave me more unaffected pleasure—affected, at all events, only by the fear that you will settle down in your Devonshire Sahara for life.

I enclose a letter which has just arrived for M$^{rs}$ Thomas, who, I hope is

46

quite well, I trust you had no difficulty in getting her consent—she was always obdurate.

> With my best wishes,
> > Believe me to be,
> > > My dear Annie
> > > > Ever sincerely yours
> > > > > WS Gilbert
>
> P.S. I die the first week in August[12]

He drew a skull and bones across the PS.

This letter makes it clear that Mrs Thomas was a stumbling-block and that Gilbert, although his tone is jocular, even facetious in the post-script, still has more than a little qualm of jealousy. Yet, in his charac-teristic way of denying and rendering comic what he felt deeply, he made a small profit from his disappointment by writing a Bab Ballad, 'Johnny and Freddy' (*Fun*, 3 August). Here two eccentric dancers com-pete for Mary Ann's hand, only to have her marry a curate who dislikes the stage.

Annie's own response to Gilbert is impossible to know. Since Gilbert was not familiar with her husband-to-be's name, the acquaintance was probably a recent one. An undated note from Miss Thomas to Mr Cudlip indicates she is delighted to go somewhere unspecified with him,[13] but she did not totally forget her former suitor during her years in her 'Devonshire Sahara'. In 1870 she asked him to become her daughter's godfather, Mrs Charles Dickens having been her son's god-mother. Gilbert replied in a joking letter (4 October) that he had 'god-fathered five infants this year & the responsibility is becoming overwhelming'—but he agreed.[14]

In 1873 the Cudlips moved to St Magdalen, Paddington, and Annie invited Gilbert to a party in January 1874, but press of work made him refuse.[15] She wrote him a congratulatory letter when *Broken Hearts* was produced in December 1875, for which he thanked her warmly.[16]

---

[12] PML. Gilbert wrote from 28 Eldon Road, which he seems to have been occupying prior to his own forthcoming marriage. At first he misdated his letter 11 June, then corrected it to July. He also omitted a word in the first sentence, which I have added in square brackets.

[13] JWS.

[14] PML. Annie addressed her letter to Sussex Villas rather than to Essex Villas, where Gilbert was now living. After her marriage, Gilbert always addressed her formally as Mrs Cudlip.

[15] Gilbert to Mrs Cudlip, 28 Jan. 1874: PML.

[16] Gilbert's letter is dated 17 Dec. from Essex Villas. No year is given, but only *Broken Hearts* fits that time and place. Annie's letter to Gilbert has not been found, but Gilbert's reply indicates its general content: PML.

A few months later (8 April 1876) he sent her a consolatory letter for a 'frightful loss' she had just sustained, presumably of a child.[17] Since Gilbert had heard of it through Florence Marryat, it is unlikely that the two households kept in touch. After eight years in London, the Cudlips returned to the country, where Pender eventually became a rural dean and made a special study of the Eucharist;[18] Annie continued to publish novels.

Many years later, a middle-aged Mrs Cudlip asked a middle-aged dramatist if he could help her daughter in a dramatic career. Rather sadly, Gilbert replied (26 May 1898) that he had severed his connection with the stage and had no influence, but he would keep his ears and eyes open. 'It will give me great pleasure to be of service to your daughter.'[19] Annie Thomas Cudlip outlived W. S. Gilbert by seven years.

In spite of his unhappiness at losing Annie, Gilbert was resilient enough to look for someone else, and he found a pretty fair-haired 19-year-old, Lucy Agnes Blois Turner, whom he had known since she was 16. Her family was a distinguished one in India, her indefatigable maternal grandfather, Sir Herbert Compton (1770–1846) having risen from enlisted soldier to Lord Chief Justice of Bombay and a knighthood in 1831. His sons continued in the Indian Civil Service, while his daughter Herbertina (1815–1913) married Captain Thomas Metcalfe Blois Turner, Lucy's father, on 24 January 1835. The Turners were a numerous clan in that part of India, and Captain Turner and his elder brother Henry Blois Turner ranked next to each other in the Bombay Engineers (of the India Company's Army), Henry eventually becoming a Lieutenant-General in the Royal Army. When Thomas M. B. Turner died prematurely in Bombay on 7 July 1847, Henry immediately went on furlough, which suggests that he accompanied his sister-in-law and her children, including the unborn Lucy, back to England. He returned to Bombay in 1851, rising ten years later to be Chief Engineer of Scinde, and left India for good in 1863.[20]

---

[17] PML.

[18] See his pamphlet *Bible Worship: or The Continuity of Sacrificial Worship* (Oxford: Mowbray and Co., 1895). Information about Pender Cudlip comes from J. Foster, *Alumni Oxonienses* (Oxford: Parker & Co., 1888), i. 324; *Clergy List* (1869, 1870), and *Crockford's Clerical Directory* (1885).

[19] PML. Sir Arthur Sullivan recorded meeting Miss Cudlip on 23 Dec. 1891: 'nice contralto voice [—] no power as yet'. By 1909 she appeared as a soprano at a Caruso Concert, Royal Albert Hall, conducted by Thomas Beecham.

[20] For Sir Herbert Compton, see C. E. Buckland, *Dictionary of Indian Biography* (London: Swan Sonnenschein & Co. Ltd., 1906), 96. For information about the Turner family, I am indebted to George C. McElroy, who consulted the Indian Army Lists and the Bombay

Born on 14 November 1847 at Blything in Suffolk, Lucy was eleven years younger than Gilbert almost to the day. Her mother did not marry again, but lived out a widowhood longer than her queen's. (Among her possessions at her death was a small envelope inscribed 'Ferns from the Himalayas'.)[21] Herbertina's brother-in-law must therefore have supplied indispensable masculine advice and perhaps financial management—a situation Gilbert used briefly in his 'Tale of a Dry Plate'. When he first met the Turners, possibly through militia connections, they were living in Curzon Street. 'I remember how kind and agreeable he used to be in the old Curzon Street days,' Lucy's cousin wrote to her at her husband's death.[22] Evidently gingerbread was a Curzon Street speciality,[23] very appealing to Gilbert's well-known sweet tooth.

Having been denied Annie, William began to feel an interest in Lucy. Engagements and marriages crept into the Comic Physiognomist's columns: 'The C.P. in Love' (2 March 1867); 'Some Engaged Men' (16 March); 'The C.P. at a Wedding' (27 April), and so on. Gilbert also gave Lucy's sister Grace a copy of his published *Dulcamara*, inscribed with 'kind regards'.[24] All this suggests an engagement in mid-March and a minimum conventional wait of six months before a marriage on 6 August at St Mary Abbot's, Kensington, by the Revd Herbert Turner, a visiting priest and probably a relative of the bride. Perhaps the PS of Gilbert's long letter to Annie, 'I die the first week in August', refers to his own marriage as well. At least it is evident that Miss Thomas was still in his mind when he married Miss Turner.

The marriage settlements suggest that there was some money on Lucy's side,[25] while, if we believe 'To My Unknown Bride', Gilbert estimated his personal resources at £300 a year, aside from what he earned. After a short continental honeymoon, the young couple began domestic life at 28 Eldon Road, Kensington. Even though Gilbert was older than his bride he was not yet 31. He assumed a jocular mantle of age, however, signing himself her 'Old Boy' when he wrote from camp and

Baptismal, Burial, and Marriage Records (microfilm) in the India Office Library. Lucy's father signed the marriage register as 'T. M. Blois Turner', the Blois connection evidently being important to the Turners. 'Metcalfe' probably came from Charles, later Lord Metcalfe.

[21] JWS. At Herbertina's death the ferns were given to her 'tweeny', later Mrs Brien.

[22] Richard Turner, 8 June 1911: WSG/BL Add. MS 49,343.

[23] A recipe for Curzon Street gingerbread is included in *Kitty's Cookery Book*, published privately by Lady Gilbert for charitable purposes during W.W.1.

[24] PML.

[25] C. Prestige, '"Everything that's Excellent": Gilbert and his Legal Circle', paper given at the conference 'Gilbert and Sullivan and their Circles', University of Leicester, 17 July 1988.

calling her 'Kitten', 'Kitty', and (in letters) 'Dearest Kits'. She was, indeed, small and delicate, 'dainty' as contemporaries described her. Even in middle age, her arms and skin would still be lovely and youthful.[26] Depending on who described her nose, it was 'a little dab' or 'a dear little nose'.[27] Her voice was gentle and quiet.[28] She called her husband 'Willie'.[29]

The newly married Kitten looks out at us from a photograph and from her husband's pencil drawing with a level glance and a prettily determined chin. Elegantly dressed in later pictures, she gives a sense of dignity and erect carriage unusual in small women. 'She pulled herself up to look tall,' her gardener's daughter said of her in middle age.[30] Mrs Gilbert's sense of fun was not as great as Mrs Cudlip's, however. At a dinner party, for instance, she said of an excellent joint of meat, 'I had it cut off myself.' Gilbert at once remarked, 'No wonder it was so tender!' Lucy did not immediately see the joke.[31]

Since her family was relatively close at hand, the young Mrs Gilbert maintained a close daughterly relationship with her mother, whose favourite she was. This continued throughout Mrs Turner's long life, and the Gilberts often saw more of the Turners and Comptons than of his own relatives. When Willie was abroad or in barracks at Aberdeen, Lucy stayed with her mother or visited other members of her family. Although she did not immediately thrust herself into her husband's theatrical circles, she was a playgoer, and in time Gilbert came to rely on her reports of deviations in the stage business of his operas.

Like Annie Thomas, Kitty enjoyed riding; she and Willie frequently rode together, and sometimes she kept him on a short rein. When, for instance, Annie, now Cudlip, offered Gilbert a pug, he perforce refused: 'I am not allowed to have more than two dogs'.[32] When he was late in

[26] Telephone interview with Mrs Brien, 27 July 1974.

[27] Personal interview with Mrs H. G. Hart (1974), daughter of Lady Gilbert's gardener ('dab of a nose'), and letter from Nancy McIntosh to J. M. Gordon [1935] ('dear little nose').

[28] Personal interview with Miss Emily Paxton (1974), formerly Lady Gilbert's maid.

[29] In the surviving fragment of a joint letter to an unknown addressee, n.d., [probably autumn 1868]: WSG/BL Add. MS 49,345.

[30] Mrs H. G. Hart. Pamela Maude, one of the children who visited the Gilberts at Grim's Dyke, remembered that Mrs Gilbert sat up very straight and had 'the kind of face that would have looked just as suitable on a child': *Worlds Away* (London: John Baker, 1964), 126.

[31] H. Orchardson Grey, *The Life of William Q. Orchardson* (London: Hutchinson & Co. Ltd., n.d.), 110.

[32] From Camp, Redhills, Aberdeen, n.d.: PML. Gilbert facetiously offered to slaughter one of his present dogs 'to create a vacancy, but I can't get at it, as they are in Leicestershire & I am in Aberdeen'.

meeting Kitty's train, he 'caught it',[33] and there was a row when Marion Terry perhaps outstayed her welcome.[34] Even an elderly Gilbert concealed an unsuccessful flutter in stocks for 'domestic reasons'.[35] For all her Dresden doll look, Kitty could make her weight felt and 'in a soft way wore the breeches'.[36] As Gilbert once remarked in *Fun*, (17 June 1865), the *soupçon* of a will of her own 'makes fair girls still more adorable, because you had not supposed temper compatible with flaxen hair'.

Yet even the happiest of marriages may have rows, and the Gilberts' marriage was happy even if Kitty was not the subdued and submerged little person some biographers have imagined. As time passed, not only did she prove an excellent chatelaine of the ever-larger houses which her husband's increasing income made possible, but she also became the centre of his happiness, indispensable to him, the one person he trusted unchangingly.[37] In spite of their childlessness, they had children about them, for Gilbert was a kind of magic uncle to the sons and daughters of friends, providing lavish chocolates, theatre boxes, and delightful parties, including what must have been one of the very first electrically lit Christmas trees.[38]

Such hospitality was, however, more than a decade in the future when they began life together in 1867. Gilbert continued to write for *Fun* and other periodicals and made use of his foothold in the theatre to turn out farces, a Christmas pantomime, and more burlesques. The first of these, 'Allow Me to Explain', 'altered from the French', joined Tom Robertson's already-running *Caste* at the Prince of Wales's

---

[33] Gilbert's diary entry, 11 July 1878: WSG/BL Add. MS 49,332.

[34] Dr Eric Midwinter suggested this possibility in a letter to the author, 20 Sept. 1989.

[35] Letter to G.B. Macmillan, 8 Jan. 1907: Macmillan Papers/BL Add. MS 54,999. Gilbert lost £246 by speculating in Caledonian Deferred and returned several cheques, Macmillan's among them, to be exchanged for open ones so that the loss would not appear in his cheque book.

[36] Conversations (1974) with the late Lilian Gordon, Mrs Hart, the local doctor, Rosalie Crutchley (Kitty's god-daughter), and the local clergyman indicate that they all found Lady Gilbert dominating.

[37] Letter from Mary Crawshay to 'Dearest Kitty', n.d. [just after Gilbert's death]. The writer also says Gilbert told her he would kill himself 'if anything happened' to his wife: WSG/BL Add. MS 49,341. Although this is a gushing letter and, under the circumstances, likely to be exaggerative, it is undoubtedly sincere.

[38] The year was 1881. *Kate Terry Gielgud: An Autobiography* (London: Max Reinhardt, 1953), 52–3. Gilbert also took Kate and her sisters behind the scenes at *Iolanthe* to show them how the fairies' lights were worked. See also Maude, *Worlds Away*, 124–45, for Gilbert's entertainment of children.

Theatre on 4 November.[39] In it, Gilbert used stock farcical situations such as confusions of identity, impossible alternatives ('My wife on the one hand and my annual income on the other!'), and a character's frantic necessity to undo all that he has just contrived to do. Sprightly dialogue reconciled *Fun*'s friendly reviewer (16 November) to 'the threadbare character of the subject', and it was 'smartly played' by Squire Bancroft and George Honey in the leading roles. Less tolerantly, E. L. Blanchard's diary dismissed 'Allow Me to Explain' as a bad farce. Obviously, Gilbert had spent little time on reworking old materials and was, no doubt, writing rapidly for additional income. On the other hand, 'Highly Improbable', which followed a month later at the New Royalty Theatre, was 'An Original Impossibility' reaching toward the style we recognize as Gilbertain.[40]

Eighteen sixty-seven was the year of the Second Reform Bill and of John Stuart Mill's unsuccessful attempt to secure woman suffrage. Gilbert's farce, therefore, includes the first examples of those bills and measures which were to mark his political satire. Here they are a Young-Ladies-in-all-the-Professions Employment Bill and a Members of Parliament Matrimonial Qualifications Bill. The first is invented by Polly, the eldest of a country MP's six daughters, who pretend to practise masculine professions in order to trick Tom, a new Member-elect. The second bill is their father's attempt to make Parliament respectable by requiring all Members henceforth to be married. There is a comic servant, Cocklethorpe, who is a female footman, dressed as a footman down to the waist and as a lady's maid from the waist down.[41]

Tom proves himself a match for the girls in more ways than one and marries Polly in order to qualify under her father's matrimonial bill. Gilbert's dialogue combines a conventional farcical catchword ('my motto') with formal diction and early examples of his stylistic trick of dislocation between modifier and modified: 'a reckless course of Sunday School teaching!'—'The gay delirium of a needlework class!'

Martha (Pattie) Oliver had just taken over the management of the Royalty, and 'Highly Improbable' was the first play she sent for licens-

---

[39] It was originally intended to open on 2 Nov.

[40] 'Highly Improbable' was never published, but a typescript of the licence copy was made and circulated by Townley Searle. This contains lines cut or changed, probably in rehearsal or during early production, but not material which was altered or deleted later. The title was originally 'Mr. Ferguson'; there were a greater number of male occupations for the girls and direct references to women's rights, while Tom's multiplicity of professions anticipates Miss Spinn's in *Randall's Thumb*.

[41] Gilbert, 'My Pantomime', *Era Almanack* (1884), 77–9.

ing. It opened on 5 December as after-piece, later moved to curtain-raiser to F. C. Burnand's long-running burlesque of *Black-eyed Susan*. Although Miss Oliver did not appear in Gilbert's piece, its cast included names which would be associated with his works to come, particularly that of Nellie Bromley, the first Plaintiff of *Trial by Jury*. Reviewers were generally amused by the spirited acting and inventive stage business, although Blanchard thought the farce 'very queer'. 'Of course, the understanding and reason are equally set at defiance,' wrote the *Athenaeum*'s critic (14 December).

While 'Highly Improbable' was running happily at the Royalty, Gilbert's first pantomime without Millward was braving the dense fog of Boxing Day. This was *Harlequin Cock Robin and Jenny Wren; or, Fortunatus and the Water of Life, The Three Bears, The Three Gifts, The Three Wishes, and The Little Man Who Woo'd the Little Maid*. Gilbert took four days to write it, for which E. T. Smith, the new Lyceum lessee and manager, eventually paid him £60. 'A pantomime of some seventeen scenes got up in ten days!' exclaimed *The Mask*,[42] and this cumbersome production included multiple ballets of flowers, canaries, and fish, a procession of birds, a march of bears, a double harlequinade, and so on *ad infinitum*. It gave Gilbert material for 'Our Own Pantomime' in *Fun* (11 January 1868), 'Getting Up a Pantomime' in the January *London Society*, and 'My Pantomime' in the *Era Almanack* for 1884. It gave E. T. Smith the questionable honour of introducing the cancan to the English stage.

Although conglomerate plots and titles were popular that Christmas, *Harlequin Cock Robin* was the most conglomerated of all. Reviewers exonerated the author, whose work they found clever, neat, and faultlessly rhymed, but they blamed the lessee's devotion to excess. Moreover, for the first and only time, Gilbert found himself in the common condition of many playwrights: utterly at the mercy of manager and stage-mechanist. Consequently, as the *Porcupine* critic remarked (4 January), 'Mr. Gilbert's smooth libretto has evidently been written merely to fill up a scene-plot'.

On opening night, however, this scarcely mattered, since the huge fountain, which required irrelevant 'front' scenes to set and strike, did not appear, and the scenery was erratic at best. It had been painted at Cremorne, and very little had reached the Lyceum by curtain time, other instalments arriving throughout the performance. In vain, critics

---

[42] A copy was not sent for licensing until 24 Dec.; it was then in a copyist's hand with interpolations and stage directions in Gilbert's hand: LC/BL.

tried to correlate what happened on stage with their books of the words—and said so in their reviews. Three scenes were entirely omitted, and the order of the rest was scrambled. The gallery, restive to begin with, protested noisily as the slow performance dragged its maimed length along until Smith apologized from the stage and rushed on the transformation scene before its time. The harlequinade pleased the audience, and the pantomime could be considered a success of sorts. Part of this success was owing to the cancan, danced by Mlle Finette and her sister—the only thing in complete working order from the beginning!

A transient mistress of James McNeill Whistler,[43] Finette had a French reputation, small feet, high heels, and a high kick. Smith had been persuaded to hire her by John Hollingshead, who wanted her for the Alhambra, which he was managing, after she had been 'sanitized' by the pantomime.[44] 'The "Can-Can" defies description, and once seen, will not easily be forgotten,' exclaimed the *Era*. Although in deference to English proprieties, Finette wore the costume 'of a dancer rather than a danseuse', as *The Times* put it, she still produced great excitement and a certain moral debate, profitable at the box-office. The *Tomahawk*, for example, was disgusted by the men who flocked to see 'the most gross and filthy exhibition that has ever disgraced our degenerate stage'.

On the second night of *Harlequin Cock Robin*, a near panic occurred when a small fire, immediately extinguished, sent dancers screaming across the stage. Fortunately, Miss Furtado (who played Jenny Wren) with great presence of mind came to the footlights and calmed the shouting, about-to-stampede audience.[45] Gilbert was not in the house.

By early January the pantomime had at last settled down; the fountain was in place, throwing its rainbow beams, and audiences were increasing. In none of this was Gilbert interested. His, or rather, E. T. Smith's pantomime, had intensified his determination to control both the stage on which any play of his appeared and the text of that play.

[43] R. McMullen, *Victorian Outsider: A Biography of J. A. M. Whistler* (New York: E. P. Dutton & Co., Inc., 1973), 54–5. Whistler did a drypoint etching of Finette in her dressing-room at the Bal Mabile.

[44] J. Hollingshead, *My Lifetime* (London: Sampson Low, Marston & Company Ltd., 1895), i. 224–5.

[45] The episode is described in letters to *The Times*, the first (30 Dec.) from Lord Londesborough, who was in the audience; the second (31 Dec.) from E. T. Smith, who naturally played down 'the momentary panic' and stressed the Lyceum's safety. The burning of Her Majesty's Theatre on 6 Dec. undoubtedly contributed to the audience's fright.

Never again would he allow doggerel lyrics of unrivalled imbecility to be foisted upon his work. He turned to happier things, specifically to the London première of *La Vivandière* on 22 January 1868, sharing the bill with H. J. Byron's *Dearer than Life* with Henry Irving in the cast.

Although announced for the New Holborn Theatre, Gilbert's burlesque appeared at the very recently rebuilt Queen's, of which Alfred Wigan was the nominal and Henry Labouchère the actual lessee. *La Vivandière* had also been renovated since playing in Liverpool with changes in dialogue, new lyrics to new tunes, and the excision of Maria's tootling cornet solo because Henrietta Hodson, the new 'Daughter' could not double in brass for Liverpool's Maria Simpson. Since Miss Hodson was Labouchère's mistress, she was, *ipso facto*, the Queen's leading lady. Fortunately she was also a good actress.

The new cast included Lionel Brough in Roberto's funereal plumes and J. L. Toole orientally costumed as a sergeant of Zouaves. Miss Everard continued as the Marchioness. The audience laughed a great deal at Gilbert's verbal pleasantries, accepted willingly the absence of slang and breakdowns, enjoyed what *The Mask* called the 'beatific' legs of Pauline Markham's transvestite Tonio, and, in spite of the late hour (11.30 p.m.), remained to applaud Gilbert and his cast. On 6 March the Prince and Princess of Wales came to the theatre and enjoyed what they saw—the first of many royal visits to Gilbert's plays.

More important than the immediate success of *La Vivandière* was the fact that critics recognized Gilbert as a reformer, whose characters were 'very comic without being in the slightest degree vulgar' (*Illustrated Times*, 18 January), who preferred airs from light French and Italian opera to music-hall tunes (*Era*, 26 January), and who showed 'refinement in the manipulation of a fantastic material' (*The Times*, 24 January). These were highly desirable qualities on a stage subject to the Lord Chamberlain's Examiner of Plays, who deleted allusions to royalty and public persons, names in holy writ, taken in vain or not, and innuendos even faintly sexual. The first of these limitations removed a certain range of satiric possibilities; the last, a certain range of incident which had hitherto been a prerogative of comedy. This made English plays 'skittish' rather than 'indecent'.[46] On the other hand, sex comedy no longer being possible, a newer comedy of words and logic-play developed, leading through Gilbert's inversions and syllogisms to Wilde's drama as epigram and aphorism, Shaw's drama as

----

[46] J. Knight, *Theatrical Notes* (London: Lawrence & Bullen, 1893), xiii.

social debate, and eventually merging with Ionesco's supra-logical 'absurdity'. If, as Gilbert later wrote, the Victorian dramatist was forced to perform a hornpipe in the fetters of censorship,[47] to dance in chains, as Nietzsche says, is the highest art, though chains produce grotesque appearances and give the hornpipe a new pattern.

But as yet Gilbert did not feel his fetters, and was, indeed, breaking those of the theatrical past. In mid-February he took a short run to Paris as 'The Theatrical Lounger' of the *Illustrated Times*. There among other productions he saw Offenbach's *Robinson Crusoe*, which he judged less successful than *La Grande Duchesse* and 'wildly improbable without being at all funny'.[48] He also spent two days finishing his next burlesque and sent it to Pattie Oliver, having set two numbers to airs from *Robinson Crusoe and L'Œil crevé*, the music of which he had just bought. Meanwhile, he thought of 'Dearest Kits' and wrote to her from his room high above the Rue St Honoré. He did not 'much like being a bachelor', but he bought some chocolate to console himself. Still he longed to be with her.[49]

Home again, Gilbert turned to his next burlesque, *The Merry Zingara; or, The Tipsy Gipsy and the Pipsy Wipsy | A Whimsical Parody on the 'Bohemian Girl'*, which replaced Burnand's *Black-eyed Susan* at the Royalty on 21 March. Brilliantly mounted, Gilbert's piece included Miss Oliver as Arline, Edward Danvers as Devilshoof, and sturdy Charlotte Saunders as the Gipsy Queen who discloses the customary impossible relationships resolving the plot. In several ways *The Merry Zingara* is a trial run for *The Pirates of Penzance*, where Frederic is to the pirates as Arline is to the gipsies, and Ruth reveals the pirates' noble identities just as, in lines deleted before production, the Queen explains that 'My gipsies all were babes of rank and worth'.[50]

[47] 'A Hornpipe in Fetters', *Era Almanack and Annual* (1879), 91–2.

[48] (15 Feb. 1868), 103.

[49] Dated 'Wednesday' from Hotel de Lille et d'Albion: WSG/BL Add. MS 49,345. Hesketh Pearson misdates this letter to 1872/3 in *W. S. Gilbert: His Life and Strife* (London: Methuen & Co. Ltd., 1957), 33–4. References within the letter itself as well as the dates of Gilbert's review in the *Illustrated Times* and of his sending his burlesque to Miss Oliver make Feb. 1868 the only possible date. Pearson also erroneously asserts that Gilbert visited Paris because he was searching for French plays to adapt.

[50] LC/BL. Both the licence copy and the published text begin with retainers drinking tea 'with the air of robbers carousing', which becomes pirate sherry in the later opera. The text of *The Merry Zingara* is a complicated one. It was published by Phillips in 1868, but exists in two states, the second of which deletes or contains substitutes for some of the lyrics in the first. Six lines of rhyming dialogue have also been deleted from the first state, in which Aline resists arrest with a dagger, which she will turn against herself if necessary. In Townley Searle's copy of the first edition, first state (PML), there is a note in his hand to the effect that this passage

Again reviewers praised Gilbert's taste in music, polished versification, and brilliant wordplay. For example, when Count Arnheim upbraids Devilshoof for stealing his daughter, the gipsy replies, 'I took her in a moment of abstraction.' Or again, the Queen delivers a speechful of Gilbert's *Fun*-liners: 'You never put gas pipes between your lips, | Or go to sea in secretary-ships. | . . . | Or hang a picture in a frame of mind.'

Nevertheless, the press's enthusiasm in general was not quite so great as it had been two months before, no doubt because, although Gilbert had refined his technique, he broke no essentially new ground. E. L. Blanchard dismissed *The Merry Zingara* in his diary as 'nothing great', but the audience loved it and demanded many encores. At the end, Gilbert appeared amidst a loud burst of applause. Pattie Oliver included the burlesque with *Black-eyed Susan*, and 'Highly Improbable' on her benefit programme, 24 June, which proved so popular that it had to be repeated the following night.

In late 1867 Gilbert had become a member of the Dramatic Authors' Society, and now was so advertised on the title-pages of his burlesques. For dramatists whose plays were on its list (and it attempted to secure a monopoly), the Society treated with provincial theatre members, assessing royalties on an appropriate scale. This arrangement had for many years been advantageous to writers, for, though the charges were not large, payments accumulated steadily.[51] Provincial managers who wanted new London successes for their theatres needed the Society's permission, and in the days when writing for the stage was highly underpaid, some such organization was necessary. Gilbert placed most of his 1860s plays on the list, taking an active part in the Society itself. In a financially haphazard occupation and remembering Emden's advice, he intended to make sure the hire was worthy of the workman.

After his first cluster of successes, however, no new Gilbert play reached the stage until December 1868. The *Athenaeum*'s gossip

---

was queried by L.C., presumably the Lord Chamberlain. Yet only a very prurient reader of plays could find anything objectionable in it; perhaps he objected to the allusion to suicide. Moreover, the Lord Chamberlain's Day Book (LC/BL) and the licence copy itself have not been annotated for required changes. It is more likely that the lines (not particularly good ones) were cut in rehearsal or early performance. The licence copy, for instance, seems more like a draft than a finished text. All further quotations from *The Merry Zingara* come from Phillips's first state.

[51] A. W. à Beckett, *Green-Room Recollections* (Bristol: J. W. Arrowsmith, [1896]), 260–1. See also D. Barrett, 'The Dramatic Authors' Society (1833–1883) and the Payment of English Dramatists', *Essays in Theatre*, 7 (Nov. 1988), 19–33.

column of 4 July announced a forthcoming Gilbert burlesque, but nothing came of it. Instead, he occupied himself with journalism and his annual three or four weeks with the militia. After three years as a lieutenant in the Royal Aberdeenshire Highlanders, he was now promoted to captain, and, as usual, his experiences furnished saleable illustrated articles such as 'A Militia Training', published in *London Society* that September. In mid-August, leaving Clement Scott as substitute reviewer for the *Illustrated Times* ('rather a heavy run of Othellos & such like lumber'),[52] Kitty and Willie spent a fortnight at Hotel Christol, the best in Boulogne. From it came another *London Society* article, 'Britons at Boulogne', published in November.

With the coming of autumn, Gilbert had hoped to be appointed regular drama critic of the *Daily News*, a post John Hollingshead was leaving and for which he offered to recommend Gilbert. To his disappointment, Edmund Yates, Hollingshead's predecessor, seemed likely to be chosen. Perhaps prematurely, Gilbert took himself out of the running: 'Yates has already a *locus standi* on the paper, besides a reputation (got God knows how) for being a talented man. So let him enjoy his ill-deserved honours as best he may.'[53] In the event, Moy Thomas, whose capability Gilbert did not question, succeeded Hollingshead, who had broader fields in view.

Meanwhile Gilbert undertook a new commission: the illustrations for his father's serial, *King George's Middy*, which ran for a year in *Good Words for the Young*, beginning in November. He also was busy again in the theatre. On 1 December he wrote to the Dalziels, who cut his woodblocks, 'I am sorry that I should be so late with [twelve sketches and three more to come], but I have been much occupied with rehearsals & other work.'[54] The rehearsals must have been the first for Gilbert's new *Robert the Devil; or, The Nun, the Dun, and the Son of a Gun*. The other work, no doubt, included contributions to *Tom Hood's Comic Almanack* and *Tinsley's Magazine*, which published his satirical article on contemporary stagecraft in January 1869, but did not pay till April. But more important than occasional articles and his continuing contributions to *Fun* was Gilbert's preparation of the first collection of Bab Ballads, discussed in chapter 5, below.

[52] Gilbert to Clement Scott from Boulogne, 25 Aug. 1868: PML.

[53] To Clement Scott, 5 Sept. 1868: PML. In an earlier, but undated, letter from Boulogne (PML), Gilbert told Scott that Hollingshead had asked him several weeks before if he would like the latter's place on the *Daily News*, but it was to be kept secret.

[54] PML.

Ironically enough, Gilbert's fourth burlesque was written for John Hollingshead, who had given up the *Daily News* to become lessee and manager of a new theatre, the Gaiety. Hollingshead was an occasional contributor to *Fun*, a well-known journalist formerly on the staff of *Household Words*, but less well-known as stage director of the Alhambra. In later years he prided himself for having, *inter alia*, invented matinées, raised dramatic pay, and abolished charges for booking seats, programmes, etc. In mid-1868, only five months before opening night, work began on his new theatre in the Strand, not far from the *Fun* office. In a day of theatre conflagrations, the Gaiety was nearly fireproof, while improvements in gaslighting eliminated the unpleasant vapour which frequently hung between audience and stage.[55] On the first night the building was topped by a large flashing electric light for publicity purposes, in anticipation of Hollingshead's favourite phrase: 'the sacred lamp of burlesque'.

The Gaiety was designed by C. J. Phipps as an elegant, commodious theatre, with a lofty stage and a considerable depth below it to accommodate huge pieces of scenery. Above the stage a frieze depicted a medieval court watching a masque, fortuitously appropriate for the legendary subject of Gilbert's burlesque. All this safety, convenience, and decoration, however, was still unfinished on the morning of 21 December. Rehearsals had been farmed out to a private drawing-room, Covent Garden, even to Evans's singing rooms, and, in Gilbert's case, to Astley's, where a hippodrama nightly was on stage! The pantomimists practised at the Alhambra. There was no time for a proper dress rehearsal, the workmen having barely finished and settled themselves to watch from the second gallery before the public was admitted.[56]

The only original thing on the opening bill, as Hollingshead himself said, was Gilbert's *Robert the Devil*. The rest had been taken from the French: the curtain-raiser (*The Two Harlequins*) by Gilbert à Beckett, the main comedy-drama (*On the Cards*) by Alfred Thompson. Thompson was also responsible for the burlesque costumes, his first and much-praised essay in design; by choosing delicate, harmonious tints rather than the customary primary colours, he achieved a fantastic elegance.[57]

[55] *The Times* (11 Dec. 1868).

[56] J. Hollingshead, *Gaiety Chronicles* (Westminster: Archibald Constable & Co., 1898), 46. The company did not occupy the stage until 3 or 4 o'clock on opening-day, and the last workmen did not leave until 6.20 p.m. Arthur Sullivan was a first-night guest of Hollingshead and perhaps met Gilbert then for the first time.

[57] Ibid. 43.

Hollingshead had given Gilbert *carte blanche* as to subject, and Gilbert had chosen Meyerbeer's spectacular romantic opera, *Robert le Diable*,[58] which, in spite of its enormous European success, was supposedly accident-prone.[59] Briefly, the opera deals with Bertram's, the Devil's, attempts to gain the soul of his half-mortal son, Duke Robert, by enticing him to evil and then presenting the customary contract. Father and son visit a ruined convent where hangs a mystic cypress branch which will give Robert access to his beloved Princess Isabella. The ghosts of faithless nuns arise from their graves and, led by their Abbess, dance wildly around Robert, offering him various temptations. Bertram is finally foiled by a time technicality, in which Alice, Robert's foster-sister, keeps her brother from signing until midnight strikes. Bertram's power ends; he disappears.

Retaining many of the incidents of Scribe and Delavigne's libretto, Gilbert turned a spirit-haunted Meyerbeer cavern into Madame Tussaud's Chamber of Horrors and demoted Bertram to 'Town trav'ller to the Gentleman below' with a touch of club-window ogler.

The supernatural elements of Meyerbeer's opera, familiar in Romantic literature, are easily susceptible of broad parody, but Gilbert treated them in a quasi-serious, sometimes satiric, fashion, more complex than he had yet attempted. The magic branch, for instance, is a policeman's truncheon, inscribed '*No eye can see the man who bears this staff*', a line much enjoyed by reviewers, satirizing, as it did, a constable's reluctance to appear to petty criminals.

In the licence copy, Robert speculates at some length on the utility of a magic device to immobilize Members of Parliament. When asked why bad men are given statues, Bertram replies, 'That's our strict rule ... | "Good deeds we write in sand—bad deeds in marble!"'

The wax figures in the Chamber of Horrors are self-divided moral pluralists, having been at some time 'broken, melted, and re-cast!' Thus King John passed for years as Mr Wilberforce, and Old Bailey, a grotesque in chains, remembers he once was Pope. Even Bertram is 'A saint by choice, a devil by compulsion!' since he must secure a daily victim. (It revolts him, but he does it.) At the final curtain, Bertram,

---

[58] In the licence copy, *Robert the Devil* has been altered to *Robert le Diable*, evidently by the licenser of plays, perhaps because persons in holy writ were acceptable in French. Reviewers used both titles, and the text, published by Phillips in 1868, uses the English title, which I have also used to distinguish the burlesque from the opera and from which all subsequent quotations come unless otherwise noted.

[59] *Era* (27 Dec. 1868), 11, gives a list of accidents.

terrified, sinks through a grave trap to be made into a waxen image 'among the dead men'. At least one reviewer found this exercise in comic horror somewhat too grim.[60] Gilbert also gave Bertram a companion, Gobetto, victim, valet, and familiar, who becomes a waxwork of himself. Two mysterious pantomimic fiddlers accompany Bertram, perhaps at Hollingshead's suggestion,[61] one of whom was John D'Auban, the future arranger of most of London's stage dances, including those of the Savoy. Still another weird effect was Grieve and Son's setting for the ghostly ballet, taken from John Martin's famous painting of Pandemonium. Flickering under coloured fires, 'it was like a design from Milton', wrote A. T. Teetgen of the *Musical Standard.*

Although laughter exorcized most of the alleged bad luck attendant on performances of Meyerbeer, the performance did not go unscathed. Hollingshead's unavoidably piecemeal rehearsals of a raw new company showed in mixed and conflicting reviews, particularly in the case of both Gobetto and Bertram, who were played by actors new to London, the latter by Richard Barker. (Barker soon forsook acting for stage-management and in 1875 began a long association with Richard D'Oyly Carte.) The ladies of the cast were excoriated by the *Will-o'-the-Wisp* as 'hopeless dummies' with nothing on their minds but their legs. (Hollingshead, of course, had no objection to legs—they gave him long runs.) In fact, only the young Nellie Farren, then beginning her long Gaiety career, as a vivacious, cheeky Robert, was enthusiastically praised by every reviewer. Gilbert, who reviewed his own burlesque in the February issue of *London Society*, agreed with them and drew a Bab illustration of Nellie in transvestite costume, insouciantly smoking a cigarette.

Having had the cancan thrust upon him, so to speak, the previous year, Gilbert now was faced with a sketchily dressed Mlle Anna Bossi, imported to dance the Lady Abbess, which she did, at times, as indecently as possible. *Fun* objected that Thompson's designs gave little work to the costumier and still less exercise to the imagination.

But the audience shared none of these strictures, for a storm of approbation burst over Gilbert at the final curtain on 21 December, late

---

[60] *Theatrical and Musical Review* (24 Dec. 1868), 151–2. Even so, this reviewer found the Chamber of Horrors the funniest thing in the burlesque.

[61] Hollingshead, *Gaiety Chronicles*, 94, said Gilbert 'was always ready to accept a suggestion if he thought it was good and reasonable'. The reviewer for *Fun* (2 Jan. 1869), 163, implied that Hollingshead borrowed the idea of the mysterious fiddlers from the music halls. On the other hand, Count Arnheim and Florestein were both said to be accompanied by appropriate musicians in the preceding *Merry Zingara* with which Hollingshead had no connection.

though the hour was. The cast improved in subsequent performances, and *Robert the Devil* ran until 15 May 1869. Then it was replaced by Thompson's *Columbus; or, The Original Pitch in a Merry Key*. In late August *Robert* returned briefly to the Gaiety, and was played in the provinces for at least three years to come. Gilbert even revised the text for an 1878 anniversary revival back at the Gaiety. In this altered version, Bertram tempts Gobetto with the traditional pleasures of Cockayne, and Gobetto explains how his master 'changed me, last night, into fourpence halfpenny—| And spent me on a pint of half-and-half.' Having been forced to taste Bertram's love elixirs, he has now engaged himself to 'seventeen spinsters, & three dozen widdies'.[62]

*Robert the Devil* was Gilbert's largest-scale work to date, and contributed to his reputation as a 'leviathan of burlesque', as the *Graphic* called him (18 April 1870). He was by now well established as a reformer and box-office draw. He had begun to make his weight felt in stage direction: a martinet but more often right than wrong, Hollingshead called him,[63] although no martinet could have completely controlled those first Gaiety rehearsals.

Gilbert had rapidly learned to adapt words to extant tunes, sometimes nonsensically but in increasingly complex rhymes and grammatical constructions. In dialogue he was still strait-jacketed by closed couplets and to a lesser extent, by puns, but he had begun to individualize the common stock of burlesque devices. He had discovered the comic possibilities of numerical extension and multiple identity. He had continued to develop parody into dramatic criticism. Two more burlesques still lay before him, one of them his best, but now, leaving the big stage of the Gaiety behind him, he turned to carving a cherry stone among the Reeds.

---

[62] One of the holograph additions to the printed libretto marked 'Prompt Book': WSG/BL Add. MS 49,316. Gobetto's multiple engagements suggest that Gilbert still had the plot of *Engaged*, produced the year before, in the back of his mind.

[63] Hollingshead, *Gaiety Chronicles*, 94.

# 5

---

# Babs, Reeds, and Druidesses

We fly to fields of fancy
Gilbert, *Ages Ago*

GILBERT began 1869 as the author of a book. Hard covers, gilt edges, bound in green and gold, 'admirable print and splendid paper',[1] *The Bab Ballads* was decidedly more impressive than the six-penny editions of his burlesques. Its publication, however, had been a toe-to-toe battle.

Gilbert had been sounding out publishers while he was still on holiday in Boulogne the summer before. At first he evidently thought of *Fun*'s proprietor, Edward Wylam,[2] but instead Wylam opened negotiations with John Camden Hotten on Gilbert's behalf.[3] Hotten was a strange choice, notorious after his fashion. Mark Twain called him 'Hottentot', and in addition to stage memoirs, collections of jokes, and reputable comic works, he published pornography, including Swinburne's occasional flagellations. (The four pages of advertisement in the first edition of *The Bab Ballads* end with one for *Romance of the Rod*.)

Swinburne himself was having a long dispute over copyright and the 'singular laxity' of Hotten's accounts,[4] while Tom Hood had been carrying on a vendetta in *Fun* against the publisher. In 1862 Tennyson had brought a formal bill of complaint against Hotten for plagiarizing and

---

[1] 'Looks into Books', *Fun* (19 Dec. 1868), 153.

[2] *The Bab Ballads*, ed. J. Ellis (Cambridge, Mass.: Harvard University Press, 1970), 24 n.

[3] Fragmentary copy of a letter from Gilbert to Wylam, 26 Aug. 1868, from Hotel Christol: WSG/BL Add. MS 49,330.

[4] *The Swinburne Letters*, ed. C. J. Lang (New Haven: Yale University Press, 1959–62), ii. 119. See letters for 19 and 28 Aug. [1870], 6 Dec. 1872, 30 Jan. [1873], Feb. [1873], and 27 Apr. 1888, for Swinburne's problems with Hotten. The poet, however, intended to remain on at least moderately amicable terms with Hotten, who had papers which might be used against him. This suggests that Swinburne believed Hotten was not above blackmail.

selling some of his early poems.[5] In fact, Hotten's attitude toward paying authors is epitomized by Ambrose Bierce to whom the publisher owed £100 for *The Fiend's Delight*. After much shilly-shallying, Hotten gave Bierce a post-dated cheque and died before it was due[6]—allegedly of a surfeit of pork-chops.

This slippery person offered Gilbert £50 for an edition of 1,500 copies of forty-four collected Bab Ballads. During September 1868 he was forced up to £90 in bills at four and six months, plus 2 guineas for a specially drawn frontispiece and title-page vignette. The edition would now be 2,000, and, if a second edition were called for, Hotten would print 1,000 copies for £50, Gilbert cannily retaining copyright.[7] The finished book would be volume ii of a 'New Series of Illustrated Works of Humour', of which Henry Leigh's *Carols of Cockayne* was the first volume.

Why did Gilbert chose to deal with Hotten? Perhaps he supposed that he and Wylam could control him. Perhaps, as has been suggested,[8] Gilbert's friend Leigh was an inducement. Perhaps he simply wanted to publish a collection of his verse and Hotten's format looked attractive. But Gilbert soon regretted his choice. Hotten rapidly set out to recoup some of the not-yet-paid £90 by quietly printing 300 extra copies. When the overrun reached 263, one of the printers, Judd, told Gilbert, who demanded payment for a second edition.[9] Hotten's plaintive excuse that he used odd sheets to print review and author's copies was hardly convincing, especially since a hundred or fewer such copies sufficed better publishers.[10]

Hotten made as much trouble as possible, holding back legitimate review copies, delaying, telling Gilbert to go elsewhere, but Bab forced him to pay something for and then to destroy the overrun, and to publish a month late on 19 December 1868. Thereafter Gilbert did go elsewhere, first to William Tinsley, who showed no interest, then to the Quaker George Routledge, who paid him £50 for an 1870 shilling

[5] The bill was brought in Chancery, filed on 30 July 1862 and amended 1 Aug. 1862: PML.

[6] P. Fatout, *Ambrose Bierce: The Devil's Lexicographer* (Norman, Okla.: University of Oklahoma Press, 1951), 104.

[7] Copy made by Gilbert of a letter from Wylam to Hotten, 9 Sept. 1868: WSG/BL Add. MS 49,330.

[8] *Bab Ballads*, ed. Ellis, 24.

[9] Ibid. 25. Copies of the original correspondence are in WSG/BL, some of which have been used by P. W. Plumb in 'The Bab Ballads: A Publishing Account', *W. S. Gilbert Society Journal*, 1 (autumn 1985), 58–62.

[10] Chatto & Windus to Gilbert, 15 Jan. 1875: WSG/BL Add. MS 49,331.

edition[11] of thirty-six ballads and continued to print successive collections until Macmillan took over in the new century. Unfortunately, affairs with Hotten dragged on at least until August 1870 when Gilbert gave him notice to appear at Marlborough Police Court, with Gilbert's letter (9 December 1868) requiring payment for a second edition.[12]

Favourable reviews of *The Bab Ballads* began to appear in early 1869. Its subtitle, 'Much Sound and Little Sense', was illustrated by the vignette of a baby preparing to thump a piano. Moreover, in a brief preface, dated October 1868, Gilbert had characteristically denigrated his work. Since the ballads had, he said, 'achieved a certain whimsical popularity among a special class of readers', he now hoped to learn whether that popularity should gratify him. He thought his 'rather clumsy' illustrations as bad as the verses, and in a sudden Gilbertian flash, he remarked that the ballads 'are not, as a rule, founded upon fact'.

This protective colouring of self-deprecation, was, of course, his preparation for failure in case critics proved hostile. As we shall see, he practised it all his life in varying degrees, which accounts in part for the generally held assumption that Gilbert was a poor judge of his own work. In June 1869, at all events, he liked *The Bab Ballads* well enough to give an inscribed copy 'To Cousin Annie [Edwards] from Cousin Schwenck'.[13] He knew she would understand his wit.

In spite of amusement, reviewers of the 'Bab's' were sometimes puzzled. 'How does he manage to get a start?' wondered M[atthew] B[rowne] of the *Contemporary Review*. He found an odd humour in 'the contrast between the mechanical and apparently causeless insanity of the conception, and the ordered, luminous, and musical sanity of Mr. Gilbert's manner'. While the *Illustrated Times* of 6 March thought that 'more *unmeaning* nonsense never trickled from human pen', its reviewer felt 'a peculiar fascination in following the author in his sensation headers of absurdity'. Some of the verses were poetry, the drawings 'little gems in their way', but he recommended deleting the preface—advice which Gilbert took in the Routledge cheap edition.

Unfortunately, the *Athenaeum* (10 April) followed a line of criticism from which Gilbert's work has never been completely free, i.e. that it lacked geniality and heart. This reviewer preferred whimsicality prompted by understanding and love like that of Charles Lamb. Heart

---

[11] F. A. Mumby, *The House of Routledge 1834–1934* (London: George Routledge & Sons Ltd., 1934), 104.

[12] Copy, 11 Aug. 1870: WSG/BL Add. MS 49,330.     [13] PML.

or no heart, however, Gilbert's whimsicalities continued to please the public.

With the 'Bab's' in print and *Robert the Devil* settled at the Gaiety, Gilbert found a stage, if not an immediate production, for his fifth burlesque *The Pretty Druidess; or, The Mother, the Maid, and the Mistletoe Bough*. This was a travesty of Bellini's opera *Norma*, which had been announced for autumn 1868, but had not appeared then. Perhaps Gilbert had become interested in this plot because his father used it for an unpublished verse tragedy, 'Morna'. Or perhaps he wanted something more tightly knit than *Robert the Devil*. Whatever his motive, his burlesque had been finished for some time before he read it on 18 March to a new company in what was to be the greenroom of a new theatre, the Charing Cross.

Situated in King William Street, Strand, the Charing Cross Theatre occupied the site of W. S. Woodin's Polygraphic Hall. '[A] walking polyglot . . . a talking Proteus', Woodin was a quick change monologist,[14] patronized by many people whose religious scruples kept them out of theatres. Gilbert knew him and had written anonymously for his entertainments, as had Robertson and Blanchard, although only the latter's contributions can be identified.

Work progressed slowly on the new theatre; in fact, three months elapsed between the first reading and the first night of *The Pretty Druidess*. Meanwhile, Gilbert had provided another string to his bow: as early as 7 February theatre columns had been promising his first German Reed entertainment. Entitled *No Cards*, it appeared at the Gallery of Illustration on Easter Monday after a Sunday of snow and coastal storm. It is unlikely that Gilbert had time that Easter to attend the annual Volunteer Review at Dover; so he probably escaped the hail and wind which beat one of the attending ships apart against a pier.[15] If not, he must have returned tempest-tossed, unless, as on a better-known occasion, he led his men back inside to a good fire.[16]

The Gallery to which Gilbert, wet or dry, now devoted his talent was another nominal non-theatre, which drew audiences from both the highly respectable and the regular playgoers. Mr and Mrs Reed were adroit in their nomenclature, for their theatre was a 'gallery', their

[14] *Illustrated London News* (7 Mar. 1857).

[15] A. R. Bennett, *London and Londoners in the Eighteen-Fifties and Sixties* (London: T. Fisher Unwin Ltd., 1924), 325–6.

[16] A. E. T. Watson, *A Sporting and Dramatic Career* (London: Macmillan & Co. Ltd., 1918), 84.

plays 'illustrations', their roles 'assumptions'—an amusing but profitable example of Victorian word-magic.

When Gilbert began to write for them, Priscilla and Thomas German Reed had been giving drawing-room entertainments for more than ten years. He had been a theatre musician and was experimenting elsewhere with what he called *opera di camera*: small chamber operas by young composers, a form which he was then alone in encouraging. Priscilla Horton Reed, Macready's protégée in her youth, had played Ariel and Lear's Fool as well as Planché's original transvestite Fortunio. Her lovely contralto voice still served her well, although her dancing figure was gone and her acting company called her 'Mama'.

The Reeds' snug little theatre at 14 Regent Street seated five hundred in a narrow, steeply raked auditorium, inclined to stuffiness[17]—a 'variegated tunnel', approached by fire-hazardous passages, according to John Hollingshead (*Daily Telegraph*, 10 March 1875). Piano, harmonium, and sometimes a harp constituted the orchestra, but composers included Molloy, Clay, Sullivan, and Alfred Cellier. Some of the best scenic artists—Telbin, Beverley, and O'Connor—designed sets for the tiny stage, while *Punch* men and members of the *Fun* gang wrote many of the plays. At first limited to a cast of three, the Reeds had now enlarged to four performers in plots of multiple identities, disguises, or impersonations.

This multiplicity suited Gilbert very well. He devised a plot in which a poor young man and a rich old one disguise themselves and compete for a charming girl. Her strong-minded aunt, in turn, pretends to be Salamanca Trombone, the Queen of Babbetyboobledore, an 'uncivilized' island, which is an early Gilbert utopia:

> Civilization takes no stride
> In Babbetyboobledore.
> There's nothing like self-respect or pride
> In Babbetyboobledore.
> They've little regard for money or birth—
> Unless it's allied to genuine worth.
> There isn't another domain on earth
> Like Babbetyboobledore.

Audiences burst into applause when Mrs Reed sang this song.

Rosa D'Erina (real name Rose O'Toole), a recent and transient newcomer, played Annabella with an interpolated Gilbert-Molloy song,

---

[17] F. Anstey, *A Long Retrospect* (London: Oxford University Press, 1936), 41.

'Thady O'Flinn'. More important was the début of Arthur Cecil Blunt as the juvenile lead. Cecil was an accomplished amateur, and his voice, sympathetic though tiny,[18] and mobile face made him worth the £10/week two-year contract he had just received.[19] Cecil's friends were in the first-night audience and welcomed the visibly nervous new-comer as he took the stage. For Cecil as Mr Churchmouse and German Reed as the rich Ellis Dee, Gilbert devised topical Siamese Twins busi-ness, the twins themselves having just been on display at the Egyptian Hall.

The score of *No Cards* was patchy, most of the numbers having been arranged or composed by Reed himself. For a short time, Cecil interpo-lated a wholly irrelevant song by a very minor composer,[20] while Gilbert inserted his 1867 Bab Ballad 'The Precocious Baby' to the tune of 'The Whistling Oyster'. Nevertheless, Gilbert's first entertainment was a success, praised for point and neatness even though it played sec-ond fiddle (or would have had the Gallery possessed one) to the other piece of the evening: Burnand and Sullivan's *Cox and Box*. This sparkling triumviretta, like Arthur Cecil, was making its theatre début, and, like him, proved a decided success. It outshone, although it did not quench, *No Cards*.

After 139 performances the double bill went to enliven the provinces in August. Gilbert's piece brought him £150 as did each of his subse-quent plays for the Reeds.[21] More important, it also brought him into an extended theatre family, whose personalities he could play with and whose style encouraged him to experiment. Furthermore, if he had not already met Sullivan at the Gaiety, it is likely that they would have run into each other in the Gallery in March or early April.

At home, Gilbert's domestic life was proceeding happily. He had pur-chased the lease of 8 Essex Villas, north of Kensington High Street, into which he and Lucy moved in early April, their preparations causing a temporary drop in his *Fun* contributions. A commodious semi-detached house, brick with stone facings, No. 8 gave them more room for entertaining, which they did with pleasure. 'I think I can promise you some good music & plenty of people you know,' Gilbert wrote in an

---

[18] Sir Charles Villiers Stanford, *Pages from an Unwritten Diary* (London: Edward Arnold, 1914), 108.

[19] Shirley Brooks, diary entry for 30 Mar. 1869. Cited by kind permission of the London Library.

[20] J. W. Safer, 'Three Husbands'.

[21] Letter to Harold Power, 8 Aug. 1877: WSG/BL Add. MS 49,338.

invitation to Planché.[22] Perhaps it was here that Gilbert's habit of nocturnal work began, when the street noises had died away. 'My usual writing costume is my nightshirt & dressing gown,' he told Frank Holl, the painter, years later.[23]

Sometime during 1869 Gilbert became a member of the Junior Carlton Club, founded five years earlier as a Conservative club.[24] The elder Gilbert having been a member of the Reform Club since 1855, this was perhaps a mild defiance. Father and son, however, continued on the best of terms, William Schwenck still illustrating William's stories. Perhaps the club's excellent cooking at a moderate cost attracted Gilbert, who was not greatly interested in partisan politics. The most likely reason, however, is that given by John Hollingshead: 'The undecided young man is caught . . ., made a member of a comfortable club, and stamped as a Tory, or Conservative for the remainder of his existence.' He cited 'the strange case' of Gilbert.[25] For whatever cause, Gilbert remained true to the Junior Carlton; in fact, he wrote one of his last cheques to it (29 May 1911).

He was also attracted to the more theatrical Garrick Club, but was blackballed, allegedly because of a confusion in identity. Asked to stand again, with the assurance of election, he refused to go through a form to compensate someone else's error. This was very characteristic, for his own excellent memory and clear logic often made him assume that men acted unpleasantly toward him by calculation rather than by simple vagueness or inadvertance. Accordingly, he became angry or felt hurt because he mistook carelessness for intentional slight. This attitude, which increased with age, exacerbated his temper and gave him needless pain. Not till 22 February 1906 was he elected to the Garrick club, thirty-seven years after Sullivan and forty-one after Burnard.

As a member of the Dramatic Authors' Society, Gilbert was also involved in the problem of enforcing provincial assessments for performances. He and others had signed a circular dated 10 December 1868, rescinding all former restrictions, thus freeing members to deal independently with provincial managers if they chose. On 21 April 1869 Blanchard recorded 'terrible discoveries' about a defalcating clerk who

[22] W. S. Gilbert to J. R. Planché, 10 June [1869]: Huntington Library, JP 99, reproduced by permission.

[23] 22 Nov. 1886: PML.

[24] *Rules, Regulations and List of Members of the Junior Carlton Club* (privately printed, 1888), 7. Gilbert's name appears as having joined in 1869 (ibid. 83). Except for William Kendal, there were no actors in this list, and no dramatists to speak of apart from Gilbert.

[25] J. Hollingshead, *My Lifetime* (London: Sampson Low, Marston & Co. Ltd., 1895), i. 55.

had disappeared. Although Gilbert remained on the Society's list for several more years, he was soon to be in an obviously better position to drive his own bargains.

In 1869, however, he was trying to promote his most ambitious work to date, a prose comedy-drama tentatively called 'Quits'. 'When do you think you will be in a position to give me an answer about the Drama?' he wrote to Hollingshead from his new library on 16 April. 'It is lying idle all this time.'[26] It continued to lie idle for another three months.

This was a difficult time for Gilbert—two plays waiting for production but unproduced. At last, on Saturday 19 June the Charing Cross Theatre opened with *The Pretty Druidess* as the last piece on a bill which began with an operatic sketch, *Coming of Age*, and featured a three-act drama, *Edendale*. The new house was small, prettily decorated in blue, white, and gold, with comfortable leg-room. Unfortunately the performance started late because of an uproarious protest from the pit, which lacked programmes. When these were showered down from stalls and circle, the disturbance subsided,[27] allowing Madge Robertson (Tom's youngest sister) to speak an inaugural address, written by E. L. Blanchard and promising

> Their entertainment will be light, but care
> Shall make it certain it is wholesome fare.[28]

And wholesome it was, although so delayed by the demonstration and first-night nerves that many spectators left before the final curtain fell past midnight. Gilbert immediately took a bow, which the *Theatrical Journal* thought in questionable taste, but the remnant of audience applauded heartily.

Shorter than *Robert the Devil*, *The Pretty Druidess* is, nevertheless, more important in Gilbert's development as a satiric dramatist. Bellini's original opera gave him the first of his invasion plots (Romans invade Gallic society) and a variant of the widespread Victorian theme of fairy love (a Druidess loves a Roman). Briefly, Norma, a Druid priestess, has secretly married the Roman Pro-Consul Pollio, who now loves the novice Adelgisa, also secretly. Discovering his infidelity, Norma is at first furious but then confesses her own broken vows. Oroveso, her

---

[26] Maggs Bros., *Autograph Letters, etc.* (Catalogue 464; 1925), 121. Both Gilbert and Hollingshead wrote later that it had been immediately produced, but that seems unlikely in view of this letter, which I assume must refer to *Quits*.

[27] *Theatrical Journal* (30 June 1869), 201–2.

[28] Programme of opening performance.

father and Arch-Druid, orders her to be burnt alive. Repentant, Pollio ascends the pyre with her, and they die together. At this point Gilbert's plot took a new turn. In anticipation of *Iolanthe*, his Druidesses all admit 'they have married Romans on the sly!' Oroveso's solution is simple—let them pass through harmless theatrical red fire. He then discovers from a long-lost card case that he is Julius Caesar in disguise, upon which Adelgisa announces she is his wife.

The tag is spoken by Norma, who pleads for 'proscribed burlesque':

> Forgive our rhymes;
> Forgive the jokes you've heard five thousand times;
> Forgive each breakdown, cellar-flap, and clog,
> Our low-bred songs—our slangy dialogue;
> And, above all—oh, ye with double barrel—
> Forgive the scantiness of our apparel!

Such an appeal was almost *de rigeur* at the end of a Victorian burlesque, as witness (*inter multa alia*) Fancy's speech ending H. J. Byron's *1863; or, The Sensations of the Past Season*:

> Frown not on our efforts, pray,
>   If you think our merit's slight;
> Come again another day,
>   Don't condemn us here tonight.[29]

Yet Gilbert had not used it before except for a line or two in *La Vivandière*. Furthermore, *The Pretty Druidess* does not contain most of the debased components Norma specifies. The Lord Chamberlain, for instance, had recently banned short ballet skirts; so Gilbert's characters were decently, but not excitingly, dressed.[30] Moreover, they did not engage in 'breakdowns' or other eccentric dances. Nor does Norma's speech seem to be Gilbertian self-protection; instead, she pleads for a form against which several contemporary critics were making a dead set. The audience, however, scarcely noticed the incongruity as they prepared to leave the theatre.

Although critics praised Gilbert for reforming burlesque, the first scene of *The Pretty Druidess* lacked 'go' on opening night with a new company. This caused *Judy*, whose new editor, Charles Ross, had mounted an anti-Gilbert campaign, to advise more boisterous conventional

---

[29] (London: Thomas Hailes Lacy, [1864]), 30.

[30] See late Jan. and early Feb. issues of *Judy* for satiric comments on the Lord Chamberlain's order that skirts be longer. Almost all reviewers remarked on the absence of short skirts in *The Pretty Druidess*.

'business' as at the Strand Theatre where ' "breakdowns" have proved very far from failure'. In spite of good reviews, Gilbert's burlesque lasted only to mid-August, when it was replaced by Burnand's *Very Little Faust and More Mephistopheles*. On 1 September *Judy* chortled, 'At length those very plain Druidesses . . . have given place to something really funny'; that is to Burnand's 'absurd tomfoolery with a coloured cotton pocket-handkerchief'.

Gilbert had scarcely seen his play begin its short career when he found himself involved in a completely unforeseen contretemps. Tom Taylor's 'new and original' drama *Mary Warner*, which opened at the Haymarket Theatre on 21 June, proved to be an unacknowledged adaptation of Dr Gilbert's novel *Margaret Meadows: A Tale for the Pharisees*. Miss Bateman was making a great success in the title role, but *The Times, Era, Athenaeum*, and other periodicals all called attention to the similarity. The *Athenaeum* even accused Taylor of lifting some dialogue from the novel. Annoyed but unabashed, Taylor wrote immediately to *The Times* on 26 June. True, he had read *Margaret Meadows*, but not while writing his own play. Dr Gilbert himself had suggested the subject to Taylor, he said, and he and the novelist were 'perfectly at one'. Taylor regretted the 'misunderstanding' by which Dr Gilbert's name was omitted.

This explanation (varied for other periodicals) did not convince the Gilberts. W.S. parodied *Mary Warner* in the 10 July issue of *Fun*, and undoubtedly advised his father to proceed to arbitration. In less than three weeks this ended in an award of £200 to Dr Gilbert and the right to have his name appear as co-author of *Mary Warner* if he chose. He did not choose. After the Haymarket season ended, perhaps prematurely on 10 July, the play continued in Miss Bateman's repertoire, her husband paying Taylor £400 for it.

The definition of 'new and original' continued to be moot for most of the century.[31] 'New' could simply mean a new translation or adaptation, while, as the *Tomahawk* had observed (30 November 1867), 'To be original you must turn somebody's novel into a piece and call it your own.' Furthermore, a novelist could not legally hold dramatic copyright of his work unless he printed and registered a dramatic version in his own name.[32] It was unfortunate for Taylor that he had chosen to use an author very much in evidence that year, Dr Gilbert having already published two books in 1869: *Lucrezia Borgia, Duchess of*

---

[31] See e.g. an *Era* editorial, 'Authors and Adaptors' (3 Sept. 1892), 13.
[32] 'Authors and Adapters', *Illustrated Sporting and Dramatic News* (26 Sept. 1874), 739.

*Ferrara* and *Sir Thomas Branston*, a novel about alcoholism. Taylor, however, continued to write 'new and original' plays, and the press continued to object. Four years later, with *Mary Warner* in mind, Dr Gilbert wrote to Hollingshead to offer help in the latter's campaign to prevent the theatrical piracy of novels.[33] Hollingshead did not succeed.

By early July the 'dead' theatrical season was approaching, and Hollingshead finally chose to produce the younger Gilbert's two-hour, three-act, serious comedy, now retitled *An Old Score*. Announced for Saturday 24 July, it appeared on the following Monday before an audience crowded with 'dramatists, journalists, and theatrical barnacles' if one read the *Porcupine*, or a fashionable audience including literary celebrities if one read the *Sunday Times*. Whoever they were, playgoers laughed—sometimes in the wrong places—and called heartily for Gilbert and Hollingshead.

Nevertheless, the performance was by no means perfect. For one thing, the Gaiety stage was too large for a tightly knit play. For another, opening lines were inaudible. Sam Emery totally misconceived his important role, and Rosina Ranoe was swamped by hers. While critics praised Gilbert's natural story, frequently brilliant dialogue, and originality of treatment, they found him cynical. No character was completely sympathetic, and John Hollingshead, looking back, acknowledged that the play was too true to disagreeable human nature. 'Playgoers have a sneaking kindness for humbugs', he wrote.[34] When Gilbert parodied himself in a *Fun* review (7 August), he praised even the bad acting and found fault with his own construction in the first and third acts.

As several reviewers pointed out, Gilbert had used an episode in the life of the late Mr Dargan as a basis for his plot. In it a hypocrite for his own selfish purposes takes a boy from the streets and puts him in an office. The boy, by his own exertions, becomes a wealthy Bombay merchant and settles his 'old score' by destroying the bills forged in his name by his 'benefactor', whom he rightly despises. The 'benefactor' has a rebellious son, who becomes the editor of a scurrilous journal, but reforms through love. Allusions to such a journal prompted an angry review in the *Tomahawk*, which assumed Gilbert was attacking its own methods. He, in turn, and perhaps mendaciously, disclaimed any intention of such an attack, and the *Tomahawk* apologized.

[33] William Gilbert (père) to John Hollingshead, 12 Mar. 1873: Huntington Library HD/75, reproduced by permission.

[34] J. Hollingshead, '*Good Old Gaiety*' (London: Gaiety Theatre Co. Ltd., 1903), 16.

Before the second night, Gilbert and Hollingshead set out to make changes, one of the few times the dramatist allowed someone else to tinker with his text.[35] But in spite of first-night cordiality, audiences did not come. Most of the other theatres were also in the doldrums, but *An Old Score* lasted only till late August.[36] Gilbert's 'cynicism' and astringency were not popular with audiences who wanted 'genial' comedy or domestic drama with comic scenes and did not share the *Stage*'s wish for a return to 'the rich scathing satire of the old comedies'. As one of the characters in *An Old Score* observes, 'From the satirist's point of view, the audience is always degenerate.'

Still, his first attempt at a full-scale comedy had been praised for readability, which meant it had literary qualities, and Gilbert no doubt went with good heart to hear Charles Dickens speak at the London Rowing Club's dinner in honour of Oxford's and Harvard's competing crews. (Oxford won the race on 27 August.) Returning, he was astonished to hear that the Gaiety was on fire. Six engines roared up, but, to everyone's relief, it proved a false alarm, caused by testing the range in the new restaurant atop the theatre. This excitement gave Gilbert a paragraph for his 'Theatrical Lounger' column on 4 September.

After *An Old Score* no new Gilbert play appeared on the London stage until 22 November, when *Ages Ago* opened in miserable weather at the Gallery of Illustration. This entertainment outran *Cox and Box*, was revived during more than ten years and occasionally abridged, was pirated in America, and was the Gallery's greatest success.

A new soprano, the long-staying Fanny Holland, had replaced Rosa D'Erina. Complimented on her clear, 'sympathetic' voice and intensity of expression, she had been giving London concerts for the last two years; now, in *Ages Ago*, she doubled the roles of Rosa and Lady Maud. In the modern framing plot, German Reed as Sir Ebenezer Tare has taken over a supposedly haunted castle, the title deeds of which appear only once each hundred years. Rosa loves the impoverished Columbus (Cecil), who is staying the night. The Scottish housekeeper Mrs MacMotherly (Mrs Reed) has second sight.

While the mortals sleep, the cast change costumes and animate as the portraits of former owners: Lady Maud, Sir Cecil,[37] Lord Carnaby

---

[35] R. Allen, *W. S. Gilbert: An Anniversary Survey and Exhibition Checklist* (Charlottesville, Va.: The Bibliographical Society of the University of Virginia, 1963), 25, 28.

[36] In the autumn *An Old Score* played Liverpool; in 1872 Gilbert revised it as *Quits!* for Marie Litton and Hermann Vezin. It still ran for little more than a month.

[37] The character was Sir Cecil Blunt in the licence copy, but evidently Sir Aubrey de Beaupre was used on stage. Mallet's contemporary book of the lyrics used both.

Poppytop, and Dame Cherry Maybud. The portraits engage in romantic interludes of their own until daybreak, when Dame Cherry leaves the title deed naming Columbus as the new owner before returning to her next hundred years' sleep. Armed with this, he gains Tare's permission to marry Rosa.

That *Ages Ago* anticipates *Ruddigore*'s revitalized ancestors has long been noticed, although Gilbert did not invent the device. Mrs MacMotherly's tale of the original wicked Sir Roger Bohun suggests Dame Hannah's later legend of the Ruddigore family curse, but the ancestors' scene of *Ages Ago* is in its own right a deft example of playing ages against relationships. 'His grandmama is seventeen, and he is sixty-five' because of the dates at which their respective portraits were painted, dates emphasized by authentic costumes. The 'old' young people pair off, while Dame Cherry and Lord Carnaby settle into a middle-aged affection, Mrs Reed continuing a line of lively Gilbertian contraltos who would extend into his full-scale librettos.

Frederic Clay, a friend of Sullivan, composed 'clever', charming music for *Ages Ago*, which almost made up in elegance what it lacked in humour. (The *Illustrated Times* of 27 November suggested Clay take a hint from Sullivan's 'eccentric scoring'.) A serious, though not a professional, musician, Clay was beginning his career of writing for the stage as well as his collaboration with Gilbert, for whom he would set three more works.

It was Clay who formally introduced Gilbert to Sullivan at the Gallery; at least that was how Gilbert remembered it. Now he asked Sullivan that invariably quoted question: what did he think of Gilbert's contention

that if a musician who is master of all instruments has a musical theme to express, he can express it as regularly upon the simple tetrachord of Mercury, in which, as we all know, there are no diatonic intervals whatever as upon the more elaborate disdiapason with the three tetrachords and the redundant note which, as I need not remind a composer of your distinction, embraces in its perfect consonance all the single, double and inverted chords.

Sullivan was a master of all instruments, but he said he would have to think it over. Of course, when he went to see Gilbert's *Palace of Truth* the next year, he recognized part of the quotation, which Gilbert had taken from an encyclopedia and adapted to blank-verse dialogue.

Reviewers were delighted by *Ages Ago*. Even *Judy*, the next March, found it 'full of charmingly fanciful dialogue' and thought it 'a pity to waste so much talent upon the goody-goodies' in the audience. But the goody-goodies had now been joined by more sophisticated playgoers, whom both Gilbert and Sullivan in their separate works were attracting.

This was the last of Gilbert's works for the stage in 1869, although he contributed 'A Medical Man' to Clement Scott's collection of *Drawing-Room Plays and Parlour Pantomimes*, published for Christmas but dated 1870. Very likely this comedietta had been written two or three years earlier when Gilbert was doing short farces. Its chief characters are Alphonso de Pickleton, a bashful playwright, and Belinda, who has answered his matrimonial advertisement. The plot involves mistaken identity, disguise, and the modesty also celebrated in *Ruddigore* and other works. At the happy ending a theatrical manager accepts Alphonso's sensation drama 'The Patriarch and the Precipice; or, The Blue Pill of Despair'. The *Era* took exception to Alphonso's five-page expository monologue, and the *Tomahawk* considered Gilbert's allusion to 'throwing up' coarse. Altogether, the collection made little stir, except perhaps among the amateurs for whom it was intended.[38]

Gilbert, as usual, contributed to *Tom Hood's Comic Annual*, but he occupied himself mostly with writing a new burlesque-extravaganza for the Qlympic Theatre.

---

[38] *A Medical Man* was produced two years later on 24 Oct. 1872, at St George's Hall.

# 6

## Burlesque into Fairy Play

Few authors have become so famous in so short a space of time

*Era* (28 Jan. 1872)

THE curtain which rose on the first performance of *The Princess* (8 January 1870) began Gilbert's most productive and innovative decade, during which he wrote more than thirty-five plays, encompassing every genre from farce to near-tragedy and including five librettos set by Arthur Sullivan. When the decade began, his work was pleasurably anticipated by most audiences; when it closed, he was the leading dramatist of the day. Moreover, he invented a new kind of fairy play which became a standard for judging all others.

*The Princess* was an experiment; Gilbert had been anxious to try, in his own words, a 'blank verse burlesque in which a picturesque story should be told in a strain of mock-heroic seriousness'.[1] When W. H. Liston, manager of the Olympic Theatre, and his wife, Maria Simpson, asked Gilbert to do a Christmas piece for them, he leapt at the chance. Choosing Tennyson's poetic medley *The Princess*, he wrote a 'respectful perversion' in time to be sent for licensing on 16 December 1869. The Olympic then circulated a statement that it intended to reform burlesque by producing work without 'meretricious accessories' such as far-fetched puns and breakdowns.

Tennyson's poem lent itself well to the dramatist's purpose. Princess Ida founds a women's university, which excludes all men—even the Prince to whom she was betrothed in infancy. He and two companions disguise themselves as girl students and enter her domain, but are soon discovered. In a tournament the Prince and his friends are wounded by Ida's brothers, after which she nurses the Prince and comes to love and accept him. They will, he promises

---

[1] Gilbert, 'An Autobiography', *Theatre*, NS 1 (Apr. 1883), 220.

Walk this world,
Yoked in all exercise of noble end,
And so thro' those dark gates across the wild
That no man knows. Indeed I love thee: come[.][2]

Gilbert retained these lines for his burlesque, although his princess speaks them to his prince, whom he christened 'Hilarion'. For Tennyson's tournament, he substituted a combat for six in which Hilarion's side is victorious. Fourteen years later, Gilbert was to carry these changes, much of his dialogue, and the reversed quotation into *Princess Ida* at the Savoy Theatre.

The critics of 1870 applauded his courage in producing a musical play which required unusual attention from the audience. The *Pall Mall Gazette* (10 January), without mentioning Gilbert's name in its long review, found that *The Princess* aimed at an older, more meritorious form of burlesque. Others called it 'healthy', a favourite Victorian encomium, which evidently meant it was free from *double entendres*. Gilbert himself in a brief correspondence overruled the *Daily News*'s objections to blank verse.

Although the playbill credited Maria Simpson (Hilarion) with directing the burlesque, Gilbert obviously had a good deal to do with it. No doubt, for instance, he coached Mattie Rheinhardt, hitherto a provincial tragic actress, now a handsome, serious Ida. Almost every review praised her for clarity of intonation, a special Gilbert consideration then and always. Ida's brothers and Hilarion's friends were, of course, transvestite roles, which Gilbert thought in retrospect, struck an epicine note. Yet characters *en travesti* were the rule in burlesque, and at least, constant to his own critical principle, he did not allow a male low comedian to play a middle-aged woman.

With his 'bold experiment' safely under way, Gilbert relaxed. Two days after the première, he and nearly three hundred other members of the theatrical profession, including Sullivan and Reed, forgathered at a farewell dinner for Charles Mathews, the light comedian, off to Australia. Such an evening of speeches, music, and conviviality was, of course, for men only; Gilbert, like most of his colleagues, would spend a lifetime attending them.

His burlesque ran till mid-April, then went to the provinces. Three years later, Gilbert suggested to Buckstone that he revive it at the

---

[2] Alfred Lord Tennyson, *The Princess*, in *Poems and Plays*, ed. T. Herbert Warren, rev. and enlarged by F. Page (London: Oxford University Press, 1971), 200.

Haymarket, but the manager put him off: 'there seems to be so much music in it'.[3] Although Marie Litton thought of producing the reform burlesque, it seems to have lain dormant until it became *Princess Ida* in 1884. Nor, despite an imitation or two, did it banish Burnand, Byron, and the rest from the theatre of the 1870s.

There was also a great deal of music in Gilbert's next two works for the stage, both of which dealt with problems in identity solved by time-juggles. The first of these was a libretto, *The Gentleman in Black*, set by Frederic Clay in an Offenbachian mood, and produced at the Charing Cross Theatre on 26 May.

Gilbert's plot is a dramatic variation of the pseudo-German supernatural tale, such as Dickens's 'The Baron of Grogswig' or his own 'The Triumph of Vice'. Its crux is the exchange of personalities for a month brought about by the satanic Gentleman:

> Otto's body, grim and droll,
> Shrine young Hans's simple soul;
> Otto's soul, of moral shoddy,
> Occupy young Hans's body.[4]

After a series of rather predictable but amusing contretemps, Hans and Baron Otto revert to their original selves when the sixteenth-century calendar reform omits thirteen days and thus ends their month of exchange prematurely.

Evidently Gilbert at first offered the role of Otto (red hair, moles like hat-pegs) to George Thorne,[5] who would one day play comic leads in Richard D'Oyly Carte's touring companies. Thorne had to decline, however; so Edward Danvers created Otto, with Emily Fowler as a girl-boy Hans.

Gilbert and Clay's attempt at English *opéra bouffe* was neither a failure nor a great success, although Fred Clay had two curtain-calls. *Judy*'s reviewer, who arrived too late for a stall, spitefully and fallaciously remarked that Gilbert the reformer had used 'broadly suggestive jokes, and dubiously *double entendres*'. But the dramatist paid no attention; he did, however, write to the *Era* (30 May) to protest what he thought was a charge of plagiarism.[6]

---

[3] 22 Oct. 1873: WSG/BL Add. MS 49,330. *The Princess* had been successfully played in Edinburgh in May 1870.

[4] The reciprocal change of ugly to handsome recalls Lord Byron's verse play *The Deformed Transformed*.

[5] G. Thorne, *Jots* (Bristol: J. W. Arrowsmith, [1884]), 43–4.

[6] Gilbert's letter was published 5 June 1870. A story by the same name had appeared

A more subtle treatment of identity, *Our Island Home*, joined the long-running *Ages Ago* at the Gallery of Illustration on 20 June. In it, the Reeds and their company used their own names but with radically altered personalities in fictitious events. Their 'son' (played by a new comedian, Corney Grain)[7] appeared as a pirate apprentice, ready to slaughter everyone in obedience to his articles. Again a question of date solves the dilemma. Reed had hoped Sullivan would set *Our Island Home* and written to ask him.[8] But Sullivan stipulated a higher price than the Gallery could afford; so Reed wrote the music himself. Yet, in spite of complimentary reviews, the entertainment left the bill after the summer tour, and Gilbert did not publish it.

During the next five years Gilbert wrote three more entertainments for the Reeds: *A Sensation Novel* (30 January 1871), *Happy Arcadia* (28 October 1872), and *Eyes and No Eyes* (5 July 1875). The first, which ran for 186 performances, parodied violent fiction with a cast whose identities again were multiple. Before the play begins each has committed some 'sin' which condemns him or her to represent exaggerated 'sensation' stereotypes within the play. At the end of each act, or 'volume', they are allowed to slip out of character temporarily and realign themselves. Thus the good governess can love the bad baronet, and the virtuous Sunday school teacher can adore the lovely, yellow-haired fiend, modelled on Lady Audley. Two of the cast were exchanged in infancy, and the baronet is really a bus conductor. In a triumph of absurdity, Gripper, the always-too-late detective, is really Chang, one of the Siamese Twins.[9]

In *Happy Arcadia* (set by Clay), the pastoral characters transform themselves into each other so that Chloe's body acts as if it were Strephon's; Chloe's personality inhabits Colin's grizzled face and rugged form, and so on. Less complex and less amusing, *Eyes and No Eyes* manipulates the idea of Hans Christian Andersen's 'The Emperor's New Clothes'. Here it is an imaginary cloak.

The summer of 1870 saw Gilbert buying an inkstand at the sale of

nearly fifty years before in *Blackwood's*, which Gilbert had not read. The critic replied (12 June) that he had referred to a different story, 'The Metempsychosis', which involved changing souls in bodies and that he had not suggested Gilbert borrowed from it.

[7] In my edition *Gilbert before Sullivan: Six Comic Plays* (Chicago: University of Chicago Press, 1967), I erroneously stated that Alfred Reed played this role, but I have since found reviews which indicate the actor was Corney Grain.

[8] 7 Mar. 1870: PML.

[9] LC/BL. Later it was probably changed to Hawkshaw, and in the 1890s to Sherlock Holmes.

Charles Dickens's effects for 11½ guineas and then going off to camp with the Royal Aberdeenshire Highlanders. The regimental motto, 'Nemo me impune lacessit', was exactly right for him. In mid-August he began to illustrate 'Madame Fortunio', which supposedly would begin in the November issue of *Good Words for the Young*. It did not appear then, however, and by 6 September Gilbert had completed only ten of the twenty-four drawings for the first section.

The Franco-Prussian War had broken out in July, prompting English journalists to flock across the channel. On 4 September Napoleon III surrendered with his immediate troops at Sedan, but France, now a republic, fought on while German armies marched toward Paris a fortnight later. On 6 September Gilbert unexpectedly and hurriedly left England as a newly appointed war correspondent for the *Observer*. Just before leaving, he wrote a quick note to the Dalziels, who were cutting his blocks, and sent them the illustrations he had completed. He crossed to France that night in a gale and, as he later learned, with an attractive female swindler, whom he innocently befriended. He even changed two pound notes (possibly counterfeit) for her into some of the gold he foresightfully carried.[10]

France was not a safe place for Englishmen at the moment. G. A. Sala, for instance, had just been seized, imprisoned, and ill-treated as 'a Prussian spy'.[11] Gilbert's cousin Sutherland Edwards, a special correspondent for *The Times*, was repeatedly arrested as a spy on the evidence of a 'naturally jovial German face' and Prussian moustache.[12] Suspicion was rampant as both the diarists Edmond de Goncourt and Felix Whitehurst repeatedly noted, the latter himself being temporarily arrested.[13] Gilbert, too, thought for a moment he might be taken into custody when a fellow traveller noticed 'Schwenck' lettered on his bag and '*The Observer*' written on his visiting card: '*cela veut dire espion*'.

Nevertheless, he arrived safely in Paris before the Germans did, taking a room in the Grand Hotel, which was being abandoned by guests and German waiters. Gilbert visited ramparts and outworks, saw trees being cut down and houses destroyed in preparation for defence. The Tuileries Gardens were occupied by horses; carts of slaughtered beef

[10] W. S. Gilbert, 'The Lady in the Plaid Shawl', pub. in *The Flag* (a fund-raising collection published by the *Daily Mail*, 1908): MS and printed copy in PML. The narrative is subtitled 'A Scrap of Autobiography', and Gilbert insisted every word was true.

[11] *Illustrated Times* (10 Sept. 1870), 166.   [12] *Porcupine* (13 Aug. 1870), 193.

[13] F. M. Whitehurst, *My Private Diary during the Siege of Paris* (London: Tinsley Brothers, 1875), i. 126–30.

were driven past; and on 13 September there was a grand review of the National and Mobile Guards.[14] For some ten days Gilbert waited for the Germans, who had not yet arrived. Then the *Observer* recalled him, presumably because he would be unable to send back reports when the city was completely besieged. So Gilbert caught the last train which left Paris, and crossed the bridge at Creil, an important junction, just before French engineers blew it up. At Boulogne he took a steamer to Folkestone—his brief career as war correspondent was over.

He returned in time to begin adapting Dickens's *Great Expectations* for the Gaiety with J. L. Toole as Joe Gargery, but this was put aside for rehearsals of *The Palace of Truth*, his first fairy comedy. (The word 'fairy' here refers not so much to character as magical conditions or situations.) Playgoers had been promised this treat for four months, but, although originally scheduled for late October, its production was delayed by an unexpectedly successful revival of *The Rivals*. It finally was staged at the Haymarket on 19 November, the day after Gilbert turned 34.

He had begun work on *The Palace of Truth* nearly a year before, when Buckstone commissioned him to write a blank verse comedy and when Palgrave Simpson suggested Madame Genlis's late eighteenth-century nest of tales within tales *Le Palais de la Vérité*.[15] Although Thomas Holcroft had translated the story in 1819, Gilbert could easily have read it in the original French. Certainly, one of its themes, masks and faces, instantly appealed to him.

Cutting characters, incidents, and whole pseudo-oriental subtales ruthlessly, he emerged with an enchanted palace in which everyone unconsciously and unintentionally speaks the truth. A music critic discloses his complete ignorance of music, a lover his fickleness, a prude her immodesty, a friend her enmity. Only Princess Zeolide meets the test of the palace successfully, disclosing a greater store of love than she has yet given utterance. Her father, the appropriately named King Phanor, owns a crystal box, 'a perfect emblem of a spotless life', which enables him to lie, until it is stolen by the outwardly virtuous and inwardly deceitful Mirza. At last, Queen Altemire breaks the crystal, and the palace is disenchanted.

---

[14] E. Goncourt, *Paris under Siege, 1870–71: From the Goncourt Journal*, ed. and trans. George J. Becker (Ithaca, NY: Cornell University Press, 1969), 60–6.

[15] Gilbert, 'Autobiography', 221. In her memoirs Mrs Kendal says that Buckstone gave Gilbert the Genlis story to dramatize, but she was writing in old age, sixty years after the event and made several errors in fact. 'W. S. Gilbert', *Cornhill Magazine*, NS 75 (Sept. 1933), 313.

Gilbert reduced Genlis's genii and other supernaturals to mortals; he deleted all her magical implements except the box and the palace, but he followed Genlis's dialogue more closely at times than the Haymarket's advertisements acknowledged.[16] Nevertheless, his moral diverged from hers, for in *Le Palais de la Vérité* complete truth destroys both dangerous errors and sweet illusions which make for contentment. Gilbert's palace, on the other hand, 'shows up human nature as it is', turning the original cautionary tale into a satire. True, Phanor says, 'Now that the place has lost its influence | We shall get on much better,' but, ironically, his courtiers have learned lessons about each other, not about themselves. Human nature cannot exist in a world of absolute truth.

In this and all his fairy plays, Gilbert was seriously concerned with the distinction between words and reality, words and truth. Here words are false shadows of things; they are to be distrusted because they are used, as in the real world, to deceive or to cheat. The palace of truth is dangerous to its inmates because it forces them, not merely to avow, but to possess true virtue if they are to pass its test. Philamir, a conceited amorist, fails until he abandons the deceptive metaphors and meretricious rhetoric with which he has hitherto wooed women. When he objects that Zeolide says only, 'I love you', she replies:

> What words could I employ, which, tested in
> The crucible of unimpassioned truth,
> Would not resolve themselves into those three?

In fact, *The Palace of Truth* is an example of what Sullivan was to call Gilbert's lozenge plot; that is, a plot in which persons revert to their real natures or become what they have only pretended to be by taking a magic pill or potion. The palace is an architectural lozenge, in which Gilbert first realized the large-scale satiric possibilities of the device.

Buckstone himself played Phanor in a 'Bashaw turban cocked on one side,' as the *Theatrical Journal* said (7 December). Now in the last decade of his life, he had trouble with blank verse, but his mouth with its jug-shaped corner,[17] his eccentric voice, his shrewdness and drollery,

---

[16] Edward St John-Brenon, 'Mr. W. S. Gilbert's Original Plays', *Grand Magazine*, 1 (Mar. 1905), 309–16. This article includes a detailed comparison of scenes, characters, and dialogue drawn from Genlis. There was an occasional suggestion in the press that Gilbert might owe something to Charles Mathews's *Truth* (1834), but characters, scenes, and plots are all different, as well as dialogue.

[17] 'Stage Faces', *Era* (30 July 1881), 14.

his chuckle and wink could still convulse audiences. Prince Philamir and Princess Zeolide were played by W. H. Kendal (not quite at home in verse either) and Madge Robertson, his wife of less than two years (already possessing a sweet silvery voice and an infinitesimal piquant lisp).[18]

Strangely enough, the critics' response to *The Palace of Truth* was 'will it run?' Even some of the majority who admired and praised the comedy feared it might be over the heads of the ordinary playgoers. Dutton Cook (*Pall Mall Gazette*) wondered if it might prove 'one of those productions which an author's friends admire enthusiastically, but which the general public avoids with almost equal eagerness'. Admitting Gilbert's cleverness, the *Theatrical Journal* (7 December) remarked that 'the vivisection of the heart . . . is not an agreeable oper-ation'. They need not have worried. Audiences responded to the irony 'so clever . . . so subtle' (the *Sunday Times*, 27 November), and *The Palace of Truth* stayed in the bills for most of a year.

Several critics commented on Gilbert's other 'daring innovation', his taking a bow before the cast appeared for theirs. He was, they conjec-tured, making a stand for the dignity of the dramatist, but, as he wrote Moy Thomas two days later, 'I went on because I was shoved on from behind. . . . My own opinion is that an author best vindicates his dignity by not showing at all.'[19]

Financially Gilbert did very well with his first fairy comedy. After some revision of fees, it paid him 4 guineas a night till 23 February and 2 guineas thereafter. On tour, Gilbert asked 3 guineas a night for at least twenty performances.[20] He had now engaged the relatively new English's Dramatic Agency to handle his plays, although he still set terms and conditions himself. Very likely Gilbert's choice of English was influenced by the fact that he was also agent for Byron, Robertson, and Buckstone among others. Certainly English did well for Gilbert; all together, *The Palace of Truth* had earned £2,200 by early 1876, count-ing fees everywhere[21]—a large sum in those days—with more to come when it was revived in 1877. Gilbert also found time to contribute fiction and pictures to *Tom Hood's Comic Annual* for 1871 and 'A Drop of Pantomime Water' to the *Graphic*, as well as his usual work for *Fun* throughout the year. He even revised *Dulcamara* for three weeks' per-formance at the Opera Comique, cutting down the broad comedy and

---

[18] 'Our Actresses', *Era* (22 Apr. 1882), 5.   [19] 21 Nov. 1870: PML.

[20] Letter to J. B. Buckstone, 30 Nov. 1870: PML.

[21] Letter from Gilbert to E. A. Sothern, copy, 23 Feb. 1876: WSG/BL Add. MS 49,338.

enhancing the music. The role of Nemorino was sung by a tenor instead of a soprano, and, as the *Era* said, the first night brought 'rapturous applause' and 'roars of laughter'.

After the happy ending of 1870, Gilbert light-heartedly began 1871 with a ball on 4 January at the Strand, where the theatre company and 'select' friends danced till nearly 7 a.m.[22] Very soon, however, he found himself engaged in a quarrel with Andrew Halliday, a popular dramatist, who accused Gilbert of vindictiveness in his parody reviews. During the previous autumn, he had burlesqued Halliday's historical drama *Amy Robsart* and his adaptation of Dickens's *Old Curiosity Shop*. Of the first, Gilbert had written, 'a good piece has been sacrificed to scenery, upholstery and pink silk stockings'; of the second, 'This piece is an outrage. Everyone concerned in it is to be pitied.' Halliday set irate pen to paper; Gilbert replied, defending himself, and this continued until Halliday determined to print the 'piquant' correspondence.[23] Yet, although promised, it never appeared, or, if it did, has sunk without a trace. Perhaps Halliday realized he might look foolish. At any rate, when his *Notre Dame* appeared in April, Gilbert was fortunately able to describe it as 'on the whole an excellent melodrama and immeasurably superior to the same author's Nell'.

With *The Palace of Truth* occupying the Haymarket, Gilbert now became house dramatist for the Court Theatre. This playhouse replaced the short-lived Belgravia on the south side of Sloane Square. Before that, it had been a chapel, the walls of which were retained while Walter Emden gutted and reconstructed the interior. The outside, however, still looked unfinished when the Court opened on 25 January under the management of Marie Litton.

Inside, however, the new house was prettily decorated in mauve, gold, and silver, its attendants in attractive livery. St George's adventures were depicted above the proscenium, with fiery-tongued dragons on each side—'not agreeable' commented the *Daily Telegraph*. Unfortunately, their fire did little to warm the fashionable first-night audience, which had gathered to see Gilbert's comedy *Randall's Thumb*. In fact, the theatre was so cold and damp that playgoers huddled together for most of the evening.

The inaugural address, spoken by Mrs Hermann Vezin, announced 'we are nothing loath, | To bring out plays of truly British growth.'[24]

---

[22] 'Soiree at the Strand Theatre', *Era* (8 Jan. 1871), 14.
[23] *Theatrical Journal* (11 Jan. 1871), 11.    [24] *Era* (29 Jan. 1871), 11.

With this purpose in mind, it is significant that Marie Litton had chosen Gilbert, three of whose plays she mounted during the year. He was the coming man, yet on opening night he refused to answer a call between acts and had to be forced to appear after the final curtain, very likely with the memory of his letter to Thomas fresh in mind.

Based on his own short story published the year before, *Randall's Thumb* also gave Gilbert material for a review of himself in *Fun* on 11 February. He praised the cast and the theatre, but described the comedy as loosely constructed and improbable, almost farcical at the end.

One of Gilbert's favourite actors, the American-born Hermann Vezin, played Buckthorpe, under Randall's vicious thumb for having supposedly committed an accidental murder. In the version played on the first night, Buckthorpe turned out to be the long-lost son of the comic couple; critics complained of this, and Gilbert wisely cut it, together with redundant dialogue. Edward Righton, a Liverpool actor, made his London début in the 'character role' of Joe Bangles, while Maggie Brennan was Miss Spinn. Anticipating the plurality of Pooh-Bah, she had been at various times a governess, a lady's companion, a Crimean nurse, a pew-opener, a missionary, a *vivandière*, a stewardess, and a Bloomer! As former pew-opener, she is able to inform on Randall's villainy. Moreover, the dialogue includes an increasingly favourite Gilbert theme—his belief that no one shielded from temptation can judge another who has been surrounded by it.

Reviewers' responses, aside from Gilbert's own, ranged from 'brilliant', 'a spontaneous overflow of wit and epigram', to *Judy's* characteristic 'a very dreadful mistake'. Almost everyone remarked on the Robertsonian effect of lovers happily stranded on an offshore rock. Although *Randall's Thumb* was not an extraordinary success, it lasted for a hundred performances, one of them attended by Princess Louise and the Marquess of Lorne, just back from their honeymoon. The comedy toured, was revived in 1872, played in America, and was seen in the provinces as late as 1888.

Yet, sadly enough, while Gilbert was winning acclaim, his old friend and mentor Tom Robertson was dying. Ill since autumn, he had managed to see his last play, *War*, onto the stage of the St James's Theatre on 16 January. It failed; indeed, its last performance on 3 February was also the day on which its author died. His was the first death since Prowse's in the old *Fun* gang, and Tom Hood served as one of

Robertson's executors. At his funeral Mrs Bancroft wept bitterly,[25] and Gilbert was startled at seeing Robertson standing on the other side of his own grave: 'The idea of a man assisting at his own funeral was dreadful, and paralysed me for a moment by its dreadful fascination.'[26] Twice more in ensuing years Gilbert saw 'Robertson', once as the defendant at the Wainwright trial for murder! He obviously had a double or doubles, for the critic Thomas Purnell also met 'him' after his death.

Tom Robertson was not a great dramatist, but he had been an important, innovative one, the best of the Victorians before Gilbert. The minute realities of his plays, his 'cup and saucer drama', made it possible for later Victorians to develop a theatre which would be a criticism of life. It is not too much to say that without Robertson or someone like him, Shaw's plays would necessarily be different from what they are. Till the end of his own life, Gilbert never forgot what he owed to Robertson.

Gilbert spent March in a legal quarrel with Arthur Sketchley over their now-defunct journal *Mrs. Brown's Budget*. The details are not very clear; Sketchley insisted Gilbert had been a full partner throughout, which Gilbert denied and called in his solicitors. There was, however, no lawsuit, and Gilbert paid Sketchley £30 rather than the £50 Sketchley asked.

On the other hand, Gilbert was more than generous to his *Fun* friend Harry Leigh, who was adapting his first libretto from Meilhac, Halévy, and Offenbach's *Les Brigands*. When Gilbert learned this, he was himself translating the same piece for Boosey & Co. Although with his present popularity, he could undoubtedly have found a theatre manager eager to stage his version, Gilbert made no attempt to do so. Instead, insisting he had adapted it only for copyright purposes, he left the way clear for Leigh's *Falsacappa*, which appeared at the Globe Theatre on 22 April. It was neatly written but not well sung, and the audience grew a little restive during the three acts. Reviewers, however, encouraged Leigh to continue writing librettos. Gilbert's translation was published, and in October announced for production at the Gaiety, but nothing came of it till 1889 when *The Brigands* returned to drive Gilbert into a lawsuit. In 1871 he simply dropped Offenbach's brigands and carabineers into his retentive memory for eight years until they resurfaced as pirates and policemen.

[25] Letter from T. F. Dillon Croker to Clement Scott, 12 Oct. 1889: Scott Papers/TM.
[26] Interview with *Daily News*, excerpt in 'Theatrical and Musical Gossip', *Theatrical Program* (24 Jan. 1885), 20.

Buckstone unexpectedly went bankrupt in April, with liabilities reported at more than £10,000:[27] 'it would almost appear that the pecuniary success of "The Palace of Truth" . . . is not so great as Miss Clementina Scott and other enthusiastic admirers of Mr. Gilbert would desire,' sneered an unidentified critic. Yet, even if Gilbert's play had failed, five months of poor houses could hardly account for quite such a sum. Arrangements were made for Buckstone to continue managing the theatre, but an irremediable part of his problem was that he was old, forgetful, sometimes vague, as reviewers and his own correspondence admitted. He conducted the Haymarket as it had been conducted a quarter-century earlier, keeping up practices long abandoned by other theatres. Before *The Palace of Truth* opened, for instance, Gilbert received a bundle of free tickets, a dramatist's perquisites in the poorly paid bad old days. Gilbert refused them.[28]

Meanwhile, of the next three pieces at the Court Theatre, only *Creatures of Impulse* was completely satisfactory, cordially received, happily reviewed, and revived in the 1890s. Another dramatization of one of his own stories, this little play shows an old fairy enchanting the other characters so that each behaves contrary to his or her own nature. The shy girl kisses everyone, the coward challenges everyone, and so on. At the end no one marries anyone, a denouement which surprised the *Era* (16 April)—it was another daring innovation. Alberto Randegger supplied the score and conducted the augmented band. A naturalized Englishman, Randegger was fourteen years older than Gilbert, and well-known as a conductor. 'His whole body [was] full of music' and 'vibrated on the podium';[29] like Gilbert, he was fastidious about enunciation.

Again a woman (Maggie Brennan) played a young man, and Edward Righton created the role of Boomblehart, the miser forced to give guineas away. He was very well received, but could not resist broadening his effects for bigger laughs, and, although Gilbert did not write his dialogue in stage 'Jewish', Righton made up as a caricature Jew. When *Creatures of Impulse* was revived the next year without Randegger's music, critics objected to his constant interpolations, such as 'Oh! Wriggling Rachel', 'Oh! Slobbering Solomon', and 'Oh! Jumping Jeremiah'.[30] Obviously Gilbert was not in control!

Gilbert's next Court piece was *Great Expectations*, adapted with the

[27] 'Law and Police', *Illustrated London News* (13 May 1871), 463.

[28] Gilbert, 'An Autobiography', 221.

[29] *Musical World* (27 Feb. 1875), 155, quoting the *Dundee Courier*.

[30] *Era* (27 Oct. 1872), 12, and (3 Nov.) 11.

permission of Charles Dickens, Jr., the novelist having been dead for nearly a year. This is the play originally intended for the Gaiety, but J. L. Toole wanted more comedy than Gilbert was willing to supply; so it went to the Court instead.

Of course, Dickens's novels were perpetually being staged; Halliday's *Little Em'ly*, for example, had recently been popular. Occasionally an adaptor chose a relatively self-contained portion of a long novel, such as Mr Pickwick's trial, and made a relatively unified play out of that. But more often, adaptors simply gave illustrations of Dickens—the high points and most popular characters of a novel held loosely together and dependent on the audience's knowledge of the original. Gilbert did neither. He followed his own principle that the dramatist must seek 'coarse, vigorous, and effective contrasts' (*Illustrated Times*, 2 May 1868), and collapsed the novel into a fairly terse melodrama while retaining much of the relevant dialogue. Miss Havisham, Wemmick, Wopsle, and Pumblechook became off-stage allusions; minor characters disappeared. 'But what the drama has lost in humour it has gained in horror,' said the *Daily Telegraph* (30 May). Horror, unfortunately, was not appropriate to the Court as a comedy house, even though John Clayton won high praise as Jaggers and Maggie Brennan made a believable Pip. At the end some of the cast responded to a feeble call, but Gilbert was not in the house.

The last of Gilbert's Court plays for 1871 was *On Guard*, a comedy, staged on 28 October. Reviewers complained that it was too 'talky', although they admitted the dialogue was sometimes brilliant. Once more Maggie Brennan played a male role, but, for the first time, unsuccessfully. Righton overacted, the audience was irritable, and when Gilbert appeared at the curtain it was to hear cries of 'Cut it down!'[31] Within the month *On Guard* was withdrawn because of so-called previous arrangements. 'Possibly the management arranged for a larger audience and they did not come,' commented the *Hornet* (22 November), which had already taken Gilbert to task for not living up to *The Palace of Truth*. *On Guard* soon slid into the realm of plays revived only for amateur and charity performances.

In May 1871 Gilbert again went for militia duty at the King Street Barracks in Aberdeen. Lodging over a baker's shop, he was watched, writing industriously, by the family over the way.[32] To amuse himself,

---

[31] *Pall Mall Gazette* (30 Dec. 1871), 9.

[32] Charles Glennie, quoted in typescript of a talk by John Malcolm Bulloch (23 Nov. 1937): LG.

he joined the Masonic Lodge St Machar on 9 June, and appropriately enough, perhaps, his seconder was connected with a lunatic asylum! Gilbert's Masonic brethren were to prove useful in popularizing his light operas, and he enjoyed their company, but there is no evidence that he attended lodge meetings regularly back in London.

By this time, Gilbert's connection with *Fun* had all but closed; his last Bab Ballad, 'Old Paul and Old Tim', had appeared in January and his last review on 27 May. Although the rate of payment had improved slightly and he may even have achieved a salary,[33] Gilbert disapproved of critics who were also dramatists, and he was now definitely a dramatist. He would still contribute to Tom Hood's comic annual until 1873, but the high and palmy days of the *Fun* gang were over.

Gilbert was back from Scotland in time to attend a *déjeuner* at the Crystal Palace on 8 July for the visiting actors of the Comédie-Française at which Lord Dufferin and a bust of Molière presided. The French actresses could not be seated with the gentlemen according to the rules of public banquets, but they had their own luncheon, complete with bouquets. Gilbert and nearly two hundred others ate their way through a sumptuous 'French' menu of *potage Colbert, saumon Almaviva, salade Sganarelle*, etc., etc.[34] There was a rumour that the Comédie would produce a French translation of *The Palace of Truth*, but it remained only a rumour.

Gilbert's real success of 1871 was his second fairy comedy *Pygmalion and Galatea*, written against time and produced on 9 December, again at the Haymarket. Rehearsals began in late October when Buckstone returned from a bout of scarlet fever, and when the fairy comedy opened in December, it confirmed Gilbert's new reputation for writing plays which could be read in the study as well as seen on the stage—the Victorian reviewers' supreme accolade.

In *Pygmalion and Galatea* Gilbert chose to amplify Ovid's tale of a sculptor vowed to celibacy, who falls in love with a female statue to whom Venus grants life. These characters were popular, both in Victorian England and on the continent, from Jean Jacques Rousseau's monologue *Pigmalion* in 1772 to George Bernard Shaw's *Pygmalion* in 1912. Victor Massé and Franz von Suppé turned them into figures of light opera; William Morris retold their story in verse, and Burne-Jones, Watts, and Gérome painted them.

---

[33] See marked copies of *Fun*: Huntington Library.
[34] 'Banquet to the Comedie Francaise', *Era* (9 July 1871), 13.

Gilbert, however, used the tale to emphasize King Phanor's conclusion that man cannot live with complete truth. Here Pygmalion laments his human limitations—like Rousseau's Pigmalion he can create statues more perfect than living beings, but he cannot create life itself. He has been married for ten years to Cynisca, a former votary of Artemis who, at their marriage, gave each the power of striking the other blind if he or she were unfaithful in thought or deed. While Cynisca is absent, Galatea, the statue, comes to life, innocent of the conventional ways and morals of the world. She is, indeed, a prototype of Shaw's New-Born in *Back to Methuselah*, who admires herself in a mirror and cannot understand why she may not say she loves her sculptor.

When she hears that Leucippus is a professional soldier, she calls him a paid assassin. When Leucippus accidentally shoots a fawn, she tells the others that he is a murderer. She drives Pygmalion's rich, vulgar patrons away by assuming they are statues modelled by a clumsy beginner. When Cynisca returns and hears Galatea's innocent comments on the sculptor's lovemaking, Pygmalion's wife blinds her husband. Only when she hears him say that Galatea is not fit to live, does she restore his sight. Plaintively Galatea returns to stone, a sacrifice to the status quo ante, as John Wellington Wells was to be in *The Sorcerer*.

The power of inflicting blindness and the name Cynisca are not original with Gilbert, although their source may have been merely subliminal. They come from another of Madame Genlis's stories, 'Daphnis and Panrose', which has for its moral the assumption that mild and uniform affection is longer-lasting than and preferable to blind, irrational love. This is a far cry from Gilbert's fable.[35]

He had been careful to have Galatea's statue modelled from the actress who played the living Galatea, but he did not insist on strict historical accuracy in costumes, which rioted in violet, scarlet, blue, and gold.[36] On the other hand, the set was a Greek interior 'realised with

[35] In the *Grand Magazine*, 1 (Apr. 1905), 484–91, Edward St John-Brenon published a second article showing parallel passages between Gilbert's *Pygmalion and Galatea* and Mme Genlis's play of the same name, which was avowedly a continuation of Jean Jacques Rousseau's 'Pigmalion'. St John-Brenon says nothing about 'Daphnis and Panrose', which Mme Genlis based on a story from Compré's *Dictionnaire de la fable*. Nor does he show that Gilbert develops his characters differently. Since Gilbert always made a point of acknowledging any source for his work, one can only assume that *The Palace of Truth* began as an adaptation, but developed into something he considered original, and that *Pygmalion and Galatea* with its new plot seemed also original. When he published the first series of his plays, he wrote in a foreword that the plot of *The Palace of Truth* was probably as old as *The Arabian Nights*, which was rather disingenuous of him.

[36] Letter to unidentified correspondent, 24 Oct. 1882: PML.

archaeological fidelity' by John O'Connor, who designed many of Gilbert's sets.

Buckstone was funny in the small role of Chrysos, the art patron, although Robert Buchanan, the dramatist-critic, objected to the 'nastiness' of his scenes, played with 'satyric unction'.[37] Kendal and Madge Robertson again played the romantic leads. 'Miss Robertson in Galatea is divine,' John Addington Symonds wrote to a friend.[38] She showed new powers of pathos as well as the irony which would mark her subsequent roles, and, although she had begun to suffer from stage fright, she concealed it well.[39] Gilbert's 'sly shafts of satire' pleased the *Era*, while the *Graphic* insisted that 'A step so bold in dramatic art might deserve some . . . praise even if it had failed. But *Pygmalion and Galatea* is in every way a success.' It had Planché's more-than blessing; Shirley Brooks thought it '*the* piece of the time' (although badly acted).[40]

The comedy coined money even when paired with such a tedious makeweight as the hundred-year-old burletta *Midas*. 'I begin to think "Pygmalion" *must* be a good piece', Gilbert wrote to Buckstone.[41] He considered himself entitled to an increase for his next work and proposed 5 guineas a night for a hundred nights, 3 guineas thereafter. He would devote at least six months to it, declining all other work, and the piece was not to be played until three days after a rehearsal in which the cast were letter-perfect.[42] Buckstone agreed, but hoped that Gilbert would not take the increase as a precedent.[43]

Other Pygmalions were rushed to the stage to take advantage of Gilbert's popularity. In January 1872 *Ganymede and Galatea* at the Gaiety was a broadly comic, lame-rhymed version of von Suppé's *Die Schöne Galatea*, with Arthur Sullivan's brother Frederic, Nellie Farren,

---

[37] *A Look around Literature* (London: Ward and Downey, 1887), 261. Buchanan also objected to Galatea's indelicacy in passing her hand up and down Buckstone's protruding abdomen (ibid. 262).

[38] To Henry Graham Dakyns, 11 Jan. 1872, in *The Letters of John Addington Symonds*, ed. H. M. Schueller and R. L. Peters (Detroit: Wayne State University Press, 1968), ii. 196.

[39] W. Baynham, 'Stage-Fright', *Theatre*, NS 2 (Apr. 1879), 175.

[40] Letter to Miss ('Torie') Matthews, 12 Feb. 1872, in G. S. Layard, *A Great 'Punch' Editor: Being the Life, Letters, and Diaries of Shirley Brooks* (London: Sir Isaac Pitman & Sons Ltd., 1907), 508.

[41] 5 Jan. 1872: WSG/BL Add. MS 49,330.

[42] Copy: 3 Jan. 1871 [1872]: WSG/BL Add. MS 49,330.

[43] 4 Jan. 1872: WSG/BL Add. MS 49,330.

and a bust of Beethoven in a Greek studio![44] In March William Brough's *Pygmalion; or, The Statue Fair* was revived at the Strand; in May, Victor Massé's *Galathée* was the most popular piece in a visiting French company's repertoire. Also in May, the Stereoscopic Company published a portrait of Kendal as the sculptor.

Amid the pleasure of his success, Gilbert made a mistake. In the preface to a privately printed *Pygmalion and Galatea*, he described it as inferior to *On Guard* but infinitely more popular because it had been adequately rehearsed. He distributed only eighteen copies, nearly half of them to the Haymarket company, as commendation for their hard work. The rest were given to personal friends, but inevitably at least one copy fell into the hands of the daily press. On 7 February 1872, therefore, Gilbert found himself writing a long letter to the *Observer*, pointing out that he was entitled to his own opinion, that his preface was not a public comment, and that *On Guard* had been hastily rehearsed with two other pieces, on a stage half-occupied by carpenters. 'I was in the position of an artist, who having to paint a large picture is permitted to see only six square inches of his canvas at a time.'

Marie Litton brought an action for libel, and Gilbert immediately called upon leading theatre people 'to prove that a three-act comedy and two farces cannot be efficiently rehearsed in ten days'.[45] Ultimately the action seems to have been dropped, but it left Gilbert even more determined to insist on sufficient rehearsals. *Pygmalion and Galatea* went on its way, the box-office rejoicing. By the 1890s it had been played everywhere from Calcutta to St Petersburg. It was much more

---

[44] *Era* (21 Jan. 1872), 13. Strangely enough, the *Era*'s 1873 supplement in its list of new plays produced in London the preceding year (5 Jan.) gave Gilbert as the author of *Ganymede and Galatea*; hence some confusion has arisen among those who have not read *Ganymede and Galatea*. Even a glance at the text (LC/BL), however, shows it cannot be Gilbert's; there are no clever rhymes, nor much fun in the verses. The grammar is very awkward, rhymes are forced, and Galatea in the burlesque plays pranks, demands beefsteak and pickled onions, loves Pygmalion's slave, and cheats the art patron of gold and jewels. Victor Massé's *Galathée* (libretto by Barbier and Carré) also engages in pranks, as well as getting drunk and smashing things. When *Ganymede and Galatea* was licensed, 10 Jan. 1872, no author for the English version was given, but it was noted as adapted from the German of Poly Henrion with music by Franz von Suppé. An advertisement for the Gaiety Theatre indicates that von Suppé's version was added on 4 Feb. 1872 to the evening bill in which *Thespis* was already running. In New York (1884), *Adonis*, with a male statue and female sculptor, proved to be a great hit, although, as the *New York Times* said, its plot was merely a framework for song, Amazonian females, dames, and repartee.

[45] Letter to James Albery, 20 Feb. 1872, in *The Dramatic Works of James Albery*, ed. W. Albery (London: Peter Davies, 1939), ii. 772.

important in its long day than was Gilbert's first libretto for Arthur Sullivan.

This was *Thespis; or, The Gods Grown Old*, the 1871 Boxing Night piece at the Gaiety Theatre. Composer and librettist had agreed in October to write a Christmas entertainment for Hollingshead,[46] but only after Gilbert's fairy comedy was produced could he give *Thespis* his undivided attention. He read it to an appreciative company on 14 December, but since J. L. Toole was still on tour full rehearsals could not take place before the eighteenth. Furthermore, most of the principals were occupied with playing several roles each in the Gaiety's current pre-Christmas programme.[47] According to Gilbert's much later estimate, the extravaganza, or 'grotesque opera', was 'invented, written, composed, rehearsed, and produced within five weeks',[48] but in his scrap of autobiography, he put it at less than three.

Consequently the Boxing Night performance, replete with interpolated comic dances and a grand ballet, was really a three-hour-long rehearsal. It took a week to shake *Thespis* down into an effective production; Sullivan conducted only on the first night, Meyer Lutz thereafter. The cast, headed by Toole as Thespis and Nellie Farren as Mercury, was popular, although on first nights Toole was always excessively, and sometimes defiantly, nervous and imperfect in his words.[49] The *Athenaeum* thought he spoke more from impulse than from text. Fred Sullivan played Apollo well, but the audience was not very responsive. It encored only four numbers, one of them Thespis's 'I once knew a chap who discharged a function' with its 'railway' orchestration. At the end hisses mingled with applause from sleepy, bad-tempered playgoers, fidgety to get away. 'Thespis; or, the Gods Grown Old and WEARISOME!' commented the *Hornet*. Nevertheless, the *Musical World* grasped the essential point of the collaboration in its 17 February 1872 review. 'In almost all conjunctions of music and words,' its critic, Shaver Silver (Sutherland Edwards), said, 'there is a sacrifice of one to the other; but in *Thespis*. . . . Sufficient opportunities have been given for music; and the music serves only to adorn the piece.'

---

[46] For Sullivan's probable reasons, see T. Rees, *Thespis: A Gilbert & Sullivan Enigma* (London: Dillon's Bookshop, 1964), 11.  [47] Ibid. 20.

[48] Letter to Percy de Strzelecki, 14 Aug. 1902, published in T. Searle, *A Bibliography of Sir William Schwenck Gilbert: A Topsy-turvy Adventure* (London: Alexander-Ouseley Ltd., 1931), 5–6. In this letter, Gilbert completely misremembered the length of *Thespis*'s run, setting it at about seven nights!

[49] J. Hollingshead, *My Lifetime* (London: Samson Low, Marston & Co. Ltd., 1895), ii. 107.

Gilbert's plot, shorn of extrinsic embellishments and irrelevant dances, is simple but gives a new twist to old patterns of burlesquing the classics. Thespis and his actors picnic on Mount Olympus where the gods have become elderly and incapable of fulfilling their divine functions. Actors and gods change places, the latter going to earth for a year, the former taking their nominal identities, while Mercury, the only young god, stays to assist them. Alas! the Thespians' experiments prove disastrous. Tipseion, a reformed drunkard, for example, is now Bacchus and makes the grapes give only ginger beer. Nicemis, Sparkeion, and Daphne confuse their human relationships with those of the deities they impersonate, while Timidas as Mars has abolished battles, thus causing universal war and upsetting the Peace Society. At the end of the year the Olympians return, discover the actors' ineptitude, and drive them out. Reduced to this basic plot, *Thespis* looks backward to French *opéra bouffe* and far forward to the Flowers of Progress who remodel Utopia in Gilbert and Sullivan's penultimate opera. Gilbert also found it more immediately useful in *The Happy Land*. It is, in fact, fundamentally a Gilbertian invasion plot in which outsiders penetrate and affect a given society, often for the worse.

As usual, reviewers wondered if the burlesque were not too recondite for a typically unruly Boxing Night audience, and Meyer Lutz also believed that musically it was too 'ultra-classical' for its hearers.[50] Soon, however, reviewers were praising the piece and audiences returning to laugh. Nor did they care that Toole changed his words every night. *Thespis* had as long a run (sixty-three performances) as most Christmas pieces, and Richard D'Oyly Carte thought of staging it at Christmas 1875 and again in 1895, but neither production eventuated. It was never revived during the collaborators' lifetimes, nor did Gilbert publish a finished text even though the only ones extant were very imperfect and practically uncorrected.[51] 'Little Maid of Arcady' survived as separately published, surprisingly bowdlerized, while Sullivan later transferred 'Climbing over rocky mountain' to *The Pirates of Penzance*.[52] This, of

[50] 'A Gossip with Meyer Lutz', *Era* (22 July 1893), 9.

[51] Gilbert to Percy de Strzelecki, 23 Apr. 1890: PML. Gilbert wrote erroneously that he had been in America when *Thespis* was published and had had no opportunity of correcting the proofs. Gilbert intended to include *Thespis* in the last volume of *Original Plays*, but died before he read proofs.

[52] See J. March, 'Part of *Thespis* Score Discovered', *Savoyard*, 20 (Mar. 1981), 25. Having examined the full score of *The Pirates of Penzance* (PML), March concludes that Sullivan cut 'Climbing over rocky mountain', as far as Edith's entrance, out of the score of *Thespis* and pasted it into *The Pirates* MS to begin with, not as a last-minute, hurried inspiration in the USA.

course, may have been the fate of other numbers to which Sullivan could have tacitly set other lyrics for the early Savoy Operas. But neither composer nor librettist admitted it, and neither the score, which was in Sullivan's possession, nor the band parts, which were in Hollingshead's, at least until 1879, have survived.

Author and composer did not feel compelled to put aside other interests in order to continue their collaboration. Instead, Gilbert plunged into the *Era*'s current controversy, ignited by Bodham Donne's having excised all political references from the current pantomimes. Donne was the Lord Chamberlain's Reader of Plays, highly intelligent, very well educated, and more generous than his antagonists thought. In a letter published on 14 January, he explained that he followed the already-established principle of cutting words or lines which were personal or personally political, as well as those likely to offend moral or religious scruples. Whatever theatre managers said, most of them found this censorship useful since it supposedly guaranteed the 'purity' of their productions.

It would be another year before Gilbert really challenged the Lord Chamberlain; so now he contented himself with writing a comment, which the *Era* printed along with Donne's. From his own experience, Gilbert said, he had gathered that an actor may 'curse' but not 'damn'; may exclaim 'Heaven forbid' but not 'Lord forbid', and may not use the German *sakrament* because it sounds like 'sacrament'! Obviously, he was thinking of *Great Expectations* and *The Gentleman in Black*. Ironically assuming Donne was required to order enough revisions to keep his office from being abolished, Gilbert remarked, 'I have no particular desire to bring about this catastrophe, but at the same time I am unwilling that it should be averted at my expense.' The tone was that of rather amused superiority, galling to Donne, who had not only passed *The Palace of Truth* unaltered, but gone out of his way to commend its author.[53]

The next week (21 January), the *Era* included the Great Mackney's music-hall song, which began, 'There's a row about the Chamberlain | Cutting down the Pantomimes'. But with the holiday season well over, the argument died out—for a while.

February was taken up with Gilbert's letter to the *Observer* in regard to rehearsals and with preparing unnecessarily for Marie Litton's abortive libel suit. After that he joined the crowds lining the streets as

---

[53] J. B. Buckstone to Gilbert, 28 Apr. 1872, printed in the *Era* (5 May 1872), 11.

the Prince of Wales, recently recovered from typhoid, drove with wife and mother to a thanksgiving service in St Paul's Cathedral. Gilbert sketched an elderly man in court uniform and sword, cocked hat in hand, and labelled it 'A reminiscence of Thanksgiving Day 27th Feb. 1872'.[54] Given Gilbert's attitude toward princes, it is hard to believe he made a special journey, but the great wave of patriotic emotion may have carried him along.

In late April Gilbert was in a cold fury because the headmasters of Harrow, having described his *Palace of Truth* as indelicate and unfit for their boys to see, took it upon themselves to delete comic scenes and dialogue from an amateur performance to which the school had been invited. Apprised of this by the woman who had chosen the piece, Gilbert defended himself, allegedly for her sake, in a letter meant for publication. It showed none of the amusement with which he had treated Bodham Donne, but was a satiric attack on persons who 'would detect indelicacy in the alphabet itself' or in 'any combination of its letters that their prurient taste might induce them to attack'. The *Era* (5 May) printed the story as 'A Dramatist under the Harrow' and included a long excerpt from Gilbert's letter. The Harrow masters should have shrivelled, but doubtless did not; how were they to know that in another thirty years or so, Gilbert would be invited to respond for the visitors at a Harrow Speech Day!

Negotiations for an American production of *Pygmalion and Galatea* had begun in April, and in June Gilbert made a hasty visit to the United States, sometimes misattributed to 1871. He intended to place both the fairy play and his new, as yet unfinished, comedy for the Haymarket and had, at first, thought of waiting till October to take over a company of his own choosing.[55] The *Hornet* for 12 June, however, reported that he had gone to America, and the *Entr'acte* for 15 June that he had arrived there. Of his five days in the United States, he spent two in Boston.

In the event, Gilbert later sold the performing rights to Lester Wallack of New York. On 1 October *Pygmalion and Galatea* opened at Wallack's Theatre with limelight effects by Prof. Tobin of the London Royal Polytechnic Institute. For its first Boston performance (23 December), the playbills announced 'The Wonderful Optical Illusion of the DISSOLVING STATUE', an effect duly patented, also by Dr Tobin. The English actress Carlotta Leclerq played Galatea.

[54] WSG/BL Add. MS 49,321.
[55] Gilbert to Mr Montgomery, 23 Apr. 1872: Harvard Theatre Coll.

Some of Gilbert's continuing American negotiations no doubt involved copyright questions, for no Englishman could copyright his works there: he had to sell or assign them to an American. In *Thespis* Gilbert and Sullivan had more or less solved the problem by appending a 'Caution to American Pirates', which specified that the copyright of words and music for the United States and Canada had already been assigned to R. M. Field of Boston. But *Thespis* did not make enough money to be worth pirating.

Gilbert was therefore pleasantly surprised at the end of summer to receive a draft for £73. 10*s*. from John McCullough's business manager. McCullough, having produced *The Palace of Truth* at his San Francisco theatre, thought Gilbert was entitled to a share of his not inconsiderable takings. Gratified, the dramatist sent a letter to the *Era* (1 September), pointing out this 'rare instance of liberality and fair dealing on the part of an American Manager, to whom the Eighth Commandment is an all-sufficient Copyright Act'. It was to remain a rare one.

Buckstone was finishing his tour and would be returning to London where the Haymarket was being redecorated. In the spring he had announced the theatre would reopen with Gilbert's new play, and in late September he wrote Gilbert to see John O'Connor and explain his views about scenery.[56] But the manager had always intended to continue with *Pygmalion and Galatea*. The theatre would not be ready till the end of October, and Gilbert's next play could be put in rehearsal in November.

Unfortunately, Buckstone found himself in a dilemma: Madge Robertson (Mrs Kendal) was pregnant and, he supposed, shortly to be confined. Kendal had not told Buckstone and denied it when Buckstone asked in June; 'he cares little for any embarrassment in which I may be placed,' lamented Buckstone, who could not be ready with another play in time.[57] He asked Gilbert's advice.

Mrs Kendal did open in *Pygmalion and Galatea*, however, to thunders of applause, but almost immediately, and, prematurely, gave birth to a son. Buckstone hastily put on *The Rivals* again for a few nights and then returned to Gilbert's play with Ada Dyas as a specially engaged Galatea. The critics liked her, and Mrs Kendal did not return till 21 December. Since Gilbert's new play was to open in early January, she must have been rehearsing it before then.

[56] 25 Sept. 1872: WSG/BL Add. MS 49,330.
[57] Ibid.

Aside from *Happy Arcadia* produced on 28 October, Gilbert staged no new work in 1872. He made up for this relatively quiet year by the tumult of the next.

# 7

## A Wicked World—A Happy Land

to relish the caustic satire of the author as he lashes the vices
which afflict mankind.

*Era* (19 Jan. 1873)

FOR his third fairy play Gilbert chose to dramatize his own illustrated story 'The Wicked World', from Tom Hood's 1871 *Comic
Annual*. The tone of this allegory, as Gilbert called it, is half-joking
even when it is serious. The narrator asserts he has chosen to write a
fairy tale because no one can prove him wrong, and he strings out the
action for much more than a year.

As he had promised Buckstone, Gilbert worked on the new play for
months, discarding the peripeteia of the former plot and concentrating
the action into twenty-four hours. The scene is fairyland on a cloud
floating above our wicked world. Gilbert envisioned the set as resembling John Martin's 1853 painting *The Plains of Heaven*: vaporous
mountains and headlands around ethereal blue and a flowering slope
on which sit white-clad angels. This picture evidently had made a great
impression on the dramatist, for five years earlier, as a reviewer for the
*Illustrated Times*, he had suggested it would make an excellent transformation scene for an improved kind of pantomime. The connection
with Heaven was also maintained in Gilbert's scenario, which specified
that the women characters '*in costume & general appearance—should
suggest the idea rather of angels than of conventional fairies. All should
be clothed in long white robes, but certain distinctions in the orna-
mentation & details of these robes may be permitted.*'[1] He designed the
graceful white woollen costumes himself. The drifting cloud is inhab-
ited by both male and female beings, between whom, however, no mortal (that is, sexual) love exists. All these virtuous creatures have one

[1] WSG/BL Add. MS 49,292.

100

fault, however, '*An overweening sense of righteousness*', arising from their freedom from sin.

While the fairy men go to meet their king in mid-earth, Selene (the queen) and her sisters discuss the world with Lutin, a serving fairy. Selene says that love is the only thing which enables mortal man to bear the evil and misery of life, although, paradoxically, love itself motivates sin and crime.[2] Curious and anxious to demonstrate their pure life, the fairy women invoke an old law which allows a mortal to come to their cloud if his fairy counterpart is absent. They are thus able to import two Hunnish knights, Sir Ethais and Sir Phyllon, and later a human Lutin.

But with men comes earthly love, followed by jealousy, malice, violence, and its other attendant emotions. All the fairies now adore the mortals. Selene and Darine compete for Sir Ethais, a Gothic cad, and only the lowly Lutin enjoys himself as a kind of Bottom in their bower. Darine deposes Selene, who is content with her kingdom in Ethais's heart, but finds that he puts knightly 'honour' (that is, fighting a duel) above sexual fidelity. As the erstwhile queen curses him, he and the others leap to earth, Sir Ethais exclaiming, 'I go to that good world | Where women are not devils till they die!'

Awaking from their nightmare of passion, the fairies reject their offstage king's proffered gift of human love. Yet, having themselves fallen into temptation, they will in future be more compassionate to man's struggle 'to defend | The demon-leagured fortress of his soul'.

That Gilbert could not depict serious love has long been an article of critical faith,[3] nor could he represent love in slow gradations of growth or nuances of expression. The convention of love at first sight was intrinsic to his theme in *The Wicked World*, but he occasionally managed to achieve something like genuine passion in isolated moments such as Selene's outcry that, being immortal, her unfulfilled love is the more terrible in its infinite duration of longing.

Gilbert was nervous about his new play,[4] so nervous that he rejected Marion Terry for the small role of Zayda, even though rehearsals had begun. The part needed an 'old stager', he said, and promised to write a play later for Miss Terry.[5] Instead he chose Marie Litton, who

---

[2] When Alfred Austin published a revised edition of his verse play *The Human Tragedy* in 1889, which began with an apostrophe to Love: 'Parent of all our woe and all our worth', Gilbert wrote him to say he had long agreed.

[3] A. Filon, *The English Stage: Being an Account of the Victorian Drama*, trans. F. Whyte, introd. H. A. Jones (London: John Milne, 1897), 141.

[4] J. B. Buckstone to Gilbert, 12 Jan. 1873: WSG/BL Add. MS 49,330.

[5] Letter to Buckstone, copy, 30 Nov. 1872: WSG/BL Add. MS 49,330.

accordingly made her Haymarket début and was praised by the *Pall Mall Gazette* for her enunciation and point. Madge Robertson and W. H. Kendal were, of course, Selene and Sir Ethais, while Buckstone played Lutin and Amy Roselle, Darine.

Even on the day of the first performance, Gilbert was anxious. 'I send you a copy of my new piece before it is damned,' he wrote to J. R. Planché with an invitation to dinner. 'It is rather a risky affair & will be either a big hit or a big failure. "Laudatur ab *hiss*" perhaps!'[6] The risk, of course, lay in the subject-matter, for no Victorian dramatist had hitherto depicted a heroine so obviously in the throes of sexual frustration. In fact, badly written letters objecting to Gilbert's play were sent to the papers.[7]

The evening got off to a bad start. Wearing a glittering green costume with little wings, Buckstone had to speak Gilbert's prologue, ending with

> But prithee be not led too far away,
> By the hack author of a mere stage-play:
> It's easy to affect this cynic tone,
> But, let me ask you, had the world ne'er known
> Such Love as you, and I, and he, must mean—
> Pray where would you, or I, or he, have been?

Gilbert was not a hack author, but once again he was denigrating himself lest the critics dislike his play. Buckstone was received with shouts of laughter and got through most of these lines glibly enough, but toward the end his memory failed. After painful efforts to recover, he left the stage,[8] and Gilbert's wry palliative remained unspoken. Nevertheless, the audience cheered the dramatist and soon were laughing 'at the shafts of wit which are levelled at the follies of the world as though they formed neither part nor parcel of it'.[9]

Many reviewers thought the play well written but unpleasant, the *Illustrated London News* cavilling at Gilbert's use of 'theological' language such as 'sin' and 'righteousness'. The *Era*, however, announced on 5 January that with *The Wicked World*, Gilbert stood foremost among dramatic authors of the day: 'his genial wit and caustic satire have made for him a reputation which will long outlive both him and us'. Joseph Knight's scholarly essay in the *Athenaeum* (11 January) even compared Gilbert's innovative combination of idyll and satire to Ibsen's

---

[6] 4 Jan. 1873: PML.  [7] 'Our Omnibus', *Era* (2 Feb. 1873), 4.

[8] T. E. Pemberton, *The Kendals: A Biography* (London: C. Arthur Pearson Ltd., 1900), 72.

[9] *Era* (19 Jan. 1873), 11.

methods in his early verse plays. Knight further raised *The Wicked World* to the level of literature by referring to Gilbert's *readers*.

Almost every reviewer complimented John O'Connor for his set, showing a bird's eye view of a medieval city through a rent in the cloud, changing to the ocean below for Act 2, and then a series of mountain ranges for Act 3, giving the effect of constant motion above the earth. The cast, too, were generally praised, although Buckstone's Lutin seems to have been more Buckstone than Gilbert. Kendal looked the part, but it was Madge Robertson's triumph. Her voice, repeatedly described as musical, her acting full of indescribable charm, she more than satisfied Gilbert. He dedicated his play to her 'In recognition of the extreme good nature | With which she has received my crude suggestions, | And the admirable TASTE with which, | In very many instances, | She has improved upon them.' Knight, however, found 'a thoroughly satisfactory rendering of blank verse' beyond Madge Robertson's reach.

Four days after the opening, Charles Lutwidge Dodgson went to see *The Wicked World*. 'I did not like it much,' he predictably wrote in his diary.[10] By then, two of Selene's longest speeches had been somewhat curtailed if Buckstone's prompt-book is a reliable guide.[11] Shortly thereafter, Gilbert sold Buckstone the autumn touring rights for £200,[12] and in March the provincial rights went for £230 to Price of Aberdeen[13]—all together a more-than-tidy sum, since Gilbert was also receiving first £4, then £3 a night for the London run. The recent success of *Pygmalion and Galatea* made the new fairy play a valuable property indeed, although, in the event, it had a run of only 175 performances.

Meanwhile Gilbert was engaged as a cheerer on the sidelines of John Hollingshead's and J. L. Toole's copyright suit: *Toole* v. [*Richard*] *Young*. Hollingshead hoped to amend the current law which allowed anyone to adapt a published novel or short story at will, thus preempting works which an author might wish to dramatize for himself. Unfortunately, Mr Justice Cockburn decided in favour of the status quo. Toole appealed unsuccessfully although Hollingshead collected supporting letters from Gilbert, Charles Reade, George Eliot, M. E. Braddon, and others.[14]

[10] 8 Jan. [1873], in *The Diaries of Lewis Carroll*, ed. R. L. Green (New York: Oxford University Press, 1954), ii. 317.

[11] PML.    [12] J. B. Buckstone to Gilbert, 12 Jan. 1873: WSG/BL Add. MS 49,330.

[13] Gilbert to L. J. Sefton, 3 Mar. 1873: PML.

[14] J. Hollingshead, *My Lifetime* (London: Sampson Low, Marston & Co. Ltd., 1895), i. 177; ii. 53. See Ch. 6, above.

But something more immediately important had Gilbert in its grasp and would lead him to a contest with the Lord Chamberlain's Office. (After all, he asked permission to dramatize other writers' fictions, and no one had yet attempted to appropriate one of his own stories.) Marie Bancroft asked Gilbert to write a 'wild' burlesque for private performance. Perfectly willing to oblige an old friend, and very likely recalling their hilarious evenings of improvisation in the 1860s, he undertook a political parody of *The Wicked World*. Although he considered the fairy play was his best work to date, he could easily see how absurd it might be if he twisted the frame of reference from love to politics. He could find absurdity in all things except himself—and sometimes even there; so it would be simple to satirize government, especially since he did not care for the current Liberal Prime Minister, William Ewart Gladstone.

Gilbert could not resist telling Marie Litton about his parody, which she immediately wanted for the Court Theatre. He refused, until a death in the family kept the Bancrofts from using it; then he let the Court have the piece. He felt a certain compunction, however: what would be the result of an author publicly burlesquing his own very serious play? In answer, he assumed a *nom de plume*, F. Tomline (later F. Latour Tomline), a long-ago byline.[15] Other problems he left to fate, which was extremely merciful.

As Gilbert remembered it, Miss Litton gave his plot to Gilbert à Beckett, a rather heavy-handed political satirist for the defunct *Tomahawk* and for *Punch*. À Beckett wrote the burlesque with 'some slight assistance' from Tomline.[16] But earlier, Gilbert also said he had called in à Beckett himself.[17] Whoever invited him, à Beckett's share was slight although he divided the fees equally with Gilbert. Perhaps he worked some of the synopses into dialogue, but it was Gilbert himself who had written the detailed scenario, then called 'Great Britain and Ireland'.[18]

[15] I have been unable to find the articles for which Gilbert used this byline. According to the *Graphic* (10 Aug. 1872), 134, worn-out sixpences called 'Tomlines' after Col. Tomline, MP, were still in circulation; perhaps this suggested the name to Gilbert.

[16] Gilbert, 'An Autobiography', *Theatre*, NS 1 (Apr. 1883), 222.

[17] Draft of letter to Frederic Clay, 7 Mar. 1873: WSG/BL Add. MS 49,330. In the draft of a letter the following day, Gilbert told Clay he had given the idea of the burlesque to Miss Litton 'to deal with as she thought proper'. Gilbert at first wrote 'handed the sketch to Miss Litton', but crossed it out.

[18] WSG/BL Add. MS 49,306.

The plot closely parallels that of *The Wicked World* except that love has now become a popular, i.e. Liberal, government. The earthlings are Mr G[ladstone], Mr A[yrton], and Mr L[owe], dressed and made up like *Vanity Fair* caricatures of their originals. The actor W. J. Hill as the albino Lowe even looked through his eyelashes over the footlights in Lowe's own way.[19] These ministers had already been subjected to constant comic attacks in *Punch* and other weeklies, Gladstone for his determination to stay in power; Lowe (Chancellor of the Exchequer) for his rudeness and parsimony; and Ayrton (President of the Board of Works) for his lack of any sort of taste. In fairyland, they sing, 'we are three most popular men, | we want to know who'll turn us out!', accompanied by an eccentric dance.

The ministers 'improve' fairyland by painting everything, even the trees, slate grey. They set up a two-party system, make Selene Prime Minister, and, when Darine asks what a ship is, they appoint her First Lord of the Admiralty. In this scene, which, in the licence copy, is a close parody of the examination scene in Tom Robertson's *School*, incompetent fairies are all given important government posts. Utter confusion reigns, and the mortals prepare to return to their earthly cabinet meeting. Crying, 'my chief, my trimming chief', Selene tries to detain Mr G., who repulses her, exclaiming, 'I seek that parliamentary world | Where friends insult us only when we're *out*.' They leave, and the male fairies return, bringing with them the gift of popular government.[20] Selene rejects it, and the burlesque ends with a chorus of 'Britons ever, ever, ever, | Shall be slaves.'

David Fisher and Edward Righton played Mr G. and Mr A. respectively, the latter eventually broadening his performance until Gilbert asked Marie Litton to speak to him. Since she was still playing in *The Wicked World* at the Haymarket, Selene was the stately Helen Barry.

Although political allusions were not unknown on the Victorian stage, *The Happy Land* was one continuous allusion at which the first-night audience (3 March) screamed with hilarity. Almost immediately the Lord Chamberlain's Office screamed too—but not with mirth. Bodham Donne, the Examiner of Plays, had, of course, read Gilbert and

---

[19] 'Merry-go-Round', *Entr'acte* (21 Apr. 1888), 4.

[20] At various stages of MS, licence copy, and prompt copy, it had been 'a Gladstone government', 'an earthly parliament', and 'a Liberal government' before being changed to 'a popular government'. These may have been à Beckett's terms; 'a Liberal government' in the prompt copy was altered to meet the Lord Chamberlain's objections. The MS (PML) shows other changes in Act 2.

à Beckett's burlesque and licensed it on 8 February. He had not seen the lyrics, but the political material was then general and not directed against individuals. On stage, however, and especially with interpolated lines, it became completely personal. 'It is nothing less than a pillory,' exclaimed the *Daily Telegraph*'s critic, very likely Clement Scott, caught between disapproval and irresistable laughter.

Viscount Sydney, the Lord Chamberlain, went to see the play for himself on 5 March. He had already heard objections from the Prince of Wales, who attended opening night and laughed heartily—at first. Lord Sydney immediately banned it although Marie Litton promised to delete make-up and names and to send the prompt copy to Bodham Donne. Assuming this was sufficient, she therefore kept the Court Theatre open on 6 March,[21] but distributed a provocative notice: 'Miss LITTON begs to inform the Public that the Lord Chamberlain has FORBIDDEN Messrs. FISHER, HILL and RIGHTON to make up their faces in imitation of Messrs. Gladstone, Lowe and Ayrton.'

The theatre closed on 7 March while Donne found eighteen pages of unlicensed matter,[22] presumably including the satiric songs. Marie Litton now confessed that the authors had 'put her up' to see how far they could go.[23] Since Gilbert had made no secret of supervising rehearsals, he obviously knew or had made the changes, and he had already objected to the principle of censorship in his 1872 letter to the *Era* (14 January): 'As I consider that I am quite as well qualified to judge of what is fit for the ears of a theatrical audience as [the Licenser of Plays] can be, I have systematically declined to take the slightest notice of his instructions.' As a matter of fact, his plays rarely needed censoring. This time he had to take notice, however, but although the offensive lines were omitted in renewed performances, they appeared, capitalized, in the printed text soon eagerly being purchased at the theatre. Moreover, in an oblique assertion of rights, Gilbert had appended a statement to *The Happy Land* to the effect that he and Buckstone sanctioned the burlesque.

[21] J. R. Stephens, *The Censorship of English Drama 1824–1901* (Cambridge: Cambridge University Press, 1980), 121.

[22] Marie Litton said Donne found eighteen pages on which alterations had been made, which is not the same as eighteen pages of alterations. Since this chapter was written, two articles by Terence Rees and Philip Plumb have appeared in the *W. S. Gilbert Society Journal*, 1/8: 229–37 and 1/8: 238–40 respectively, giving other details of the 'Happy Land' controversy. Dr Rees particularly discusses the political background and the provincial performances of this burlesque. See also E. Righton, 'A Suppressed Burlesque—The Happy Land', *Theatre*, NS 28 (Aug. 1896), 63–6.

[23] Stephens, *Censorship of English Drama*, 121.

Tomline's identity proved a challenge. Shirley Brooks confidently believed he was Henry Labouchère;[24] the licence copy gave his name as A. N. Tomlin; reviewers called him an unknown, but the *Athenaeum* (8 March) and others suspected Gilbert. 'How very like Mr. Gilbert Messrs. Tomline and à Beckett are!' one of them remarked. Gilbert found himself casting about for explanations when Fred Clay took it upon himself to deny publicly that his friend had any part in the play. In consecutive drafts of a letter to 'Claydides', 'Gilbertides' admitted some 'slight' collaboration and asked Clay to respect his anonymity. In the second draft he said he had no pecuniary interest in the piece, which was not the case.[25]

A letter from F. Latour Tomline appeared in the *Daily Telegraph* for 7 March, countering the press's general argument that a victim had no means of appealing from stage caricature as he had from printed satire: 'the imagination refuses to picture Messrs. Gladstone, Ayrton, and Lowe standing in front of a stationer's window, and hissing a "Punch" cartoon', but they could come to the playhouse and hiss.

This question of why the stage alone was debarred from political satire engrossed the press for the next month. Editorials argued that theatres might sink into party dissension or explode into riot; others, that the audience's good taste was censor enough. Some suggested that the Lord Chamberlain was showing political bias himself or that, by interfering, he had made the Ministry look more ridiculous than the burlesque had. Only a few reviewers failed to be amused, however, among them Burnand, who wrote Shirley Brooks that *The Happy Land* was 'coarse rubbish'.[26] His notice in *Punch* (15 March) decided that ten minutes were enough to a piece in which 'vulgarity and rudeness often do duty for repartee'.

The Lord Chamberlain joined in with an explanatory letter to the papers, urged perhaps by Sir Lawrence Palk's announcement that he would put a question in the House of Commons.[27] In short, the nose of authority had been gloriously pulled, and in the less scrupulous provinces the verisimilitude of make-up continued. The uproar was even thought to have helped defeat the Liberals in the next election. For, as Joseph Knight summed it up afterwards, *The Happy Land* was the nearest approach to Aristophanes seen on the Victorian stage.[28] Of

[24] Diary, 7 Mar. 1873: London Library.     [25] 8 Mar. 1873: WSG/BL Add. MS 49,330.

[26] Brooks, Diary, 7 Mar. 1873: London Library.

[27] 'The Happy Land', *Era* (9 Mar. 1873), 11.

[28] *The Stage in the Year 1900: A Souvenir* (London: Spottiswoode & Co. Ltd., 1901), 41.

course, *Punch* said it was Aristophanes with a whip and bludgeon. In July there was an approving allusion to *The Happy Land* in Parliament, in reference to a dispute between Ayrton and Lowe.[29]

With two plays running concurrently, Gilbert was negotiating for a third, fourth, and possibly a fifth—a comedy for Mrs John Wood, which was delayed until 1874. No wonder he refused Stephen Fiske's invitation to contribute to the *Hornet*, a periodical he disliked anyway. He had already decided to adapt Labiche and Marc-Michel's farce *Le Chapeau de Paille d'Italie*, under the title 'Hunting a Hat'. He may even have finished it when he wrote to Marie Litton about terms in late March: £3 a night, eighty nights guaranteed from 1 July.[30] But he did not reckon that *The Happy Land* would last till 14 November, which it did. (The Viceroy walked out on it in Calcutta a year later, and it was banned in Melbourne in 1880!) The new piece was held over.

Nevertheless, it was not an altogether pleasant time for Gilbert. He had been given into custody by a Metropolitan Railway stationmaster to whom he was making a complaint. True, he received an apologetic letter from the railway, but the episode was annoying. He used it much later in another adaptation, *On Bail*.

More serious was his lawsuit against the *Pall Mall Gazette*. Some two weeks after its 6 January review of *The Wicked World*, the paper had published a slashing denunciation of Gilbert and the play, signed AMUETOS. The review had called Gilbert's work indecorous; the letter called it indecent. Gilbert sued for libel. 'I have worked hard & zealously for the purity of the stage,' he wrote to Planché, 4 June, asking for his help.[31] Amuetos had called *The Wicked World* coarse, gross, vulgar, offensive, as well as indecent; he even said that there were lines in it unfit to be spoken in any theatre. Gilbert felt his honour was attacked. 'A charge of deliberate indecency is morally akin to a charge of deliberate dishonesty,' he later wrote to the *Era* (7 December). In *The Happy Land*, he had attacked Gladstone for not maintaining England's honour, and his own was very important to him: 'if it be a sin to covet honour, | I am the most offending soul alive,' he once quoted in giving an autograph.[32] Gilbert expected his suit to be heard in late June, but it hung fire till November. He had five months to grow angrier when he had time to think about it.

[29] *Hansard's Parliamentary Debates*, 3rd ser., ccvii. 30 July 1873, col. 1274.
[30] 27 Mar. 1873: WSG/BL Add. MS 49,330.
[31] 4 June 1873: Harvard Theatre Coll.    [32] PML.

It did not help that Buckstone, touring with *The Wicked World*, reported that Gilbert's fairy play 'does not seem to be understood by the many'.[33] Nor did Gilbert like hearing that heavy rainstorms had reduced business in Birmingham,[34] although this did not affect him financially. He was now writing a serious play, but put it aside briefly to *épater* the Lord Chamberlain again. Turning back to Meilhac and Halévy, he hastily adapted their recent one-act farce *Le Roi Candaule*, which had lately appeared in London, untranslated yet censored.

Gilbert significantly called his 'very free and easy version' *The Realm of Joy* (later *Realms of Joy*). Meilhac and Halévy's play satirized hypocrisy and bourgeois prudery in the dilemma of a *pater familias* who brings his adolescent daughters to a naughty operetta, only to send them into the corridor whenever a *risqué* song begins—thus unconsciously exposing them to the attentions of flirtatious young men. There is also a scrambled quadrangle of two males, one wife, and one mistress, whom Gilbert sanitized by making both women wives— thereby producing a situation anticipating Shaw's *Overruled*.

In *The Realm of Joy* the improper off-stage play is *The Happy Land*; Gilbert had only to equate politics with sexual morality, a confusion not infrequent in his—or any—society and to exaggerate the French characters a little further. He, too, satirized audience hypocrisy, as, for example, in Jopp's speech saying that he has seen this 'infamous attack on beloved public servants' eighty-four times, but 'We don't come to see the piece, we come to see the spectators, we come to moralize over the depravity of human nature'. The 'beloved public servant' was 'The Lord High Disinfectant', regarded by Society 'as a discreet and loving father who shall determine what is fit for them to hear'.

Bodham Donne was loath to license *The Realm of Joy* (at first ironically called 'A Political Recantation'). Its references to the Lord High Disinfectant seemed to him intentionally and grossly offensive.[35] He kept the Royalty Theatre waiting to construct the necessarily elaborate set till the last possible minute.[36] But Lord Sydney had learned caution. He would not again advertise a play by banning it; so he approved *The Realm of Joy* and directed Donne merely to make the 'usual

---

[33] 19 Aug. 1873: WSG/BL Add. MS 49,330. Buckstone wrote from Dublin.

[34] Buckstone to Gilbert, 22 Oct. 1873: WSG/BL Add. MS 49,330. Buckstone wrote from Birmingham.

[35] Donne to Spencer Ponsonby, 11 Oct. 1873: PRO.

[36] [Miss V. Donne] unsigned letter to Charlie [Donne], n.d.: PRO.

corrections'. 'What "the usual corrections" can be in a piece so *utterly incorrigible* . . . passes my understanding,' Donne exploded.[37]

Nevertheless, the farce appeared at the Royalty on 18 October to an audience screaming with delight and (said the *Athenaeum*) some hisses. Again Gilbert had disguised himself as Tomline, but his identity, if not an open secret, was distinctly ajar. The *Era* (19 October), for instance, thought he had been 'somewhat audacious' and called him by name.

On opening day Gilbert received a letter from Marie Litton, enclosing cheques and irritation. She had asked earlier if he would reduce his fee when the still-running *Happy Land* was revived, not an unusual arrangement. In a bad mood, Gilbert wrote an imperious negative, to which Marie bitterly replied that *she* had not made great sums from his plays. She protested 'against your writing to me as if I were a mere dependant on your consideration & liberality'.[38]

Even allowing for her possible exaggeration, this was an unattractive side of Gilbert. He was determined not to give in on a financial question, particularly on one dealing with the theatre. He could be extraordinarily generous on many occasions, but he insisted on the payment he felt his work deserved. It had been only seven years since Emden told him never to sell a good piece for £30. He had come a long way since then, and he intended to go much farther, far beyond the slipper and pipe domestic comfort that a Blanchard could afford and that Gilbert had already left behind. Self-deprecating as he might be, he knew the market value of his plays. Marie Litton's letter touched him on the raw, exposing all his family stubbornness. (Her letter also shows that Gilbert was now acting as sole author of *The Happy Land*.)

If, however, he had been peremptory, he made great amends with his next Court play, an 'Eccentricity' in three acts, which opened on 15 November, the day after the burlesque closed. This was the long-delayed 'Hunting a Hat', retitled at Marie's suggestion and now known as *The Wedding March*, to capitalize on the current interest in *Lohengrin*.

Gilbert's adaptation is a model of how a French farce could be intelligently suited to the English stage. To begin with, the original plot needed very little 'moral' revision. It depended on split-second timing, on rapid intrusions and concealments, on frantically invented expedients and mistaken identities, and on the pursuit of a crucial object: a hat

[37] Stephens, *Censorship of English Drama*, 122.
[38] 18 Oct. [1873]: WSG/BL Add. MS 49,330.

of Italian straw. (To use Gilbert's names), Leonora hangs the hat on a tree while engaging in a small *tête-à-tête*. Woodpecker Tapping's horse eats it. Although it is his wedding-day, he is forced to find a duplicate hat lest Leonora's monomaniacally jealous husband, General Bunthunder, be aroused. Woodpecker's wedding party has assembled; his bride's father is highly irascible, and his bride has an intrusive male cousin. All these persons, including deaf Uncle Bopaddy, constantly follow Woodpecker in his desperate quest, constantly mistaking their surroundings for the mayor's office, a restaurant, etc. Woodpecker, in turn, has to invent wild excuses and deceptions to keep them quiet and ignorant. Finally he discovers that Bopaddy's wedding gift is an identical straw hat. All is saved at the last moment through a series of *commedia dell'arte lazzi*. The inventive bridegroom (named, incidentally, from Tom Moore's ballad, 'The woodpecker tapping the hollow beech tree') may now claim his bride.

Although Victorian farce had often hard work to find non-sexual equivalents for the sexual French plots it borrowed, in *Le Chapeau de Paille d'Italie* sexuality is merely lagniappe, and Gilbert did not need it. He could invent such laughable business as Uncle Bopaddy's flirtation with two milliner's doll-heads, a moment of Chaplinesque mime. In fact, *The Wedding March*'s innocence 'might fairly be tried by a jury of spinsters', purred the *Daily Telegraph* (17 November); its laughter is 'continuous and healthy', praised the *Standard*.

Gilbert's preface to the published play set forth his comic principle very clearly: 'the success of the piece depends principally on the absence of exaggeration in dress and "make-up"'. The fun came from 'the most improbable things being done in the most earnest manner by *persons of every-day-life*'. 'Fun—why there is enough fun in *The Wedding March* to make half-a-dozen ordinary farces,' exclaimed the *Era* (1 February 1874). Revived and re-revived, it was one of Gilbert's most frequently played successes and brought him £2,500.[39]

On 27 November his libel suit against the *Pall Mall Gazette* came before Mr Justice Brett and a special jury in the Court of Common Pleas. Gilbert had enlisted Bancroft, Blanchard, John Oxenford of *The Times*, Buckstone, William Chippendale of the Haymarket, and W. G.

---

[39] The audience hissed a burlesque hymn at the end of the 1882 revival, however, thinking it a caricature of the Salvation Army. Since the licence copy merely ends with 'Final chorus', words unspecified, one cannot tell. It is unlikely Gilbert would have written a new chorus nine years after the first production.

Wills, author of *Charles the First*, to testify for him as to *The Wicked World*'s freedom from coarseness and indecency. As part of his testimony, Gilbert deposed that the *Pall Mall Gazette* in reviewing his plays, referred to him by name only when it found the play unsatisfactory.[40] Unfortunately, Buckstone, who could not resist making his testimony a comic turn, may have lost the suit for Gilbert. Asked to read some lines of the play as he had delivered them on stage, he looked around the court and said in a stage whisper to the barrister representing the newspaper, 'I can't, sir! I'm too shy!'[41] Laughter swept through the court, but Buckstone's joke had unintentionally implied that the lines were indecorous. Among alternatives, Mr Justice Brett asked the jury to consider the possibility that both letter and play were innocent, the first of malice, the second of indecency. In that case they were to find for the defendant. This is what the jury did, although the *Pall Mall Gazette* implied that the foreman was confused and the jurymen did not believe Gilbert was guiltless. Gilbert thought this in the worst possible taste,[42] but was satisfied that the trial proved *The Wicked World* was not indecent although he had to pay the defendant's costs.[43] Foolishly, however, he wrote to *The Times* on 4 December to protest against the 'gratuitous assumption' of carnal love in his play, which made him seem strangely naïve, especially when he was preparing to rehearse a play about two fallen women for early 1874. In fact, this drama, *Charity*, was at first scheduled for production in December 1873, and in mid-November Gilbert and Buckstone had a troubled correspondence about it. Buckstone had intended to produce someone else's three-act play briefly at Christmas, which Gilbert considered insulting to himself and threatened to place the matter in his solicitor's hands. Buckstone gave in, and while Gilbert's letters have an unpleasant accusatory tone, they are also the letters of a dramatist standing firm for what he considers his rights.

Imitations of *The Happy Land* meanwhile challenged the Lord Chamberlain. In Robert Reece's *Richelieu Redressed* at the Olympic, Righton 'made up' as Gladstone, and George Canninge's Duke of Orleans resembled Disraeli, although this had to be changed. 'You must be aware from what happened about "Happy Land" that these "makes

---

[40] Gilbert was not the only dramatist who sued the *Pall Mall Gazette*; Dion Boucicault e.g., sued but settled out of court.

[41] *Pall Mall Gazette* (31 May 1911), 2.

[42] Letter to Moy Thomas, 9 Dec. [1873]: PML.

[43] Letter to the Editor, *Era* (7 Dec. 1873), 7.

up" are not allowable,' Spencer Ponsonby wrote to the manager.[44] Still the play hit hard, and the audience riotously approved. In December Gilbert à Beckett's *In the Clouds: A Glimpse of Utopia* 'took off' John Bright. Gilbert had begun a small vogue.

[44] To Henry Neville, 29 Oct. 1873: PRO.

# 8

## Problem Plays and Sweethearts

I believe in the morality of God Almighty, not that of Mrs. Grundy.

W. S. Gilbert

THE year 1874 began with two failures and a death. The failures were Gilbert's proto-problem plays: *Charity* at the Haymarket Theatre, beginning 3 January, and *Ought We to Visit Her?* at the Royalty, 17 January. The death was that of Euphrosyne Parepa-Rosa, which altered the direction of Gilbert's creative life although he did not know it at the time.

He had been working on *Charity* for a long time and had even composed it in 1872.[1] 'Composed', however, seems to have meant, at most, outlined a plot, for in his letter to Buckstone on 10 January 1873, he promised to 'think out' the plot which became *Charity*. At first he conceived it as an older-style 'woman's play' like *Leah* or *Lucrezia Borgia*. 'My experience of Mrs. Kendal suggests to me that she has considerable & hitherto unsuspected tragic capabilities,' he wrote. He thought of creating a powerful part for her: 'a passionate vindictive devil with some *one* accessible weak point—such as love for a child or for some other *woman*'.[2]

As Gilbert worked out his scenario, however, Mrs Kendal became, not a passionate devil, but a fallen angel: Mrs Van Brugh, ostensibly a widow, who devotes her time and fortune to social work, especially to rehabilitating outcast women. The 'devil', played by Miss Woolgar, is Ruth Tredgett, a thief and a prostitute. Ruth's experience of prison visitors' charity has been unhappy:

There's ladies come odd times. I call to mind one—come in a carriage *she* did. Same story—poor, miserable, lost one—wretched, abandoned fellow-creetur, and that. She called me a brand from the burnin', and wanted to stretch out a

[1] Gilbert to Moy Thomas, 3 Jan. 1873 [1874]: PML.
[2] 10 Jan. 1873: WSG/BL Add. MS 49,330.

hand to save me, *she* did. Well, she stretched it out, ... and, fool-like, I took it, and kissed it. She screeched as tho' I'd bit her!

Mrs Van Brugh takes her hand, saying, 'You are a woman who wants help, and I a woman who will help you.'

Mrs Van Brugh's daughter Eve is engaged to Fred Smailey (Mr Kendal), rigidly righteous and disapproving of his mother-in-law-to-be's religious tolerance.

MRS. V. B. There are but too many starving men of all denominations, but while I'm hunting out the Churchman, the Jew, the Catholic, and the Dissenter will perish, and that would never do, would it?
FRED. That is the Christianity of Impulse. I would feed him that belonged to my own church, and if he did not belong to it, I would not feed him at all.
MRS. V. B. That is the Christianity of Religious Politics.

Fred's father is both a villain and a humour character, having invented a noble Roman ancestor, Caius Smaileius, whom he invokes to justify himself. Resentful that he did not inherit Mrs Van Brugh's fortune, he investigates her marriage, and forces her to confess she was a mistress, never a wife. Eve is consequently illegitimate. Rising to the moral occasion, Dr Athelney, a colonial bishop-elect, takes the women into his own home. Paradoxically, society cuts Mrs Van Brugh for being what she is and cuts Smailey for having exposed her; Fred twists out of his engagement to Eve. Ruth Tredgett, however, who has recognized Smailey, procures evidence that he once forged a burial certificate, and he is arrested. Mrs Van Brugh, Eve, and Ruth prepare to accompany Dr Athelney and his son to the bishop's Australian see. There, in a newer, freer society, they will teach lessons of hope, kindness, and, greatest of all, charity.

While 'sinners' were often sent to Australia in such Victorian works as *David Copperfield*, Gilbert's conclusion is a very liberal one. Mrs Van Brugh and her illegitimate daughter go as companions fit for a bishop, and Gilbert implies that Eve will eventually marry his son. His heroine, who says, 'I will be punished no further', is very different from the grovelling self-abasement of such sinners as Lady Isabel in *East Lynne*, whom Mrs Kendal played later the same year. 'I have not known one moment's peace since I became a guilty creature,' cries Lady Isabel; and 'all my future life spent in repentant expiation can never atone for the past, never, never'.[5] She dies of moral necessity and shame. Indeed,

[5] T. A. Palmer, *East Lynne*, in L. R. N. Ashley (ed.), *Nineteenth-Century British Drama* (Glenview, Ill.: Scott Foresman & Co., 1967), 395, 379.

shame was an important element in serious Victorian drama, and Gilbert is nowhere so advanced as when he finds unkindness worse than unchastity.

As he told himself in a preliminary statement of purpose, he intended to depict

the bitter injustice shown by society against a woman who has *once* gone wrong. . . . When the damning fact comes to light, her character is utterly blighted in the eyes of the world—her penitence goes for nothing—her subsequent good deeds, her remorse, her pure life—all go for nothing. Society looks upon her as plague stricken—a pariah—a leper. . . . But in the case of a man, the verdict of society is in the opposite direction. He may violate faith with every woman who will listen to him and no harm to him comes of it.

Or, in a dialogue note which put it more succinctly:

You forget that the rules that apply to a man & to a woman in such a case are widely different. You forget that *I* am a man—and it would be monstrously unfair to judge me by the rules that society has framed expressly for you.[4]

In short, Gilbert attacked the almost sacrosanct double sexual standard.

A second theme in *Charity* is one Gilbert had earlier touched on, but not so thoroughly developed. That is, the importance of environment in determining morality. Ruth, who 'never had no father', explains:

I were brought up to be a thief. Every soul as I knowed was a thief, and the best thief was the best thought on . . . Well, it was *in* prison and *out* o' prison . . . I sometimes thinks as if they'd bin half as ready to show me how to go right as they was to punish me for goin' wrong, I might have took the right turnin' and stuck to it afore this.

Moved almost to tears, Dr Athelney says, 'as a clergyman of the Church of England I feel bound to tell you that—that your life has been—has been what God knows it couldn't well have helped being under the circumstances.' Mrs Van Brugh adds, 'Who shall say what the very best of us might not have been but for the accident of education and good example?'

Although Smailey was Ruth's first seducer long ago, he now sits as a magistrate and atones for his sins by showing no mercy to offenders brought before him: 'it's all topsy-turvy!' Ruth exclaims. Even Smailey's imaginary ancestor is not merely laughable, although Caius Smailieus caused the critic William Archer to exclude *Charity* from the

---

[4] WSG/BL Add. MS 49,292.

'New Drama'.[5] In *Charity* and *Ought We to Visit Her?* both, ancestor worship encourages cruelty to one's contemporaries.

Much of the public and critical reaction to *Charity* was uncharitable. Part of this may have arisen from the intrusion of farce upon the serious plot. 'Tragedy pure and simple, never flourished at the Haymarket,' Buckstone wrote to Gilbert when the latter first suggested a heavily dramatic play. He asked for a strong, pervasive comedy element;[6] so Gilbert perforce built up the role of Fitz-Partington, for him. This detective of many disguises recalls Gripper in the recent *Happy Arcadia* and elicited the usual laughter, but at the expense of plot. At least one reviewer, moreover, thought Buckstone's part was too slight!

The *Era* (25 January), while praising acting and dialogue, regretted that Gilbert did not provide 'a more satisfactory termination' since the present ending was not in harmony with the spectators' 'notions of dramatic justice'. The dramatist would have had greater success had he not 'evinced a . . . scornful disregard of certain conventional laws in writing for the stage'. But Gilbert's purpose had been to challenge those laws, not merely disregard them. Audiences accustomed to ostracism or death for stage sinners were prepared to pity but unaccustomed to admire. Even ten years later the *Era* (21 March 1885) editorialized against Gilbert for advocating a dramatist's freedom to treat adultery as he chose. Nor was the 1874 evening improved by an old, indifferently acted after-piece, *Raymond and Agnes.*

Although she was too young for the role, the pit rose enthusiastically, waving hats and cheering, at Mrs Kendal's confession scene. Gilbert himself wrote to her that 'Whatever success the piece may eventually achieve will have been mainly due to you'.[7]

He was bitter. 'Pieces written with anything like an earnest purpose seldom seem to succeed. Motley's our only wear, nowadays,' he wrote to a Mrs MacHarness, who had praised *Charity*.[8] Buckstone was meanwhile losing £150 a week—more than £200 by late February[9]—and withdrew Gilbert's play in March. Interestingly enough, it was more successful when toured by Wilson Barrett, especially in Liverpool, Bradford, and Edinburgh. Augustin Daly produced it in great style with Ada Dyas and Fanny Davenport at the Fifth Avenue Theatre in New York for forty-two nights, a good run in America. But this gave Gilbert

---

[5] *The Old Drama and the New* (London: William Heinemann Ltd., 1923), 278.
[6] 12 Jan. 1873: WSG/BL Add. MS 49,330.
[7] 30 Jan. 1874: PML.   [8] 17 Feb. 1874: PML.
[9] J. B. Buckstone to Gilbert, 25 Feb. 1874: WSG/BL Add. MS 49,330.

no pleasure, for Daly added characters and revised the text without asking his permission (not that he would have given it). Nor would an American court issue an injunction. In a review which might have been written, *mutatis mutandis*, by Dickens's Jefferson Brick, the *Evening Post* declared

It is questionable whether the full force of the cutting sarcasms against the snobbery and hypocrisy of English life can be fully appreciated at this side of the Atlantic, where, happily, the evils which are attacked have not yet taken root and flourished in our comparatively new society.

Although Gilbert liked 'strong' women characters—Mirza in *The Palace of Truth*, Cynisca, Selene, Mrs Van Brugh—after *Charity* he ceased to write them. Not even the forthright Jane Theobald in his next play, *Ought We to Visit Her?*, rose to their stature. In this problem play, however, he once again disregarded conventional attitudes, this time in order to deal with the actress question.

Even though plays about virtuous actresses were fairly popular, Victorians still tended to assume the worst about them. If not promiscuous themselves, they were tainted by association with the stage, and for decades 'actress' had been a euphemism for 'prostitute'. In 1877, for instance, the Free Church's Revd S. Runsie Craig preached an anti-theatre sermon (as reported in the *Era*), asking, 'Would you look upon a ballet dancer as a desirable visiting acquaintance, or allow a low comedian to share the innocent joys of your domestic circle?' Advanced Edwardian critics sometimes objected that Victorian players had been too concerned with asserting their respectability ('ladylike' and 'gentlemanly' were among the most gratifying adjectives a Victorian reviewer might use). But to attract new audiences, the fight for social recognition was essential.

In 1874 Gilbert, intending both to reform and defend the stage, entered the battle willingly and, some reviewers thought, wilfully. His play was based on Mrs Edwardes's very popular novel, serialized in *Temple Bar* in 1871; in fact, her name appeared with his in the programmes. Symbiotically, she had quoted from a serious Bab Ballad, 'Only a Dancing Girl' (1866), in which Gilbert portrayed the domestic virtue of a tawdry chorus girl, while satirizing the rouged, respectable matrons who despise her. Mrs Edwardes's heroine Jane is a sanitized version of Bab's dancer. Leaving the stage before making a professional début, she marries Francis Theobald, gentleman and gambler. They live abroad until he inherits an English house in Chalkshire and, returning, discovers Jane is outside the pale of local society. He resumes a semi-affair with Lady Rose Golightly, whose rank procures for her the social position her behaviour does not merit. At the end of the novel Jane nearly elopes with a duke, but is saved by providentially reading a chance leaf of an old sermon. Gilbert radically altered this conclusion, eliminating both duke and sermon. Unlike Mrs Edwardes, who tacitly accepts a double sexual standard while criticizing a double social one, he accepted neither.

Choosing episodes which showed the hypocrisy of the Chalkshire ladies, Gilbert emphasized their attitude: 'Mr. Theobald is not to be punished for being the husband of an actress, and Mrs. Theobald *is* to be punished for being the wife of a gentleman!' Jane, who in Gilbert's version, has appeared on the stage, is bright, natural, spontaneous, and proud of her former profession. As she declares, 'At heart I've never given up my old associates, or my love for them, or my belief that their lives are as good as other lives.' Gilbert based Jane's first-act assertion of loyalty on the novel, but he went further in the last act. Lady Rose herself acknowledges the superiority of Jane's background: 'I am not of your honest, unaffected, true-hearted world—it would have been better for me if I had been!' This obeisance before the theatre is pure crusading Gilbert. The *Athenaeum* (24 January) took leave to doubt her lines, but they are what makes *Ought We to Visit Her?* an unusual play. At the end the Theobalds plan to return to the continent where Mrs Grundy is not 'such an utter brute'.

Although the first night was a success, and Mrs Edwardes and Gilbert bowed from their private box, the *Era* (25 January) wondered if 'the dramatic dish is not a little too strongly flavoured for English taste'. It was, in spite of Henrietta Hodson's charming performance as Jane. Nor did *Ought We to Visit Her?* improve in its country tour. The *Era*'s Liverpool critic referred to Jane as 'ultra-peculiar' and to the moral tone as 'not very healthy'. Nevertheless, Mrs Edwardes thought of dramatizing her novel *Archie Lovell* 'with the help of a well-known theatrical writer', who may have been Gilbert. The plan came to nothing, and F. C. Burnand, who had not asked her permission, adapted her novel.

After ten months of hilarious successes in 1873, Gilbert was chagrined that serious plays on which he had worked hard should have short runs and adverse criticism. He wrote no more problem plays until *The Hooligan* in the last year of his life, although he continued to raise social questions even in his comic librettos. The next year in *Trial by Jury*, his male chorus echoed Smailey as they sang:

Oh, I was like that when a lad!
    A shocking young scamp of a rover,
I behaved like a regular cad;
    But that sort of thing is all over.
I'm now a respectable chap
    And shine with a virtue resplendent,
And, therefore, I haven't a scrap
    Of sympathy with the defendant!

Ruth Tredgett's upbringing recurs in *Iolanthe* (1882) in a song deleted after opening night; having suggested Parliament consider the problems of 'Dingy Drury Lane! | Soapless Seven Dials!', Strephon sings two more stanzas:

Take a tipsy lout
    Gathered from the gutter—
Hustle him about—
    Strap him to a shutter:
What am I but he,
    Washed at hours stated—
Fed on filagree—
    Clothed and educated?
      He's a mark of scorn—
        I might be another,
      If I had been born
        Of a tipsy mother!

Take a wretched thief
    Through the city sneaking,
Pocket handkerchief
    Ever, ever seeking:
What is he but I
    Robbed of all my chances—
Picking pockets by
    Force of circumstances?
      I might be as bad—
        As unlucky, rather—
      If I'd only had
        Fagin for a father!

The critic William Beatty-Kingston objected. These points jarred 'upon the ear and taste alike' in a professedly comic opera.

Not only did *Charity* and *Ought We to Visit Her?* fail to attract audiences, but a third, the libretto for *Trial by Jury*, did not even reach the stage. Mme Parepa-Rosa, Gilbert's childhood friend, for whom he had translated the 'Laughing Song', and whom he had called 'glorious Parepa' in *Fun*, was dead.

After making a reputation in two worlds, she had married Carl Rosa, a violinist, as her second husband. German by birth, Rosa was nevertheless devoted to the cause of English opera, especially as sung in the rich soprano of his wife. Although in 1871 Parepa-Rosa spent four months recuperating from having a stillborn son, her voice was unaffected, and she was still unapproachable in such roles as Donna Anna, Norma, and Leonora. Her acting, however, was more in tone with sprightly parts: Maria, Martha, and Aline. Even though she had become ample of figure—sumptuous, an American reviewer said—she was 'as quick and lively as any of her slimmer competitors'.

In 1873 the Rosas brought their American earnings permanently to London, where Carl assembled a touring company and took Drury Lane for an 1874 season. His great drawing-card was to be his wife's performance of Elsa in the English première of *Lohengrin*. But Rosa also wanted to emphasize native genius; so he asked Gilbert for a libretto which Carl would set himself.

Pleased at this commission from the husband of an old friend, Gilbert set to work. Characteristically, he expanded his one-page 'Trial by Jury', already published in *Fun*, into a one-act libretto, satirizing a breach-of-promise suit. He could hardly have intended the role of the Plaintiff for Parepa-Rosa, however, for she would devote herself to Elsa. 'Little Hersee', Rose Hersee, petite and pretty, would probably have sung the Plaintiff in the Gilbert–Rosa piece. But Hersee lost her chance; Rosa never wrote the music. Instead, his wife began a painful illness that autumn and died while her doctors were calculating the probable length of her convalescence.

On 26 January 1874, her heavy oak coffin was lowered into a grave at Highgate Cemetery in the presence of half the musical world: Sir Michael Costa, Santley, Ganz, Patey, Randegger, the Carl Rosa chorus members, and Gilbert, among many others. While clods fell on the camellias, azaleas, and violets, he mourned the death of a friend and of a collaboration, for Rosa left his company to finish its last two weeks without him and then disbanded it. The projected Drury Lane season was abandoned, and with it the production of *Lohengrin*. Gilbert put his manuscript away.

Indeed, he had little time to think about it, for between Parepa-Rosa's death and her funeral another of F. Latour Tomline's adaptations

121

was produced at the Globe Theatre. This was *Committed for Trial*, a version of Meilhac and Halévy's *Le Reveillon*, which had just been played in French at the Holborn Theatre. The plot is familiar to twentieth-century audiences from Strauss's *Die Fledermaus*, another adaptation, which achieved the popularity that Gilbert's lacked.

Amusing enough but not distinctive, *Committed for Trial* was chiefly remarkable for omitting the naughty midnight supper with its masks and graces which had given the play its original title. (He restored it in a revised version in 1877, since, as *The Times* said, everyone knew what had been omitted anyway.) The Globe production was notable for introducing Arthur Cecil to the professional stage, having left the German Reeds in search of a wider scope. As a gaol-bound husband, having a little fling *en route*, he overacted, but still was received enthusiastically. Opinions of the adaptation itself ranged from the *Athenaeum*'s 'wittier than the original' to the *Entr'acte*'s 'thoroughly contemptible'.

Salvaging a joke or two for later operas, Gilbert relaxed at the eighteenth anniversary festival of the Dramatic, Equestrian, & Musical Sick Fund Association, held in Willis's Rooms on 18 February. The festivities consisted of a good dinner, toasts, and a long report; hardly a rollicking occasion even though actresses led by Mrs Stirling joined the tables of actors, playwrights, and managers.

Gilbert had already written his next piece for the Court Theatre, yet another adaptation, *The Blue-Legged Lady*, this time taken from a *pochade* by Labiche and Marc-Michel. As a curtain-raiser for *The Wedding March*, this brief farce reproduces the chaotic rehearsal of a piece in which a princess has fallen into a dyer's vat and has emerged with sky-blue legs. Members of the cast played themselves, stepping in and out of character; in fact, most reviewers believed that the anonymous author was W. J. Hill, who acted that role in the play.

The blue legs did not run, and Gilbert forgot the piece quickly and entirely. About this time he suggested a new prose comedy to Buckstone, who was still receptive in spite of his losses from *Charity*. Evidently the chief character was to be a man the life of society in public, but a tyrant at home—someone not unlike F. C. Burnand if family accounts are reliable.[10] Buckstone knew such a person and liked the idea very much, but 'write it at your leisure', he told his dramatist.[11] As

[10] In a 1971 interview Monica Burnand, one of Sir F. C. Burnand's grandchildren, described all his family, except for her father and herself, as being terrified of him.

[11] 3 Mar. 1874: WSG/BL Add. MS 49,330.

soon as he had time, he would make an arrangement about the fees he still owed Gilbert. Never completely clear about money, in old age Buckstone had become worse: 'my head is so queer—since my sun stroke 2 years ago,' he wrote to Gilbert on 23 January 1875, asking if his remaining debt was £141.[12] It took Gilbert a long time to receive his money in £10 instalments. But at that he was luckier than Robert Buchanan, whose *A Madcap Prince* was performed at the Haymarket that year and who had to issue a writ against Buckstone—'confound him!'—for his fees.[13] Gilbert never wrote the projected comedy, although he was to have two more plays presented at the Haymarket.

So far it had not been a very rewarding year. Gilbert had tried to go beyond *The Wicked World* into the real one with innovative plays which audiences would not attend. Turning back to adaptation, he had produced nothing to equal the delicious absurdities of *The Wedding March*. He now tried a more congenial subject—topsy-turvydom, in a libretto of that name with music by Alfred Cellier.

Gilbert and Cellier's extravaganza was intended for the new Criterion Theatre for which H. J. Byron was manager, author, and actor. This playhouse was part of the large complex of the Criterion Restaurant and had been built into it almost as an afterthought. Designed by Thomas Verity for Spiers and Pond, the restaurateurs, the plans originally called for a small concert hall. During construction, this was changed to an eight-hundred-seat underground theatre with air pumped in by machine. Lavishly used ornamental tiles lent unusual charm to lobby and staircases.

After a debate about the licence, the Criterion opened on 21 March with Mrs Wood in Byron's *An American Lady* as the main piece. *Topsyturvydom* was intended for the curtain-raiser, but the decorators had not quite finished, complete rehearsals were impossible, and only the comedy was played on the first night. When it did appear, once more a Gilbert piece was said to be too complex for the audience: 'clever, but rather remote,' the *Athenaeum* called it, 'an exercise rather than an amusement'. Yet it is a significant step in Gilbert's development, his first attempt to make the theme of topsy-turvy inform an entire play. He had postulated the principle in his Bab Ballad 'My Dream', four years earlier almost to the day: a systematically reversed world in which virtue is vice, soldiers are shot for being courageous,

---

[12] WSG/BL Add. MS 49,331.

[13] H. Jay, *Robert Buchanan: Some Account of his Life, his Life's Work and his Literary Friendships* (London: T. Fisher Unwin, 1903), 232.

judges practise crime, etc. From this and other Bab Ballads as well as such songs as 'Babbetyboobledore', Gilbert was to develop his vision of a double world: one part consisting of things or principles as they are, the other consisting of ideas about or attitudes toward these things and principles; a world of truth and a world of what we think is reality—two separate worlds which are only intermittently synonymous.

The opening scene of *Topsyturvydom* is laid in England at a peak of universal perfection. A ministerial Topsyturvyite, Crapolee, visits Mr Satis, an MP, and discusses his native land where people are born old and gradually youthen, are born wise and gradually forget everything, and where 'Folly is honoured, wisdom despised—disreputable wealth is courted, honest poverty contemned.' The Topsyturvy government is, predictably, made up of persons wholly unfit for their posts. Crapolee invites Satis to visit his country, warning him that 'Extremes meet and the difference may not be so great as you suppose.'

The rest of the play takes place in Topsyturvydom, where the chandelier rises from the floor and the furniture is on the ceiling. Except for the soprano, the inhabitants' hair is coloured to match their clothing. Detestation is a compliment and the national anthem a hymn of hate. There, Satis falls in love with Tipto, the King's pretty young grandmother, who refuses to give up reading Newton's *Principia* in spite of her age. But, having thoughtlessly insulted the King's mother, Satis is appalled to find that his unpleasantries are taken for a marriage proposal. He refuses, and the King orders him to be executed. Crapolee, however, suggests a fate worse than death. Let him marry Tipto and spend the rest of his life in uninterrupted bliss. All exclaim, 'Oh, horror!'

Fanny Holland, the soprano of Gilbert's German Reed pieces, sang Tipto, and most reviewers liked her song about always forgetting 'that I mustn't remember, | But never remember I ought to forget.' Nevertheless, once again a Gilbert piece had a short run. At least the Reeds were still reviving *Ages Ago*!

For the rest of the spring Gilbert put nothing new on stage. Perhaps he overcame his dislike of Shakespeare idolatry long enough to take Kitty to the charity *tableaux vivants* at Cromwell House in April. His sisters Maude and Florence were there and among the most effective figures in the tableaux John O'Connor and others arranged from Shakespeare's plays. Their brother must have been writing, however, for in early May he sent a note to Irving to say, 'I have conceived what I think would be a tremendously powerful part for you. Do you care to hear more about it? If so, make an appointment.'[14] Irving forgot to reply, and Gilbert began writing the play for H. J. Montague. After Gilbert had finished about an act and a half, Montague went unexpectedly to America. The dramatist then tried Irving again without success, although he had evidently liked Gilbert's idea.[15] Gilbert went no further. Summer came on hot and grew hotter. Gilbert often spent late Sunday breakfast at John Clayton and Palgrave Simpson's house in South Kensington, where actors forgathered.[16] Then at a June or July performance of Lecocq's *Giroflé-Girofla* he ran into Richard D'Oyly Carte, who asked if he had anything available for use as a 'filler'. Carte was importing French *opéra bouffe* for the London Opera Comique and hoped to establish a permanent company for light opera, produced with the attention to detail which marked even mediocre continental performances. Gilbert approved of this intention and had *Trial by Jury* still on his hands; so he offered it to Carte. At the moment, however, the would-be impresario had no composer ready to set it, and since his next production, *La Branche cassée*, lasted only about six weeks, he lost his lease of the theatre.[17] But he did not forget *Trial by Jury*.

In the tropical heat of July, Gilbert paid his 1½ guineas to join the overflowing crowd at a goodby banquet for J. L. Toole, off to tour America. He went to camp as usual; then, by 12 September, the *Athenaeum* reported that he was engaged in the composition of a new play for the Prince of Wales's Theatre. This time, it was—at last—a winner.

But not without casting problems. Gilbert had written specifically for the talents of Mrs Bancroft and John Hare, now a close friend who even named his eldest son after the dramatist, and whose daughter was Gilbert's god-daughter. Hare's speciality lay in playing men twice his age or more. He was adept at turning his boyish face into an old one, an ability which Gilbert intended to exploit. His *Sweethearts* was a two-act 'Dramatic Contrast' in which Hare and Mrs Bancroft would be young in Act 1 and middle-aged in Act 2.

The plot is simple. Harry Spreadbrow, leaving for India, tells Jenny Northcott he loves her. A kind of perverse coquetry keeps her from showing her feelings till he has left. In Act 2 thirty years later, Harry

[14] 3 May 1874: Irving Corr./TM.   [15] 28 Aug. [1874]: Irving Corr./TM.

[16] Sir Johnston Forbes-Robertson, *A Player under Three Reigns* (London: T. Fisher Unwin Ltd., 1925), 113.

[17] G. C. McElroy, 'Whose *Zoo*; or, When Did the *Trial* Begin?', *Nineteenth-Century Theatre Research*, 12 (Dec. 1984), 42–4.

returns from India and meets Jenny, also unmarried. He does not remember her last name correctly and laughingly tells her that his infatuation for her faded in a week. He remembers giving her a camellia. No, she says, a rose, producing the withered flower she has kept for thirty years. Kissing Jenny's hand, Harry declares, 'the serious interest is only just beginning'.

In spite of Gilbert's having tailored the role for him, Hare rehearsed badly, especially in the first-act touches of pathos. Bancroft reluctantly concluded he would not do, although Gilbert hoped that the actor still might redeem himself. He saw what Hare lacked and promised to rehearse the play over and over again with him, emphasizing particularly the pathetic parts.[18] Wait till Saturday to decide, Gilbert urged, but by Saturday Bancroft and Hare had had a painful interview; Hare had proposed and Bancroft accepted terms to ease him out of the role,[19] and Hare had left the Prince of Wales's, where his reputation had been made.

Evidently Marie Litton hoped he would join her company and sent him a message through Gilbert. Her invitation came to nothing, for Gilbert reported that Hare would not accept any London engagements: 'I fancy he has views of some special kind with which I am unacquainted.'[20] Hare did indeed have views; by the next March he had become manager of the Court Theatre. Meanwhile Charles Coghlan played Harry Spreadbrow at the Prince of Wales's.

Produced on 7 November, *Sweethearts* was balm for the irritations Gilbert had felt. The *Era* (15 November) hailed him as if he had been long absent and was glad he had not laid aside his witty, poetic pen. Here was a play which did not require thinking about social problems, a Robertsonian play (on the same bill as Robertson's *Society*), a play the scenery of which was right side up! Here, too, were deft performances, Mrs Bancroft's worthy, as everyone said, of the Comédie-Française itself. Here was Gilbert's triumphal re-entry. The cast was repeatedly cheered, and the author eagerly called for. He was not there; his first-night bogy was beginning to close in.

Gilbert distilled the plot of *Sweethearts* into a song lyric which Sullivan set the next year. Chappell's gave the composer £700 for it, and it did very well in drawing-rooms. The play ran, toured, was revived,

---

[18] Letter to S. B. Bancroft, copy, 8 Oct. 1874: WSG/BL Add. MS 49,330.

[19] S. B. Bancroft to Gilbert, 10 Oct. 1874: WSG/BL Add. MS 49,330.

[20] 16 Oct. 1874: WSG/BL Add. MS 49,330.

served as one of Mrs Bancroft's farewell performances in 1885, and was done by the Kendals for a Command Performance at Osborne House in 1887.

Gilbert's pleasure at the enthusiasm which greeted his dramatic contrast was not, however, utterly unalloyed. The *Hornet* had begun a campaign against him, repeatedly calling him 'dead Gilbert' and referring to his ghost walking nightly at the Prince of Wales's. Its reviewer (11 November) remarked on Gilbert's shrunken reputation, his cynicism 'even in the silent tomb', and 'his idea of studying human nature', which was 'to look down into the dirty cavity where his heart ought to be, and imagine that all other men are like himself.' It was petty, it was silly, it was maddening!

Small wonder then that when Tom Hood died on 20 November, leaving the Bauble, as the editorship was called, to Henry Sampson, Gilbert formally broke with *Fun*. The news of Hood's death had 'knocked [him] over', and he offered to supply more contributions until the Dalziels (now *Fun*'s proprietors) could make other arrangements. Within a week he learned that Sampson, who had been Hood's more than assistant for some time, had also worked for the *Hornet*, and while Gilbert admitted that a young man did not always have the opportunity of choosing his employment, his own self-respect would not permit him to work under Sampson. Otherwise, he wrote to the Dalziels, he would have been glad to contribute, even at a loss.[21] He sent in two columns for the next three numbers as his last. These were a three-part parody of *Hamlet*, entitled 'Rosencrantz and Guildenstern', beginning 12 December. Yet even this was perhaps not written immediately for *Fun*—Gilbert had recently read a Hamlet burlesque to the Court Theatre company. Marie Litton did not accept it, however; so he used it to say goodbye to an association of more than a decade.

The year ended with the publication of 'The Story of a Twelfth Cake' in the *Graphic* Christmas number and of another Gilbert and Sullivan song, also published by Chappell & Co. 'The Distant Shore' tells how the kindly Wind offers to take a message to a maiden's faraway lover. In its haste, the Wind accidentally sinks the ship in which the lover is returning; the maiden dies of grief, but now walks hand in hand with her love on a distant shore. It is a sentimental song with irony at its core, completely appropriate to follow *Sweethearts*.

[21] 30 Nov. 1874: PML.

127

# 9

## Operatical, Comical, Tragical

in all his work we feel that there is an 'awakened' intellect, a
thinking brain behind it

William Archer

WHEN, prompted by Richard D'Oyly Carte, Gilbert read *Trial by
Jury* to Arthur Sullivan on a cold March day in 1875, none of
them realized how deeply they were committing themselves to each
other. For the rest of their lives they would be devoted, though not
always exclusively, to producing and reviving what came to be called
the Savoy Operas.

By now, Gilbert was so thoroughly identified with wit that colum-
nists were beginning to ascribe to him jokes he had never uttered. He
was not yet the Great Cham of Victorian comedy, but he was on the way.
Of the three 'reliable' dramatists—Byron, Albery, and Gilbert—named
by the *Illustrated Sporting and Dramatic News*, he was the 'most brilliant', and, if *Charity* and *Ought We to Visit Her?* had somewhat dulled
his reputation, *Sweethearts* and *Trial by Jury* more than regilded it.

Carte, at the time business manager for Selina Dolaro, needed an
after-piece for her production of *La Périchole* at the Royalty Theatre.
He remembered Gilbert's unperformed piece for Carl Rosa, and he
thought of Sullivan, who was committed to set a libretto for Dolaro.
Although Sullivan had been very successfully pursuing the career of a
young composer-conductor (a symphony, hymns, overtures, songs), his
real love was the theatre. He had already written music for *The
Tempest* and *The Merchant of Venice*, while he and Burnand had done
*Cox and Box* and *The Contrabandista*. Then, too, he was collecting and
being collected by Royals, especially the Duke of Edinburgh, whose
Duchess had improvised the butterfly net which hung over Sullivan's
mantelpiece. Sitting near it, perhaps, Sullivan now screamed with
laughter as Gilbert read his libretto aloud. Characteristically the

128

dramatist gave the effect of 'a man considerably disappointed with what he had written'.[1] But Sullivan, who always knew at a glance whether he could set any particular words,[2] immediately agreed to collaborate. He quickly composed the score; they rehearsed the cast, and *Trial by Jury* was on the boards in three weeks.

While Sullivan composed music, Gilbert père and fils attended a copyright meeting to organize a new Association to Protect the Rights of Authors at home and abroad. At a second meeting the dramatist joined a working committee of Hollingshead, Taylor, and Wilkie Collins, among others. Yet, although a Royal Commission on copyright was set up in 1875, it took three years more to make a report, and dramatic copyright continued to be more lax than that for literature.

From the first, *Trial by Jury* aroused what *The Times* called 'almost boisterous hilarity'. Since it had no spoken dialogue, its creators billed it as 'A Dramatic Cantata', which piqued critical interest. The absurdity of the plot was contained in an impeccably realistic courtroom set; the costumes were contemporary. Even when the Plaintiff entered with her bridesmaids in wedding attire, it was, as a critic said, real wedding attire.

But this realism only underlined a libretto in which there were no conventional romantic leads and no real love at all. Before the trial for breach of promise opens, Edwin, the Defendant, tells the Jury that, while he once loved Angelina, the Plaintiff ('My riches at her feet I threw—'), he has now become 'Another's love-sick boy'. In turn, the Plaintiff attempts to make them increase the damages, while the Defendant insists he would prove a worthless husband. The Judge, first smitten by a bridesmaid, then by Angelina, admits openly that he himself has jilted a 'rich attorney's | Elderly, ugly daughter'. At last, to expedite matters, he decides to marry Angelina himself. Although Edwin wonders if 'They'll live together . . . In manner true?', the cantata ends ebulliently as plaster cupids in Bar wigs descend from the flies.

Even in this happy work, however, Gilbert began the serious lyrics which were to 'ground' his librettos. Angelina sings, 'Sunshine, if eternal, | Makes the roses fade:' and 'Winter hath a beauty, | That is all his own.'

Sullivan's music bubbled with wit and good humour and parodies of Handel and Italian opera. So well suited was score to words that *The*

---

[1] R. Allen (ed.), *The First Night Gilbert and Sullivan* (New York: The Heritage Press, 1958), 28.

[2] Letter from Sullivan to à Beckett, 13 Oct. 1874: PML.

*Times* (29 March) thought they seemed to have 'proceeded simultaneously from one and the same brain', as Wagner's operas did. The cast featured Fred Sullivan, whose contrasting gravity and flirtatiousness were irresistible and who made up as Lord Chief Justice Sir Alexander Cockburn. If Nelly Bromley's voice as the Plaintiff could not match Rose Hersee's, it did not really matter. Nor did the audience greatly care if W. H. Fisher's voice as Edwin was rather tired after singing the male lead in *La Périchole*.[3] Reviewers now reprobated the Offenbach operetta for its daring, tipsy heroine. Gilbert was daring too, said the *Era*, but in a different way: 'He ventures into fields where no previous dramatists have entered. . . . He says things which many of us may have thought, but which no one has dared to express.'

Hardly had the collaborators taken their curtain-calls, and before they put on false beards to mingle with the supers in a later performance, than Gilbert was off to play Leucippe in a 2 April performance of *Pygmalion and Galatea* he supervised at the West Riding Lunatic Asylum.[4] Gilbert loved acting even before lunatics. More than a thousand well-behaved patients were in the audience, and front seats were taken by county families. At the end of the play, visitors, patients, and nurses whirled in a ball, sometimes graceful, sometimes uncouth.[5]

Gilbert's next production, which opened on the heels of *Trial by Jury*, was an extravagant three-act farce, *Tom Cobb; or, Fortune's Toy*. For it, Gilbert returned to the stage of the St James's Theatre, now managed by Marie Litton, where he had made his first dramatic success. By now, the theatre was physically run down, the red baize entrance door so creaky that the *Illustrated Sporting and Dramatic News* said that only enthusiasts would force their way through it more than once a season. Fortunately, audiences braved their way for *Tom Cobb*.

In this version of 'Tom Poulton's Joke', Tom Cobb, penniless, feigns death for three months, leaving behind a mock will in favour of his sweetheart, Matilda O'Fipp. His rival Whipple, a surgeon, derisively names a dying pauper after Tom, a pauper who leaves a miser's golden horde. Matilda and her rascally father claim it and refuse to recognize Tom when he tries to resurrect. O'Fipp chooses a new name for him from *The Times*, and he becomes Major-General Arthur Fitzpatrick, a

---

[3] *Hornet* (31 Mar. 1875), 17.

[4] 'Modern Treatment of Lunacy', *Lancet*, 1 (10 Apr. 1875), 521.

[5] *Orchestra* (May 1875), 315. In Dec. 1875, H. J. Byron's burlesque *Aladdin; or, The Wonderful Scamp* was performed at Colney Hatch Asylum for more than 1,000 lunatics and some 200 visitors.

soldier-poet engaged to Caroline Effingham, whom he has never seen. She, however, is suing him for breach of promise. 'The huckstering men of law appraise my heart-wreck at five thousand pounds!' she says.

The Effingham family is aesthetic and 'intense', given to grouping itself picturesquely at every opportunity, while Caroline's brother Bulstrode is a moodily Byronic law clerk. When Tom, as Fitzpatrick, agrees to continue the engagement, the Effinghams hail him as a deep thinker and write down his banal utterances. Then O'Fipp finally reveals Tom's true identity, and he proves to be the very man for whom Bulstrode's employers have been searching. The dead pauper was his grandfather and has left him a £1,200 bank account as well as the gold. Turning to Caroline, Tom asks, 'you loved me as a penniless, but poetical major-general; can you still love me as a wealthy, but unromantic apothecary?' She replies, 'I can! I can love you as a wealthy anything!' The family arranges itself in a final group.

Everyone was amused by the rapturous Effinghams, even the *Hornet!* The *Era* praised Marie Litton's Caroline for her serious air in the midst of absurdity, and her enormous hat especially charmed critics. As Tom himself, E. W. Royce was amusing but rather stiff. '[S]pontaneous, but, for the most part, cruel,' the *Illustrated Sporting and Dramatic News* said of Gilbert's wit; 'The humour is irresistable but always cynical.' The dramatist was growing weary of this insistence on his cynicism, especially since it seemed inapplicable to *Tom Cobb*. He collaborated with Sullivan that spring on a song, 'The Love that Loves Me Not', which was ironic, but definitely not cynical.

In a lively vein, Gilbert and Kitty attended a fancy-dress ball given by 'Nous Autres', a group of nine, mostly non-theatricals, but including Sullivan as well as Gilbert. Some two hundred guests danced from 11 p.m. to 4 a.m. with a supper break at 1 a.m. Kitty and William's costumes were among the best: she as *vivandière*, he as medieval jester. Mrs Kendal came as Marguerite, and the artist Marcus Stone as Robespierre.

About the time that Gilbert started off for his summer barracks at Aberdeen, the last of his German Reed pieces, *Eyes and No Eyes*, was produced at St George's Hall. Ingenious but less individual than its predecessors, it at least provided a good part for Mrs Reed as an ageing coquette. Mr Reed, however, had retired from acting and had been replaced by his son Alfred. After completing his duty with the militia, Kitty and her Old Boy went to Trouville and Boulogne, where they had fine weather and splendid bathing, after which Gilbert returned to a busy autumn.

Occasional paragraphs began to appear, announcing that Gilbert and Sullivan were working on a new opera for Carl Rosa, who had recovered sufficiently from his wife's death to be interested in opera again. Gilbert could not even promise to think about it until January 1876, so plans went no further. The Royal Aquarium scheme, however, went much further. It began for Gilbert on 28 September when he lunched with Wybrow Robertson, Marie Litton's husband and managing director of the scarcely formed Royal Aquarium and Garden Society—a luncheon which would prove costly in irritation. At this time Gilbert merely contributed 5 guineas and allowed his name to be used as patron, on the assurance that 5 guineas made him a life member. Sullivan had accepted the post of musical director, and later Gilbert spent a certain amount of time carrying on correspondence on the Aquarium's behalf.

After a summer's touring, Selina Dolaro brought *Trial by Jury* back to London, where the *Musical World* even described Fred Sullivan as 'transcendent'. Transferred to the Opera Comique early the next January, it elicited the *Daily Telegraph*'s chauvinistic prophecy that the collaborators would establish an English form of *opera buffa*, suited to English audiences, actors, and 'that sense of decency which still belongs to the national character'.

In October 1875 Gilbert was trying to interest the Adelphi Theatre in reviving *Great Expectations* in spite of its original lukewarm reviews. The Adelphi, however, preferred an adaptation of *Martin Chuzzlewit*, in which Gilbert might make fine play with Pecksniff. He secured permission, but did nothing—he was too busy. Carte was thinking of reviving *Thespis* at Christmas and then touring it, in which case Gilbert and Sullivan would have to revise it first. Again nothing happened. Carte's backer backed away. It's 'astonishing how quickly these capitalists dry up under the magic influence of the words "cash down",' Gilbert told Sullivan.[6] Unfortunately, out of three possible stage works since September, Gilbert had salvaged nothing.

Sad news arrived from Calcutta that autumn: English, Gilbert's agent, had died there suddenly of a heart attack at the age of 39. Although Gilbert continued for a while with English's associate Blackmore, he found the latter less congenial, even incompetent. 'You

---

[6] Copy, 23 Nov. [1875]: WSG/BL Add. MS 49,338.

must surely see that a licence given to a Manager to give one or more performances of a piece, in January, should not be taken, as a matter of course, to hold good for the following June,' he wrote, controlling his exasperation. Blackmore asked if he were to continue as Gilbert's agent. Not 'if you demand 10 per cent on all fees that pass to me through your office,' Gilbert replied.[7] After mid-June 1876 he began to conduct business for himself and to continue to represent Sullivan in their dealings with Carte.

The next unpleasant thing which happened was Gilbert's name being drawn for jury duty. He replied that as a practising barrister he was exempt, and then he looked around for somewhere to practise as briefly as possible. What he found was the Wainwright hearing at the Southwark Police Court. Henry Wainwright, having killed and dismembered his mistress, had been arrested with parcels of her body in a cab. A barrister acquaintance of Gilbert's, named Besley, was appearing for Wainwright and willingly gave Gilbert a nominal brief for 12 and 13 October. After 14 October when the murderer was sent to the Old Bailey for trial, Gilbert could explain that his name should not be on the jury list when he was called for special duty.[8]

He had been a footnote to a famous case, and that was enough. More important, he had won time in which to finish his last fairy play, *Broken Hearts*, for John Hare at the Court Theatre, which Hare had renovated. Gilbert had completed Act 1 by mid-September while Hare was still on holiday. Nevertheless, he drove ahead, pouring himself so intensely into his play that on the last page he wrote, '*Finished Monday, 15th November*, 1875, *at* 12:40 *a.m.* THANK GOD!'

As rehearsals began, Gilbert dashed into a small characteristic episode in private life. An Italian organ-grinder, Paoli Frati, ground away under the windows of Essex Villas. '*Basta!*' cried the dramatist. First, a penny, demanded Frati. Gilbert gave him in charge, and at Hammersmith Police Court the organ-grinder apologized through an interpreter. Whereupon Gilbert asked if he could plead in Frati's defence and, when refused, quixotically paid the Italian's 10-shilling fine.[9] Then he went back to rehearsals.

The new play was medieval in setting, a sombre fairy-tale. Lady Hilda, her frail sister Vavir, and two other ladies come to the Island of

[7] Copy, 16 June [1876]: WSG/BL Add. MS 49,338.

[8] Copy, 13 Nov. 1875; addressee illegible: WSG/BL Add. MS 49,338.

[9] 'Mr. W. S. Gilbert and the Organ Grinder' and 'Topics of the Week', *Era* (28 Nov. 1875), country edn., 6, 11.

Broken Hearts for refuge, all but Vavir having been disappointed in love. Hilda mourns a prince, loved from afar, but drowned in shipwreck. Yet, since women's hearts must love, she now adores a fountain; Vavir, a sundial, and another lady, a mirror. The only man on their island is the deformed Mousta, whom Gilbert described as a mixture of Caliban, 'the Softy', and Danny Mann, the hunchbacked henchman of *The Colleen Bawn*. He might have added Quasimodo as well. Mousta studies spells like the recipes of Macbeth's witches in order to make himself handsome for Hilda.

To this island comes Prince Florian, the object of Hilda's broken heart, not drowned after all, but wrapped in a veil of invisibility. Like so many of Gilbert's young male characters, he is a cad and amuses himself by pretending to be the spirit voice of fountain, sundial, and mirror. Vavir innocently falls in love with him, but, upon seeing Hilda, Florian exclaims, 'oh, wilful, wayward heart, | Bow down in homage—thou art caught and caged!' After Mousta steals and then gives up the magic veil, Florian gently undeceives Vavir, who dies beside her sundial. With a shriek Hilda falls upon her body.

Although *Broken Hearts* was Gilbert's closest approach to tragedy, it appeals to sentiments rather than to passions. Women—and men—in the audience wept, but it seems unlikely that they underwent the catharsis of tragedy. Instead, pathos imbued the blank verse which was smooth and serviceable, but rarely poetic.[10] Since Gilbert did not care for Shakespeare, his model was French rather than the Elizabethan English imitated by his contemporaries. Nevertheless, most reviewers found *Broken Hearts* poetic. Certainly Gilbert thought it his best play, but he could not help writing a self-deprecatory note to Clement Scott just before the opening: 'I have been so often told that I am devoid of a mysterious quality called "sympathy" that I determined in this piece to do my best to show that I could pump it up if necessary—with what success remains to be seen.'[11]

Rehearsals were sometimes stormy, for Hare's temper matched and even on occasion exceeded Gilbert's. He preferred to direct the plays he produced, while Gilbert insisted on stage-managing his own pieces. As if there had not been difficulties enough, Bruce Gordon, the scene-painter, fell ill, and was replaced by a designer named Phillips, reputed

---

[10] William Archer calculated that Gilbert had written at least 9,000 lines of blank verse, not one of which had 'the smallest metrical beauty': *English Dramatists of To-Day* (London: Sampson Low, Marston, Searle & Rivington, 1882), 161.

[11] 6 Dec. 1875: PML.

to be very sensitive and to throw his brush at the scene if annoyed. Gilbert therefore gave up his idea of the sun setting behind the dying Vavir: 'fancy the effect of a comic sunset if Phillips were too often annoyed'.[12] He did insist on real water for the fountain. Fortunately, when *Broken Hearts* opened on 9 December, reviewers praised Phillips's light effects.

The cast was excellent. Bessie Hollingshead, Gilbert's third choice for Vavir, was so touching as to win a special curtain-call. Perhaps Gilbert had intended Hare to play Mousta, but the role went to George Anson in a proto-Deadeye make-up. The Kendals were, of course, Florian and Hilda, she in pink velvet with slashed sleeves.[13] Both the *Era* and Joseph Knight disliked her final shriek in an ending Knight felt should be pianissimo, and sometime during rehearsals or early production, Gilbert and the Kendals had a serious and mysterious quarrel.

Although the *World* (15 December) disapproved of magic as a plot device, the *Era* had already reported that Gilbert and Hare took their call in 'something like a tempest of congratulatory cheers'. For E. L. Blanchard, *Broken Hearts* was 'a perfect fairy poem', while Knight (in the *Athenaeum*) described it, together with *Pygmalion and Galatea* and *The Wicked World*, as 'the most important contribution to fairy literature that has been supplied by any dramatist, or indeed, any writer, since the commencement of the seventeenth century'. Exploring, as they do, the anguish of love, they are indeed Gilbert's bitter comedies, and echoes from them haunted his creative life.

Small wonder, then, that Gilbert was furious when Clement Scott printed a not very funny jest of Burnand's: 'I'm just off to see Gilbert's "Broken Parts".' 'Burnand's attempt at wit is silly and coarse,' the wounded dramatist wrote, 'and your desire to bring it into prominence in the worst possible taste.'[14] Moreover, it might injure the success of the play. Nevertheless, *Broken Hearts* ran for seventy-eight performances, while in Boston, William Gillette, the future depictor of Sherlock Holmes, played Florian gracefully.

Concurrently with preparing *Broken Hearts*, Gilbert issued his first volume of *Original Plays*, dated 1876 but released in late 1875. He had been negotiating with Chatto & Windus since January and had drawn

---

[12] Ibid.

[13] G. Kingston, *Curtsey while You're Thinking* (London: Williams & Norgate Ltd., 1937), 60. Miss Kingston wore Madge Robertson's costume when Gilbert chose her, aged 15, for an amateur performance of *Broken Hearts*.

[14] Mrs C. Scott, *Old Days in Bohemian London* (London: Hutchinson & Co., n.d.), 70–1. Some versions of the incident say 'Broken Tarts', but 'Parts' is probably correct.

five woodblock illustrations, which were not used after all. In addition to his first three fairy plays, the volume contained *The Princess*, *Trial by Jury*, and—stubbornly—*Charity*. The *Standard* gave him the supreme accolade when it said that *The Palace of Truth* and *Pygmalion and Galatea* 'may be read and enjoyed as poems by persons who have never entered the walls of a theatre'.

In December and January Gilbert was engaged in an argumentative correspondence with Wybrow Robertson over the payment of 2 more guineas for his first annual subscription to the Royal Aquarium and Summer and Winter Garden Society. Both Gilbert and Hare distinctly remembered his assurance that they would have to pay nothing more; so Gilbert refused, dismissing a letter from Henry Labouchère, executive committee chairman, as 'a disgraceful quibble',[15] which it was. He resigned. Two years later, when Robertson and Labouchère had violently fallen out, he attended (doubtless with a certain pleasure) the trial in which Robertson sued Labouchère for libel.

During the autumn Gilbert had already begun work on a play for E. A. Sothern, the more-than-famous creator of 'Lord Dundreary', a ridiculously comic character in Tom Taylor's *Our American Cousin*. Although Sothern occasionally played romantic roles, he was essentially a clown yearning to be Romeo. Unfortunately he had a habit of commissioning or buying serious dramas in which pathos and comedy mingled, only to be too nervous to stage them. Coping with Sothern's ambivalences, Westland Marston, the playwright, remarked, 'The difficulties of finding him constant to any particular design was, I believe, an experience which I shared with many other dramatists.'[16] He certainly shared it with Gilbert, who had promised Sothern a play by 15 January 1876. Within a month of the deadline, however, he requested six weeks' extension: 'I really want to make a big thing of the piece.'[17] He did, but when *Dan'l Druce* was performed at the Haymarket in September, Sothern was not in the cast.

As 1875 ended, Gilbert asked Mrs Reed if her copyist would write out *Ages Ago* for him to send his mother and sisters Florence and Maude in Algiers, where they wanted to get up an amateur performance.[18] (Characteristically Gilbert did not keep many copies of his own works

---

[15] Letter to Sullivan, copy, 25 Jan. 1876: WSG/BL Add. MS 49,338. Labouchère said arrangements made before the society was formed did not count.

[16] *Our Recent Actors* (Boston: Roberts Brothers, 1888), ii. 211.

[17] Copy, 15 Dec. 1875: WSG/BL Add. MS 49,338.

[18] Copy, 30 Dec. 1875: WSG/BL Add. MS 49,338.

on hand; he frequently asks a correspondent to return the single copy he has sent.) The Reeds' copyist obliged, but overcharged. Gilbert paid half of what he asked.

He spent the first two weeks of 1876 feeling 'very seedy indeed', a phrase he used to describe a general malaise, perhaps a severe headache. It often required rest in bed or on a sofa, and it is likely that Gilbert's 'seediness' included migraine. Dr Oliver Sachs, for instance, finds the 'Nightmare Song' in *Iolanthe* a description not of a nightmare, but of a migraine delirium, with eleven migraine symptoms in its lines.[19] In the later 'When you find you're a broken-down critter', which finally found a place in *The Grand Duke*, the 'Black-beetles . . . cutting their capers, | And crawly things never at rest' suggest the visual hallucinations of migraine.

By late January, however, Gilbert was himself again, and on 2 February he went to a benefit matinée at the overheated Strand Theatre to see Arthur Clements's burlesque of *Broken Hearts*, entitled 'Cracked Heads'. Years later the American actor Joseph Jefferson remembered it as one of the funniest burlesques he ever saw. Loose-legged Edward Terry played Monsta, and Lottie Venn was Tilda, who loves a pump; Lady Vapid loves a clock. Bessie Hollingshead and the Kendals were there too, evidently enjoying it, but Scott's review in *Concordia* exploded: 'Turn everything into ridicule; reduce every idea to vapid chaff. . . . if the author and the artists who seriously conceived and executed *Broken Hearts* think so little of their art as to welcome this as a good parody, there is very little more to be said about the matter.' He forgot that he himself had disseminated Burnand's rude joke.

Carte wanted another opera, but was still fluctuating. At this point, Sullivan went to Paris, leaving Gilbert to write to Carte that with the chance of a good theatre, 'we'll work like Trojans. But we can't hold ourselves at your disposal whenever you want us.'[20] In May they thought of doing a piece based on *The Wedding March* with Fred Sullivan as Woodpecker Tapping, but once more the plan fell through. *Trial by Jury*, however, after playing since January at the Opera Comique, was happily touring, now with W. S. Penley, the future 'Charley's Aunt', as the Foreman.

Meanwhile Gilbert was corresponding with Sothern in America about a new play for which he had a character and a title, 'The Ne'er-

---

[19] *Migraine: Understanding a Common Disorder* (Berkeley and Los Angeles: University of California Press, 1985), 22.

[20] Typed letter and signature, copy, 11 Mar. 1876: WSG/BL Add. MS 49,338.

Do-Weel'. He asked 2,000 guineas in two instalments for ten years' exclusive rights, and, strangely enough, suggested that he use the pseudonym 'R. J. Moore'. Sothern agreed to the price but not to the name, and Gilbert eventually gave in. Although he did not say so, it seems likely he wanted to see what the reception of the play would be, shorn of the associations his own name inevitably brought. Furthermore, he had offered to let Sothern revise the piece as he chose, so 'R. J. Moore' could not set a precedent for English actors rewriting W. S. Gilbert.

A new club now appeared on his horizon—the just-founded Beefsteak Club, 'the Steak' as habitués would call it—which Gilbert paid 8 guineas to join. Sullivan joined too, as did Irving, Toole, Corney Grain, Hare, Kendal, Burnand, Labouchère—two hundred of 'the better class of "Bohemianism"', all well-known and 'clubable'. Originally a room with print-covered walls and a long dining-table in King William Street, the Club eventually moved to Green Street. Its hours were 3 p.m. to 3 a.m., and at first it was essentially an after-theatre meeting place. In the coming decades it was convenient for Gilbert to wait there during Savoy first nights which he could not bring himself to attend.

Family matters for the elder Gilberts came to some kind of a head in late spring 1876, as Schwenck tried in vain to deal with his parents, who had been steadily growing apart. Mrs Gilbert did not find home agreeable, although they were living at 14 Pembridge Gardens, an attractive three-storey house, light, decorated with plasterwork, and with carved grapes and vines twisting about the stairs. She had been in Algiers; now she was in Paris.

In her absence, her husband became so dangerously ill that Schwenck, Jane, Alfred, and a doctor all wrote urging her to return. Instead, she remained abroad while her son pretended that she had come home and was assiduously enquiring after his father.[21] Evidently Dr Gilbert did not see his wife, but went to Salisbury to recuperate, leaving Schwenck to cope with his mother. Neither parent would discuss the cause of their latest quarrel, and Anne had refused her son's offers of reconciliation or a solicitor. Since Dr Gilbert had assigned their house and £400 a year to her (and another £400 to their unmarried daughters), he had left only an income of £150, which he intended to augment by continuing to write books and articles.

---

[21] Letter to 'Madam' [Anne Gilbert], copy, 6 June 1876: WSG/BL Add. MS 49,304.

Unfortunately, his doctors now told him that would be impossible. Schwenck therefore suggested that Anne Gilbert allow her husband two rooms where he could live quite separately or that she forgo some of her allowance.[22]

On 1 June Anne gave a rather grudging consent which she withdrew four days later. Schwenck had tried to mediate and failed. His father had been too autocratic for too long; his mother no longer cared, and none of the three was skilled in the art of smoothing things over. Dr Gilbert spent the rest of his long life with Jane and Alfred, visiting Schwenck, Kitty, and the Reform Club from time to time. Anne Gilbert disappears. If she wrote to Schwenck, he followed the family custom and destroyed her letters. She continued to live in Pembridge Gardens with Florence and Maude, however, until March 1888 when she died, aged 76, from asthma and 'intestinal stricture'.

While this family embranglement went on, Gilbert was also arranging for alterations in his new house, 24 The Boltons. He wanted, among other things, a new marble fireplace in the master bedroom, two rooms thrown together, and double-glazing to muffle the sound of nearby church bells.[23] Later he proposed a small fernery. The Gilberts moved in by 23 July; it was suitable for a writer of 2,000-guinea plays, even though he did have to borrow from the bank to buy the leasehold. The neighbours, including Jenny Lind next door, were congenial, and the nearby vicar was forward-thinking on social questions. The Gilberts approved of their new dwelling and lived there for seven years.

Gilbert's next work for the theatre had already appeared in the provinces on 1 July. This was *Princess Toto*, another collaboration with Frederic Clay, opening in Nottingham. Clay bought the acting and publishing rights for £525, very useful to Gilbert just then, to whom the copyright would revert after ten years.[24] Kate Santley was not the best choice to create Toto, but Clay's 'humble pen [had] always been at her disposal' since she 'immortalized' a song for him.[25]

This three-act opera was the most ambitious of the Gilbert–Clay collaborations. The libretto deals with the absurd adventures of an utterly absent-minded, impulsive princess, Toto, who marries two husbands (one in infancy, one in disguise). She joins a mock-brigand band of

[22] Letter to 'Dear Mama', copy, 29 May 1876: WSG/BL Add. MS 49,304.

[23] Typed letter to J. Houle, copy, 3 June 1876: WSG/BL Add. MS 49,338.

[24] Gilbert, typed letter to 'Dear Claydides', copy, 7 June 1876: WSG/BL Add. MS 49,338.

[25] Letter from Frederic Clay to George Grossmith, n.d. [1877]: George Grossmith's letter album, PML.

meek courtiers, from whom she is enticed away by her father and two ministers disguised as Red Indians. Calling themselves 'the Consequential Vulture' and 'the Unmitigated Blackbird', they speak in parodies of *Hiawatha* and the novels of James Fenimore Cooper. (Gilbert also borrowed the lyrics from a song in his translation of *Les Brigands*.) At last all identities are disclosed, and Toto's two husbands are successfully reduced to one. Nottingham liked it, especially the parody, and Santley toured successfully, not bringing it to London until October.

That busy summer Gilbert was absent from camp for a fortnight with his Commanding General's permission. In late July, however, he was billed for full 'messing', including some £7 for beer, which he never drank. Captain Gilbert was willing to pay for the 'abominable' food if all other absent officers were likewise billed, which, however, was not the case.[26] Moreover, the Colonel made the mistake of saying that other bills had nothing to do with Captain Gilbert, who paid and resigned.[27] Eventually he was persuaded to soldier on for two more years, but at Gilbert's death, Colonel Innes told a reporter that 'we did not think him very distinguished then'.

The fortnight's leave, so provocative of annoyance, was evidently spent roughing out Sothern's new play *The Ne'er-Do-Weel*, a sketch plot of which he sent to Sothern in America. As usual, the actor wanted a serious drama, but he could not give up the idea of comedy; Gilbert, struggling to meet his requests for changes, worked more closely and deferentially with him than with any other actor. He toyed with the idea of a half-humorous, half-pathetic scene in which the ne'er-do-weel would regret parting with his dog. 'Perhaps you possess such a dog . . . whom you could trust not to over-act?' Gilbert asked, half-whimsically.[28]

He was saturated with the piece, saw John O'Connor about a scene plot, and hoped that Sothern, whether or not he liked the play, would recognize that Gilbert had conscientiously done his best.[29] The actor had already paid him £1,000, although Gilbert had a small fear that the play might not really be his best. He was right, but Sothern's veering requests made it worse than it might have been. Sothern never played it.

---

[26] Typed letter to Lord Inverurie, copy, 25 July 1876: WSG/BL Add. MS 49,338.

[27] Letter to Capt. Gordon Alexander, copy, 17 Oct. 1876: WSG/BL Add. MS 49,338.

[28] Letter to E. A. Sothern, copy, 26 Oct. 1876: WSG/BL Add. MS 49,338.

[29] Letter to E. A. Sothern, copy, 15 Dec. 1876: WSG/BL Add. MS 49,338. To protect the English rights to *The Ne'er-Do-Weel*, Gilbert temporarily thought of engaging the Bijou Theatre in Westbourne Grove for one night, not advertising his name, and charging admission at the door. 'No one will come, & no harm will be done.' Sothern did not agree.

In the meantime *Dan'l Druce*, the earlier play Sothern had not taken, opened at the Haymarket on 11 September 1876, with Hermann Vezin in the title role. Gilbert had chosen his initial situation from George Eliot's *Silas Marner* and so could not avoid producing something like Eliot's ending; however, the rest of the play was his own. He set it in the seventeenth century for plot credibility, but made no attempt at historicity except for what he supposed was the language of the period.

The plot centres on Dan'l, a drunkard and a miser since his wife eloped with a fine gentleman; he thinks of his gold as something he himself has created. Sir Jasper Coombe and his sergeant, Reuben Haines, escaping from the Battle of Worcester, find Dan'l's cottage, send him for food, take his money, and leave behind Sir Jasper's tiny girl with a note saying the gold has taken this form. When Dan'l returns, he hails the child as sent by Heaven to save him.

Fourteen years pass: Dan'l is a hale old blacksmith, and the child a 17-year-old, trembling on the edge of first love. Sir Jasper has just returned as the generous local squire with Reuben as his bailiff, whereupon, recognizing them, Dan'l begins an elaborate plot to keep Dorothy. Reuben, villain-cum-comic relief (and overacted by Odell),[30] expresses his own lasciviousness in words which reviewers found Shakespearean, but which sound like a trial run for Jack Point's patter in *The Yeomen of the Guard*:

I will so coll thee, coax thee, cosset thee, court thee, cajole thee, with deftly turned compliment, pleasant whimsy, delicate jest and tuneful madrigal—I will so pleasantly perplex thee with quaint paradox, entertaining aphorism, false conclusion and contradiction in terms . . . that thy wedded life shall seem one never-ending honeymoon[.]

The complications which follow are conventional stage devices of recognition, overhearing, misunderstanding, and cross-purposes, used rapidly and skilfully to move the plot along. In the last act Dorothy chooses to stay with Dan'l and to marry her childhood sweetheart; in fact, she really is Dan'l's daughter, for Sir Jasper was the seducer of Dan'l's wife. Only one reviewer managed to be surprised.

---

[30] On 13 Sept. Gilbert wrote to Odell, explicitly pointing out his undesirable exaggerations in manner and make-up; that the actor habitually over-acted is indicated in a letter (17 Dec. 1872) written to him by H. B. Farnie, 'bitterly complaining' at Odell's interpolated buffoonery in *L'Œil Crèvé*: PML.

On opening night each act was cheered and the customary storm of applause burst when a smiling Gilbert and the cast took their calls. Vezin as Dan'l was 'the noble center of a noble play', as one reviewer put it. He was an actor not only of great emotional power, but of intellectual stature, and played in the 1884 revival as well. In fact, Vezin included it in his provincial repertory as late as 1890. As Dorothy's suitor the very young Forbes-Robertson looked picturesque and acted well, although the *Era* did not like the way he showed his teeth. But the delight of the play was Marion Terry. Gilbert had promised to write her a play, and Dorothy Druce was one of her first important roles. She had a cool, demure charm, different from her sister Ellen's warm glow, but 'quaint' and 'delicious', to use her reviewers' favourite adjectives. Gilbert had not been able to resist giving her a touch of pretty vanity, and the *Era* declared her speech about her new shoes was in itself worth a visit to the Haymarket:

I am rejoiced that I am decked in my new gown—it is more seemly than the russet, in which, methinks, I did look pale. Geoffrey a man!—my old playmate a man! Pity that I have not my new shoes, for they are comely; but they do compress my feet, and so pain me sorely. Nevertheless, I will put them on, for it behoveth a maiden to be neatly apparelled at all seasons.

In general, critics responded to *Dan'l Druce* as to a major play, albeit an imperfect one. They saw domesticity as a new line for its author and were impressed by his revelation of heart, praising him for becoming thoroughly human. Only *Punch* found the love scene 'namby-pamby'. Early in November Gilbert went to Liverpool to rehearse a second *Druce* company with Marion Terry's younger sister Florence as Dorothy and Henry Forrester as Dan'l; by the time Forrester died in 1882, he had played Gilbert's blacksmith more than three hundred times.

The play ran for 119 performances in London. Rumour and the *Saturday Programme* said Gilbert had been paid £700 for the American rights. Nevertheless it had only a limited success there. Although E. L. Davenport did well in Philadelphia, the Shakespearean actor Lawrence Barrett failed in New York even after clergymen, doctors, dentists, and policemen were offered free tickets. The *Dramatic News* explained that 'The older civilization rather likes the quiet flow of a play like this, which we, demanding a more sensational or stirring treatment, will vote tedious.'

Three weeks after the Haymarket première, Kate Santley brought *Princess Toto* to the Strand, where it lasted only till 25 November in spite of dances arranged by John D'Auban and wonderfully fantastic costumes. As the music critic of the *Athenaeum* explained in 1881, the cast treated it as if it were an *opéra bouffe* of more than ordinary vulgarity, nor did Kate Santley understand Gilbert's wit. Ironically, *Toto* left the Strand to make room for Arthur Clements's burlesque 'Dan'l Tra-duced, Tinker', which proved very dreary.

On 24 October Gilbert and many other dramatists and actors were invited to a Dramatic Banquet given by Lord Mayor Cotton, who had been working his way through the arts until he arrived at the Stage. Tom Taylor, W. G. Wills, and W. S. Gilbert all answered the toast to dramatists: the first was pedantic; the second urged a national theatre, but the third spoke with 'admirable point, keen humour, and unexpected eloquence' (according to the *Era*). First Gilbert compared the Drama to a provincial Richard Third: 'it may not be very good or very strong, but it "takes a long time in dying" '. Last, he pointed out happily that at least six London theatres were now performing *English* pieces. (This insistence on originality caused Gilbert to refute, by giving relevant dates, the *Era*'s suggestion in November that Meilhac and Halévy's *La Boule* was the germ of *Trial by Jury*.)

The year 1876 ended happily enough for Gilbert, except that a further quarrel was brewing with Henrietta Hodson, which would give him trouble in 1877. *Fifty 'Bab' Ballads* (dated 1877) had been published, for which he had written a new preface, promising that any ballads showing 'evidence of carelessness or undue haste' had been withdrawn. Furthermore, he agreed on 16 December to write an original three-act play for the comedian John S. Clarke. Gilbert asked a minimum of 1,000 guineas within twelve months, 1,500 within eighteen, Clarke to have ten years of absolute acting rights. He admitted they were high terms, but, as he wrote, 'I never scamp my work, & whatever I do is the best of the kind that I *can* do.'[31]

All that was left was to wish the Terry sisters a tongue-in-cheek 'decent, sober, temperate & respectable Christmas, undisfigured by extravagance & untainted by excess'.[32]

---

[31] Copy, Dec. 1876: WSG/BL Add. MS 49,338.     [32] 20 Dec. 1876: PML.

# 10

## Storms and Clear Sailing

I am never known to quail
At the fury of a gale

       Captain Corcoran

GILBERT began 1877 as a member of the executive committee for Henry Compton's benefit matinée. Poor Compton, a dryly humorous actor, was now incurably ill, and, in fact, died the next September. Gilbert, along with the theatrical world, attended his funeral at Brompton Cemetery. The dramatist had offered, *faute de mieux*, to write a short address to be spoken at the benefit, but there was no room in a programme which began with William Creswick in a scene from *Othello* and ended, four hours of dramatic excerpts later, with *Trial by Jury*. Sullivan conducted this (and incidental music for the entire afternoon), while Gilbert had a non-speaking role as the Associate. When the benefit took place on 1 March, it realized something like £3,250, Gilbert contributing both money and time.

For Sullivan, January was a sad month. His brother Fred, who had been ill for nearly four weeks, died on the eighteenth, leaving Arthur to write 'The Lost Chord' out of sorrow and to care for his pregnant wife and seven children. Fred's stage career had been relatively brief, albeit successful, and his death left Gilbert and Sullivan without a leading comedian. Gilbert and Fred Clay followed his flower-smothered coffin to the grave, which was also his father's, in Brompton Cemetery.

While not attending executive sessions or funerals, Gilbert was turning *Committed for Trial* into *On Bail* as rapidly as possible for Charles Wyndham, star and manager of the Criterion Theatre. It was not a happy association. Wyndham refused to allow enough time to rehearse the complicated stage business, and Gilbert had to force him to advertise *On Bail* as an adaptation, not an original play. In the event, it ran for only five weeks, beginning 3 February, and *The Times* (5 February) wished Gilbert's name were associated with a better class of work. James Albery's adaptation *Pink Dominos*, which began almost immediately at the Criterion, and which Gilbert disliked, was far more popular and naughtier.

Meanwhile Gilbert, who had been anxiously awaiting Sothern's verdict on *The Ne'er-Do-Weel*, was upset to learn it would not do. Sothern would let him keep £500 as a forfeit, but he felt the comedy could not be acted by the inadequate American companies with whom he often played. Gilbert was astounded. Sothern had never said a word about pick-up companies before, and he had approved the elaborate sketch plot which the dramatist had sent him.[1] But it was useless to argue: the actor's nervousness had again overcome him. At first Gilbert intended to repay the £1,000 advance from author's fees, but later said he would mortgage his newly acquired property; 'damn the mortgage, I accept your word,' Sothern wrote.[2]

By this time *Dan'l Druce* had closed, and Gilbert, always foresightful, had already suggested a revival of *Pygmalion and Galatea*. Marion Terry, in the flush of her success as Dorothy Druce, would play Galatea, for which role Gilbert was already privately coaching her. As Cynisca, Buckstone suggested Henrietta Hodson, but Gilbert refused because they were not on speaking terms. What the dramatist did not know, and what Buckstone did not tell him, was that in October Miss Hodson had joined the Haymarket company as leading lady. She claimed Galatea as her right, and in late 1876 had begun a battle royal which would reach its climax in June 1877.

Hodson and Gilbert's reciprocal antipathy had started during the snappish rehearsals of *Ought We to Visit Her?* in 1874. He had made a mild joke at her expense; she had called him a 'floody boul' and told him to go home to bed. Angrily Gilbert flung away, ran into Marie Litton, and told her what had happened.[3] He then found himself about to be sued for slander and apologized unwillingly, after a fashion. Miss Hodson distributed his apology broadcast. In late November 1876 he and another playwright, Frank Marshall, had a casual conversation in which Gilbert repeated his view that a director must be able to speak to his leading lady. Evidently Marshall passed on the conversation to his intimate friend Henrietta, with exaggerations which he later said were

[1] Letter to Sothern, copy, 30 Jan. 1877: WSG/BL Add. MS 49,338.
[2] 18 Mar. 1878: WSG/BL Add. MS 49,331.
[3] Letter to Marie Litton, copy, 4 Feb. 1874: WSG/BL Add. MS 49,338.

unintentional.[4] Again Hodson threatened to sue, but this time Gilbert did not apologize even though she said he did.

Since, however, it was her professional right, he agreed to let her play Galatea whereupon she shifted to Cynisca in which she did very well. Gilbert had taken the precaution of asking Henry Howe, actor and stage-manager at the Haymarket, to make sure he was not discourteous to Miss Hodson during rehearsals, but Henrietta called this 'a studied insult'. (At the end of the season, the company presented Howe with two inscribed tankards as compensation for his arduous duties during an 'exceptionally trying season'.) Gilbert disregarded Hodson when the play commenced, but wrote to Marion Terry to congratulate her for realizing his concept of Galatea so completely.[5]

When in February a revival of *The Palace of Truth* was mooted, Gilbert suggested Marion for Zeolide and Henrietta for Mirza. Again Henrietta demanded Zeolide, and Gilbert agreed if Buckstone would engage a 'strong' actress for Mirza. On 10 February, learning that Hodson's engagement would not be renewed next season, Gilbert asked for, and received, a note saying he had not influenced Buckstone's decision. 'You are fully capable of either having dictated it to him or of having forged it to suit your own purposes,' Henrietta flared.[6] It cost her the role—whether Zeolide or Mirza did not matter. At this point a completely different play was temporarily produced, called *Flame*, which starred the wife-to-be of a print-seller named Graves, who subsidized the Haymarket. *Flame* soon went out, and *The Palace of Truth* reappeared. Although Buckstone, again playing Phanor, could not remember his lines, it ran till the end of May, the *Era* (22 April) summarizing it as 'furnishing fun without buffoonery, comicality without stupidity, and drollery without exaggeration'.

Even while Gilbert amused himself on 6 March by attending the annual benefit of G. W. Moore (Moore and Burgess Minstrels), followed by a supper party and ball, he felt embattled on a second front. 'Am I the victim of a delusion? Or are you annoyed with me about anything?'

[4] Letter from Gilbert to Marshall, recapitulating their conversation, copy, 12 Dec. 1876: WSG/BL Add. MS 49,338. Marshall was the editor of the *Henry Irving Shakespeare*, short-tempered and intolerant of chaff: A. W. à Beckett, *Green-Room Recollections* (Bristol: J. W. Arrowsmith, [1896]), 178–81. His huge, pasty face caused him to be nicknamed the 'Boiled Ghost'. H. Furniss, *Some Victorian Women: Good, Bad, and Indifferent* (London: John Lane, 1923), 49–50.

[5] 21 Jan. 1877: PML.

[6] 3 Mar. 1877, repr. in W. S. Gilbert, *A Letter Addressed to the Members of the Dramatic Profession in Reply to Miss Henrietta Hodson's Pamphlet* (privately printed [1877]), 15. The *Era* (27 May 1877, 9–10) published Miss Hodson's answer to Gilbert.

he wrote to Clement Scott.[7] Someone unnamed had told Scott that Gilbert denigrated Scott's reviews, which made the emotional critic turn cold and aloof to his hitherto friend. Gilbert insisted he had never 'said one word behind your back that I would not cheerfully repeat before your face . . . I always speak openly, without fear or favour.'[8] This was true; he was crotchety, as he himself admitted; he might exaggerate in a fit of anger; but he lacked the temperament for what he called 'social treachery'.

While still in his unpleasant mood, Scott submitted an anti-Gilbert article to the new society journal *Truth*, of which Henry Labouchère was owner, editor, and dramatic critic. Horace Voules, Labouchère's assistant, returned it, but suggested they would 'be glad if you saw your way to give us a good strong slashing article on Gilbert's Great Expectations at the Aquarium next Saturday'.[9] On good terms again with Gilbert, Scott presumably declined. Reviews for this brief revival were tepid anyhow, although the *Theatre* acknowledged that the adaptor had aimed at something higher than mere illustration.

As Voules said, *Truth* had been slashing Gilbert 'pretty severely', and no wonder, for Labouchère's mistress was Henrietta Hodson. Although later she was called 'Mrs. Labouchère', she was really the wife of a non-theatrical man named Pigeon, from whom she eloped with Labby. They were, in fact, not married until the autumn of 1887 and were likely the couple Gilbert had in mind when he punned that a reviewer was always 'blowing his own strumpet'. Late in life, the dramatist wrote to a friend that he could never understand Labouchère's hostility until he remembered he had '*introduced him to the woman who is now his wife!*'[10]

Labouchère loved dissension, was a 'dirty' fighter, a disputatious MP, and, from the first, delighted to involve *Truth* in litigation. The next July, for instance, he maligned James Davison, music critic of *The Times*; F. W. Hawkins, editor of the *Theatre*; and Henry Hersee, critic for several papers, over a difference in opinion about an opera début; then he invited Davison to bring an action.

Miss Hodson's next step was the publication of 750 copies of a twenty-two-page pamphlet: *A Letter from Miss Henrietta Hodson, An Actress, to the Members of the Dramatic Profession, Being a Relation of the Persecutions which She has Suffered from Mr. William*

---

[7] 7 Mar. 1877: PML.      [8] 8 Mar. 1877: PML.
[9] 15 Mar. 1877: Clement Scott Papers/TM.
[10] To Mrs Talbot ('Cousin Mary'), 13 Oct. 1905: Talbot Corr./PML.

*Schwenck Gilbert, a Dramatic Author.* In it she portrayed Gilbert as quarrelsome, vain, an intriguer, and a boaster. She said he liked to humiliate actresses, and W. H. Kendal was on the verge of writing a denial that Gilbert deliberately reduced Madge to tears, when Gilbert himself wrote to say Henrietta's accusation was untrue.[11] Hodson described how he brought friends to rehearsal and talked loudly with them whenever she was on stage. This was, of course, an absurd charge since Gilbert was the last man in the world to allow distractions during rehearsals, and, besides, Cynisca is never on stage alone; so if Gilbert spoiled her scenes, he would also unavoidably spoil those of other actors and actresses, including Marion Terry. These accusations suggest the possibility that Labouchère wrote this part of Hodson's pamphlet himself, if indeed he did not write it all. Certainly the rhetoric suggests his authorship.

In contrast to this beastly Gilbert, Henrietta presented herself as a long-suffering believer in promises of amendment, hitherto a keeper of the peace, but now determined to expose a tyrant. Her solicitor George Lewis was a personal friend, and she quoted his letters on the case and many others, most of which the *Era* and the *Theatre* printed during May and early June. They also printed excerpts from Gilbert's answering pamphlet: *A Letter Addressed to the Members of the Dramatic Profession in Reply to Miss Henrietta Hodson's Pamphlet*, published on the advice of 'two eminent counsel'. In it, Gilbert, too, reproduced letters, including one which Henrietta had 'quoted' from Howe, a paragraph of which Howe denied writing. Buckstone had lost and misremembered another letter of which Gilbert had a pressed copy; George Lewis had mislaid the dramatist's so-called letter of apology. Again, Gilbert had the pressed copy which showed he had been neither slanderous nor apologetic.

In these pamphlets, the weight of evidence is with Gilbert, although both were obviously anxious to put themselves in the best possible light. Buckstone was forgetful, confused at times, and anxious to take both sides. Howe, while trying to make peace, finally agreed with Gilbert, and, since Howe was a Quaker, he probably told the truth when he said he noticed nothing strange about rehearsals. Moreover, Henrietta loved to denigrate any available person. Lillie Langtry, later her protégée, told Mme Ritz that Henrietta's tongue was sharper than

[11] Copy 25 Apr. 1877: WSG/BL Add. MS 49,338. Gilbert also wrote to Miss Brennan that Hodson lied when she said in her pamphlet that he had tried to prevent Miss Brennan from playing in *Ought We to Visit Her?*

sword or pen.[12] Some years earlier there was a rumour she would be sued for spreading slander of a sexual sort,[13] while Margaret Scott found her, after she retired from the stage, surrounded by a Victorian 'School for Scandal' which congregated 'to tear one another to shreds. If you entered with a character, you emerged without one.'[14] Nevertheless, the *Theatre* congratulated Miss Hodson on her courage, and *Truth*, of course, repeated her accusations, while sneering at Gilbert as an incompetent dramatist (which would be Labouchère's line for the next twenty years). Gilbert, in turn, wanted to sue, but his counsel advised against it even though the article was written by someone 'adept in the art of offensive comment and criticism'.[15]

This battle, trivial though it may perhaps seem, is nevertheless significant, first, because it was an episode in the contest between actors and dramatists for control of the stage, intensified because Gilbert directed his own plays. 'I have the misfortune to differ altogether from Miss Hodson's views as to the functions of a dramatic author at rehearsal,' he wrote wryly.[16] Second, Hodson's depiction of Gilbert was a caricature still taken for granted with little investigation.

On the same day that the *Theatre*'s last Hodson–Gilbert column appeared, Arthur Sullivan wrote to Richard D'Oyly Carte that he and Gilbert would do a two-act opera: advance royalties to be 200 guineas on delivery of the manuscript; nightly royalties to be 6 guineas.[17] Carte was now the manager of the Comedy Opera Company (Limited), which he had set up in 1876 in order to finance the production of a full-scale work by Gilbert and Sullivan. Frank Chappell (not one of the Chappell publishing house), George Metzler, and E. H. Bailey, who held a street-sprinkling monopoly, were among its directors; as manager Carte would have a salary of £15 a week and an interest in the profits.[18]

Richard D'Oyly Carte was 33 years old in 1877, having left the paternal business of Rudall and Carte, musical instrument makers; set up an agency for singers; organized tours; and involved himself in

---

[12] M. L. Ritz, *Cesar Ritz: Host to the World* (London: George C. Harrap & Co. Ltd., 1938), 173.

[13] Shirley Brooks, diary entry, 16 Dec. 1873: London Library.

[14] Mrs C. Scott, *Old Days in Bohemian London* (London: Hutchinson & Co., n.d.), 107. Nevertheless, Mrs. Scott was fond of Henrietta in her later years.

[15] Quoted by H. Pearson, *Gilbert: His Life and Strife* (London: Methuen & Co. Ltd., 1957), 71.

[16] *Letter Addressed to the Members of the Dramatic Profession*, 6.

[17] 5 June 1877: DOYC/TM.

[18] Extracts from letter from Richard D'Oyly Carte to George Metzler, 4 July 1877: DOYC/TM.

managerial schemes. Even before *Trial by Jury* he had perceived the value of a lasting collaboration between Gilbert and Sullivan and worked to bring it about. His sense of meticulous staging even from childhood made him respect Gilbert, while his own experience as a composer of songs and an *opera da camera*, 'Dr. Ambrosius, his Secret', endeared Sullivan to him. 'Faithful affection was always a strong element in his character,' his sister said;[19] furthermore, unlike most managers, he was an artist *manqué*. Now he was about to become the third member of what would be called 'the triumvirate'.

But before the new comic opera could be produced, Gilbert staged at the Haymarket the comedy he had promised John S. Clarke, now the manager. Sullivan was working hard as head of the new National Training School of Music and composing incidental music for Charles Calvert's Manchester production of *Henry VIII*. He had also begun to have excruciating attacks of kidney stone and did not even attempt to compose *The Sorcerer* score until late August. *Trial by Jury* was still being played as a recital at the Aquarium Theatre, which advertised 'Sullivan's Cantata TRIAL BY JURY every evening. THE LIVE WHALE now on public view every Day.'

Gilbert's 'farcical comedy' *Engaged* opened on 3 October 1877 to a less-than-full house, divided between laughter and hisses. In this satire on the profit motive, love, honesty, and unselfishness are inextricably connected with money, for, as its heroine Belinda tells Belvawney: 'I love you madly, passionately; I care to live but in your heart, I breathe but for your love; yet . . . you must give me some definite idea of your pecuniary position . . . business is business'. Or, as virtuous Angus tells his mother-in-law-to-be: 'What wi' farmin' a bit land, and gillieing odd times, and a bit o' poachin' now and again; and what wi' my illicit whusky still—and throwin' trains off the line, . . . I've mair ways than one of making an honest living'.

Cheviot Hill, rich but niggardly, compulsively proposes marriage to every woman he meets, always in the same words: 'you are the essence of every hope; you are the tree upon which the fruit of my heart is growing—my Past, my Present, my Future—you are my own To Come.' When he buys Maggie Macfarlane's affection from Angus for £2, 'ye'll be happier wi' him,' says the lowly Scot, 'and twa pound is twa pound'. But Cheviot is also engaged to Minnie Symperson, whose father will inherit his fortune if he dies. Symperson therefore urges Cheviot to

---

[19] Notes signed Blanche Mornington, 2 May 1908: DOYC/TM.

commit suicide, even prematurely appearing in deep mourning for him (thus anticipating Jack Worthing in *The Importance of Being Earnest*). Told that Cheviot consents to live, Symperson exclaims, 'It's not business, sir—it's not business.'

Throughout the play, all the characters say openly what would ordinarily be hidden and admit what in Victorian society would be inadmissible. This particularly Gilbertian technique had begun in *The Palace of Truth*, but *Engaged* more closely resembles *Trial by Jury* in the openness of its satiric dialogue, mitigated in the cantata, however, by rhyme and music.

Now, with a dramatis personae who could not plead musical mitigation, *Engaged* met the fury of critics who intended to show their own sensitivity at its expense. 'Nauseous . . . repulsive', howled *Figaro* (10 October). 'For heartless, cold-blooded, brutal cynicism the play has never perhaps been equalled. . . . You do not naturally expect good taste from Mr. Gilbert,' buzzed the *Hornet*. 'Mr. Gilbert pains when he laughs and takes a delight in vivisecting the human heart,' lamented Clement Scott in the *Daily Telegraph*, once more laughing in spite of himself. Other periodicals, the *Observer* and the *Academy* for instance, enjoyed and praised. 'Our Captious Critic' of the *Illustrated Sporting and Dramatic News*, who saw the comedy twice, sensibly asked, 'Where is this bitter, heartless cynicism they talk so much about? . . . why this talk of diseased minds, deformed imagination, wicked scepticism, sardonic hatred of the entire human race . . .?' To him, *Engaged* seemed 'riotously humorous, whimsically incongruous', and utterly comical. When a *minissimus* playwright, William Muskerry, accused Gilbert of plagiarizing his unpublished one-act play, the *Era* asked, 'Does Mr. Muskerry positively mean to imply that *he* has written, or could write, so striking a play as *Engaged*?'

Except for George Honey, acting broadly as Cheviot, the cast understood a new principle of comic acting which Gilbert had begun to inculcate—that of playing comically without letting the audience see that the actor knows he is funny. As Belinda, Marion Terry demonstrated an absolute command of this technique, uttering her lines with an irresistible seriousness which surprised reviewers who thought of her only as an *ingénue*.[20] In America, E. A. Sothern realized too late that Cheviot

---

[20] According to Pearson (*Gilbert: His Life and Strife*, 68), Amy Roselle had signed a contract to play in a Gilbert piece, but in September 1877 she refused to appear although she had already signed a contract. Gilbert threatened to sue her, so she agreed, but wrote 'from your continued impertinent conduct towards me and the gratuitous insults you insist upon heaping

Hill was exactly the part he had been looking for. He decided to play it in New York, but illness intervened.

By now, Carte had a theatre, and rehearsals were under way for *The Sorcerer*, although the score was still incomplete. The London Opera Comique was then less than 10 years old, essentially underground, and reached by a covered passage and steps down from the Strand. There were entrances in two other streets; so it met minimum fire regulations, although it was cramped backstage.[21] Smallish, but airy, the auditorium was prettily decorated in white, blue, and gold, but the stage backed on that of the Globe Theatre so that actors on one might hear lines spoken on the other.

Carte's agency provided some of the principals, while others were newcomers or old standbys. Giulia Warwick (Constance) had sung with Carl Rosa and on the concert stage; Richard Temple (Sir Marmaduke) had just played in Benedict's *The Lily of Kilarney*. Alexis was a former amateur tenor turned professional, George Bentham, also known as Signor Bentami; he had appeared at Her Majesty's, and Sullivan may have met him when they both took part in the 1871 Triennial Gloucester Music Festival. The Australian soprano Alice May (Aline) had just made a provincial operatic début, but was really an *opéra bouffe* singer. (In time to come, she would foolishly say *The Sorcerer* had been especially written for her!)

Mrs Howard Paul, who had played everything from Lady Macbeth to Offenbach's Grande Duchesse and was now touring with her own entertainment, accounted for three roles herself. She agreed to play Lady Sangazure; a young actor in her company, Rutland Barrington, would be Dr Daly; and she advised George Grossmith not to turn down the title role which Sullivan offered him. Technically a non-professional entertainer, Grossmith appeared at working men's institutes, the YMCA, and other virtuous organizations. 'I should have thought you required a fine man with a fine voice,' the wispy, nervous Grossmith

---

upon me . . . [*ellipses his*] I can only think you wish me to cancel my engagement. . . . I must refuse to recognize the existence of men who have behaved in such an extremely ungentlemanly manner.' The only play which fits the date is *Engaged*, in which Miss Roselle did not play, although the role she might have had, Maggie Macfarlane, was played by a newcomer. Pearson gives no source for this quotation, and it is not now in WSG/BL. To what Miss Roselle refers is difficult to discover since she was always one of Gilbert's favourite actresses and less than two years before, he had given her a copy of *Original Plays*, 1st ser, with a long, very complimentary, inscription: PML. She had not appeared in a Gilbert play since 1874.

[21] C. Prestige, 'The Early Operas' First Home', *Gilbert & Sullivan Journal*, 6 (May 1951), 223–4.

said. 'No, that is just what we don't want,' answered Gilbert in an often-quoted anecdote. The last of the principals, Harriet Everard (Mrs Partlet), had played in some of Gilbert's early burlesques and was a good character actress in such roles as Mrs Corney.

In Temple, Grossmith, and Barrington, the triumvirate had the nucleus of what became a permanent company. Probably Everard would have made a fourth had she not died prematurely in 1882. Although Temple's acting range was wider than the others', Barrington, so steady and stolid-y, played effectively against Grossmith, so agile and whimsical.

In the plot, which Gilbert derived from his 1876 *Graphic* short story 'An Elixir of Love', Aline Sangazure and Alexis Pointdextre sign their marriage contract amid village rejoicings. In youth, his father Sir Marmaduke loved her mother Lady Sangazure, and their asides tell us their fires are not quenched, merely banked. Mrs Partlet's daughter Constance loves the kindly, sentimental, but oblivious rector Dr Daly.

Alexis, a social reformer and egotist, believes that marriage, irrespective of age, rank, or wealth, is a universal panacea. Consequently, he summons John Wellington Wells to provide a Patent Oxyhydrogen Love-at-first-sight Philtre, which he proposes to add to the communal teapot.[22] After a spectral incantation, parodying the Wolf's Glen scene of *Der Freischütz*, the philtre is administered to the unsuspecting villagers and gentry.

Act 2 opens with a chorus of ill-assorted couples singing:

> Happy are we in our loving frivolity,
> Happy and jolly as people of quality;
> Love is the source of all joy to humanity,
> Money, position, and rank are a vanity;
> Year after year we've been waiting and tarrying,
> Without ever dreaming of loving and marrying.
> Though we've been hitherto deaf, dumb, and blind to it,
> It's pleasant enough when you've made up your mind to it.[23]

---

[22] E. L. Blanchard's Friar Bacon is perhaps a prototype of John Wellington Wells. The Friar is a 'Licensed Dealer in Black Art', makes up love potions, provides conjuring tricks, and gives private lessons in parlour magic: *Harlequin and Friar Bacon; or Great Grim John of Gaunt and the Enchanted Lance of Robin Goodfellow* (London: Music-Publishing Company, 1863), 11. Blanchard wrote under the name of Francesco Frost.

[23] R. Allen (ed.), *The First Night Gilbert and Sullivan* (New York: Heritage Press, 1958), 63.

The potion has caused Constance to love a deaf old notary; Sir Marmaduke, the pew-opener Mrs Partlet; and Lady Sangazure, the Sorcerer himself. Forced by Alexis to drink the potion, Aline loves Dr Daly. The antidote, it seems, is the sacrifice of either Alexis or Wells to Ahrimanes. Popular opinion chooses Wells, who swallows poison, bids farewell, and sinks through a trapdoor amid red fire while winding his watch, cleaning his glasses, putting on his gloves, and brushing his hat. When the curtain rises again for the final picture, he throws up first his hat and then a shower of business cards.

Gilbert had intended a second supernatural episode in which John Wellington Wells calls up Ahrimanes or, alternatively, his own ruling spirit, to discover the antidote. Mrs Paul was to double this ghostly figure, veiled in black, but the scene was sensibly deleted. This meant, however, a rather hurried conclusion. Other numbers were also cut, including one which Gilbert thriftily reworked for a duet in *Iolanthe* five years later:

> Thou art the day, & I—the hour—
> Thou art the idol—I the throng—
> Thou art the tree and I the flower—
> Thou art the singer—I the song.[24]

The plot of *The Sorcerer* burlesqued not only supernatural traditions of opera and melodrama, but also Alfredo's denunciation scene in *La Traviata*. Throughout, Gilbert gained laughter by changing his dramatic equations: for instance, a speech about conferring upon a rich man 'the great and priceless dowry of a true, tender, and loving heart' is delivered, not by some rustic beauty, but by an aged pew-opener. John Wellington Wells is not a Dr Dulcamara, but a meek little salesman touting his trade catalogue. (Perhaps unexpected reversals like these encouraged the *World* to find the opera 'splenetic'.)

Sullivan's music was delightful, although he did not have enough time to write an overture for first night. (He used the 'Graceful Dance' from *Henry VIII*.)[25] Several reviewers, however, admonished both Sullivan and Gilbert for wasting their talents, *Figaro* even complaining there was nothing in *The Sorcerer* which could not have been written by 'any theatrical conductor engaged at a few pounds a week'.

---

[24] Part of a ballad for Aline ('Have faith in me') in an early holograph version of the libretto, possibly in a copyist's hand. BL Add. MS 53,193.

[25] A. Jacobs, *Arthur Sullivan: A Victorian Musician* (Oxford: Oxford University Press, 1984), 111. Later Cellier compiled an overture from tunes in the opera.

Most notices were much better than that, and attendance was excellent. Carte had to apologize on the first night for Bentham's sore throat and swollen face—in fact, the tenor proved generally less good than expected, and after four months was sent out with Carte's first touring company. George Power took his place in London. At the end of January Giulia Warwick replaced Alice May.

The lion's share of praise went to Rutland Barrington's flageolet-playing clergyman and to George Grossmith's sorcerer, chugging round the stage in an absurd crouch with the enchanted teapot—a piece of 'business' he invented and Gilbert immediately approved. Amusingly enough, neither Barrington nor Grossmith was a singer, Barrington consistently a little flat, and Grossmith, as the *Saturday Review* remarked, possessing the talent of 'singing correctly, expressively, and pleasantly without having any particular voice'.

Altogether, the first night on 17 November was a happy birthday-eve present for Gilbert. After audience cheers and applause, he and Sullivan came forward to bow to the audience and then 'bowed to each other with a mock gravity that was irresistibly comic' to the *Sportsman* and everyone else. The triumvirate's hearts and pockets were gladdened by a six-month run; indeed, so gladdened was Gilbert's that he sent Sullivan a sketch plot of the next opera, which would become *HMS Pinafore*. He had already decided on parts for Barrington, Everard, and Grossmith; on doing away with a *comprimaria*; on a 'kind of "judge's song"' for Sir Joseph; and on sailor costumes specially made in Portsmouth.[26] As in the set for *Trial by Jury*, visual accuracy would provide a right-side-up for topsy-turvydom. By 8 January 1878 the prose scenario was ready to read to Carte, and Gilbert asked for a note agreeing to terms. The directors of the Comedy Opera Company tried unsuccessfully to reduce the guarantee on the new piece.

Gilbert spent Christmas Eve at the Drury Lane rehearsal of E. L. Blanchard's pantomime *The White Cat*, chatting with Blanchard himself, Hollingshead, and G. A. Sala. On New Year's Day 1878 he lunched with Henry Neville, leading actor and manager of the Olympic Theatre, and Lord Londesborough, its owner, to discuss *The Ne'er-Do-Weel*, which Neville promised to put into immediate rehearsal with Marion Terry as the female lead.

Gilbert then had a small but sharp disagreement with General Turner, who had tried to insist upon seeing the Gilberts' marriage settlement before paying Lucy a legacy of £150 from her aunt. Having consulted his solicitors, Gilbert refused. He was also nettled by the fact that John Hare at the Court Theatre had produced an old Tom Taylor play, *Victims*, instead of a new Gilbert one and had accused Gilbert of insulting him in a remark made on stage-management. After *Broken Hearts* he evidently decided never to let Gilbert direct a full-length play at the Court again, thus excluding him from a stage which had once been a source of income and, under Hare, a source of artistic hopes. With the appearance of *Victims*, the *Observer* remarked that Hare's search for a modern comedy had evidently been in vain. Gilbert wrote a letter to the editor, pointing out it need not have been, and to Hare he addressed a long letter, denying he had insulted the manager: 'You should know me well enough to be aware that, when I have anything to say, I talk *to* people—not of them.' Hare complained that Gilbert did not attend the opening night of *Victims*. It would have been humiliating, Gilbert replied: everyone knew he would have written a comedy for Hare if asked. Still, he would continue to be Hare's friend.[27]

With all this, he had also been practising for a charity pantomime at the Gaiety. Written by himself, Robert Reece, Burnand, and Byron, it was played by amateur actors and, since no lady could appear on a public stage, by professional actresses. Mlle Rosa, a charming Columbine from a dancing family, partnered Gilbert as Harlequin. Trained by John D'Auban, he was a dazzling success when *The Forty Thieves* was performed on 13 February. His 'trips' and 'window-leaps' were almost professional, no mere feat for a man 6 feet high. He danced a hornpipe; he mimed Harlequin's love of Columbine and of mischief; he 'gave one an idea of what Oliver Cromwell would have made of the character'.[28] And he also provided a special parody of the 'Judge's song' from *Trial by Jury*. The pantomime realized almost £700 for the Royal General Theatrical Fund, and was given twice more, at Brighton on 9 March and again at the Gaiety on 10 April to benefit wives and children of seamen killed in the sinking of HMS *Eurydice*.

Even though Gilbert moved the opening of *The Ne'er-Do-Weel* further ahead to 25 February, extra rehearsals could not save it. The first act-and-a-half went well, although Neville was better in the serious scenes than those lightly comic. (*Punch* thought Sothern would have been better, and Sothern might well have carried it off.) But when a

[27] Copy, 30 Jan. 1878: WSG/BL Add. MS 49,338. Gilbert addressed Hare by his real name, Fairs.

[28] J. Hollingshead, *My Lifetime* (London: Sampson Low, Marston & Co. Ltd., 1895), ii. 124.

character tied hand and foot for plot purposes left the stage in 3-foot high hops, the audience hooted. Further on, Gilbert realized he had himself made a mistake in construction,[29] and reviewers did not like his 'unfeminine'—that is, independent—women. 'Mr. W. S. Gilbert seems perverse in his belief that a woman who is deepest in love is the least reserved,' Scott primly observed in the *Telegraph*. The audience guyed another scene till George Anson lost his head and repeated his lines over and over to a storm of hisses. In short, as the sympathetic *Sunday Times* put it, 'a very clever play experienced a fate more disastrous than often awaits a piece of mere stupidity'.

Kitty, her mother, and Mrs Hare had all been to the first night; Gilbert spent the evening backstage. The next day he was unable to work, and the day after 'rather seedy', but well enough to take Kitty to a fancy-dress ball, where he saw Neville and proposed to reconstruct the piece. And reconstruct it he did, at least to some extent. *The Ne'er-Do-Weel* was withdrawn on 2 March, as a programme note explained, so that the author could revise the second half.

With its title changed to *The Vagabond*, the play was back on stage 25 March, and, according to Gilbert, went magnificently, ending with two tremendous calls for him. He had, however, 'planted stalls' with friends, and a good deal of the crammed house was 'papered' with free seats. This time reviewers were less hostile, but *The Vagabond* did not have the run Neville envisioned.

Gilbert resigned his commission in the Royal Aberdeenshire Highlanders that spring. There was the prospect but not the certainty of their being permanently on duty, and, willing though Gilbert thought he was, he felt he could not give up his career for a possibility.[30] Moreover, it is unlikely that Gilbert would have chosen soldiering when he was still receiving managerial requests for new plays. Much as he had once enjoyed the masculine life in barracks or under canvas, his interest had already begun to wane. Colonel Innes raised no objection (perhaps he said a private hallelujah), and Gilbert left the Highlanders with the honorary rank of major and the right to wear his uniform.

That settled, he and Sullivan went to Portsmouth on 13 April, lunched aboard the *Thunderer* and inspected ships for the set of *HMS Pinafore*. Gilbert made sketches of the *Victory* and the *St Vincent*, after which he spent two days working at the scene model and then took it to

[29] Gilbert to Sothern, copy, 1 Apr. 1878: WSG/BL Add. MS 49,338.
[30] Gilbert to Col. Innes, copy, 6 Apr. 1878: WSG/BL Add. MS 49,338.

Carte for the carpenters to work from. He was still writing lyrics and dialogue, and Sullivan, in full swing of composition by Good Friday, wrote to his mother that the new opera 'will be bright and probably more popular than the Sorcerer, but it is not so clever'.[31]

During this year Gilbert saw a great deal of Marion Terry, both in and out of the theatre, as well as something of her sister Florence. Marion was his protégée; they walked down the Strand together after a *Ne'er-Do-Weel* rehearsal, stopping for buns and ginger beer. Both Terrys were friendly with Kitty, whom they resembled in being fair and looking delicate. In her own family, Marion was 'the lady', so much so that Gilbert had written an angry letter the year before to Richard Barker, who wanted to replace her with a more sexually appealing actress, one who would attract men to the theatre he was managing.[32]

Florence, Marion, and Mrs Gilbert occasionally went out together, and Marion was a house-guest at the Boltons, where Gilbert coached her not only in roles for his own plays, but in others such as *The Two Orphans*. Kitty and he went to see her in this and in *The Crushed Tragedian* in which Sothern, back in London, was acting. Both Gilberts took her to Brighton with them, where Gilbert read aloud to Kitty and Marion in the evening, as he did at home, frequently choosing a Dickens novel.

On 20 April Gilbert took more manuscript to Sullivan; then on Easter Sunday Kitty, Marion, and he went to Paris by the night boat, a foggy but calm passage. In Paris they found good rooms at the St James Hotel where the women promptly slept, leaving Gilbert to walk around and buy Callot etchings. Then for the next three days they perambulated the boulevards, visited touristy places, and met John Hare also on holiday. Gilbert went to the Louvre while Kitty and Marion shopped.

On the evening of 24 April they were off to Brussels, where, after visiting Waterloo, Gilbert went to bed with 'a furious headache'. Luckily, he was well enough next day to see the cathedral and the lacemakers, where he bought Kitty some lace. For himself, he purchased gloves and a silver watch. After two days of sightseeing in Antwerp, the three returned to Brussels, Gilbert having rows with intrusive old ladies in the trains. On the morning of 29 April they reached home: 'nothing opened by customs'.

Gilbert's diary for 1878 is still extant, and frequently during the first half of the year, it shows small 'x's in the left-hand margin. After that

---

[31] PML.    [32] Copy, 18 Dec. 1877: WSG/BL Add. MS 49,338.

there are only a few such marks. He was not a discursive diarist, often noting merely a street name, not what he had done there. Some of the 'x's occur beside entries in which 'NH', 'Not Hill', or 'nh' appears, presumably referring to Notting Hill Gate, where the Terrys were living. Others appear beside evenings spent at home, others beside references to streets. The immediate question is, of course, whether, like more than one male Victorian, Gilbert used a mark to indicate a sexual experience. This is possible, but unlikely unless he were visiting other women as well as Marion and Kitty, which seems improbable. Furthermore, a few marks accompany entries which are completely devoid of anything that could accommodate copulation. Nor is it likely that, given Victorian propriety, Gilbert would bring a mistress or at least a frequent sexual partner into his wife's house.

Not that Gilbert was sexually unattractive. At 41 he was an imposing figure, tall, straight-backed, muscular, always well dressed. 'I should like to pose as a misogynist if I could—but I can't. I have often tried it, but without success,' he wrote to an American friend in 1880.[33] He always liked pretty women, women with intelligent minds under their delightful hats. Yet his personality was evidently more flirtatious than passionate. A kiss, perhaps, an arm around the waist in a cab, seems to have been enough for him.[34] The marks in the diary remain a mystery.

When the Gilberts returned from the continent, not quite a month remained before the première of *HMS Pinafore; or, The Lass that Loved a Sailor*. Sullivan had already asked for an increased male chorus, and the collaborators continued to work, in Sullivan's chambers on 1 May, at the Boltons on 5 May. Gilbert felt 'seedy' again. Music rehearsals were taking place, and he relaxed by playing tennis before breakfast. Then, with the first night less than two weeks away, they decided to cut Mrs Howard Paul's part.

The plot of *HMS Pinafore* is a fairly simple one. Captain Corcoran's daughter Josephine loves Ralph 'the smartest lad in all the fleet', but is also loved by the parvenu Sir Joseph Porter, First Lord of the Admiralty (not First Sea Lord). When Josephine and Ralph plan to elope, aided by the entire crew, Dick Deadeye, a grotesquely deformed sailor, informs the Captain, who intercepts them. Sir Joseph condemns Ralph to a dungeon, but Little Buttercup, a bumboat woman, explains that she once

---

[33] Undated fragment of a letter: Harry Ransom Humanities Research Center, The University of Texas at Austin.

[34] E. Midwinter, 'W. S. Gilbert: Victorian Entertainer', *New Theatre Quarterly* (Aug. 1987), 279.

practised baby-farming and her nurselings included Ralph and the Captain. She mixed them up, and so the Captain is really Ralph and Ralph the true Captain: a Gilbertian reversal which treats acquired characteristics as if they were innate.

While Sir Joseph believes that love levels all ranks, he draws the line at a common seaman's daughter. Ralph and Josephine are free to marry; Sir Joseph marries his cousin Hebe, and the former Captain pairs off happily with Little Buttercup, whose love according to Gilbert's preliminary prose narrative is 'as tender & romantic . . . as if she were the heroine of the piece'. The age difference in which Ralph is simultaneously as old as the Captain and young enough to be his son-in-law parodies the variable age of Thaddeus in *The Bohemian Girl*, while Little Buttercup's confusion of infants, as Gilbert himself once pointed out, resembles Azucena's in *Il Trovatore*.

Hebe was to have been Mrs Paul's role. George Grossmith had already told her it was too small, and Sullivan twice informed Carte there was nothing for her to do. He wanted a voice for concerted pieces only. In the licence copy, Gilbert had done his best to build up some unnecessary lines for her, borrowing the repeated interjection 'Crushed again!' from *On Bail* to pad her part. Now he cut them.

Although she had signed a contract for £10 a week, Mrs Paul left. Her once-glorious contralto, like her health, was no longer dependable; she had been ill in December 1877, and Rosina Brandram had to substitute for her at a few hours notice. Mrs Paul died on 6 June 1879 after a week's severe illness, only 46 but looking much more elderly. In her place a young concert singer, Jessie Bond, became Hebe, who is little more than a chorus leader in the final version of the opera.[35]

The pace of rehearsals quickened. Accompanied by Kitty, Gilbert spent his days in the theatre and invited Marion Terry to the dress rehearsal—after which he began an additional night run-through, which lasted to 4.45 the next morning. When, on 25 May the curtain rose on the quarterdeck of *HMS Pinafore* with Portsmouth in the distance, 'Every block and rope . . . is in its place,' exclaimed the *Standard*. Happy music bubbled from the pit where Sullivan was conducting, so

---

[35] In her *Life and Reminiscences* ([London: John Lane, 1930], 59–60), Jessie Bond said that Mrs Paul was to interpolate 'turns' of her own into *HMS Pinafore*, but that she left in high dudgeon because Miss Bond's voice was better and she, not Mrs Paul, was to sing in concerted numbers. This is a mistaken memory, for Mrs Paul's role was to be tiny from the first and Gilbert would never have allowed the insertion of 'turns', presumably from her former entertainments, into a work of his own. The only remnant of Mrs Paul left in *Pinafore* is Sir Joseph's reluctance to marry Hebe, who, as played by her, would have been middle-aged.

happy that the audience could not guess it had been written between bouts of devastating pain.

Although Rutland Barrington had a heavy cold, his first number was encored, and other encores followed, including a repetition of the first-act finale. Grossmith's Sir Joseph was made up as Lord Nelson. The new soprano, Emma Howson, born in Tasmania, had sung with her family's opera troupe across the United States and studied in Italy before coming to England; pure-voiced and intelligent, she was far superior to Alice May.[36] Her Ralph, George Power, was also an improvement on Bentham.

Reviews were good, although Sullivan was again admonished not to waste his talent. Only *Figaro* was actively malign, while *Truth* merely dismissed the libretto as another Gilbert failure; the *Athenaeum*, amused but not ecstatic, thought *Cox and Box* superior to the new opera. Burnand must have read that notice with pleasure, perhaps with the hope it could still be 'Burnand and Sullivan'; *Punch* ignored *Pinafore*.

Although it lacked the miniature perfection of *Trial by Jury*, this fourth Gilbert libretto for Sullivan was satirically far more complex than its immediate predecessor. Elements of its plot were suggested by such Bab Ballads as 'Captain Reece', in which the hero of the title does his duty even unto marrying his daughter, sisters, cousins, aunts, and aged mother to members of his pampered crew; 'General John', in which Private James and General John change names and ranks because the private has 'a glimmering thought' they were exchanged at birth; and 'Woman's Gratitude' which satirizes the assumption that the face is an index to the mind:

> Men, absolute iniquity
>    With bandiness assess,
> And physical obliquity
>    With moral twistiness.

This is Dick Deadeye's case in *Pinafore*. He looks like Quasimodo, and his messmates hate him for it. Although he speaks the plainest common sense, 'From such a face and form as [his] the noblest sentiments sound like the black utterances of a depraved imagination.'

---

[36] Miss Howson later sang Patience in the USA; her brother John played Grossmith roles and, in his Bunthorne costume, impersonated Oscar Wilde before the crowd at a train stop during the poet's American tour. For the 500th performance of *Pinafore*, the Opera Comique management gave Miss Howson a gold ring with 'Josephine' written on it in diamonds.

In the shifting social status of his characters, Gilbert parodied Victorian 'equality' drama, particularly its prototype, Bulwer-Lytton's *The Lady of Lyons*, first performed in 1838 and revived for at least fifty years thereafter. Its haughty heroine Pauline spurns a worthy peasant, Claude Melnotte, who asks: 'am I hump-backed—deformed—hideous? A coward—a thief—a liar? Or a dull fool—a vain, drivelling, brainless idiot? What am I then—worse than all these? Why, I am a peasant!'[37] He has even taken lessons to make himself worthy of Pauline. When, after many complications, Pauline learns to love Claude, she finds he has become a Napoleonic marshal and her social superior. Thus, too, Ralph Rackstraw, a Melnotte at sea, calls Josephine 'proud lady' and 'haughty lady' when she seems to spurn him, promises to educate himself, and asks: 'Is not my love as good as another's? Is not my heart as true as another's? Have I not hands and eyes and ears and limbs like another's?' Josephine, in lines later cut, superciliously describes the 'mean and sordid lives' of his relations.

Or to choose another example, in Tom Taylor's 1865 drama *The Serf*, Countess de Mauleon adores the virtuous and talented peasant Ivan, until at last, abandoning her pride, she confesses her passion. Luckily, Ivan's supposed father announces on his deathbed that Ivan is really the son of Prince Bariatinski, stolen in infancy. The joyful countess brings down the curtain (and the house) with the specious assertion that 'Love Levels All'.

Another kind of popular theatre appears in Sir Joseph Porter, who in an earlier version was office-boy to a cotton-broking firm and rose to be a travelling salesman, in a progression reminiscent of Caseby's in *An Old Score*. Sir Joseph is obviously devoted to melodramas glorifying the British tar. Following their libertarian traditions, he tells the *Pinafore* crew that they are any man's equal—excepting his. He writes a song for them ('A British tar is a soaring soul'), full of the sort of belligerent stage directions found in Dick's *The Actor's Handbook* for amateurs, and other publications of the sort. Sir Joseph believes that all sailors should dance hornpipes and teaches Captain Corcoran to dance one on the cabin table. Falling in with these views, Ralph rises 'in manhood's glorious pride', insisting, 'I am an Englishman—behold me!' The Boatswain compliments him in Handelian measures for resisting 'all temptations | To belong to other nations'.

[37] G. H. Lewes (ed.), *Selections from the Modern British Dramatists* (Leipzig: F. A. Brockhaus, 1867), 62.

For two days after the opening, Gilbert and Sullivan tinkered with *Pinafore*, putting some dialogue into recitative, cutting an on-stage hornpipe, and temporarily deleting Barrington's serenade. Then Sullivan went to Paris as a British Commissioner for the International Exhibit there, while Gilbert sounded Henry Neville out about reviving *Broken Hearts* with Marion Terry as Lady Hilda and Florence Terry as Lady Vavir. He also read Neville the projected plot of a Faust play. Neville preferred Faust.[38]

Gilbert then felt 'seedy' and ill for several weeks, perhaps with migraine. He even considered a trip around the world, but got only as far as Margate, which he visited on 9 July. Finding the Terrys and their mother there, he wrote to Kitty to join him.

After five more days of bathing, walking, and picnicking, the Gilberts went on to Le Havre and as far as Rouen. They ran into John Hare and his wife again, bathed, and had an excellent late breakfast at Trouville: sole *vin blanc*, chicken, an *entrecôte* with potatoes, and green beans.

Back in London, a blazing summer was melting everything, including audiences for *Pinafore*. At Covent Garden the Promenade Concerts began on 3 August with Sullivan and Alfred Cellier as conductors, Sullivan playing selections from *The Sorcerer* on opening night. By 16 August the weather had begun to cool: 'good for the Concerts & the "Pinafore",' Sullivan wrote to his mother.[39] On the twenty-fourth he conducted Hamilton Clarke's medley of tunes from the opera, repeating it for at least three nights, each to increasing pleasure. Although an *Athenaeum* review accused Sullivan of being a much more listless and inanimate conductor than the vigorous Cellier, the concerts helped keep *Pinafore* afloat for some 700 performances. Carte was able to send out a second and a third company to tour the provinces.

Gilbert was now working hard at *Gretchen*, his Faust play for Neville, beginning to think out a new libretto for Sullivan, rehearsing *The Wedding March* revival at the Folly Theatre, and preparing *Sweethearts* for Brighton. As a quick-money set-off for *Gretchen*, he suggested to Selina Dolaro that he adapt another Labiche play for her at the Folly. She agreed.

---

[38] Diary entry for 18 June 1878: WSG/BL Add. MS 49,332. Neville wanted the play by Nov. 1878, but Gilbert did not finish it, nor could Neville put it on then. *Gretchen* did not open until March 1879.

[39] 16 Aug. 1878: PML.

On 24 November he relaxed briefly by going with Kitty to one of James McNeill Whistler's Sunday breakfasts, where Albert Moore, the painter, and others joined them. Gilbert also attended the trial of *Whistler* v. *Ruskin* which followed and in which the artist sued the critic for denigrating his works. He was contemptuously awarded 1 farthing damages, the smallest possible sum.

After this, Gilbert saw the year out with a daily stint of translating Labiche's *La Cagnotte* for Dolaro. He had produced only two new plays in 1878, and one was a failure. The other has lasted more than a hundred years.

# 11

## Not Poetic, but Aesthetic

such caricature as only a man of genius could indulge in.

*Era* (4 Apr. 1880)

AFTER working for a few days on *La Cagnotte*, Gilbert put it aside, although *Fun* erroneously announced it would be performed at Easter. *HMS Pinafore* had reached 180 performances and the Opera Comique had temporarily closed, ostensibly for repairs and redecoration, but really for putting in new drains. It would open again in February 1879. Gilbert's concern was now with the staging of *Gretchen*, and he wrote to Neville to see if it could be produced before 1 March in accordance with the understanding they had reached in late 1878. Otherwise, he would withdraw it. His letter included a rather depressed sentence: 'Possibly you may agree with me that, under any circumstances, this will be the wisest course to pursue.'[1] But, after all, he did not withdraw it even though it was not produced until 24 March.

Very soon Gilbert encountered difficulties with Neville. The dramatist had stipulated costumes by Alias; the manager chose the cheaper May, who, Gilbert had said after *The Sorcerer*, would never again dress a piece of his. They disagreed on set designers and on who should play Gottfried, until Gilbert wrote that unless he had unquestioned rights of casting and staging, '*I will not put my foot within the walls of the Olympic.*'[2] Unfortunately, he had not put these stipulations in writing.

Gilbert's temper was further exacerbated by a bout with W. H. Kendal, who said in the Beefsteak Club that he did not believe Gilbert had repaid Sothern for *The Ne'er-Do-Weel*. Armed with a letter from Sothern, Gilbert demanded an apology, which Kendal refused to give

[1] Copy, 13 Jan. 1879: WSG/BL Add. MS 49,330.
[2] Copy, 3 Feb. 1879: WSG/BL Add. MS 49,330.

on the grounds he had said nothing.[3] The Kendals had both been *personae non gratae* since their mysterious falling out during *Broken Hearts*, and Gilbert had not liked the way Madge played Lady Hilda. Then in 1877 they played *Sweethearts* in the provinces without his permission, and, when he wrote to object, Kendal's manager sent him unpleasant letters, telling him to stop writing. For all his success as a gentlemanly light comedian, Kendal had a streak of off-stage coarseness, demonstrated in a vulgar song he sang at the Prince of Wales's 1882 dinner for actors. The Prince did not like it.[4]

Madge Kendal, too, as Ellen Terry once said, could 'with all her pure Victorian look . . . be the very devil'.[5] Although she was the better actor, she doted on her husband and thought it was 'real *impudence* for Gilbert to put anyone in any part Willie has played'. It must be 'unpleasant', she wrote to Sullivan, 'to see such a handsome fellow after one had just looked in the glass at oneself'[6]—wifely devotion indeed, for if photographs may be trusted, Kendal was by no means handsomer than Gilbert. For his part, the dramatist thought Madge and Willie were turning Hare against him.

Certainly, Hare and Gilbert had fallen out in an exchange of angry letters. Gilbert had been ill and recovered just in time to learn the Hares would not keep a dinner engagement because, John said, Gilbert had behaved coolly to his wife. He defended himself, and Lucy wrote to Mary Hare, but the long friendship was broken. Mrs Kendal, whose husband was now in managerial partnership with Hare, asked Sullivan 'if you can, make the G's & the Johnny's friends again—because they really like each other'.[7]

Whatever Sullivan did—if he did anything—did not reconcile 'the G's & the Johnny's'. That task was finally performed in February 1883 when Hare, at last realizing his burst of temper had been at fault, sent his little daughter as an emissary to Gilbert, who at once capitulated: 'Let our quarrel die & be buried,' he immediately wrote to Hare.[8]

On a more cheerful note, *Engaged* was playing in New York, where it brought Gilbert $897.75 for the last week in February. 'Send me over

[3] Letter from Gilbert to Chairman of Beefsteak Club, copy, 3 Mar. 1879: WSG/BL Add. MS 49,338. John Hollingshead, who had heard Kendal, was Gilbert's informant.

[4] P. Magnus, *King Edward the Seventh* (London: John Murray, 1964), 220.

[5] S. Blow, *Through Stage Doors* (Edinburgh: W. & R. Chambers Ltd., 1958), 135. It was rumoured that in their later years, she browbeat Kendal.

[6] Madge Kendal to Sullivan, signed 'Madge Grimston', Kendal's real surname, n.d. [1877]: PML.

[7] Ibid.  [8] Copy, 3 Feb. [1883]: WSG/BL Add. MS 49,332.

any MS of plays you want sold as soon as possible,' Horace Wall, Gilbert's agent, wrote;[9] but, he added later, 'Let me impress this upon you, tragedy is over. Comedy, musical pieces good here for 2 years at least.'[10] *Princess Toto* was playing in New York from mid-March, but Gilbert got nothing from it. Nevertheless, he sent rough copies of *Gretchen* to Wall.

Gilbert had spent eight months working on his tragedy, the idea for which came from a picture, *Regrets*, he had once seen. In it two priests walk through a field, the elder reading his breviary, the younger looking wistfully at a pair of youthful lovers. In April 1878 he had bought a life of Goethe and a copy of *Faust*; in June he and Kitty went to hear Gounod's opera at Covent Garden. By mid-June he had seen it twice, but now it bored him; so the next time, he left and went backstage at the Haymarket to see Sothern.

With rehearsals for *Gretchen* beginning, Gilbert attached a note even to the privately printed copies: 'The leading idea of this play was suggested by Goethe's "Faust". The author is indebted to that work for the scene between Mephisto and Martha in Act II. In every other respect the dialogue is original.' In a second, public note he pointed out that Goethe's *Faust* was not a stage play, but a philosophic treatise on human nature in dramatic form. He asked to be absolved from a charge of intentional irreverence. He was, in short, nervous about the response.

In changing the title, Gilbert also changed the balance of the plot. His Faustus is always a young man, disillusioned in love, who becomes a priest. He makes no compact with the Devil, who nevertheless shows him a vision of Gretchen. 'Spirit of purity, I come to thee!' Faustus exclaims. Gretchen herself has seen Faustus in a dream, and wakes to find that Gottfried her soldier-cousin and his friend, is about to confide her to his care.

Of course, Faustus seduces her, while promising marriage. But when Gretchen learns he is a priest, she is horrified and cries, 'Thou lovest my body, and I love thy soul!' Gottfried, returning from battle, proposes marriage, and is rejected. When he learns why, he intends to kill his false friend, but they are reconciled during Gretchen's long deathbed scene, for which Faustus reverts to his monk's habit. As day breaks, Gretchen dies, still loving Faustus:

---

[9] 3 Mar. 1879: WSG/BL Add. MS 49,334.
[10] 11 Mar. 1879: WSG/BL Add. MS 49,334.

> I can turn my head, but not my heart—
> And I can close mine eyes, but not my heart—
> And still my foolish tongue, but not my heart—
> So, Faustus, it is meet that I should die!

Again, Gilbert's blank verse was efficient, but generally prosaic. The best lines are Mephisto's, who, shorn of his supernatural power over Faustus, becomes a kind of anticlerical *raisonneur*. Marion Terry was Gretchen; H. B. Conway, Faustus; and Frank Archer, Mephisto. Mrs Bernard Beere, then at the beginning of her career, played Lisa, seduced and abandoned, whom Gretchen befriends in her own days of innocence. Here and in Gottfried's refusal to blame his fallen cousin, Gilbert again shows that charity which was a cardinal virtue for him.

Seldom, said *The Times*, had a play been anticipated with such curiosity. The first night went enthusiastically with a curtain-call louder than had ever before greeted the dramatist. In no other Gilbert play, the *Sunday Times* exclaimed, was the satire so scathing and the versification more powerful. Other reviews were lukewarm, and *Truth* characteristically called it trash. Within ten days the box-office receipts had sunk from the opening night's £142 to a mere £32.[11]

The failure of Gilbert's attempt at tragedy was assisted by elements outside the play as well. The season, for instance, was Lent, 'that fearfully dull time', as Sothern once called it.[12] At first the weather was wintry with slight snow, which changed on the second night to constant sleet. Over Gilbert's remonstrances, Lord Londesborough decided to withdraw *Gretchen* on the evidence of five nights. He had no intention of losing money. Neville did not renew his lease, and by mid-April Fanny Josephs was installed as lessee of the Olympic, playing a drama translated from the French. When Gilbert published *Gretchen*, he added a bitter preface to show the kind of 'encouragement' dramatists might encounter. In America, Horace Wall appreciated the tragedy 'as a grand brain production', but wrote that audiences there did not want blank verse or old subjects.[13]

Gilbert had briefly thought of continuing the Bab Ballads and began a new series in *Time*, a periodical just started by Edmund Yates. After contributing 'Jester James' in April and 'The Policeman's Story' in May, however, he let the series lapse. Neither ballad was among his best,

---

[11] Nightly Accounts Olympic Theatre: WSG/BL Add. MS 49,334. The exact figures were £141. 15s. 0d. and £32. 11s. 6d.

[12] Letter to Gilbert, 27 Oct. 1875: WSG/BL Add. MS 49,331.

[13] 15 Apr. 1879: WSG/BL Add. MS 49,334.

although the second ironically demonstrated the inequality of rich and poor in a court of law. He also abandoned his projected version of *La Cagnotte* (The Money-Box) after having finished two acts and a page or two of the third. Almost on impulse, he passed it on to William Yardley, who had been Clown to Gilbert's Harlequin the year before. Yardley, too, seems to have done nothing with it, and an unknown, completely untalented third person finished it under the title of *Lord Mayor's Day*. The play appeared anonymously at the Folly Theatre on 30 June, and would have been a resounding failure had it succeeded in making any sound at all. Gilbert disclaimed it.

*HMS Pinafore* was now causing a furore in the United States without much reimbursement for either Gilbert or Sullivan. Their only profit came from voluntary donations of $500 each from the Broad Street Theatre in Philadelphia and from Oliver Ditson and Co., who published the piano score. John Ford, the impresario, sent them each £50 apiece—a gesture which allegedly determined Gilbert to insist on Ford as manager for their American visit. Having cast his bread upon the waters, joked the *Era* two years later, it 'speedily returned to him buttered on both sides'.

Meanwhile, their opera was performed by church choirs and juvenile troupes with interpolated songs such as Hebe's promise:

> I will polish up your sword,
>    And I'll keep your buttons bright;
> Yes, I will, upon my word,
>    And I'll nurse you when you're tight.[14]

A male actor undertook Little Buttercup in New York, and a woman, Ralph Rackstraw. The *Pinafore* craze brought the Boston Ideals into being to sing it, it was translated into German, the Purim Association performed it, but none of them paid royalties to its author and composer. Perhaps it was fortunate that Gilbert drew 'Sir Bevis' in a sweep and the horse won the Derby at 20 to 1![15]

Gilbert had begun a new libretto, which newspapers called 'The Bold Burglar' (but which was really *The Pirates of Penzance*), when the triumvirate decided to go to America in the autumn. Carte supposed it was his idea, but Sullivan insisted it was his—he had received

---

[14] *The First and Only Miniature Pinafore Company*, undated advertising pamphlet 1878, unpaginated: Harvard Theatre Coll.
[15] Letter from F. A. Marshall to H. J. Byron, 28 May 1879: JWS.

so many invitations to come over and conduct *Pinafore*. Gilbert was a little uneasy.

Sullivan was now too ill to conduct the Promenade Concerts, which would begin again in August. He took himself to Paris, where he endured an operation for crushing a kidney stone. Carte, meanwhile, left in July for a preliminary look at the United States and to audition possible chorus members. He could do this rapidly, playing their accompaniments himself, listening to a few bars and a scale, and noting a quick opinion: 'Good form for *Buttercup*', 'Pretty, but poor voice', 'Useful man to have'.[16]

He had left a friend, Michael Gunn, to deal with affairs at the Opera Comique while he was away. Gunn therefore soon found himself in the midst first of a legal, then of a physical, struggle. By a contract signed the previous November, the Comedy Opera Company were to receive net profits from *Pinafore* for six months, beginning on 1 February 1879. After that, Carte could make independent terms for his own benefit. Before sailing, Carte gave formal notice that the Company's rights ended on 31 July. But *Pinafore* was too remunerative an enterprise to be given up: the Directors had already made £16,000 from it.

At first the Comedy Opera Company tried legal means—an application to restrain Gunn from managing the theatre. This failed, as Richard Barker, the stage-manager, wrote to Gilbert, who was out of town. The Company then prepared to produce a rival *Pinafore* and began to lure chorus members away from the Opera Comique.

Nothing happened for ten days. Gilbert returned and sent out men with sandwich boards bearing the statement that the Opera Comique performances were the only ones authorized and directed by himself and Sullivan, but he was not at the theatre when on 31 July during the second act of the opera, a riot broke out. Three Directors, a solicitor, and a belligerent gang appeared at the stage entrance to carry off the props, contrary to the terms of the lease. Barker was called to the stage door in time to hear 'Now then, boys, now's your time' and to be knocked down a flight of stone steps. Pulling himself together, he sent for the police and refused to let the solicitor take away even a token bucket.

Men crowded into the gas room from which the lighting was controlled, and a tumult of voices reached the audience.[17] Miss Everard valiantly continued her part until someone shouted 'Fire!' and the audi-

---

[16] New York *Sun* (26 July 1879).

[17] 'The Fracas at the Opera Comique', *Evening Standard* (12 Aug. 1879). Most London papers reported this episode at varying length.

ence rose to rush through the long tunnel—a potential death-trap. Fortunately, Grossmith made himself heard across the footlights, explaining and reassuring; others joined him until everyone returned to his seat. The police arrived, quieted the uproar, and the show continued.

By the time the Directors involved received summons to Bow Street Police Court, the Comedy Opera Company was performing *Pinafore* at the Imperial Theatre, and crowds were going to see both productions. Not until March 1881 did the final confrontation take place before Mr Justice Fry in Chancery. By then the question had been reduced to whether the Company's right to play *Pinafore* extended *ad infinitum* or only to the end of the original run. In addition to testifying themselves, Gilbert and Sullivan had collected fifty-one theatrical witnesses prepared to attest the run had been broken when the Opera Comique closed over Christmas 1878.

After listening to Irving, Bancroft, and several others, the judge decided in favour of Gilbert and Sullivan, but they received nothing.[18] The Comedy Opera Company had at last been scuttled by its own greed and was in liquidation. By the time it sank, Carte had already produced two more Gilbert and Sullivan operas. '[P]oor Frank Chappell', Sullivan wrote of the partner of Metzler's publishing company, 'was led to go against me. Result, he lost my future publications, which meant thousands & thousands of pounds.'[19]

While Richard Barker was tending his injuries, Gilbert broke the neck of Act 2 of *The Pirates of Penzance*. He wrote to Sullivan before leaving for Trouville: 'I've made great use of the "Tarantara" business in Act 2. The police always sing "Tarantara" when they desire to work their courage up to the sticking point. They are naturally timid, but through the agency of this talisman, they are enabled to acquit themselves well.' He mentioned this so Sullivan might treat it as an important feature, but 'I need not say that this is mere *suggestion*—If you don't like it, it shan't be done.'[20] This last sentence is characteristic of Gilbert's willingness now, and throughout their joint career.

---

[18] C. Prestige, 'Sir Joseph Porter KCB: A Solicitor and his Litigation', *Law Society's Gazette* (24 May 1978), unpaginated. Some of this material, tracing the steps of the legal proceedings, was also used and amplified in id., 'Ten Battles Off Spithead', *Gilbert & Sullivan Journal*, 10 (autumn 1979), 289–94.

[19] Sullivan's general diary entry, 1881: B/Y. Prestige (above) says that Gilbert and Sullivan waived their right to anything but token damages of 1s. (5p in present coinage).

[20] 6 Aug. 1879: PML.

Carte returned to England well pleased; he had engaged the Fifth Avenue Theatre and arranged with J. T. Ford to produce the new opera. He had whetted American curiosity by telling a *New York Times* reporter that 'Gilbert and Sullivan have set their hearts upon making it the great effort of their lives'. (In London, a columnist signing himself 'H.P.' hoped Gilbert would not go to the States: 'His libretti are splendid, but his manners are bearish. . . . he will ruin the speculation.' Gilbert did go, was unbearish, and the speculation proved very successful!)

With all three members having now returned to London, they were able to discuss business arrangements to come. They decided to form a partnership, each contributing £1,000 and dividing the profits equally after expenses which would include Carte's salary of £15 a week and the others' 4 guineas apiece for each performance. This agreement was to be in effect as long as Carte held the Opera Comique.[21]

On 25 October Gilbert, Sullivan, Alfred Cellier, Blanche Roosevelt (their soprano), and her husband sailed from Liverpool aboard the *Bothnia*. A week later Carte and the other principals followed on the *Gallia*, after Carte had all but missed the boat. Thanks to the machinations of the Comedy Opera Company, he was arrested for a minor debt as he stepped off the train in Liverpool. With a view to harassment, the company had also procured a judge's order that Carte could not leave England under penalty of £250. After four hours in custody and frantic telegraphing, Carte managed to free himself[22] and caught the *Gallia* with five minutes to spare and a temper equally short.

In the meantime Gilbert and Sullivan had been enjoying their passage. Sullivan found friends aboard, and their group were 'most cheery & happy—the envy of all the other passengers evidently'.[23] No one was seasick; Gilbert kept them laughing, and they reached New York on 5 November. Even before they docked, reporters from the *New York World* and *New York Herald* came aboard to give the collaborators their first taste of an American interview. Gilbert was described as wearing a reddish-grey tweed suit and purple tie, half-hesitating in manner, a little reserved, but breaking into jokes and half-chuckles. Sullivan, 'a natty vivacious gentleman', in grey suit and black tie, twinkled, laughed, and, like Gilbert, had a slight smoker's nervousness. Between them they charmed the press, who asked about the new opera:

---

[21] Undated memorandum in Gilbert's hand: DOYC/TM.

[22] Letter from Beyfus & Beyfus, Carte's solicitors, to *Truth* (13 Nov. 1879). The *Era* (30 Nov.) said that Carte caught the boat by five minutes.

[23] Sullivan to 'Dearest Mum', 4 Nov. 1879: PML.

I  One of Gilbert's many self-caricatures, this one drawn in an autograph album. *Reproduced by permission of the Bodleian Library*, Oxford, MS Autogr. e. 13, fo. 51ʳ.

II  The rising dramatist of the early 1870s. *From the collection of David Stone.*

**III** Herbertina Turner, Gilbert's mother-in-law, who outlived him. Lucy was her favourite child and constant visitor. *Author's collection.*

IV H. J. Byron, first editor of *Fun,* who never blotted a pun. *Author's collection.*

V Gilbert's sketches on a blank page in his bound volume of *Fun.* At the left the young Squire Bancroft appears, probably in his role for Robertson's *Caste. From the collection of Peter Joslin.*

VI  Hermann Vezin and Marion Terry
in the first production of Dan'l Druce,
Blacksmith. *From the collection of
David Stone.*

VII  Madge Robertson (Mrs
Kendal) sees herself in a mirror as
the animated statue in *Pygmalion
and Galatea* and exclaims: 'I could
look in this mirror all day long.'
*Author's collection.*

VIII    The Princess Toto. *Author's collection.*

**IX**    Dressed in a burlesque version of a brigand queen's costume, Kate Santley appears in Gilbert and Clay's Princess Toto. *Author's collection.*

**X**  Sullivan leads a procession, the third member of which is Arthur Cecil.
*Author's collection.*

**XI**  Emma Howson, the first Josephine: 'one of the brightest, liveliest little ladies imaginable', said the *Era. Author's collection.*

**XII**  'The beautiful Miss Fortescue post-Savoy.'
*Author's collection.*

**XIII** Sheet music cover for 'If you go in', depicting Durward Lely, George Grossmith, and Rutland Barrington. 'A bat-like *pas*, executed by Grossmith at the close of the third verse, is excruciatingly funny' (review of *Iolanthe* by William Beatty-Kingston, *Theatre* (Jan. 1883). *Author's collection.*

DAYS WITH CELEBRITIES. (288.)
A DRAMATIST.—A FIRST NIGHT.

**XIV**   A cartoonist's view of a Gilbertian first night. *Author's collection.*

10th Dec. 86

Dear Mr Holl –

I received a letter from you [following] your telegram. I shall be very delighted to hear from you when your arrangements for them your enclosed ... [for you] to see me.

... will take care that my inevitable business shall interfere to prevent by coming to you ... Whenever it is convenient for you & [   ] Gilbert to make an appointment ...

for you & [   ] Gilbert

J. Holl R.A.

XV  One of Gilbert's letters to the artist Frank Holl, who painted his portrait. *Author's collection.*

XVI  Lucy Gilbert, wearing the pearls for which her husband had exchanged less expensive diamonds: a photograph formerly in the possession of her mother. *Author's collection.*

XVII  The assured dramatist in mid-life. *Author's collection.*

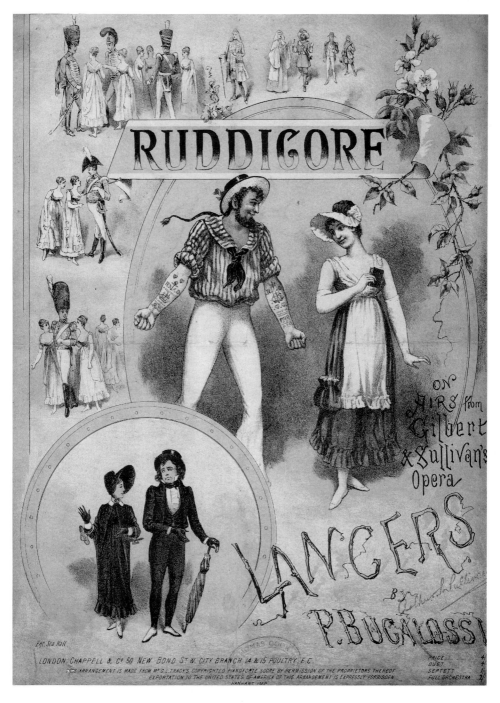

**XVIII**  Bucks, blades, ancestors, and bridesmaids surround Durward Lely (Richard Dauntless) and Leonora Braham (Rose Maybud). The lower vignette shows the reformed Sir Despard and the somewhat chastened Mad Margaret (Barrington and Bond) in Act 2. *Author's collection.*

MR. D'OYLY CARTE TO MESSRS. GILBERT AND SULLIVAN:—"NOW, HURRY UP WITH SOMETHING NEW, GENTLEMEN, PLEASE! WE'VE HAD QUITE ENOUGH REVIVALS!"

**XIX** In spite of Carte's urging, *The Yeomen of the Guard* did not reach the stage of the Savoy Theatre until October 1888. (*The Entr'acte*, May 19, 1888) *Author's collection.*

XX The audience came to admire, but laughed when she said, 'Let us pray.' (*Brantinghame Hall*) *Author's collection.*

XXI Gilbert prepares to chastise Clement Scott, who gave *Brantinghame Hall* a bad review. Mrs Kendal, who criticized dramatic critics in articles for *Murray's Magazine*, assists. (*The Entr'acte*, December 22, 1888) *Author's collection.*

**XXII** The antagonists of the 'carpet quarrel' by the cartoonist Alfred Bryan. (*The Entr'acte,* May 24, 1890) *Author's collection.*

"THE PASSING OF ARTHUR."

SIR ARTHUR SULLIVAN TO MR. D'OYLY CARTE:—"COME AWAY AND DON'T NOTICE HIM!"

RE-UNITED, OR THE HAPPY SAVOYARDS.

**XXIII** Together again for *Utopia (Limited). (Judy,* October 11, 1893) *Author's collection.*

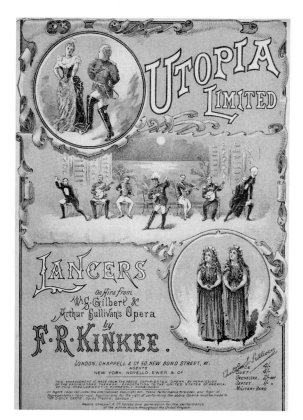

XXIV  Sheet music cover, showing Rutland Barrington and Rosina Brandram; the Utopian cabinet meeting *à la* Christy Minstrels, and Emmie Owen and Florence Perry as the royal twins. *Author's collection.*

XXV  Sheet music cover, showing Charles Kenningham as Captain Fitzbattleaxe in a tender moment with Nancy McIntosh as Princess Zara. The villainous Wise Men lurk glumly upper right. *Author's collection.*

**XXVI**   Arthur Playfair as the dancing corporal in *His Excellency*. Gilbert insisted on spurs.
*Author's collection.*

'the idea is pure melodrama taken seriously,' Gilbert told them; 'It's a sort of *reductio ad absurdum* of melodrama'. Then they landed and encountered American customs. 'This is horrible,' exclaimed Sullivan; 'they pitch your things everywhere.' 'Can't I tip him?' whispered Gilbert as hundreds of his cigars were confiscated.

Although each had or made friends in New York and Fred Clay was there to produce *Princess Toto*, the collaborators naturally saw a good deal of each other away from the theatre. Later Clay told George R. Sims that Gilbert made jokes about Sullivan in front of strangers,[24] but if he did, that did not divide them. Their friendly voices echo in a letter Sullivan wrote to his mother: 'Gilbert's here impatient for his dinner—he sends you "as fervid a message as I can put on paper with the sincere wish that you are happy and comfortable". Those are his words.'[25] Perhaps dinner was seafood at Dorlon's where Dickens and Thackeray in their day had eaten oysters.

Soon after Gilbert and Sullivan arrived, the Lotus Club gave them a lavish dinner. More than a hundred guests, including Clay and Cellier, heard them hailed 'as men who have used their undoubted genius to increase the happiness of their kind'.[26] Although very nervous, both made witty speeches, Gilbert's particularly touching on the need for international copyright. On another day, in contrast to the luxurious Lotuses, Gilbert visited an American prison.[27]

The company began rehearsing on 11 November; on 1 December they produced *HMS Pinafore*, the orchestration and stage business being, of course, new to New York. Sullivan conducted, while Gilbert, in costume, moved among the chorus, supervising the action. Afterwards led to the footlights by Sullivan, he made a short curtain speech among the flowers thrown by the audience. Reviewers were quick to note transatlantic changes. American choruses, for example, sang 'He said damme' very loudly, while the newcomers sang it almost in a whisper. Notices were good, although not superlative—critics already had their own favourite American productions—so the triumvirate did not make much money after the first week.

The orchestra, too, was a problem, for it threatened to strike unless each player's weekly wage was raised to $25. This ploy had succeeded

[24] G. R. Sims, 'Gilbertian Memories: Some Personal Reminiscences', *Referee* (4 June 1911).

[25] 12 Dec. 1879: PML.

[26] Unidentified US newspaper [1879] in Gilbert's press-cuttings book: Theatre Cuttings (1)/BL.

[27] Mr Sergeant [William] Ballantine, *The Old World and the New* (London: Richard Bentley & Son, 1884), 85–6.

with Colonel Mapleson's grand opera, but Sullivan announced he would bring over his own orchestra and meanwhile would conduct from the piano himself with Cellier at the harmonium. It was an unlikely threat, but a secret union meeting on 5 December decided the opera was merely an extravaganza and did not warrant increased pay. Carte, equally adamant, had been waiting outside the room, and communicating with the union through the hallway.

Everything now centred on preparations for *The Pirates of Penzance*, but to Sullivan's chagrin and momentary despair, he had left the musical sketches for Act 1 behind. He flung himself into composing from memory, and Gilbert allegedly suggested he use 'Climbing over rocky mountain' from *Thespis*.[28]

After the final dress rehearsal ended at 1 a.m. on 30 December, Sullivan, Clay, Cellier, and Gilbert went back to Sullivan's lodgings to work on the still unfinished overture. Cellier and Sullivan finished putting it together while the other two copied band parts, an episode which demonstrates that Gilbert could write music clearly enough to be useful. After he and Clay left at 3 a.m., Cellier and Sullivan went on till 5.[29] Sullivan's reaction the next day made him ill until he took the baton in his hand for the performance, a nervous response which continued for a lifetime and was the equivalent of Gilbert's inability to see his own works performed.

The house was filled with fashionables, including an Astor and a Vanderbilt—all wildly enthusiastic and interrupting the performance with laughter and applause. Praise was lavished on Signor Brocolini (John Clarke of Brooklyn) as the Pirate King, J. H. Ryly as the Major-General, and the massive Alice Barnett as Ruth. Blanche Roosevelt's notices were good, although several critics found her voice thin and not always true. But she was very pretty, and egotistically, like Alice May, told an interviewer that the piece had been written expressly for her. Only the tenor Hugh Talbot was a blot on the production, not knowing his lines, forgetting his music, and making-up badly. 'We shall, I think, have to get rid of him,' Sullivan wrote to his mother.[30] They did, several weeks later, but not before he tried to pick a fist-fight with Gilbert. He still did not know his lines.

Meanwhile, in Paignton, a touring *Pinafore* company, with one day's

---

[28] Letter from Gilbert to Percy de Strzelecki, 14 Aug. 1902: PML.

[29] Sullivan to 'Dearest Mum', 2 Jan. 1880: PML. He also described the scene in his diary, 30 Dec. 1879: B/Y.

[30] 2 Jan. 1880: PML.

rehearsal had given the first English performance of *The Pirates of Penzance*. It should have been on 29 December, but the music for Act 1 did not arrive in time; so it was delayed till the thirtieth. It was, unavoidably, a pick-up performance to an audience of forty-seven people and receipts of £3, but it secured British copyright. American copyright, however, presented a much greater problem. The triumvirate had decided to stand on proprietary rights as owners of a valuable property. Therefore they did not publish the libretto or vocal score, and Gilbert sold his performing rights to Sullivan's American friend Sugdam Grant for a nominal $100, since only an American could have an enforceable copyright. Gilbert asked his own legal friend, Samuel Barlow, to draw up the arrangements.[31] Even so, John Stetson, the Mr Malaprop of American managers, copyrighted the title for three months himself. Somewhat belatedly, Carte sent out touring companies trained by Gilbert and Sullivan, who also conducted and stage-managed the first Philadelphia and Buffalo performances.

Back in London, Richard Barker and Alfred Cellier's brother Frank, left in musical charge, put on a children's *Pinafore* for seventy-eight matinées over Christmas. Cast from juvenile professionals, it delighted audiences and reviewers, who were especially charmed by Emilie Grattan (Josephine) and Effie Mason (Buttercup)—'a child', wrote the *Globe*, 'not so tall as an ordinary walking-stick'.[32] Charles Dodgson found the performance very pretty, but it grieved him to hear little girls sing 'He said "damme".'

Although the authentic *Pirates of Penzance* did not strike the United States with the dazzling force of pirated *Pinafore*, it brought much more money to its creators. Often referred to as '*Pinafore* on land', its action is more complex and its music more operatic and parodistic of grand opera. The plot turns on the age of Frederic, a pirate apprentice, who will be out of his indentures on his twenty-first birthday, but who was born in Leap Year and, by a legal quibble, is only 5 and a little bit over.

Frederic longs for respectability. In a verse deleted before production, he sings:

---

[31] William Schwenck Gilbert to Mr Barlow, 9 Jan. 1880: Huntington Library, BW Box 134, reproduced by permission.

[32] So popular was the children's *Pinafore* that it returned in late December 1880 for a limited number of performances. In 1884–5 a children's *Pirates of Penzance* was performed at the Savoy.

> Oh do not spurn the Pirate's tear,
>> Nor deem his grief unreal & frothy
> He longs to doff his pirate gear
>> And turn tall-hatty & broad-clothy.[33]

Nevertheless, his duty compels him to join the pirates' attack on Major-General Stanley's newly-purchased castle.

Like Sir Joseph Porter, Major-General Stanley is incompetent; his patter song tells us frankly that his military knowledge 'Has only been brought down to the beginning of the century'. He cannot 'tell at sight a chassepôt rifle from a javelin'; he is not acquainted with sorties, surprises, modern gunnery, tactics, or elemental strategy, but he understands equations and the square of the hypotenuse, as well as integral and differential calculus. In short, the Major-General is a sly reference to Major-General Turner, Kitty's uncle, an engineer, not a fighting man.[34] His opposite number, the Pirate King, belongs to the 'robbing round' tradition, a satiric theme which stretches through the century from Lord Byron's *Don Juan* to Shaw's *Widowers' Houses*. Plaché's Brigand Chief (1829), for example, intends to purchase a title and live 'as honest, perchance, as the prince who plunders his own subjects'.[35] Autolycus' song in William Brough's *Perdita; or, The Royal Milkmaid* (1856) tells us that

> The shopkeeper who gives short weight,
>> Is robbing all round, all round, all round;
> The grocers who adulterate,
>> Like me go robbing all round.[36]

Gilbert himself had given Doro such a song in *Princess Toto*:

> There are brigands in every station,
>> And robbers in every rank;
> Some plunder the wealth of a nation
>> Some modestly pillage a bank;
> Some brigands are bubble directors,
>> And others may wear a fez hat;
> They're out of the reach of inspectors,
>> But they're none the less brigands for that.

---

[33] PML.

[34] Colin Prestige pointed out the identification and George McElroy the appropriateness of the song to an engineer: both in conversation with the author.

[35] *The Brigand* (London: John Dicks, 1829), 13.

[36] (London: Thomas Hailes Lacy, 1857), 19.

So, when the Pirate King sallies forth to seek his prey:

> I help myself in a royal way:
> I sink a few more ships, it's true,
> Than a well-bred monarch ought to do;
> But many a king on a first-class throne,
> If he wants to call his crown his own,
> Must manage somehow to get through
> More dirty work than ever *I* do [.]

Sullivan, the friend of Royals, set this without a qualm, and in London Royals happily came to hear it, from the Prince of Wales down. But unlike other robbers, Gilbert's pirates are sentimental about orphans and never attack a weaker party. When Frederic feels himself duty bound to destroy them, the Pirate King asks only, 'let our deaths be as swift and painless as you can conveniently make them'.

Yet of what use is the pirates' probity? They cannot make piracy pay. Everyone, including the Major-General, practises on their innocent credulity. The world outside the pirates' lair is a cheating world indeed. When, at the finale, the overthrown policemen charge the triumphant pirates to 'yield, in Queen Victoria's name', the outlaws put patriotism above advantage and immediately kneel because 'with all our faults, we love our Queen'—a Gilbertian reversal of melodramatic priorities. But Ruth, the piratical maid of all work, reverses the reversal by confessing that the pirates are 'all noblemen who have gone wrong!' The Major-General delightedly gives them his daughters, remarking, 'Peers will be peers'.

While Gilbert was still in New York, he was astonished to find Augustin Daly advertising a revival of *Charity*. He wrote to Daly, asking by what right he proposed to play it.[37] Then he wrote to at least two local papers disclaiming any responsibility for the play 'in its forthcoming debased condition'. Daly had constructed his own version, and no copyright law protected Gilbert. In fact, his presence in New York very likely increased Daly's box-office. In a moment of irritation Gilbert told a reporter that he and Sullivan would live in New York nine months in the year in order to benefit from American copyright.[38]

He was, however, increasingly anxious to return to stage the London première of *The Pirates of Penzance*, a willingness to leave exacerbated, perhaps, by a love-letter which he had unexpectedly received. Undated, without salutation, and signed 'Cynisca', it was from an

---

[37] 9 Feb. 1880: Folger Y.C. 4068(2).     [38] *Era* (22 Feb. 1880), 7.

actress whom Gilbert was presumably rehearsing. On cheap lined paper she wrote to explain the 'folly' of her feelings for someone she might never see again. She had never loved before, even though she had been married to a husband whom she left after the American Civil War. 'From that time, I encased myself in cast iron'—until she met Gilbert. Now, fascinated by his ability, she realized that she loved him; when he told her he was going back to England, her feelings 'were worse than death!' Cynisca remembered everything Gilbert had said or done—she could have learned anything from him, but she insisted she had never had an impure thought connected with him. 'Think of me with respect,' her letter ends, 'for I deserve it, there is no shame in the feeling I bear you—Good by—'.[39] This was the only love-letter Gilbert preserved, so it may have been significant to him—or it may have survived among his papers merely by accident. He obviously did not respond sexually, for Cynisca's tone is valedictory, nor is there any reason to suppose she interested him except professionally.

By 3 March he and Sullivan had given up thoughts they once had of going on to Cuba and were ready to sail home. After encountering three gales they arrived in England ten days later, flushed with victory, as the *Theatre* said. Kitty met them in Liverpool after four months away from her husband. In the meantime Carte's secretary Helen Lenoir (Helen Cowper-Black) went to America, first to assist, then to replace, him. After briefly attempting a stage career, she had turned to management and was one of the first business women. In fact, her executive power probably exceeded D'Oyly's, and for several years she was his 'American brain', as Matthew Arnold called her.

London rehearsals began, and on Saturday 3 April the Opera Comique was crammed for the first London performance of *The Pirates of Penzance*. Unfortunately, however, one of the most popular performers was missing from the cast. Four days before, a piece of falling scenery had hit Harriet Everard, injuring her so badly that Emily Cross had to be rushed in as Ruth. She had occasionally substituted for Everard as Buttercup, but did not know the new score. Poor Miss Everard, although she sang at some performances, never completely recovered. Gilbert felt very sorry for her and, when Barker refused her admission backstage, wrote to her that he would take care she was treated with perfect courtesy thereafter.[40] She died in 1882 of tuberculosis.

[39] WSG/BL Add. MS 49,331. This letter is dated 'Feb [1880]' in two different pencils and hands.   [40] Copy, 9 July 1880: WSG/BL Add. MS 49,338.

Critics were kind to Cross, and the audience responded enthusiastically to the new opera, especially to Rutland Barrington in the tiny, but important, role of Sergeant of Police. Marion Hood's silvery voice made a brilliant success of Mabel, while Richard Temple's Pirate King embodied the burlesque-picturesque and George Grossmith's patter song was encored every night. Three weeks later, sadly enough, he was literally pulled out in mid-performance to attend his unexpectedly dying father, who had collapsed at a Savage Club dinner. Frank Thornton filled in at the Opera Comique, one of the competent singing actors Carte had been accumulating for small roles, understudies, and alternates.

At this time Gilbert broke with Horace Wall, his American agent, and went over to Samuel French. Apparently Wall had attacked Carte in 'a most disgraceful manner' in a letter to Gilbert, and the librettist felt loyal to his impresario.[41] In May Carte himself agreed to pay Gilbert and Sullivan £2,900 for assigning him exclusive rights to play their three recent operas in Great Britain and Ireland.

On 4 June James Robinson Planché died in his eighty-fourth year, and Gilbert was among those invited to the chapel in Brompton Cemetery. Planché had not been his mentor, but he was Gilbert's forerunner, who acknowledged the younger man as his heir to Fairyland. With his death, the older generation of playwrights suddenly seemed long ago and far away. Five weeks later Tom Taylor died, and preparations were already under way for a benefit to raise funds for the elderly John Maddison Morton, author and adaptor of innumerable farces, including *Box and Cox*, but now 'in distressed circumstances'.

In addition to contributing 20 guineas (more than anyone else did), Gilbert was on the organizing committee for the benefit, with Byron, Burnand, Reece, Hollingshead, and others. He suggested sending a memorial in Morton's favour to Lord Beaconsfield—which went unanswered. Finally, on 21 July in a bill selected from Morton's plays, he appeared as Adolphus Swansdown in *Woodcock's Little Game*. It was at first rather a laconic, but later a jealous, role in which Gilbert won a commendation from the *Era*. Sullivan conducted *Cox and Box* on the same programme.

Although *The Pirates of Penzance* was still doing very well, Gilbert began to cast about for a new subject: 'I suppose an idea will come in

---

[41] Letter to Sothern, copy, 20 Apr. 1880: WSG/BL Add. MS 49,338. Gilbert wrote to Wall on 28 Apr., severing the connection.

time—it always has hitherto!'[42] While thinking it over, he sailed the *Pleione*, his second yacht. He had bought the first, the *Druidess*, in 1878 and sold it in 1879; and he was already making plans for his third, ordered from John Harvey, whose son was allowed to use the *Pleione*'s library when it was laid up at Wivenhoe. Gilbert liked the studious adolescent and helped him in his ambition to become an actor, recommending a drama coach, telling him something about acting, and asking Marion Terry to speak a friendly word to young John when he was hired for utility at the Court Theatre. Gilbert also asked Charles Wyndham if he could 'do anything for this young shaver?'[43] Wyndham sent him on tour, and Gilbert's protégé eventually became Sir John Martin-Harvey, famous for his performances of Sydney Carton.

In July 1880 Sothern had paid what was to be a flying visit to England before producing Gilbert's *Foggerty's Fairy* in New York. The comedy had been tailored for him after he refused *The N'er-Do-Weel*, and the dramatist promised to have set designs and alterations finished by the beginning of August. 'Unfortunately they are now useless to me for many months if not for ever,' Sothern wrote sadly from Hove on 30 July.[44] He had been so dangerously ill that his doctors insisted he could not act for at least a year. Would Gilbert secure the English copyright for him? Sothern had already paid over £2,000 for the piece, which Gilbert ultimately bought back from Sothern's sister and legatee Mary Cowan. The actor never appeared in *Foggerty's Fairy*—he died in January 1881, shortly after Gilbert's last interview with him, and so great had been his reputation for playing elaborate practical jokes that some of his friends did not attend his funeral for fear he would turn up as chief mourner! After nearly a year of dealing with her late brother's affairs, Mrs Cowan wrote to Gilbert that 'of all the people with whom I have had any dealings in reference to money . . . you have treated me with the greatest kindness & fairness'.[45] J. L. Toole thought of playing Foggerty, but could not agree to Gilbert's terms.

Sometime, probably during the early summer, the dramatist performed a labour of friendship at Sullivan's behest. The composer had been chosen to conduct the prestigious triennial Leeds Festival, for

---

[42] W. S. Gilbert to Mrs Barlow, 20 Mar. 1880: Huntington Library, BW Box 134, reproduced by permission.

[43] *The Autobiography of Sir John Martin-Harvey* (London: Sampson Low, Marston & Co. Ltd., n.d.), 48. See also ibid. 37, and facsimile letter between pp. 46 and 47.

[44] WSG/BL Add. MS 49,331.       [45] 12 Dec. [1881]: WSG/BL Add. MS 49,332.

which he was also to supply a new work of his own. For his text he chose an almost intractable poetic drama, Henry Hart Milman's *The Martyr of Antioch* (1822), and asked Gilbert to arrange it and turn some of Milman's blank verse into rhyme. Gilbert made suggestions, cut passages, and produced competent but not individualized rhymed verse.[46] At its first performance, 15 October 1880, *The Martyr of Antioch* was warmly applauded although reviewers expressed several caveats. Nevertheless, as the *Leeds Daily News* said, 'one cannot help regretting that [Sullivan] should neglect this style of work to pour his soul into comic opera'.

Gilbert supposed Sullivan's acknowledgement in his preface to the vocal score would be payment enough for his 'humble services', but the composer also gave his librettist an eighteenth-century silver chalice, suitably inscribed. Thanking him, Gilbert alluded to *The Martyr* as a success 'which, I suppose, will endure until music itself shall die'.[47] It was, perhaps, too great a supposition.

By November Gilbert had worked out two-thirds of his new comic libretto. Using his own Bab Ballad 'The Rival Curates' (as well as others), he changed the curates to aesthetes and then back to curates, until, after writing epitomes of some dialogue and several lyrics, he became increasingly uneasy about clerical satire and reverted to poets.[48]

Certainly Aestheticism was a subject which preoccupied the comic press in the late 1870s and early 1880s; in fact, the development of a burlesque aesthetic vocabulary, iconography, and personality became almost a monomania with *Punch* and was taken up by *Fun* and other competitors. Few movements in literature or the fine arts have provoked such a concentrated popular sneer. Nor has parody of literature ever been so closely allied with parody of painting. The personal eccentricities of Rossetti, Whistler, and the young Oscar Wilde; Robert Buchanan's attack on 'The Fleshly School of Poetry'; the unconventional pictures exhibited in the Grosvenor Gallery; Swinburne's alliteration; the merging of art, literature, and interior decoration by the younger Pre-Raphaelites—all these and more stimulated philistine comic writers to create caricature 'aesthetics', identified by their

---

[46] See A. Sullivan, *The Martyr of Antioch* (new edn.; London: Chappell & Co Ltd., n.d.). Sullivan's preface warmly acknowledged Gilbert's help.

[47] Copy, 3 Dec. 1880: PML.

[48] The fragmentary draft of the 'Rival Curates' libretto is published in J. W. Stedman, 'The Genesis of *Patience*' in J. B. Jones (ed.), *W. S. Gilbert: A Century of Scholarship and Commentary* (New York: New York University Press, 1970), 285–318.

unconventional costumes, their long hair, their strange works of art, and especially by their language, archaic, artistic, allusive. Ruskin himself had unintentionally contributed the 'blessed and precious in art', which *Punch* continually echoed with 'Distinctly Precious, Blessed, Subtile, Significant, and Supreme!' (26 July 1879) or 'How Consummate! How Perfect! How Supreme, Precious and Blessèd! Nay, how Utter!' (25 December 1880).

*Punch*'s best-natured allusions to aesthetes were such punning fillers as the suggestion Gilbert should write a 'Pater Song' instead of a patter song (23 April 1881), but the tone could be deliberately insulting as in 'Harlequin King Cultchaw' (7 January 1880), where the Peri of Pimlico, O—— W——, reclines in a roomy flowerpot amid lavender fire. Jellyby Postlethwaite, best-known of the pre-Gilbert aesthetes, appeared primarily in George du Maurier's long series of *Punch* cartoons. Sometimes he looks epicene; he sits up with a sick lily; his friend Pilcox is an apothecary-sculptor, while the acquaintances of his culturine patrons resemble Wilde, Rossetti, *et al.* In du Maurier's 1878 prose narrative 'The Rise and Fall of the Jack Spratts', the aesthetic Spratts 'reform' by living in suburbia, surrounded by formerly artistic friends who are now cigar-smoking businessmen.

These caricatures were important in training theatre audiences to recognize their counterparts on stage, and before Gilbert and Sullivan's *Patience* opened on 23 April 1881, several satiric plays had already appeared. Tom Taylor's *Victims*, for example, had redirected its blows from Tennyson to Swinburne. In John Hollingshead's *The Grasshopper* (adapted from *La Cigale*), Pygmalion Flippit was a version of James McNeill Whistler, who attended a rehearsal and approved the dialogue.[49] James Albery's *Where's the Cat?* contained what was probably the first stage picture of Oscar Wilde and ran for over a hundred performances.

While Sullivan was still composing *Patience*, his former collaborator F. C. Burnand entered the field with an enormously popular farcical comedy, *The Colonel*, produced at the Prince of Wales's Theatre on 2 February 1881. Another adaptation, it satirized aesthetic hypocrisy and drew so heavily on *Punch*, of which Burnand had recently become editor, that *Fun* declared he should acknowledge du Maurier as co-author. Burnand's Professor of Aesthetics, Lambert Streyke, whose aim is

---

[49] 'En Passant', *Theatre*, NS 1 (19 Dec. 1877), 327. For further discussion see T. Reff, *Degas: The Artist's Mind* (New York: Harper & Row, 1976), 19–20, and Appendix: 'The Caricature of Whistler in *The Grasshopper*', 36.

money, not art, bilks gullible women for a gallery of 'inaccessible genius', aided by his nephew Basil Giorgione. Happily, an American colonel arrives and discredits the hypocrites, whereupon 'the ladies return to the garments of civilization, and the play winds up merrily with the discomfiture of the Aesthete and the triumph of common sense,' according to *Punch*'s reviewer. Oscar Wilde called it a dull farce, and hoped for something better from Gilbert and Sullivan. He asked George Grossmith to reserve a box for him on opening night,[50] and the audience allegedly hooted at him when he arrived.

Sullivan, having enjoyed his *dolce far niente* in Nice, again had to finish in a rush at the last moment. He had even suggested postponing the opening, but Gilbert demurred; so by 9 April Carte was able to announce the first night and advertise that seats would be allotted in reply to written applications in the order in which they were received.

Visually, *Patience* was very much on the side of aestheticism. Gilbert at first wanted du Maurier to design the costumes, but in the end did them himself; he also considered Walter Crane as set designer. Apprehensive at first, Crane decided that Gilbert wanted 'something really beautiful as a setting' and sketched a garden scene for him. Although the tried and true John O'Connor was finally chosen, Crane thought he detected traces of his garden in O'Connor's attractive glade where Bunthorne and Grosvenor admire their reflections in a pool.[51]

Unlike Burnand and the others, Gilbert devised stage pictures in the styles of contemporary painters. His procession of damozels, for instance, recalled Leighton's *Daphnephoria* (1878) and Burne-Jones's, *Design from Romance of the Rose* (1881). Lady Jane was Whistler–Japanese: 'a gigantic nocturne in black and peacock green', as the *Referee* described her. The *Sporting Times*, however, was displeased at Jessie Bond's Pre-Raphaelite red wig and 'gaudy' blue dress, as well as the 'sickly' greens of other costumes. Nevertheless, most critics agreed with the *Pall Mall Gazette*, which declared Gilbert's aesthetic costumes exquisitely beautiful, unlike the vulgar raw reds,

---

[50] n.d., in Grossmith's letter album: PML. Wilde told a New York reviewer (*Daily Tribune*, 8 Jan. 1882) that he and a party of friends went to the first night of *Patience* and 'laughed, or jeered, at it as it deserved'. E. H. Mikhail (ed.), *Oscar Wilde: Interviews and Recollections* (London: Macmillan Press Ltd., 1979), i. 40. Wilde told a Philadelphia interviewer, however, that *Patience* 'has done our cause no harm . . . I enjoyed it very much'. (Ibid. i. 45.)

[51] W. Crane, *An Artist's Reminiscences* (New York: Macmillan Co., 1907), 236. It is unlikely that O'Connor borrowed from Crane, who also wrote that Carte had consulted him about the planning and decoration of the Savoy Theatre, only to disregard his suggestions.

yellows, and blues of the chorus's dresses when they become everyday young girls.

Gilbert's libretto differed from its predecessors in the absence of the antagonism Taylor and Burnand had so clearly shown. His rival poets have plenty of money: Bunthorne's family castle stands in the background; he pays his taxes, cherishes his receipts, and admits that if he had the Elysian Fields, he would let them out on building leases. His rival Archibald (originally Algernon) Grosvenor, an Idyllic Poet and Apostle of Simplicity,[52] immediately announces he is a man of property, who despises money. Both pursue the only woman in the opera who has neither social rank nor fortune. Gilbert thus eliminated many unpleasant elements in earlier plots. No one finds Bunthorne is a sham (although he admits it when alone), and at the end he is even prepared to carry on with his lily. The sincere Grosvenor discards aestheticism only on compulsion.

Furthermore, the philistines of this opera, the Heavy Dragoons, are just as dependent upon the attractions of costume as are the poets. They count on their uniforms to 'attract the fair', and when the fair are not attracted, the officers don knee-breeches, long-haired wigs, and pose awkwardly in imitation of the poets. In short, like Bunthorne, they are aesthetic shams.

*The Times* commended Gilbert for avoiding any distinct personal references, although Bunthorne's poems parody Swinburne's style. Rossetti, however, after reading the reviews, decided Bunthorne, the Fleshly Poet, was a direct attack on himself. Nobody, however, as Max Beerbohm remarked, could have looked less like Rossetti than Grossmith did.[53] Whistler, too, saw something of himself in Bunthorne, specifically his famous white lock of hair in Bunthorne's wig. Nothing loathe, he wrote a congratulatory note.

The opening night went splendidly. The *Athenaeum* found Gilbert's libretto 'as near perfection as possible'; the *Pall Mall Gazette* considered the stage management 'beyond all praise', and he had managed to find a permanent resting place for 'Crushed again!' cut from the dialogue of *Pinafore*. Several critics, however, took umbrage at Lady Jane's 'Silvered is the raven hair,' sung by massive Alice Barnett. 'Unnecessary

---

[52] Gilbert to Lady Katherine Coke, 13 Apr. 1881: cited here by kind permission of Catherine Ashmore. Lady Katherine wrote to Sullivan to say that there was really an Algernon Grosvenor, whereupon Gilbert immediately promised to change 'Algernon' to 'Archibald'. He had chosen 'Grosvenor' to suggest the Grosvenor Gallery.

[53] *A Note on 'Patience'* (London: 1918), unpaginated pamphlet [3].

and disagreeable,' said the *Pall Mall Gazette*, hearing her lament that 'There will be too much of me | In the coming by and by!' The *Sporting Times* warned, 'Gilberto, dames who are not bony | Have not the air of Giorgione.' To salvage her melody, Sullivan arranged with Hugh Conway (F. J. Fargus) to write new words: 'In the twilight of our love, | In the darkness falling fast'. Gilbert had grudgingly agreed, but scarcely a dozen copies were sold with Conway's lyrics.

On the day after the première, Sullivan told Carte he would collaborate once more with Gilbert, but after that he intended to do a grand opera for Covent Garden.[54] He had heard the voices of too many critics urging him to do serious music. A new opera was not needed for a long time, however, for *Patience* had a run of over eighteen months, during which Carte moved it from the stage of the Opera Comique to that of his newly-built Savoy Theatre. It spawned popular songs, Christmas cards, even an aesthetic teapot, and to mark its first anniversary the management presented a bouquet tied with ribbons of aesthetic colours to every lady in the stalls and circle.

Gilbert spent the spring of 1881 corresponding with John Harvey about his new yacht, nearly twice the tonnage of his *Pleione* and luxuriantly furnished even if marble in the baths had to be given up and the upholsterer had trouble cutting the carpet to please Gilbert. At first he intended to call her the *Vavir*, but changed to the *Chloris*, and after sailing her, he found she needed more ballast and finally a lead keel. He was having trouble with his belongings these days. He bought a clock-watch which lost three or four hours at a time, and upholsterers botched his order for making an ottoman look like a sofa. When his coachman got a bargain at a horse auction, Tattersal's wrote to say the sale was a mistake. He sent back the watch and the ottoman, but kept the horse.

He was not in the best of all possible moods when Fred Clay began to rehearse a revival of *Princess Toto* in September. Clay intended to open at the Opera Comique after Carte's company left for the Savoy, but said nothing to Gilbert since the latter had sold him all rights for ten years. Gilbert thought Clay discourteous and requested him to play the piece exactly as written without gags or interpolations.[55] Then he sent a letter to Clement Scott, disclaiming all responsibility for its staging, although, he scrupulously added, *Princess Toto* would not necessarily

---

[54]  Diary, 24 Apr. 1881: B/Y.

[55]  19 Sept. 1881: WSG/BL Add. MS 49,338. Gilbert also reminded Clay that he had lent the musician the words to 'We wouldn't be out of the fashion' for use in the USA only.

be the worse for that.[56] But it did not run long, and John Hollingshead, who had taken over the management of the Opera Comique, said that producing it cost him nearly £7,000. The crowds that Clay hoped for had gone to see the electric light at Carte's new theatre.

[56] 5 Oct. 1881: PML. Permission of Catherine Ashmore.

# 12

## At the Savoy

Two themes continuously occupied him, the melodrama and the
fairy-tales of his epoch. . . .

TLS (21 Nov. 1936)

IN July 1881 Carte showed Sullivan over his new theatre. The musician was pleased with everything except the pit entrance, 'which
must be altered'.[1] For D'Oyly it was the culmination of four years' hopes
and eighteen months' work. Although the Metropolitan Board of
Works conditionally approved plans in April 1880, its formal assent was
not given until more than a month later. Carte had purchased the freehold of part of the ancient manor of the Savoy in the Strand, and proposed to erect a theatre entirely illuminated by electric light, which, he
was convinced, was the lighting of the future. The site itself was waste
land, sloping down from the Strand where Rimmel, the perfumer's
shop, on one hand and Burgess's fish-sauce shop on the other, scented
the air. Carte's architect, C. J. Phipps, was a noted designer of theatres,
and the acoustics of the Savoy (called the Beaufort in earlier stages)
were excellent.

After the first rehearsal, on 6 October Gilbert, Sullivan, and Carte
arranged that the rent of the theatre would be £3,500 a year, Carte
insuring the building and scenery; all three, the costumes, music, and
hand properties. Also on the sixth Carte issued a preliminary pamphlet,
promising to devote the Savoy to works by Gilbert and Sullivan, and
describing its 1,200 Swan lamps, powered by four large engines. If they
failed, gas had been laid on everywhere and could instantly light the
theatre.

Unlike other theatres, the Savoy was free-standing on all four sides,
and none of its 1,292 seats had a restricted view. Decorations were
restrained Renaissance, and there was no painted drop curtain; instead,

---

[1] Diary, 31 July 1881: B/Y.

a great golden pair of curtains drew up to the sides: 'a cataract of pure gold . . . radiant and etherial', as the *Athenaeum* described the effect. Nevertheless, on opening night (10 October) the stage itself was still lit by gas and would be for some weeks to come. Although *Patience* now had a new set and an augmented chorus, it was the electric lights in the auditorium which the public came to see.

After 'God Save the Queen' had been sung and Carte had asked indulgence for Barrington's sore throat, the gas sunburner was lowered, and the pear-shaped electric bulbs instantly filled the theatre with light, which, unlike gas, was noiseless, odourless, and without ill effects. The audience cheered. At the dress rehearsal, the lights had 'the jumping toothache';[2] but now, on the first night, they merely wobbled at times and went out completely only once. They were soon under better control, however, with the installation of accumulators.[3] Some critics found them soft, some harsh. The *Morning Post*, for instance, was offended by the distinctness of outline, and one must remember that the Savoy, like other Victorian theatres, did not lower its house lights during a performance. Gilbert, of course, was learning to use the new lighting, having by force of circumstance become a pioneer in that as well. 'Do you know if I can get the swan lights in ground glass?' he asked Carte; 'I mean the bulb *ground* instead of clear. And if so would you mind ordering two or three for me to try?'[4]

Even while experimenting, he was looking ahead to the opera which would replace *Patience* and on 19 October visited Sullivan with the idea of *Iolanthe*; 'funny but at present vague,' was Sullivan's opinion.[5] So, setting his plot aside 'to clear', Gilbert concerned himself with a revival of *Engaged* at the Court Theatre, now managed by John Clayton. Marion Terry and Kyrle Bellew played their former roles; W. H. Denny would be Angus, and H. J. Byron, now turned actor, had been specially engaged for Cheviot Hill.

Byron was a much quieter actor than George Honey, who had been such a noisy blot on the first production of *Engaged*, but his idea of rehearsing differed radically from Gilbert's, and neither knew that Byron was in the early stages of the tuberculosis which was to kill him two and a half years later. He came late, left early, and drove Gilbert to despair. Clayton wanted to play the piece as soon as possible, but by 23

[2] Letter from Godfrey Turner to Clement Scott, 9 Oct. 1881: Clement Scott Papers/TM.

[3] G. Grossmith, 'Light that Failed', *Evening Standard and St James Gazette*, [8 Dec. 1906], 4.

[4] n. d. [1881]: DOYC/TM.

[5] Sullivan, Diary, 19 Oct. 1881: B/Y.

November Byron neither knew a word of the third act nor had more than 'a glimmering of the other two'.[6] In palliation of an old friend, Gilbert admitted that the part was heavy and that he was not surprised, but he insisted on a perfect rehearsal before consenting to its production. A week later, he was as satisfied as it was likely he could be, and reviewers found Byron a great improvement over Honey. When he spoke the line, 'I am full of anecdote, and all my anecdotes are in the best possible taste,' the house, remembering Byron's own plays, cheered heartily.

Once again critics commented on Gilbert's cynicism although the *Academy* found the 1881 audience more responsive to his point of view. The *Athenaeum* asserted forthrightly that his 'satire of humanity is every whit as relentless as that of Gulliver and needs no vindication. . . . the feeling it produces is akin to that derived from the contemplation of Hogarth'. Overstated perhaps, but not when compared with contemporary Victorian comedy.

Cheviot Hill was Byron's last stage appearance; he gave up the role on 4 February 1882 because of a bronchial attack. On 11 April 1884 he died after a long illness. Let his epitaph be a sentence published earlier in the *Theatre*: 'He brought out Mr. T. W. Robertson and discovered Mr. Gilbert, and has never been jealous of anybody.'

While *Engaged* was in rehearsal, Gilbert was also at long last preparing *Foggerty's Fairy* for production by Charles Wyndham at the Criterion. On opening night, 15 December, Sullivan's diary described it as 'Brilliantly clear & ingenious, but unsatisfactory—like a dream.' Gilbert had again adapted one of his own short stories, in this case telling how Freddy Foggerty, by eating a sugar ornament, can blot out any past event and its consequences. This plunges him into new situations with new and confused alignments until he is finally able to return to his original self.

'Never did actor express bewilderment with a more natural air,' exclaimed the *Era* critic of Wyndham, but audiences were also bewildered by the plot, which asked them to remember simultaneously what Foggerty *was* in contrast to what he *is*. 'It perplexes when it should amuse,' the *Athenaeum* said, conceding that it brimmed over with cleverness and sparkled with wit. Only the first act elicited incessant shouts of laughter, however, and there were hisses during the third. Gilbert had chosen to print a quatrain by Voltaire and his own translation of it in the programme:

---

[6] Gilbert to John Clayton, copy 23 Nov. 1881: WSG/BL Add. MS 49,338.

Demons and fays are banished, hand in hand.
Stern Common Sense has ousted Necromancy:
Though Fact, alas, now lords it o'er the land:
Trust me, there's something to be said for Fancy!

His audience, however, preferred music with their fancy. Five days after *Foggerty's Fairy* opened, Gilbert, Sullivan, and Carte signed a new agreement, and Gilbert went home with Sullivan to show him some numbers for their next collaboration. If Foggerty's fairies did not attract, Iolanthe's would. 'Every age is matter-of-fact to those who live in it. Romance died the day before yesterday. To-day will be romantic the day after to-morrow,' a fairy tells Foggerty. But *Iolanthe* would be set between 1700 and 1882, and its supernaturals would be timeless and topical.

The year ended with the Savoy stage electrically lit for the first time at a 28 December matinée. After Act 1, Carte made a short speech, and Mr Keppler, the electrician, broke a light bulb wrapped in gauze without igniting it. Thereafter Carte's advertisements emphasized the safety of incandescent lamps. Two days later, Carte gave gold lockets and inscribed gold-headed canes to the principal ladies and gentlemen and a week's double salary to the chorus. Then he sailed for six weeks in New York, where *Patience* had just been performed for the hundredth time.

During January 1882 Gilbert continued to work on the lyrics of *Iolanthe*, temporarily called 'Perola' until Irving's permission could be secured to use the final title. (He and Ellen Terry had played in Wills's *Iolanthe*, adapted from Hertz's *King Rene's Daughter*.) Gilbert also was investigating the new theatre's finances, writing Carte a growl to the effect that advertising costs were exorbitant and that, even with electric light, the gas bill was higher than at the Opera Comique. Nightly costs were nearly £130, which would be serious if business dropped. He proposed regular meetings to check accounts.[7] Such growls were to recur now and then for the next eight years, until they broke into a roar.

It is quite possible that in realizing his dream and in the excitement of owning the world's first electrically lit theatre, Carte had not been careful about expenses. Sullivan, now in Egypt, agreed they should reduce advertising costs immediately, but neither he nor Carte wanted a weekly financial meeting.

Having had his growl, Gilbert turned towards arranging for a

[7] 14 Jan. 1882: DOYC/TM.

February matinée of *Broken Hearts* at the Savoy. He asked Hermann Vezin to play Mousta; Marion Terry would be Vavir; and Kyrle Bellew, Florian. Unluckily, the night before the performance, Bellew was injured in a stage accident, which cut his chin to the bone, and Gilbert found himself on stage as a romantic leading man. 'Mr. GILBERT feels that nothing short of the extreme urgency of the situation would have justified him in placing himself in a position which he is so little qualified to fill,' read the indulgence slip. At 45 he was hardly a *jeune premier*, but several reviewers thought he made a handsome prince. Announced as merely reading his role, Gilbert dressed it, acted it, and was cheered at the final curtain. He was, however, admired more in the dryly comic passages than in the romantic ones: 'Florian is rather a difficult nut to crack,' he had written a month earlier.[8] Yet he had cracked it, and Marion Terry had played Vavir.

Instantly, however, he realized she was in difficulties with the Bancrofts in whose company she was playing; a rumour had spread that she and Squire Bancroft were lovers. In a much-revised draft of a letter to his friend Mrs Twiss, Gilbert showed his indignation that Miss Terry alone should be held guilty for 'an act in which she had an accomplice who was, at the very least, as much to blame as herself'.[9] Gilbert despised a double sexual standard and accordingly believed they should be condemned together or acquitted together as a matter of common justice. He and his wife, he told Mrs Twiss, had known Marion Terry intimately for some years and thought she needed an advocate. Marguerite Steen, the biographer of the Terrys, believed much of this 'scandal' could be ascribed to Ellen Terry's sense of mischief,[10] but it was enough to set a rumour afloat that the Haymarket actors refused to appear with her and that she had been turned out of the theatre.[11]

Life was full of annoyances for Gilbert that spring. He stopped an orchestral rehearsal of Henry Stephens and Edward Solomon's *Lord Bateman* held at the Savoy because they sent out invitations using Carte's name and hoping for free publicity along with their free space. Perhaps Gilbert used his undoubted authority too hastily, but Carte, returning from America, endorsed his veto. In the meantime Stephens and Gilbert carried on a correspondence in the *Era*, where Stephens was unpleasantly personal towards everyone at the Savoy except

[8] Letter to Miss Boughton, 21 Jan. 1882: PML.
[9] 22 Feb. 1882: WSG/BL Add. MS 49,332.
[10] *A Pride of Terrys* (London: Longmans, 1962), 259–60.
[11] Gilbert to Arthur Blunt (Cecil), 22 June 1881: PML.

Sullivan. After all this, *Lord Bateman* proved a failure when it reached the Gaiety stage on 29 April. 'Dull', the *Era* called its libretto; 'There is no invention and no humour.' Nor was it helped by E. W. Royce falling in a fit on-stage at a performance.[12]

Another irritating production also failed—Lingard and Searelle's *The Wreck of the Pinafore*, a so-called sequel to the opera in which the characters realign themselves, Josephine pursuing Sir Joseph, for instance. *Fun* described it as 'indeed a wreck' and the audience as unruly.

Always interested in new mechanical devices, Gilbert now invented an inexpensive contrivance for holding a telephone to one's ear at any angle. Although he offered it to the United Telephone Company Limited, they were not interested.[13] Nevertheless, and however the receivers were held, Gilbert installed telephone wires to the Savoy for himself and Sullivan a year later. The United Telephone Company also lent telephones to use for stage instructions in *Iolanthe*, and Gilbert's private phone number in the new house he would soon build was 8505.[14]

After the pinpricks of the spring, summer was tranquil. He continued to write and revise the new libretto, and Sullivan, still sad and upset over his mother's death on 27 May, began the music. While sailing the Devon coast, Gilbert went to meet his collaborator in Exeter to give him the manuscript of most of the second act. Sullivan went abroad in August—forgetfully—and had to write his secretary to send him his diaries, his morphia injector, and toothpaste. But by later September rehearsals were being held, and after one of them, Gilbert took Sullivan to see his new house being built in South Kensington. The composer was impressed with the large, well-designed building—'will be splendid', he wrote in his diary.

The dress rehearsal a month later, attended by the press, was very satisfactory, although Sullivan finished the overture only two days before. On 25 November, just as he left for the theatre, he received a letter from his broker, confessing financial ruin and the loss of Sullivan's £7,000 on investment deposit. He bravely went on to the Savoy, had a tremendous reception, and conducted the first performance. Gilbert, after checking everything backstage, had gone to stride along the Embankment until it was time to return for his bow with his collabo-

[12] He evidently became paralysed; a Gaiety benefit under the patronage of the Prince of Wales produced approximately £1,500 for him in 1883. Gilbert was on the benefit committee.

[13] Copy, 27 Mar. 1882: WSG/BL Add. MS 49,339.

[14] *Three Victorian Telephone Directories* (London: David & Charles Reprints, 1970), 173; Sullivan's number was 3084, and the Savoy Theatre's, 2602.

rator amid first-night cheers. By now, he could not bear to see the public performances of his own works;[15] so he did not know if a forgetful fairy said 'Perola' when speaking of 'Iolanthe'.

The press were struck with pleasure at the spectacle before them. In Act 1, the chorus of peers marched in resplendently, garbed by Ede and Son, robe-makers to Her Majesty and the House of Lords. 'Every coronet was correct as to its spikes, balls, and strawberry leaves,' exclaimed the *Echo*. Diamond bands crossed the fairies' bodices, and, in the second act, electric stars shone in the hair of the Queen and the principal fairies. (Two weeks later, all the fairies were illuminated.) '[T]oo dazzling to be pleasant,' grumbled *Lloyd's*, in the minority.

The Queen of the Fairies wore a helmet and silver corselet, suitable to Alice Barnett's Wagnerian proportions; like Wotan, she carried a spear on which the fairy law was written. As romantic leads Richard Temple and Leonora Braham (Strephon and Phyllis) were Dresden shepherd and shepherdess. Grossmith had one of his best roles as Lord Chancellor, while Barrington and Durward Lely were two Lords in love with Phyllis. Jessie Bond's Iolanthe, Strephon's fairy mother, was unusually quiet for her with a completely serious song: to show she could be, Gilbert said.[16]

Act 2, which took thirty minutes to set, was immediately applauded for its realistic re-creation of Palace Yard, Westminster. The scene was moonlit, and Gilbert insisted the moon must be steel-blue, not yellow. 'Oh he keeps on about that blasted moon!' said a weary electrician.[17] But he was repaid when the *St James's Gazette* noted the difference between the white moonlight and the street gas lamps on stage.

In a hilarious topical reference, the Queen of the Fairies raised her arms to a figure sitting in the dress circle and sang:

> Oh, Captain Shaw!
> Type of true love kept under!
> Could thy Brigade
> With cold cascade
> Quench my great love, I wonder!

[15] Arthur Wing Pinero likewise refused to attend the opening nights of his plays. On first nights, J. M. Morton paced Waterloo Bridge 'like a halfpenny suicide', waiting for a boy to bring him the verdict. J. Hollingshead, *My Lifetime* (London: Sampson Low, Marston & Co. Ltd., 1895), i. 191.

[16] Quoted in *The Life and Reminiscences of Jessie Bond* (London: John Lane, 1930), 109.

[17] R. A. Flicker in conversation with the author, London, 4 Apr. 1975, quoting the late Henry Pearce, who as a boy was frequently backstage at the Savoy, where his father worked on the lighting.

The figure was Captain Shaw himself, head of the London Fire Brigade, and friends sitting near him burst into laughter at what may have been a reference to his feeling for Lady Colin Campbell, who sat beside him. (Four years later, in a sensational divorce case, Captain Shaw was unsuccessfully accused of committing adultery with Lady Colin.)[18]

As to the opera enclosed in the splendid frame of the Savoy stage, opinions were mixed. Gilbert and Sullivan were no longer a startling innovation, although *Iolanthe* had a more complex libretto and a more advanced score than its predecessors. Reviewers, even while they praised, frequently commented on repetition of style. ('I used to invent a perfectly fresh character each time for George Grossmith; but he always did it in his own way,' Gilbert once remarked.)[19] Almost everyone, including Sullivan, thought the second act needed compression, and one reviewer called both acts 'unwholesome'. Yet the audience clearly enjoyed itself, and the opera ran for 398 performances.

For the plot and some of the characters of *Iolanthe*, Gilbert drew on the great body of fairy literature of the nineteenth century. His women's chorus satirizes the fairies who begin many pantomimes by singing such songs as

> Hither, hither, hither, hither,
> Trip, fairies, hither, trip, trip.
> Here come at our mystic call,
> Ye troops of elfins, one and all.[20]

Flitting onto the stage like Wilis, Gilbert's fairies sing:

> Tripping hither, tripping thither,
> Nobody knows why or whither;
> We must dance and we must sing,
> Round about our fairy ring!

Celia tells us that

---

[18] G. H. Fleming, *Victorian 'Sex Goddess'* (Oxford: Oxford University Press, 1990), 142. Lady Colin was Sullivan's guest.

[19] P. Fitzgerald, *The Savoy Opera and the Savoyards* (London: Chatto & Windus, 1899), 115. The Lord Chancellor, whose 'series of judgements in F sharp minor, given *andante* in six-eight time, are among the most remarkable effects ever produced in a Court of Chancery', may be a reference to Viscount Alverstone, who was an excellent baritone and a member of the Madrigal Society.

[20] E. L. Blanchard, *Tom Thumb; or, Merlin the Magician, and The Good Fairies of the Court of King Arthur* (London: Music Publishing Co. Ltd., [1860]), 9.

> If you ask the special function
> Of our never-ceasing motion,
> We reply, without compunction,
> That we haven't any notion!

This willingness to follow a convention they do not understand links them with the male chorus of mindless peers, for both groups perform stereotypic functions without thinking. Pantomime fairies are tutelary spirits; so Gilbert's Queen promises to aid Strephon and sends him into Parliament, where, by magic influence, he becomes the leader of both parties and proposes to throw the peerage open to competitive examination.

The plot of *Iolanthe*, however, fits into the weeping as well as laughing fairy tradition, expressed in serious, often poetic works delineating the bittersweet or tragic love of a fairy (sylph, water spirit, Pleiad, or mermaid) for a mortal. La Motte Fouqué's novel *Undine*; Théophile Gautier's scenario for *Giselle*, and August Bournonville's ballet *La Sylphide*, for instance, were all performed, imitated, and burlesqued on the English stage. Often the supernatural being sacrifices herself for the beloved or secures a happy ending by divesting herself of fairyhood, as in Ross Neil's 1875 *Elfinella*; so Iolanthe is banished to the bottom of a stream for marrying a mortal, by whom she has a son—immortal down to the waist, but his legs are human. Her proposed later self-sacrifice for his sake also links her to tragic fairy heroines.

But this is a comedy. Just as Iolanthe again incurs death by revealing her identity to her husband, the Lord Chancellor, her predicament is extended to the entire female chorus. They have (off-stage) married the House of Lords, and are now fairy duchesses, marchionesses, countesses, viscountesses, and baronesses. The perplexed Fairy Queen cannot bring herself to 'slaughter the whole company'; so the Lord Chancellor alters the law to read 'Every fairy shall die who *don't* marry a mortal.' In a parody of fairy love, the Queen proposes to Private Willis, and, instead of the fairies losing their wings, the mortals gain them, and all fly away to fairyland. 'We will arrange | Happy exchange—| House of Peers for House of Peris!'

Gilbert mingled this fairy play with a satire on politics, both current and general. Strephon is a Tory, but his legs are 'confounded Radicals'; Private Willis muses that when MPs vote, 'They've got to leave that brain outside, | And vote just as their leaders tell 'em to.' Lord Mountararat sings that Britain's rays will shine bright 'while the House of Peers withholds | Its legislative hand, | and noble statesmen do not itch | To interfere with matters which | They do not understand'. The Lord Chancellor tells us the law has no kind of fault, but almost immediately he also tells us that honesty is a new and original plan.

In Rutland Barrington's song 'De Belville was regarded as the Crichton of his age' (cut after production), De Belville is a famous poet, painter, and inventor, who unfortunately makes no money until his wealthy cousin dies. Inheriting his fortune, De Belville becomes an MP with 'a taste for making inconvenient speeches in the House'. To reward him the government takes him from the Commons and puts him in the Lords (where he will never be heard from again). In 'Fold your flapping wings' (also cut, but later than Barrington's number), Gilbert again, as we have seen, developed his favourite theme of environment making the thief.

By now, Carte's new system of printing a house plan as well as seat numbers on tickets had been in operation for a year and had cut down markedly on delays and confusion in finding places. During the run of *Iolanthe*, he introduced the queue system already practised in France and the United States. Hitherto those who wanted unreserved seats massed at the door, pushing, even fighting to be first inside. After a near-accident in the crush outside the Savoy's pit entrance, Carte wrote to *The Times* (1 January 1883) that he had received private complaints as well as a letter from the Lord Chamberlain's Office, which made him decide that the old habit of struggling for entrance was too dangerous. The English public would not submit to being disciplined he was told, but when Carte tried out the new plan, they readily formed into a line, two by two, and went in quietly.

Gilbert staged no new work that year, but he was kept busy dealing with builders for his new house. Although another libretto would not be needed for a year, he began to discuss it with Sullivan in late January 1883. On 8 February they signed an agreement with Carte in which they granted him sole performing rights for five years. Carte was to pay Gilbert and Sullivan each one-third of the net profits, deducting expenses of producing each of the operas, these to include an annual £4,000 theatre rental, lighting, and repairs incidental to performances. Sullivan drove Gilbert to the Savoy, and recorded that they had 'a slight breeze & explanation en route', a foreshadowing of things to come.

At this time, however, the 'breeze' was still without force, and on 13 March Gilbert was invited to the anniversary festival of the Royal Society of Musicians with Sullivan in the chair. Hollingshead, the younger Charles Dickens, and George Augustus Sala were there too, proposing toasts and answering to 'Literature and the Fine Arts' and to 'Music and the Drama'. Replying to this last, Gilbert again took occasion to reiterate the popular view of Drama as an invalid kept alive by transfusions of French stage blood. This would continue, he said, till the British playgoer learned to discriminate between author and adaptor, between the manager who produced original plays and 'the manager who sought ignominious safety in translation'.

Clement Scott had published a recent article in the *Theatre*, taking exception to Gilbert's essay on 'Unappreciated Shakespeare'. According to Gilbert, British audiences did not see Shakespeare because leading actors cut his plays to make themselves more prominent. Consequently, they had 'no real appreciation of the merits of their most distinguished poet'. In answer, Scott, fanatically devoted to Henry Irving, told Gilbert in the January *Theatre*, 'No, no, my dear Mr. Gilbert, if authors, modern authors, clever authors, would only allow their plays to be altered more than they do, to be cut and trimmed more than they will, the stage and the public would be the gainers'—a personal blow at Gilbert, who did not allow actors to revise his lines.

Scott was also against Carte's new queue system, yet he asked Gilbert to write a brief autobiography for the April issue of the *Theatre* and to send along a picture of himself. 'Of course, if you wish it,' Gilbert replied. 'I will go to Bassano & so violate a hideous oath never to encounter a photographer again.'[21] He had not taken umbrage at Scott's attack, and when he sent the article, he remarked, 'It seems dreadfully egotistical—But when one has to write about oneself, I suppose that is inevitable.'[22] It was not so egotistical after all: he recorded failures as well as successes.

He and Sullivan dined at each other's houses, Gilbert being among the guests at Sullivan's birthday party on 13 May, when the Prince of Wales, the Duke of Edinburgh, Burnand, a Rothschild, and others heard selections from *Iolanthe* by special telephone from the stage of the Savoy. (The superintendent had worked until 11.30 the evening before, arranging transmitters, etc.)[23] On 22 May Sullivan went to Windsor Castle, where he was knighted by Queen Victoria, along with George Grove and George Macfarren; Gilbert had to wait twenty-four years before becoming Sir William, since musicians were taken much more seriously than dramatists.

---

[21] 16 Feb. 1883: PML. Gilbert did not go to Bassano, however, but to the *Theatre*'s regular photographer.

[22] 19 Mar. 1883: PML.       [23] Sullivan, Diary, 12 May 1883: B/Y.

In June 1883 Henry S. Leigh died, that man 'of rare wit . . . without one atom of application'—another of the old *Fun* gang.[24] It was now a different paper from the time when they all lived in Bohemia; its great days were over, and it had sunk back behind *Punch*. With Byron's death the next year, Gilbert would be left as the only considerable literary survivor of *Fun*'s first decade, but, in spite of a touch of gout, he had no intention of dying like them before he reached 50.

Carte was now puffing the coolness of the July Savoy in what Gilbert called 'thermometrical advertisement'; he suggested that the manager quote temperatures outside the theatre as well as inside, 'Because degrees in the abstract convey no idea to many people—but when they are compared with the temperature outside, they will understand that the difference is very slight.'[25]

At this time the Gilberts were spending the summer at Eastbury Park near Watford, from which he frequently commuted to London. He had news for Carte a week later: Miss Fortescue, who played Celia in *Iolanthe*, was going to be married and leave the stage at the end of the run. She wanted it kept secret, and, strictly speaking, Gilbert should not have informed Carte. In spite of playing such tiny roles as she had, Miss Fortescue pleased reviewers, one of whom thought she should have greater opportunities. She was attractive enough to be called beautiful, and her fiancé, Lord Garmoyle, was the son of a rigidly righteous former Lord Chancellor, Lord Cairns, raised to an earldom through his own exertions. His intelligence and tenacity were not inherited by Lord Garmoyle, but there is no reason to suppose that Miss Fortescue did not love him. Her father was dead, and, if Gilbert did not stand *in loco parentis* to her, he felt a certain avuncularity for the actress, which would be demonstrated when Lord Garmoyle jilted her in 1884.

Sullivan had been resting in Carlsbad in June on doctor's orders; back in England in July, he stayed with the Gilberts at Eastbury, played lawn tennis, and went through the libretto of the new opera with Gilbert. As usual they made alterations and modifications until Sullivan liked the new piece very much. Having sketched a number at Carlsbad, Sullivan now set to work, although not steadily, and by November played Carte the whole of Act 2. The triumvirate then met to discuss casting and decided against retaining Barrington, but changed their minds in a few days, perhaps on Gilbert's representation. Barrington's stolidity of man-

---

[24] *The Brothers Dalziel* (London: Methuen and Co., 1901), 282.
[25] 1 July 1883: DOYC/TM.

ner was very useful to him, very likely more useful indeed than Grossmith's nervous agility.

While this was going on, Gilbert had become involved with the repertoire of Mary Anderson, 'La Belle Americaine', who had taken the Lyceum while Henry Irving and his company were in America. She had played Gilbert's Galatea in New York, an interpretation which the partisan critic William Winter described as 'The soul of the child . . . incarnated in the consummate purity of the woman'. Now she intended to include it in her first London season.

On 21 September she wrote to Winter that she had just had a long chat with Gilbert. There had been rumours in New York that he would not let her play Galatea, but Anderson said they were without foundation. 'He is a charming man and said I could do what I liked with Galatea and it would be right'[26]—but what she liked proved subject to his inspection. They met again to go over the part, 'so he may be certain that I will do nothing wrong in his play. . . . he is taking this precaution because I don't want him to be at the rehearsals'.[27] ('I am not easy to shoulder aside,' Gilbert wrote to an acquaintance.)[28]

Miss Anderson asked Winter to contradict reports published in New York that she feared Gilbert would humiliate her: 'There never was a more courtly charming gentleman.'[29] She wrote to her stepfather that she liked him very much; 'most people think him a cynic but it is seldom one meets so companionable and sympathetic a man'.[30] Nevertheless, when rehearsals began, this sympathetic gentleman refused to allow 'a dark effect' when Pygmalion was struck blind. 'There should be some sign from heaven but he won't have it at all—'.[31]

Gilbert read his one-act play *Comedy and Tragedy* to Miss Anderson on 19 November; she was delighted with it, and it went into rehearsal before she appeared as Galatea in mid-December. Reviews for that performance were mixed, but all conceded her great beauty, the *Era* calling her 'the most faultless of Grecian marbles'. *Punch* had already objected to her transatlantic 'tricks' of long pauses and drooping eyelid, but a roar of acclamation greeted her before she spoke and

[26] [21 Sept. 1883]: Folger Y.c.61 (41a).

[27] To William Winter, 5 Oct. 1883: Folger Y.c. 61 (43).

[28] To Mrs Saker, 2 May 1884: PML. Although the dates do not coincide for either *Pygmalion and Galatea* or *Comedy and Tragedy*, Gilbert specifically refers to Mary Anderson by name in this letter.

[29] 6 Oct. 1883: Folger Y.c.61 (89b).          [30] 22 Oct. 1883: Folger Y.c.61 (44b).

[31] Mary Anderson to William Winter, 23 Nov. 1883: Folger Y.c.61 (49a).

another roar of applause echoed when she took her bow with Gilbert. Yet the memory of Mrs Kendal's performance was still green, and both the critic of the *Athenaeum* and Clement Scott in the *Illustrated London News* preferred the womanliness and pathos of Anderson's predecessor.

Gilbert himself thought Galatea should be more human: 'When Galatea is a statue, she cannot be too statue-like: when she comes to life, she cannot be too womanly,' he wrote to Clement Scott on 10 December.[32] Yet he insisted that Miss Anderson played it as she did with his full consent. He had intended the play to be 'modern in style', however, and strongly objected to Alma-Tadema's arrangement of her draperies. Although as a painter, Tadema was the nobbiest Roman of them all, he did not understand that stage figures must move. 'I believe that Tadema wanted Miss Anderson to play the part in a marble wig throughout,' Gilbert wrote, joking but exasperated.[33] The best acting from his and several others' point of view, was Amy Roselle's as Cynisca. (In Chicago, the artist Frank Millet told the *Tribune* that he, not Alma-Tadema, had designed the Galatea costume.)

By the time Mary Anderson's season ended in early April, she had played the role 106 times and was preparing to take *Pygmalion and Galatea* to the provinces. It had earned a tame burlesqe in H. P. Stephens's 'Galatea; or, Pygmalion Re-Versed' at the Gaiety, with Nelly Farren as the sculptor, and Edward Terry, the statue.

While he was being courtly to Mary Anderson, Gilbert was being antipathetic to Lillian Russell, who had been engaged to play the title role in *Princess Ida*. Another 'Belle Americaine', she had already appeared in Gilbert and Sullivan's pirated operas, straight or burlesqued, in New York, and she had also broken a contract, or contracts, to run away to England with Edward Solomon. When Gilbert, Sullivan, Carte, and Frank Cellier went to see her first-night performance in Stephens and Solomon's *Virginia and Paul* on 16 July, the composer thought she had great aptitude even though she was not very cultivated. 'Could be made into the most valuable singing actress,' he noted in his diary. She already had such sexual magnetism that choosing her for the intelligent, reserved Ida was rather strange.

But when rehearsals began in November, she did not want to be made into an actress; she considered she was one already. Her publicity

---

[32] PML. Gilbert thought Anderson's conception was 'artistically more beautiful, but dramatically less effective, than Mrs. Kendal's'.
[33] Letter to Clement Scott, 12 Dec. 1883: PML.

was very favourable, and the *Daily News* prophesied that her 'rich, full, and sympathetic voice, agreeable presence, and lively style of acting will render her a valuable acquisition to the company'. Then she missed a rehearsal without informing Gilbert she would not be there. Whether this was an individual coaching session or a full rehearsal or both is not clear, but her absence infuriated Gilbert. Although she wrote an apology, her attitude seems to have been 'I think I have had enough rehearsals', and in her much later memoirs she hints that the librettist had sexual reasons for private nocturnal conferences.[34] This explanation was no doubt self-flattering, but, as Arthur Jacobs says in his biography of Sullivan, it seems far-fetched. Perhaps Gilbert was particularly exacerbated by having earlier met at a fancy-dress ball a chorus member, Miss Heathcote, when she was supposedly too ill to appear at the theatre. 'The matter is aggravated by the fact that she might easily have gone to the ball *after the theatre*. I think we must get rid of Miss Heathcote,' Gilbert wrote to Carte.[35]

The triumvirate discussed Lillian Russell's lapse, but since Gilbert said, 'I won't speak to her, & she shan't play in any piece of mine,' nothing could be done.[36] They sent her a letter offering to release her because of 'ill health' unless she could assure them she would improve enough to keep her engagement. Against advice from the press, she did not take advantage of this loophole, but sued Carte for breach of contract, a suit finally settled out of court eleven months later.

It was now ten days before the first performance of *Princess Ida*. Leonora Braham, cast as Lady Psyche, was rushed into the title role; Kate Chard would replace her. Illness had taken Alice Barnett out of *Iolanthe* in October; so Lady Blanche would be played by Rosina Brandram. Fortunately, the men in the cast kept well, attended rehearsals, and stayed in the roles for which they had been cast. Rehearsals continued.

Both Gilbert and Sullivan found December 1883 distracting for personal reasons—Sullivan because Fred's widow, married again, was leaving with the children for California. Her son Herbert, however,

---

[34] 'Lillian Russell's Reminiscences', *Cosmopolitan* (Mar. 1922), 126. The Reminiscences ran monthly from Feb. to Sept. 1922.

[35] 6 Dec. 1883: DOYC/TM. Since she was cast for a tiny role in *Princess Ida*, she was probably let off with a reprimand, but not kept in the company after 1884.

[36] Sullivan, Diary, 23 Dec. 1883: B/Y. On 26 Dec. Gilbert, Sullivan, Carte, and the Savoy solicitor tried to persuade her to sign an additional clause in her contract, presumably having to do with rehearsals, but she refused and left.

remained in London with his uncle. Furthermore, Sullivan suffered a 'terrible grief' in the sudden paralytic stroke which felled Fred Clay as he walked home from a performance of his own *Golden Ring*. (A year later Clay could walk but not speak; he lived for another five years, and at his private funeral Sullivan was one of the chief mourners. Gilbert evidently did not attend.)

Gilbert's distraction was his new house, 19 Harrington Gardens, which was not ready until late in the year. Beatrix Potter, who lived in the Boltons, wrote in her journal that his house was 'said to contain twenty-six bedrooms with a bath-room to each (fancy twenty-six burst waterpipes). It is a very handsome house with its marble court, but I should doubt the comfort of the little latticed-windows.'[37] (There were only twelve bedrooms, counting the servants', and four bathrooms— although in a private house four bathrooms were indeed a luxury.)

Sullivan had already been taken over it a second time and found it 'very original, comfortable & beautiful'. Original it was indeed. Designed by Ernest George, its gable still rises step after step to a crowning model of Sir Humphrey Gilbert's ship *The Squirrel*; squirrels decorate a pair of the steps, the entire front producing an effect both fantastic and curiously domestic. No. 19, electrically lit, had a telephone, double-glazing, and a ceiling-high alabaster-hood chimney-piece. The oak stair is carved in a Dutch fashion with hounds emerging from tendrils, while a legend over the dining-room door tells guests: 'All hope abandon, ye who enter here,' and yet he did not lose his cook! The drawing-room boasts Puck's lines, 'And those things do best please me | That befal preposterously.' It was, in short, a Gilbertian house.

As the new year of 1884 began, final rehearsals of *Princess Ida* went on. Mary Anderson, invited to one, wrote to William Winter that it was great fun 'to watch the anxiety of Gilbert & Sullivan . . . they had been there for some time & were evidently hungry and when they were offered sandwiches to see them take a tremendous mouthful and in midst of a *chew* to stop and yell at the ballet was better than any farce I ever saw'.[38]

After two dress rehearsals, one lasting seven and the other eight hours, Sullivan was seized with excruciating neck and shoulder pain. Nevertheless, fortified by morphia and black coffee, he arrived at the

---

[37] *The Journal of Beatrix Potter from 1881 to 1897*, transcribed L. Linder (London: Frederick Warne & Co. Ltd., 1966), 58.

[38] 5 Jan. 1884: Folger Y.c.61 (51b). There is no ballet *per se* in *Princess Ida*; Anderson probably meant the chorus.

theatre on 5 January, conducted the brilliant opening performance (which ran very late), took his bow with Gilbert, and fainted.[39] It took him nearly a month to recover, after which he left for the continent.

The new opera, particularly the music, was well received, even though critics noticed that much of the blank verse dialogue came from Gilbert's earlier burlesque of Tennyson. In fact, some excitement and amusement were caused by the presence of a Tennysonian figure in the audience. He proved, however, to be H. J. Lincoln, the music critic of the *Daily News*, who 'makes up very successfully after the unkempt bard', according to the *World*.

Even though women's colleges had been founded by this time, Gilbert was not quite prepared to take Tennyson's pro-feminist princess completely at her own word. Moreover, the whole subject of women's education had now become as hackneyed as comic weeklies could make it. The satirist therefore encountered an almost insuperable problem in technique. It was his habit to show the fallacious or absurd bases of what his contemporaries took seriously. Yet the subject of a female college offered no real fallacy in itself, while a great many Victorian males took it anything but seriously. For instance, a reviewer in *Ashore and Afloat* complained that in a burlesque one expects everything to be topsy-turvy, whereas Tennyson's world was topsy-turvy to begin with. Gilbert therefore could neither attack the thing itself successfully nor expose popular misconceptions of it. Consequently, there are fewer flashes of Gilbertian unconventionality in this opera.

Some critics admired this change in tone, preferring 'Gilbert the beautiful to Gilbert the cynical' as did the *Sunday Times*. Yet there were regrets for the lack of 'smartness' and 'wild fun'. The *Figaro* even reported that some frustrated galleryites called for a hornpipe when King Gama's sons appeared.

If *Princess Ida* lacked 'wild fun', however, it still possessed satire in such numbers as Lady Psyche's song, ending 'Darwinian man, though well-behaved, | At best is only a monkey shaved!' and in Ida's stupid brothers' chorus:

> Bold, and fierce, and strong, ha! ha!
>     For a war we burn,
> With its right or wrong, ha! ha!
>     We have no concern.

[39] Sullivan, Diary, 5 Jan. 1884: B/Y.

Other lyrics were touched with a fanciful elegance or a muted sadness as in 'The world is but a broken toy, | Its pleasure hollow—false its joy'.

Sullivan had been given what he longed for: a straightforward plot, nothing supernatural, and human interest in the story of how a princess finally learns to love her prince. 'Sir Arthur Sullivan should really write a grand opera,' said *Truth*, dismissing Gilbert with 'The task of a librettist is a humble one.' And writing a grand opera was what the knight frequently said he intended to do.

In his closest approach as yet, his numbers were sung on sets which out-splendoured those of *Iolanthe*. The women's academic dresses were velvet brocades over plain undergowns in chocolate and salmon, purple and peach, and other contrasting combinations, with Jessie Bond in primrose and black. ('You have played Melissa admirably,' Gilbert wrote to her.)[40] Hasty though her promotion to princess had been, Leonora Braham delighted the audience with her delivery of blank verse, and Durward Lely as Cyril was praised for his vivacious kissing song. The only complaints about the cast were that Barrington was not peppery enough as King Hildebrand while Grossmith as King Gama was completely absent during the second act of this three-act opera. Gama, the librettist told the actor, was meant for Gilbert himself: 'I thought it my duty to live up to my reputation.'[41]

On 26 January 1884 *Comedy and Tragedy* at the Lyceum joined Gilbert's *Princess Ida*, already running at the Savoy, and *The Palace of Truth*, revived at the newly opened Prince's Theatre. Based on a story of the same name, published in Clement Scott's collection *The Stage Door*, this tense little drama is dominated by Clarice, an eighteenth-century actress, persecuted by the amorous Duc d'Orléans. She has married an aristocratic soldier, D'Aulnay, who turns actor for her sake, and who at last succeeds in challenging the duke at a supper party contrived for that purpose. As her husband and would-be lover fight in the garden, Clarice improvises first a comic, then a tragic, recitation to keep her guests from knowing what is happening outside. Hearing a cry, however, she becomes distraught in earnest while her unwitting guests applaud her wonderful acting. Her husband enters, having fatally wounded his opponent. (Dramatic, but not historical!)

For the most part, first-night reviewers preferred Miss Anderson's comedy to her tragedy; *Under the Clock* said she relapsed into her American twang, but forgave her for her intense power. First appearing

[40] 19 Jan. 1884: PML.
[41] G. Grossmith, 'Recollections of Sir W. S. Gilbert', *Bookman*, 40 (July 1911), 162.

in an amber robe, diamonds blazing on throat and hands, she was indeed beautiful, as she read her bitter lines:

I am an actress—by law proscribed, by the Church excommunicated! While I live women gather their skirts about them as I pass. When I die I am to be buried, as dogs are buried, in unholy ground. In the mean time, I am the recognized prey of the spoiler—

A mild controversy arose because the designer, Lewis Wingfield, had not powdered Anderson's hair, which was dressed in a tower of auburn curls. Nevertheless, she wrote to Winter that *Comedy and Tragedy* was a great success, people waiting three or four hours for admission to the pit or gallery.[42] In 1890 the sculptor Alfred Gilbert (no relation) was so deeply impressed that he went night after night and eventually used Gilbert's title for a work of his own.[43]

Miss Anderson played Clarice until 5 April, closing then only because she refused to appear on stage during Holy Week. Thereafter Gilbert's play became part of her repertoire in England and the United States, and she opened her second Lyceum season with it, later in 1884. Once again, Gilbert was charged with borrowing a play from the French in spite of the praise for the dramatic vigour of his dialogue. As usual he wrote to the newspapers, saying his play had been constructed years earlier and offered first to Miss Litton, who felt she could not act so strong a role as Clarice.

Scarcely had he time to relax after staging *Comedy and Tragedy* than Miss Fortescue needed his help. She and Lord Garmoyle had come to the opening of *Princess Ida* and seemed very much in love, while for months, comic papers had been enthusiastic over her exchange of perihood for a peer's son. Yet in late January Lord Garmoyle broke their engagement. No doubt Gilbert was one of the first to learn this, and he arranged for her to play Dorothy in a revival of *Dan'l Druce* at the Court Theatre in March. He also sent her to his current solicitors, Bolton & Mote, and very likely counselled her to sue for breach of promise. Being, as Sullivan said, somewhat *emancipiste*, Miss Fortescue did sue in spite of still loving the egregious Garmoyle, who had almost immediately left England to travel in the East.

Newspapers and theatre periodicals which had sympathized with the forsaken young woman, now were angry when she proposed to continue

[42] 1 Feb. 1884: Folger Y.c.61 (90). Anderson added that Clement Scott had treated her shamefully and was rumoured to have taken a large bribe from an English actor to denigrate her. The bribe seems unlikely.

[43] R. Dorment, *Alfred Gilbert* (New Haven: Yale University Press, 1985), 131.

her career. Gilbert was drawn into—or entered wilfully—a correspondence in the *Era* defending the actress, but newspaper paragraphs continued until the case reached the courts in November, when Lord Garmoyle was still away. He did not defend, and with the £10,000 she received, Miss Fortescue founded a theatre company, which toured for many years, often performing works by Gilbert. Although her career there had been brief, she always thought of herself as 'an old Savoyard', and Gilbert was friendly to her till the day of his death.

Gilbert was also having his first real difficulties with Sullivan. On 29 January, before leaving for the continent, the composer told Carte he would write no more for the Savoy. In spite of this, two months later Carte notified him that audiences for *Princess Ida* were dwindling and they would probably need a new opera next autumn. Therefore he was giving both Sullivan and Gilbert their contractual six months' notice to produce one. Sullivan, now in Brussels, refused again, saying he would write to Gilbert about it when he returned.

This was a mistake on Sullivan's part, for Carte, obviously disturbed and worried, told Gilbert, who was surprised and hurt by learning Sullivan's decision second-hand. He wrote immediately on 30 March, reminding his colleague that their five-year agreement with Carte (which still had four years to run) required that they supply a new opera on six months' notice; should they fail to do so 'we are liable with him for any losses that may result from our default'. Gilbert had already made progress on a new libretto; he supposed he had written twice to Sullivan about it, and was waiting only for the latter's approval of the plot and musical situations: 'is it acting fairly towards me to allow me to devote so much of my valuable time to the construction of a libretto, having made up your mind, all the while, that nothing will induce you to set it to music when it is written?'[44]

Sullivan replied that he had come to the end of his tether. 'My tunes are in danger of becoming mere repetitions of my former pieces, my concerted movements are getting to possess a strong family likeness and I have rung all the changes possible in the way of variety of rhythm.' He asked again for 'a story of human interest and probability' and denied Gilbert had told him anything about the new libretto.[45] Strangely enough, Sullivan evidently did not consider that their last opera had possessed 'human interest', even , at times, some degree of tenderness.

What Gilbert was offering now, however, did not. It was a sketch

[44] PML. Later, Gilbert conceded he might have misremembered the letters.
[45] 1 Apr. 1884: PML.

libretto Sullivan had rejected before *Iolanthe* and which he called 'the lozenge plot', so understandably dear to Gilbert's heart. Consequently he was both hurt and angry:

When you tell me that your desire is that I shall write a libretto in which the humorous words will come in a humorous situation, and in which a tender or dramatic situation will be treated tenderly and dramatically, you teach me the ABC of my profession. It is inconceivable that any sane author should ever write otherwise than as you propose I should write in future.[46]

In reply, Sullivan wrote a long, carefully considered letter, going so far as to say there was much he liked in the new piece, but more he disliked. It would, he insisted, remind everyone of *The Sorcerer*. 'After 20 years' hard work in my career, I am not going to depart from a principle I have always acted upon, viz., never to force myself to try to do that which I feel I cannot do well.' He would like to do a piece along the lines of *Pygmalion and Galatea* or *The Wicked World*, for instance, and would telephone Gilbert as soon as he came back to London.[47]

A long face-to-face conversation, however, produced a complete deadlock, and on 12 April Gilbert wrote that he still could not 'discover in what the subject I proposed is defective'. He was anxious and wanted it settled without giving in. 'What do you say to this?' he asked. 'Write your next opera to another man's libretto. I will willingly retire for one turn. . . . It may be . . . that a new man with a new style will start a new train of musical ideas.'[48]

But who was there? Burnand was really a burlesque writer, even though he fancied himself as a librettist; Stephens had been badly received except for *Billie Taylor*; Leigh was dead, and H. B. Farnie was adroit in adaptation rather than original work. When Gilbert offered to revise his proposed piece to include a serious and tender interest, Sullivan agreed to read it—foolishly, because he knew nothing would make him swallow the lozenge.

Gilbert had supposed all was now clear, but on the sixteenth he had a tooth pulled: 'my head & face have been aching all day,' he wrote, 'to that extent that I can't collect my thoughts sufficiently to sketch out Act 2'.[49] Nevertheless, he managed to make changes in the plot along the lines he believed Sullivan had agreed to, only to be told in Sullivan's letter of 2 May that he could not accept even a revised plot. On 3 May Gilbert answered with reluctance: 'I cannot consent to construct

---

[46] 4 Apr. 1884: PML.      [47] Draft letter, 7 Apr. 1884: PML.      [48] PML.
[49] PML.

another plot for the next opera.'[50] The wheel had come full circle: Sullivan's refusal to write for the Savoy had become Gilbert's refusal.

On 5 May Gilbert wrote a six-page, carefully reasoned letter, setting out the steps in their disagreement. He remembered, however, that Sullivan had agreed to the lozenge plot in unmistakable terms; Sullivan remembered the opposite. Gilbert objected to the possibility of writing libretto after libretto 'on approval' until he hit upon one which pleased Sullivan, but he was willing, if Carte was, to let the composer set a grand opera. He would even accept 'the subordinate position which the librettist of such an opera must necessarily occupy' if that would help Sullivan. A grand opera, of course, could not be performed at the Savoy—it had neither the company nor the audience for that kind of piece; so now Gilbert faced the termination of a partnership 'which I hoped would have existed in some form or other—grave or gay, as the case might be—for many years to come'.[51] Sullivan answered, 'correcting Gilbert's erroneous statements' (as he said), and evidently accepting the end of their collaboration.

But it did not terminate. Neither really wanted to divorce himself from the other; so Gilbert wrote to ask if Sullivan would set a plot without the supernatural. 'I gladly undertake to set it without further discussing the matter, or asking what the subject is to be,' Sullivan replied.[52]

It was rather difficult for Gilbert to begin again: 'The old plot took so firm a hold on me that I cannot get it out of my mind.'[53] He suggested they revive *The Sorcerer* and *Trial by Jury* after *Princess Ida*. Although he thought it would take a month to get over the effects of the lozenge, it was actually less than two weeks before he conceived a new possibility, prompted perhaps by the Japanese sword on his wall, not by the opportune falling of that sword as legend has it. By 20 May he told Sullivan the first idea of what would be *The Mikado*; 'I think the subject excellent—funny,' recorded the composer.

Out of their first serious quarrel had come what is generally considered their happiest opera. Yet it was not completely a quarrel—their letters, while firmly committed for or against the points in question, still contained complimentary sentences, praising each other as composer or librettist. Sullivan was wrong to think he could break a contract by a simple refusal, but right in rejecting Gilbert's complex scenario, not because of the supernatural, but because it was too complicated for audiences who had trouble with *Foggerty's Fairy*.

[50] PML.    [51] PML.    [52] 8 May 1884: PML.    [53] 9 May 1884: PML.

Gilbert went off yachting for four months, writing first to Burnand, who had asked him for an article for *Punch*: 'I am simply lost in astonishment that you who have for so many years, systematically decried my work, should think it deserving of insertion in the columns of your paper.'[54] On the other side of the Atlantic, Lillie Langtry's performance of a life-coloured Galatea was attracting large audiences, especially because of the Jersey Lily's own life-colouring.

Gilbert missed the explosion at the Junior Carlton Club, when an incompetent dynamiter mistook its tradesmen's entrance for that of Adair House next door, currently occupied by the Intelligence Department of the War Office. The club's kitchen was unusable, its ironwork shattered, and some of its servants injured. Windows were broken upstairs, but none of the members of the club was hurt. A second mistaken blast hit Sir William Watkin Wynn's house nearby, but at the last explosion, the dynamiters finally hit the target they intended—Great Scotland Yard.

By September, however, Gilbert had returned in time to attend a thought-reading session at the Savoy Theatre, given by Stuart Cumberland. Amid applause he was invited to the stage, where he admitted he was 'too hard-headed' for Cumberland's purposes. The mind-reader was nevertheless able to read the number on a banknote correctly at the second try and to reconstruct a murder he had asked Gilbert to think of committing.

*Princess Ida* lasted only ten months and was replaced by the proposed double-bill on 11 October. Sullivan conducted on the first night. New and elaborate stage business now closed *Trial* with a quick trick change to a transformation scene, where the Plaintiff mounted the Judge's back *à la* fairy. Act 2 of *The Sorcerer* had been somewhat revised in music and text, and boasted in Lely and Braham much better interpreters of Alexis and Aline than Bentham and May had been. Critics had forgotten how good it was, some even proclaiming it the best in the series. L.T. in the *Daily Telegraph*, however, could not resist a flick at both Gilbert and the audience in finding that 'the absence of true sympathy is missed but by a few'. Encore after encore was demanded until *Trial* did not begin until 11 p.m. In the interval, 'the gods' sang, 'We won't go home until morning.' Finally Gilbert and Sullivan were given two curtain-calls, and the *Topical Times* commented, 'Mr. Gilbert has a heavenly smile, which he evidently keeps for first nights.'

[54] 27 May 1884: PML.

Perhaps he displayed it at the Mansion House a few nights later, when the Lord Mayor gave a dinner for the new Society of Authors which Walter Besant had helped bring into being. Gilbert responded to the toast of 'The Drama'. Hearing sometime later that a fellow author, the dramatist Robert Reece, was in financial difficulties, Gilbert sympathetically sent a cheque for £50 to Wilson Barrett, who was collecting money for Reece's relief. Gilbert asked, however, that he be put down as giving only £20 and the rest ascribed to 'any initials your fancy may suggest. Everything I do is so misrepresented, that I am afraid it will be ascribed to swagger if I give more than that sum.'[55]

Sullivan dined with the Gilberts on 20 November, and the collaborators went through the first act of their next opera; 'made several important suggestions, with which Gilbert agreed,' Sullivan wrote rather smugly in his diary. Whether the suggestions are part of the finished *Mikado* is impossible to say.

[55] 10 Dec. 1884: Harry Ransom Humanities Research Center/The University of Texas at Austin.

# 13

A Short Chapter on Method

I never scamp my work
Gilbert to J. S. Clarke
(16 Dec. 1876)

WHILE Gilbert writes and revises *The Mikado*, let us consider his method of composition and stagecraft on the threshold of his greatest success.

To the Victorian stage he had brought an original mind and a passion for thoroughness and authenticity; a perception of human limitations, both those which are inevitable and those which can be overcome; a capacity for playing seriously with words and ideas; some observation of practical but innovative stagecraft; a determination to make drama once again a major art form while simultaneously reforming the stage; an energetic mind and a temperament able to enforce the production of what that mind conceived. If his originality sometimes became eccentricity, his pattern repetitive, his mind dogmatic, and his temperament peremptory, that should not deter us from recognizing in his work the satire of an iconoclast who, paradoxically, was not a revolutionary.

In a day when closet drama was extolled and popular playwrights needed to be prolific to supply a voracious stage, works for the theatre were generally considered inferior, even trivial, compositions. Indeed, Gilbert's rapid rise was in some measure owing to the fact that 'he has given us plays . . . which we keep by us and read,' as the *Era* pointed out (28 January 1872). He himself thought that dramatic composition did not require 'the highest order of intellect', but demanded 'shrewdness of observation, a nimble brain, a faculty for expressing oneself concisely, a sense of balance, both in the construction of plots & in the construction of sentences'.[1]

Of all the Victorian dramatists, Gilbert cared most for form, which he arrived at by days and nights of experiment: 'I only write after

---

[1] Draft of Speech: WSG/BL Add MS 49,293.

11 p.m. when everyone has gone to bed,' Gilbert told Frank Holl, the painter,[2] and he always used a goose quill pen. Like Sullivan, Gilbert usually worked until 2 or 3 a.m., assisted by cigars (a dozen and a half a day) and a 'peg' or two. He preferred his own room, for, if he tried to work elsewhere, 'pictures and things distract my attention when I look up'.[3] In later life he wrote stretched out in a leather chair, his feet on a stool, his manuscript in his lap. Then he smoked less and drank lemon squash.

He might derive the idea for a play from 'A chance remark in conversation, a little accidental incident, a trifling object'—any of which might start a train of thought.[4] Out of these stimuli developed the 'motives', as the Victorians called themes of his librettos and plays. Gilbert told the *Pall Mall Gazette* (16 May 1884) that there were many ways of starting a plot and that he had tried them all. If, for instance, he occasionally intended to exploit a certain actor, his first consideration was character and the variety of 'dramatic lights' in which the actor could appear to best advantage. 'If I have a distinctive doctrine to urge upon the audience, the principal question to consider is the special constellation of characters which will best exploit my purpose.' Often he began with the last act ('then, probably he puts it first, and so gets it all wrong again,' said *Punch* in one of its Gilbert-baiting moods).

As the actual composition of the play began, Gilbert allowed the idea or plot to mould itself 'in the odd hours of the day or night, until it becomes coherent'. At first this moulding took place 'in cabs and railway carriages, aboard ship, or during quiet strolls in the Park';[5] then it moved to paper, occasionally to loose sheets, but more often to plot-books—the notebooks in which Gilbert jotted down ideas, sketches for plots, lyrics, bits of dialogue, and finally the successive drafts of the scenario.[6] More than his contemporaries, he adhered naturally to the unities of French drama, including that of the single plot.

[2] 22 Nov. 1886: PML. In the 1870s when he was writing for other theatres as well as the Opera Comique, Gilbert also worked by day, mostly in the morning, and in summer often wrote in a tent erected in his garden.

[3] Interview given to New York newspapers on Gilbert's arrival in Oct. 1879.

[4] Excerpt from unidentified interview, 21 July 1893, repr. in P. Fitzgerald, *The Savoy Opera and the Savoyards* (London: Chatto & Windus, 1899), 114. In 'A Stage Play' (1873), Gilbert gave a craftsman's description of how a three-act comedy should be written.

[5] 'W. S. Gilbert Ashore', n.d., unidentified newspaper cutting.

[6] All plot-books referred to in this chapter are in WSG/BL, except for the *Iolanthe* plot-book which is in PML; some excerpts from it appear in L. Baily, *The Gilbert and Sullivan Book* (rev. edn.; London: Spring Books, 1966), 226–9.

He doodled Babishly while he paused for thought, and his own self-caricature often peers sternly or perplexedly from a margin or verso. Some of his notes were very brief, such as a one-page fragment about a kidnapped princess for whom a deaf-and-dumb girl is substituted; or the plight of three old maids in charge of a bouncing romp; or the never-developed paradoxical situation in which a widow tries to keep her second husband from knowing she was married before, while at the same time she tries to prevent her first husband's friends from learning that she has married again. Sometimes the note sets out a variation of Gilbert's lifelong preoccupation with the true versus the false, as in a late plot-book where a fairy gives a beloved mortal some coins which make all sham things real.

Usually, however, Gilbert began by developing an outline, which often resembled a legal brief. He worked it out for several, often many, pages, successively breaking off and starting over again as new situations or complications occurred to him. If he began with characters, they too passed through a series of modifications in which possibilities were examined, revised, or discarded in recurrent transmutations which connected the final plot to the original brief by a complex associative and logical process. Ultimately there might be little or no discernible resemblance between the germ of a play and its final shape. For instance, *Iolanthe*, as we know it, begins only after twenty-eight pages of experimentation.

First, Gilbert posited a fairy sent to earth on a mission, who married a solicitor (a faint reminiscence of the story version of *The Wicked World*, and 'The Fairy Curate'). Both are banished from fairyland. Beginning again, Gilbert made the solicitor a barrister, who is elected king of fairyland, but can still practise law on earth where the fairies influence the jury. He becomes famous for his successful defence of witches.

In a few pages 'A body of fairies have come to earth. They have fallen in love with the Northern Circuit. First act ends with marriage, rejoicings. The second act, complicated consequences of this.' Gilbert immediately changed this situation to 'Fairies, on earth, see with distress the amount of misery caused by legal proceedings, politics and religious strife. They determine to fascinate & marry leading counsel—ministry.' Eventually he sketched a utopian situation in which the fairies establish a millennium and 'all professions that flourish on human weakness wither & die'.

213

The bar are more affected than anybody
They combine against fairy rule—
Eventually fairies marry bar—
Human happiness secured thereby

This fairy government is obviously an after-image of the politicized *Happy Land*, but with the fairies in intelligent control.

Gilbert left the plot but continued to gnaw his satiric bone in a proto-Shavian 'Bill for abolition of all Existing Institutions, having for its object the reduction of Civilization to its first principles'. Meanwhile, he found his way to the final version of *Iolanthe* by changing the fairy's barrister-son to an Arcadian shepherd and by replacing the Northern Circuit and the ministry with the House of Lords, the fairies now influencing legislation instead of verdicts.

Oblique though this approach may seem, it is essentially logical and systematic, and very clearly reflects Gilbert's legal turn of mind and training. In these early drafts, for example, characters are rarely given names, but are designated by numerals or letters of the alphabet:

Perhaps Nymph A is in love with mortal & employs Nymph B to take her form & make love to him on her behalf. Nymph A is bashful—that is why she employs Nymph B. Nymph B assumes form of Nymph A & makes outrageous love to mortal.

This alphabetical nomenclature continues into finished works such as 'See how the Fates their gifts allot' in *The Mikado*, where 'A is happy—B is not. | Yet B is worthy, I dare say, | Of more prosperity than A!'

Gilbert seldom wrote dialogue until he had settled his plot as much as possible, although he often indicated the lines along which dialogue might proceed. These skeleton conversations, which he called 'epitomes', are generally brief:

Enter Toto. She is depressed. She has dreamed that she was married—to a young and beautiful Prince Doro. Of course it was only a dream but still a marriage is a marriage & Barberini will be her husband while she is awake & Doro her husband when she is asleep.

Before going further with dialogue, Gilbert customarily wrote out his play as a short story, including epitomes of conversation. Then he decided where the act divisions were to fall, if he had not already done so, and modified the story where necessary. He put the narrative aside for perhaps a fortnight, after which he rewrote it without referring to the first version. Then he compared the two, noted omissions and additions carefully, put both versions aside, rewrote again, and repeated the process—perhaps a dozen times.

When at last Gilbert addressed himself to the actual dialogue and lyrics to be spoken or sung on stage, he might begin writing anywhere, revising repeatedly in order 'to ascertain in how few words my full meaning could be adequately expressed'.[7] In the penultimate version of *The Mikado*, for instance, Pitti-Sing's first speech to Nanki-Poo reads: 'and we've been shut up in a stupid old school, learning ridiculous lessons that will never be the least good to us afterwards.' Gilbert reduced this to 'and we've been at school'. Nevertheless, his dialogue, however tersely expressed, is essentially deliberate, balanced, and formal, a verbal order imposed upon the disorderly ego drives of his comic characters.

Gilbert composed verse more rapidly than prose and with fewer revisions. In his notebooks, many lyrics appear at once in what is essentially their finished form, and many changes involve the substitution of a new line altogether more often than they show him experimenting with individual words. Occasionally, however, Gilbert thought out a lyric on paper, as in this very sketchy draft in the *Iolanthe* plot-book, reproduced here in part with his crossings-out and writings-in:

> <pre>                  born              bank
>       A gentleman may break his ~~neck~~
>                 And all his creditors
>       ~~His bank~~, ~~his~~ and ~~all his~~
>                       born
>       A gentleman ~~may~~ may break his heart
>       ~~A gentleman may~~
>                     & theres an end on't
>                        may
>       But a gentleman ~~must~~ not break his word
>                    Though all the world depend on't
>       A gentleman born may forfeit life
>             For mutiny,        or treason
>       A gentleman born may leave his wife
>                ~~There~~   For many a wholesome reason
>       A gentleman born may ~~break~~ his troth
>             And              neatly
>       But if a gentleman ~~may not~~ break his oath
>             His character's gone completely</pre>

---

[7] To George Bainton, 24 Sept. 1888: PML.

His extraordinary metrical skill which enabled him to express the same content in a variety of metres and rhyme schemes, was so regular in its stresses that a composer could treat his lyrics in a variety of ways and they would still be singable. 'Never a weak syllable or a halting foot,' Sullivan said in an interview with the *New York Mirror* (3 October 1885). In verse, Gilbert's straightforward syntax and meaningful content carried singers along. He himself held the unfashionable view that

English is (next to Italian) the very best of all European languages for singing purposes, provided that the song-writer will take into consideration the requirements of the singer & reject words & phrases that involve a harsh collocation of consonants & a succession of open vowels.[8]

Gilbert's piecemeal approach to dramatic writing made it difficult for him to work up an intense emotion (although he might do single speeches well), but it was well suited to librettos, to the farce of ideas, and to satiric comedy in the timing of which he was unsurpassed. His technique did not urge him forward to fuse his materials in the heat of composition, but the unremitting labour of his file-like intelligence produced a balance and, at its best, a perfection of form in which the structure composed of innumerable separately conceived and polished parts gave the effect of inevitable unity.

The physical embodiment of his work, too, was in a form as perfect as he could make it after he had gained control, and at the Savoy a very tight control, of his theatre. 'The supreme importance of careful rehearsing is not sufficiently recognized in England,' Gilbert had written in his privately printed preface to *Pygmalion and Galatea*: 'As far as my experience shows anything, it shows that when my pieces have been carefully rehearsed they have succeeded, and when they have been insufficiently rehearsed they have failed.'

He believed that any author incapable of directing his own plays was at a great disadvantage and that his stage directions were as much a part of the play as the dialogue itself. For Gilbert, no manager had a right 'to interpose between me and the realization of my ideas'.[9] Consequently, his contracts and stipulations included provisos that he was to be paramount in stage management in the widest sense. In short, he was a man of broader practical theatrical experience than any other important

---

[8] Letter to William Archer, 5 Oct. 1904: Archer Corr./BL Add. MS 45,291.
[9] Letter to John Hare, n.d. Gilbert made the same point in a letter to Hare, 30 Jan. 1878: WSG/BL Add. MS 49,338.

dramatist—for not even Shakespeare designed costumes for his own plays. Gilbert often did, and supervised the sets as well.

This passion for control over every aspect of production arose both from his temperament and from the condition of the Victorian stage as Gilbert found it, and as he had criticized it in his *Fun* reviews. Even in the 1870s a London manager could still tell a playwright that his place was not on the stage as director, but in a box to watch the performance and make alterations suggested by the stage-manager,[10] that stage-manager sometimes being a hybrid prompter, actor, and call-boy. A quarter of a century later, Gilbert wrote to Henry Arthur Jones to say that he would gladly join any united attempt 'having for its object the annihilation of the present dictum—that when an actress hires a piece she can alter it as she pleases'.[11]

At the Savoy, Gilbert therefore preferred to use relative or absolute novices, who had 'no bad tricks to unlearn'.[12] On these he could vigorously impose his own style (which *Punch* unpleasantly described as a kind of marionette-like accuracy). Savoy rehearsals began six weeks before opening night, although changes had to be made and remade during Gilbert's shifts of lyrics and Sullivan's last minute composition. The cast rehearsed a new opera from 11 a.m. to 4 p.m.—'and we are very rigid, too,' D'Oyly Carte told a reporter from the *New York Sun* (26 July 1879). He himself usually attended, with a basket of business papers beside him. Of course, the cast was generally playing the 'old' opera at night as well.

Gilbert worked painstakingly, spending hours in practising tiny movements and facial expressions until Sullivan complained that the chorus was worn out by having to repeat the music constantly while an exit or entrance was worked out.[13] Reporters liked to watch Gilbert rehearse, and they give a picture of him as surprisingly graceful in movement and gesture, never still for a moment. 'When he was not speaking, he was acting; when he was not acting, he was speaking, and he was nearly always doing both.'[14] Scorning the director's chair placed for him, he was among the chorus, showing them how to hitch their trousers for a song of the sea, or demonstrating embraces to the

---

[10] R. Reece, 'Stage-Management', *Theatre*, NS 3 (1 Nov. 1879), 207.

[11] 1 July 1899: PML.

[12] 'A Chat with Decima Moore', *Era* (16 Dec. 1893), 11. Decima Moore created the role of Casilda in *The Gondoliers* without previous stage experience, but much coaching from Gilbert.

[13] Letter to Carte, 26 Mar. 1889: DOYC/TM.

[14] 'Gilbert as Stage Manager', *Philadelphia Times* [Mar. 1880].

principals, finishing with his usual comment, 'something like that'.[15] As the *Liverpool Post* observed (9 December 1889), every character on the Savoy stage had first been sketched on that stage by Gilbert in his own person.

Although he had a reputation as a martinet and believed that 'The principle of subordination must be maintained in a theatre as in a regiment,'[16] he was by no means an explosive director. Only wilful stupidity aroused his wrath, and he was sarcastic rather than abusive.[17] He took endless pains to teach actors who were trying to fulfil his instructions and kept them up to the mark after opening night through the reports of his wife, a Savoy *habituée*. There was, however, no compromise on texts of librettos. An actor who introduced an unapproved gag might be fined half a week's salary. Not for Gilbert the inventive comedian who might, like J. L. Toole, delay the action of a play for fifteen minutes while he gave imitations of popular actors.

Since a significant part of the plot, including exposition, and much of the satire, was contained in the lyrics, sung words had to be as clearly articulated as spoken ones. Sullivan might object that his music had to be kept down so that Gilbert's words could be heard, but the dramatist mounted to the topmost gallery and shouted, 'Please, ladies, open your mouths. The poor people who sit up here won't hear.'[18]

Before he commenced work with his cast, Gilbert had already thought out most of their stage positions, movements, and business which did not depend too closely on the music. He used his famous miniature stage with scene models which were sometimes diminutive versions of the full sets, but more often rough scale models, showing essential platforms and physical masses. His 'actors' were little blocks of wood (3 inches high for men, 2½ inches for women), painted in various

---

[15] J. M. Gordon, unpublished memoirs: LG.

[16] Copy of letter to Cairus James, 11 Dec. 1889: DOYC/TM. James, playing Ko-Ko in Touring Co. B, insisted on introducing '*inappropriate, exaggerated and unauthorized* "business" '.

[17] Gilbert's legendary irascibility seems to have been exaggerated for the sake of many a good story; J. M. Gordon, first a singer and then stage director of the company, remembered his losing his temper only once, and even George Grossmith, made nervous by Gilbert's incessant demands for perfection, did not find him abusive. James Wilbraham wrote to the *Morning Leader* (2 June 1911), defending Gilbert as a director: 'he was exceedingly strict at rehearsals . . . but I never heard him make use of bad or even offensive language to the ladies and gentlemen of the Savoy company'. Wilbraham had been with the company for eight of its best years, in the chorus and occasional small parts.

[18] R. A. Flicker in conversation with the author, London, 4 Apr. 1975, quoting the late Herbert Pearce; several actors reported similar incidents.

colours to indicate voice ranges. Manipulating his wooden cast, Gilbert experimented with effects which he sometimes had printed for the actors' use. Very early in his career, he had begun printing his plays 'as manuscript' when it was an innovation to put the full text into the actors' hands. Hitherto, performers, after hearing the whole play read, had only the 'sides' of their own lines and cues to work from.

Although dances were left mainly to John D'Auban to work out, the librettist often specified the type he wanted: 'Now a gavotte perform sedately', for instance, or 'Dance a cachuca'. Gilbert, moreover, still supervised the details. When, for example, D'Auban at a *Mikado* rehearsal showed the girls 'how to run into position and curtsey—with fists closed and index finger up, Gilbert shouted, "No! No! D'Auban, that's a Chinese attitude of the hands and fingers." ' He himself demonstrated 'Japanese' gestures.[19]

Aside from his insistence that comic actors should be serious however absurd their lines, which was his most important contribution to Victorian acting, Gilbert's most innovative staging was probably his treatment of the chorus. Before *Trial by Jury* the conventional chorus of the light musical stage was perfunctory and often parodied. As Burnand wrote in *Alonzo the Brave; or, Faust and the Fair Imogene*:

> Wine, oh! divine, oh! that is the thing
> An Operatic Chorus should sing,
> Wave o'er our heads the cups full of air,
> Action impossible if wine were there.[20]

'They earn their bread by going in a crowd, | To sing their humble sentiments aloud,' a character says in *Dulcamara*.

But although in his burlesques Gilbert accepted this kind of chorus, he soon began to change it from a group of repetitive bystanders to one of participants. For instance, he took as great pains to motivate and arrange chorus entrances and exits as those of leading characters.

I am rather bothered as to how to get the girls chorus on. There are two gangways . . . by which they ought to enter, but that will involve their coming up from *below* the stage—(as though from the level of the water). . . . Could they sing [the barcarole] *under* the stage—someone giving them the time?

he wrote to Sullivan in regard to an 1887 revival of *H.M.S. Pinafore*.[21] He also devised *enchainements* of choral gesture and even wrote words for choristers to say if a babble of sound were necessary.

[19] J. M. Gordon, unpublished memoirs: LG.
[20] (London: Thomas Hailes Lacy, n.d.), 30.   [21] 26 Oct. 1887: PML.

The Gilbertian chorus is tied to plot and satire by its leaders, such as Lords Mountararat and Tolloller or Colonel Calverley, who are also major characters in their own right and/or by secondary, minor leaders such as Celia, Leila, and Fleta. Its members furnish the bodies of confrontation so frequent at the close of Act 1; Major-General Stanley, for instance, surrounded by his daughters, produces a Union Jack while the Pirate King at the head of his band produces a Jolly Roger. Peers and fairies advance alternately on each other, fairies threatening peers with their wands. Without the chorus Katisha could not be silenced, Pooh-Bah's mendacity supported, or Sir Ruthven forced to commit a daily crime. Each member, as the *Licensed Victualler's Mirror* said (3 July 1891), was an actor interested in the progress of the piece.

Finally, the chorus was important to the air of decorum so often significant in Savoy staging. Its members marched 'dignified and stately'; they bowed politely; they begged pardon. 'Everything moved directly and precisely within well-defined limits,' remembered a critic in the *World* (11 December 1906); 'everybody on the stage behaved as if he or she were a person of fastidious breeding. . . . Everybody was trained to look serious, sedate, and demure over the funniest things, and to do them as if they were inevitable.' Such behaviour lent dignity to eccentricity, but it also furnished a box for eccentricity to burst out of— thereby providing that unexpectedness which more than one critic recognized as a peculiarly Gilbertian effect.

Chorus members tended to stay with Gilbert and liked to work with him. The Savoy offered them long stretches of certain employment,[22] although its rehearsals were demanding; James Wilbraham, for example, was a member of the company from 1883 to 1891, mostly as chorister. Gilbert needed the chorus in his own way as much as Sullivan did, and under his tutelage it developed a character which was found nowhere else.

[22] T. C. Davis, 'The Savoy Chorus', *Theatre Notebook*, 44 (1990), 26–38.

# 14

## The Mikado and After

odd suggestions, novel fun, and grotesque caricature
*Era* (21 Mar. 1885)

AS 1884 ended, Gilbert attended rehearsals for the children's matinées of *The Pirates of Penzance*, which, he said over-
enthusiastically, had never before been properly performed. Sullivan,
rather nervous at a dress rehearsal, found the first act a revelation.[1]
Then he went back to composing *The Mikado*. Gilbert, however, began
to prepare for a large party he and Kitty were to give on 14 January. But
first, in remarkably good spirits he made one of the four hundred guests
whom Augustus Harris had invited to the cutting of the Twelfth Night
Baddeley Cake (after chicken and champagne) and to a ball on the
stage of the Drury Lane Theatre. As the actor James Fernandez sliced
the cake with a silver dagger, an unnamed lady allegedly murmured, 'I
wanted that bad(de)ly.'[2]

The great treat which the Gilberts intended to give their guests was
the production of Act 2 of *Patience* in their drawing-room. Sullivan and
Frank Cellier were to play the piano and harmonium, for which a
rehearsal was held on 12 January. Gilbert had fitted up a stage; borrowed scenery from the Savoy; and engaged Grossmith, Temple, Lely,
Miss Fortescue, and others to appear with Sybil Coke, an excellent amateur, as Patience. The fifteenth, cold and snowy, saw a matinée repetition of the performance for a second party.

The rest of January was less satisfactory. Gilbert found himself
embroiled in a newspaper dispute over Burnand's attack on the morality

---

[1] *Lady's Pictorial* (3 Jan. 1885).

[2] 'Midnight Revels at Drury Lane', *Pall Mall Gazette* (7 Jan. 1885), 4. The Baddeley Cake
is served every Twelfth Night, a tradition begun by Robert Baddeley, pastry cook and member
of David Garrick's company, who left £100 to be invested and the interest used to buy an annual
cake for the actors of Drury Lane.

of the stage, 'Behind the Scenes', just published in the *Fortnightly Review*. With surprising readiness to foul his own theatrical nest, Burnand, both of whose wives had been actresses, described the inevitably degrading effect of the stage on young female innocents who attempted to earn their living there. (Daughters of theatrical families, strangely enough, he considered could remain pure in the same atmosphere.)

John Hollingshead, interviewed at once, told the *Pall Mall Gazette* that he himself wanted pretty girls with good figures and stage presence for the Gaiety. If a masher in the audience wanted this too he might come repeatedly to see it. If a lively young girl winked at the stalls, one could not padlock her eyes, said Hollingshead. This so scandalized the *Standard* that it 'went for' him in a long leader.

On the other hand, Gilbert, when asked for immediate comment by the *Daily News*, thought 'semi-nude burlesque' was fortunately on its last legs after nearly destroying a 'charming class of entertainment' in which Mrs Bancroft, for instance, had begun her career. There was little use, Gilbert said, for an author to write a clever burlesque if half-naked women were unable to speak his lines, but blurted them out 'with the manners and accent of kitchen maids'.

This, of course, brought a letter from Hollingshead (*Pall Mall Gazette*, 26 January), pointing out that Gilbert's own burlesque *Robert the Devil* had opened the Gaiety years ago, that every theatre in London had at some time or other been 'a so-called "leg theatre"' (untrue), and that the Gaiety had shown catholic tastes in bringing out Gilbert's first prose comedy, *An Old Score*. Hollingshead ended with an assertion that the Gaiety's songs and dances were as inoffensive as Gilbert's own and his chorus (as distinct from his showgirls) was drawn, with very few exceptions, from the same class. By now the combatants seemed to have forgotten Burnand. Gilbert read Hollingshead's letter on the same day that he wrote to E. Bruce Hindle, who had just published a paper, 'W. S. Gilbert, Playwright and Humorist', and had sent him a copy. The dramatist was not in a good mood, and Hindle harped on a string which made his temper vibrate. Sitting down to answer, he admitted the fairness of the article in general, but added:

I must ask you to forgive me if I show some hesitation in accepting the critical utterances of a gentleman who concludes that an author must necessarily be destitute of 'tender-heartedness & soul' because he writes a play in which personages who are deficient in these qualities are held up to ridicule & contempt.

Your paper is an excellent example of off-hand criticism—often right—often wrong—but always cock-sure.[3]

On the next night, 27 January, the first chorus rehearsal for *The Mikado* took place; Gilbert attended it as a matter of course, and the last weeks of preparation now began. Almost immediately Sullivan learned that his sister-in-law Charlotte had died in Los Angeles where she and her children had gone with her shiftless second husband. Plunging into further composition, scoring, and rehearsing, Sullivan could not leave for America. Furthermore, he had been made conductor of the Philharmonic Society in late February and even left the end of a dress rehearsal at the Savoy to prepare for a Philharmonic Concert. He also cut the twenty-ninth anniversary dinner of the Dramatic and Musical Sick Fund, held at Willis's Rooms on Ash Wednesday (18 February). Gilbert, Carte, and Grossmith attended, however; John Hare presided, and the 270 guests included the Earl of Kilmorey, Sir Frederick Leighton, and Dr Morell Mackenzie. Afterwards Grossmith, Hermann Vezin, and others took part in a musical and dramatic smoking concert, which compensated to some extent for the disappointing food.

Sullivan sent word that he was indisposed although his diary shows he was scoring. Gilbert therefore responded alone to a joint toast of 'Music and the Drama', proposed by Comyns Carr, who amusingly remarked that the librettist had now decided to write the music and Sullivan the words of their next opera. Again Gilbert commented adversely on managers who preferred to import French plays. Continuing the theme of his 1879 article 'A Hornpipe in Fetters' (*Era Almanack*), he admitted that English plays lacked strong dramatic interest because they had to be written to be morally suitable for a hypothetical 15-year-old girl, so easily and unnecessarily alarmed that English plays could contain nothing which might make her blush. Although Gilbert did not object to her and even considered her a wholesome influence, he believed that her effect on English drama should be frankly admitted.[4]

No doubt most of his audience had read Burnand's *Fortnightly* article—in fact, Carr referred to an 'authority' who recently criticized the stage. Gilbert's emphasis on the moral nature of English drama could not help but be taken as an oblique reply. But it was more, for in it

[3] PML. Hindle wrote again, explaining his viewpoint, and Gilbert, without agreeing, sent him a 'courteous & kindly letter' in return.

[4] Gilbert's speech is given in full in 'The Dramatic and Musical Sick Fund', *Era* (21 Feb. 1885), 14.

Gilbert demonstrated the conflict within his own responses—the increasing strait-lacedness which made him welcome the hypothetical girl was set against the wish to have all emotions open to him as a dramatist.

It was now less than a month to the première of *The Mikado*, and Sullivan continued to compose until the night before the dress rehearsal. The company, rehearsing all day and playing a double bill at night, were exhausted. 'Sing the music with the same ease on the first night as you'll sing it after a hundred nights,' Sullivan told them. 'You're presuming, of course, that the opera will run for a hundred nights?' Gilbert remarked facetiously.[5]

On 11 March the collaborators had a row about stage business, and Gilbert evidently made some changes for the sake of the music. The second dress rehearsal on 13 March, however, went very smoothly except for Grossmith's feeling ill and nervous, which also hampered his performance in Act 1 on opening night. At the last moment Gilbert decided to cut the Mikado's solo, 'A more humane Mikado'. In principle he was right, for Ko-Ko, the Lord High Executioner, also has a punishments' song, but in practice he was utterly wrong, for the Mikado's punishments are more ingenious than Ko-Ko's, while his refrain

> My object all sublime
> I shall achieve in time—
> To let the punishment fit the crime,

was to prove the most often-quoted passage for more than a century. The chorus and Richard Temple, who saw his only solo vanishing, pleaded for its retention, and Gilbert let it stay. Soon thereafter he moved Ko-Ko's 'little list' further toward the beginning so that more time would elapse between the two solos.

Finally, on a misty Saturday, 14 March 1885, Sullivan wrote in his diary that the new opera was received 'with every sign of real success— a most brilliant house [including the Duke and Duchess of Edinburgh]—tremendous reception'. A huge crowd had queued for hours, waiting for the cheaper seats, and many departed angrily when there was no more room.

The opera which the audience saw was not quite in its present form. Gilbert had verbal changes still to make, as well as repositioning lyrics. Yum-Yum's 'The sun whose rays' was at first in Act 1 where she had no breath to sing it; it had to be moved to Act 2. At first this number was

---

[5] J. M. Gordon, in 'New Stories of Gilbert and Sullivan', *Strand*, 70 (Dec. 1925), 647.

not even intended for the soprano, but for Jessie Bond, the Pitti-Sing, as Gilbert's holograph copy shows.[6] It is basically a soubrette's song, and transferred to Yum-Yum it made her seem more assertive, as she sings, 'We really know our worth, | The sun and I!' Go-To, for some time unnamed, was hastily invented because Frederick Bovill, the Pish-Tush, could not reach the lowest notes of the madrigal in Act 2. (Simply a voice, Go-To does not appear in revivals if Pish-Tush has a sufficiently deep register.)

Although at first Gilbert had intended to set his libretto in the England of Henry VIII, he very rapidly saw the visual possibilities of *japonerie* as popularized by the Aesthetic Movement. So, retaining the idea of an executioner having to cut off his own head, he moved the scene to a never-never Japan.[7] There the upside-down laws he invented—for instance, girls are not of age till they are 50—could seem at home, while the satire under its Japanese robes was really directed against the English themselves, even down to Pooh-Bah's allusion to Professor Tyndall's atom.

Gilbert was fortunate in that a Japanese exhibition opened at Knightsbridge on 10 January, where, under the aegis of Tannaker Buhicrosan, a Japanese village was re-created: its hundred inhabitants going about their characteristic occupations in houses, shops, and a Buddhist temple. They made fans, lacquer, and pottery, wrestled, and performed a Japanese play. From this exhibition came little maids and an interpreter to demonstrate Japanese gait, giggles, and fanmanship to the Savoy cast. Further help, very likely including the genuine Japanese song 'Miya sama', was provided by Algernon Mitford, formerly Secretary of the British Legation at Tokyo and later Lord Redesdale.[8] 'I must thank you again for your invaluable help,' Gilbert wrote to him three days after the first performance. 'I have received two letters from Europeans recently resident in Japan (both strangers to me) complimenting me on the fidelity with which the local characteristics are reproduced.'[9]

Durward Lely, playing Nanki-Poo, was also complimented by the *Illustrated Sporting and Dramatic News* for 'his heroism in sacrificing some of his personal attractiveness to the exigencies of a Japanese make-up in the matter of hair and eyebrows'. Rutland Barrington's

[6] Millar Bequest/BL Add. MS 54,315.

[7] 'A Chat with Miss Lenoir', unidentified New York newspaper, [*c*.23 or 24 Oct. 1885].

[8] P. Seeley, 'The Japanese March in "The Mikado"', *Musical Times* (Aug. 1985), 456.

[9] 17 Mar. 1885; Gloucestershire Record Office, D2002 7/1/1. Deposited by Lord Redesdale.

eyebrows were even better, according to the *Academy*: painted at the proper angle over 'highly intelligent and . . . wicked little eyes'. The three little maids were beautifully and more or less authentically dressed: Leonora Braham (Yum-Yum) in salmon-pink silk, Sybil Grey (Peep-Bo) in green-blue crepe, and Jessie Bond (Pitti-Sing) in white satin with a gigantic obi which she did her unrehearsed (and unrepeated) best to waggle—in a refined way. Katisha's black and terracotta costume was allegedly two centuries old, while Wilhelm had designed the men's costumes from 'Japanese authorities'. To foil American pirates Carte had cannily sent an agent to Paris to buy up Japanese costumes and materials there; he had already secured them in England in addition to the stage costumes themselves. The Savoy sets, as reviewers noted, resembled an Oriental fairyland or fanscape.

Surprisingly enough in view of its original long run (672 performances) and recurrent revivals, several critics took *The Mikado* to task. The *Topical Times*, for instance, though enchanted by the visual effects, complained that Gilbert was repeating himself under a specious air of novelty. The *Pictorial World* thought it doubtful that this new opera would enhance the reputation of either author or composer, while the *Athenaeum*, although delighted by the piece, again objected to the waste of Sullivan's genius. The *Daily News* even printed an extraordinary rumour that at least one of the numbers had been written by an American citizen in order to secure copyright in the United States. For the most part, however, press and audiences were charmed by Gilbert and Sullivan's most popular opera.

A significant, although perhaps unconscious part of their pleasure was the fact that three popular theatrical types, individualized by Gilbert, appeared as leading characters: the plurality figure (Pooh-Bah), the pantomime tyrant (the Mikado), and the 'dame' (Katisha).

The comic use of plurality (one person possessing or acting in two or more distinct, often contradictory aspects, capacities, or relationships), of course, long antedates the nineteenth century as Bottom, Launcelot Gobbo, and Harpagon's coachman attest. Yet this character did not come fully into its own until the nineteenth century when the facets of personality increased and more elaborate conflicts or antitheses were set up on and off stage. Quick-change artists flourished in the theatre, while Lewis Carroll's Alice remembers 'trying to box her own ears for having cheated herself in a game of croquet she was playing against herself'. As a territorial pluralist, Dickens's Wemmick is dry as dust at the office, but whimsically expansive at home.

A plurality character always quoted as the antecedent of Pooh-Bah is Planché's Baron Factotum, the Great-Grand-Lord-High-Everything in *The Sleeping Beauty in the Wood* (1840):

> As Lord-High Chamberlain, I slumber never,
> As Lord-High Steward, in a stew I'm ever,
> As Lord-High Constable, I watch all day,
> As Lord-High Treasurer, I've the deuce to pay.
> As Great Grand Cup Bearer, I'm handled queerly,
> As Great Grand Carver, I'm cut up severely.[10]

The one function omitted from this punning list is plot function, for Factotum never carries out his multiple duties.

Gilbert's equivalent of these lines is spoken, not in *The Mikado*, but in *La Vivandière* where Tonio is appointed

> Head Constable of all the Royal Towers;
> Chief Councillor of European powers;
> Chancellor too, of every King's resources;
> Field Marshall of all continental forces;
> Lord Admiral of all terrestrial seas;
> Governor too, of all our colonies;
> Prince of a dozen countries, here and there;
> Duke of most places, Earl of everywhere!

Again we never see this character in action.

Since the 1860s Gilbert had been refining and subtilizing his technique, and three plurality characters appear in the two operas which precede *The Mikado*. In *Iolanthe* the Lord Chancellor's clash of capacities leads him to speculate:

The feelings of a Lord Chancellor who is in love with a Ward of Court are not to be envied. What is his position? Can he give his own consent to his own marriage with his own Ward? Can he marry his own Ward without his own consent? And if he marries his own Ward without his own consent, can he commit himself for contempt of his own Court? And if he commit himself for contempt of his own Court, can he appear by counsel before himself, to move for arrest of his own judgement?

Strephon, too, half-mortal, half-immortal, exemplifies a kind of horizontal plurality, and in both cases conflicting characteristics are essential to plot. In *Princess Ida*, on the other hand, plurality is amusing but not relevant, being a variation of the older form. When Ida's women

---

[10] *The Extravaganzas of J. R. Planché, Esq., (Somerset Herald) 1825–1871*, ed. T. F. Croker and S. Tucker (testimonial edn., London: Samuel French, 1879), ii. 73.

warriors are loathe to fight, she announces successively that she will herself perform the duty of her fusiliers, surgeon, and maker of gunpowder, while playing several band instruments simultaneously to drown the shrieks of the wounded. The arrival of her brothers to fight for her makes all this unnecessary.

Pooh-Bah, however, is Gilbert's archetypal pluralist. As Lord High Everything Else, he immediately enumerates his offices: First Lord of the Treasury, Lord Chief Justice, Commander-in-Chief, Lord High Admiral, Master of the Buckhounds, Groom of the Back Stairs, Archbishop of Titipu, and Lord Mayor, both acting and elect, all rolled into one. Later, in conversation with Ko-Ko, Pooh-Bah adds Lord Chamberlain, Attorney-General, Chancellor of the Exchequer, Privy Purse, Private Secretary, Ko-Ko's Solicitor, Leader of the Opposition, Paymaster-General, Lord High Auditor, and Chief Commissioner of Police. In Act 2 he is also Master of the Rolls, Judge Ordinary, Secretary of State for the Home Department, Lord Chancellor, Registrar, and Coroner. Furthermore Pooh-Bah treats his family pride as a separate individual whom he must mortify. 'Ha! ha! Family Pride, how do you like *that*, my buck?' he says as he accepts a large cash 'insult' from Ko-Ko.

With increase of posts comes increase of conflicts between the posts. When Ko-Ko consults Pooh-Bah about celebrating his wedding at public expense, Pooh-Bah advises him to observe due economy or to chance the consequences of extravagance or not to violate the law—depending on whether Pooh-Bah is at the moment acting as Chancellor of the Exchequer, Private Secretary, Solicitor, or Lord Chief Justice. Separation of function is maintained visually by Ko-Ko's pulling Pooh-Bah from side to side of the stage to escape being heard by whichever of Pooh-Bah's selves has just spoken.

Moreover, several of Pooh-Bah's offices are essential for working out the plot in Act 2. It is Pooh-Bah who supplies the information that Yum-Yum will be buried alive if Nanki-Poo marries her before he is beheaded. It is Pooh-Bah as Coroner who gives Nanki-Poo's false death certificate. It is Pooh-Bah as Archbishop who marries Yum-Yum and Nanki-Poo to get the 'dead' man out of the way. And it is Pooh-Bah as Registrar who marries Ko-Ko and Katisha, thus saving Ko-Ko's life and his own. No doubt Gilbert might have worked out an equally intricate plot without Pooh-Bah, but it would have been neither as neat nor as satiric.

The Mikado, in turn, evolved from the bad-tempered monarchs of pantomime, whom Gilbert more than two decades before had described

as capricious tyrants, battering in their courtiers' heads with their scep-
tres, brutally disregarding human life, bullying their dependents, and
flirting unscrupulously.[11] Such a king, Rumbustical surnamed
Rampageous, for example, bashed and blustered his way through E. L.
Blanchard's pantomime *Riquet with the Tuft; or, Harlequin and Old
Mother Shipton* (1863). Entering in a 'rage outrageous', Rumbustical
describes himself in emphatic song:

> *I* am a Monarch with whom it's the toss of a
> *Shilling*, if one of my guards feels the loss of a
> *Head*, when I'm any way angry. . . .
> *Even* my daughter I shan't feel the loss of her—
> Don't I take everything like a Philosopher?[12]

Other representative tyrants include Brooks's Timour the Tartar,
whose cure for his own headache is to split someone else's skull, and
TOO-SLO-BI-ARF, a Chinese Emperor, *'very irascible, very self-willed, very
conceited'*, who cuts off his cook's leg for a 'leguminous atrocity'.[13]

Hildebrand of *Princess Ida* is a quieter variant of the type, but it is
the Mikado whom Gilbert made uniquely his own—cloaking his
tyranny and cruelty with legality and etiquette. For the traditional
royal caprice, Gilbert substituted the Mikado's firm adherence to his
own laws, however idiosyncratically predicated: the extraction of a
quack's teeth by terrified amateurs, for instance. Or the laws are wildly
disproportionate: flirting is alone punishable by death (except for the
traditional crime of encompassing the death of the Heir Apparent,
which involves 'something humorous, but lingering, with either boil-
ing oil or melted lead').

Unlike his predecessors, including Hildebrand, the Mikado never
loses his temper. In him the pantomime monarch's brutal disregard of
human life is refined to a detachment which expresses itself, not as
despotic abuse, but as utter non-humanity, embodied, however, in terms
of perfect etiquette. His willingness to execute his only son initiates the
plot; when, later, he supposes that son has been beheaded, he does in
fact exemplify Rumbustical's 'Don't I take everything like a
Philosopher?' 'Dear, dear, dear!' the Mikado remarks, reading the death
certificate; 'this is very tiresome'. Richard Temple, the creator of the
role, evidently caught the tone exactly, and the *Era*'s second review (12

[11] 'The People of Pantomime', *Fun* (14 Feb. 1863), 212.

[12] (London: Music-Publishing Company, 1863), 10.

[13] L. Buckingham, *Harlequin Novelty; and the Princess Who Lost Her Heart* (London:
Thomas Hailes Lacy, n.d.), 2, 14.

September) praised the 'lordly indifference' with which he told Ko-Ko, Pooh-Bah, and Pitti-Sing that they were to be executed. The Mikado has, in fact, moved from the sphere of pantomime to that of Gilbert's favourite Dickens, where he is related to Sir John Chester with his exquisite manners and cold heart and to the Marquis St Evremond.

The Mikado's daughter-in-law-elect, Katisha, also began in the knockabout tradition of pantomime and burlesque, where male comedians played 'dames' ranging from Mother Goose to a slapstick Katherine of Aragon. Dames long for youthful love and are robustly revengeful when slighted. They dye their hair and pinch or pad their figures as they pursue reluctant men. In his reviewing days, however, Gilbert objected to males frolicking in female 'unmentionables', and thereafter he preferred to use women comedians, who were perforce less slapsticky. When he collaborated with Sullivan, they agreed to have no transvestite roles, and it is now an article of dubious faith that Gilbert treated his dames with unusual cruelty, even making them admit their lack of beauty. Yet, in the same situation, male dames would have caused laughter, not compunction by such confessions. Interestingly enough, no reviewer cavilled at Gilbert's elderly amorous men such as Sir Marmaduke or the Lord Chancellor, and the so-called 'hatred' of elderly women is another of the fallacies attached to the librettist's personality.[14]

Katisha, however, was intended to be grotesque since she provides the reason for Nanki-Poo's flight from his father's court. (Even so, more than one reviewer and Gilbert himself remarked that Rosina Brandram, playing the role, tried to look old and ugly and failed.) She is tough, resilient, a little bloodthirsty, and knows she is plain. Like pantomime dames she attempts to separate young lovers, but is so forceful in her own right that her romance is more interesting than theirs.

At some stage, Gilbert evidently considered Katisha as a more commonplace rival for Yum-Yum since, in an unused lyric, Nanki-Poo sings:

> I love two maids in different ways—
>   'Tis many a lover's wont—
> The one enchants with beauty's blaze—
>   Which you—the other—don't.
> My love for her defies the storm
>   Its bark can ne'er be wrecked—

[14] See J. W. Stedman, 'From Dame to Woman: W. S. Gilbert and Theatrical Transvestism', in M. Vicinus (ed.), *Suffer and Be Still: Women in the Victorian Age* (Bloomington, Ind.: Indiana University Press, 1972), 20–37.

> My love for you, though not so warm,
> Takes calmer, purer, holier form—
> Affectionate respect!

The second stanza tells us that

> loving hearts but seldom wane,
> But e'en in middle age, retain
> Their youthful tenderness![15]

Instead of these golden threads among the silver, however, Gilbert ultimately chose to give Katisha herself two serious solos, each a variation on the paradox of love and death:

> The hour of gladness
> Is dead and gone;
>
> .    .    .
>
> And all has perished
> Save love, which never dies!

and

> Hearts do not break!
> They sting and ache
> For old love's sake,
>     But do not die,
> Though with each breath
> They long for death
> As witnesseth
>     The living I!

Characteristically, Gilbert used the dame to satirize, not the middle-aged follies which his contemporaries conventionally ridiculed, but the premium which Victorians placed on youthful beauty as the most desirable personal quality in marriage. Ruth, Lady Jane, and Katisha all point out that they are superior to the rose lips and bright eyes of 17-year-olds in everything except appearance. And if Yum-Yum (an embryonic Katisha who really knows her own worth) triumphs in her loveliness and marries a prince, Katisha, 'tough as a bone', triumphs in her ugliness and marries the comic baritone—which is much better! Rosina Brandram, Lady Blanche in *Princess Ida*, sang Katisha's songs seriously, and *The Mikado* was the making of her career.

After Gilbert and Sullivan had bowed hand in hand to a delighted audience and after Sullivan had visited Gilbert on 16 March to make

[15] WSG/BL Add. MS 49,306.

changes, all went smoothly for some two months until Gilbert precipitated a quarrel with Carte in late May.

The dramatist wanted more business consultation and a larger practical voice in the running of the theatre. The manager in answer cited the terms of their agreement by which he was to deal with the business of production. Gilbert immediately took Carte's words at their most unpleasant face value, writing on 1 June:

I am at a loss to express the pain & surprise with which I read your letter.

As you decline to permit me to have any voice in the control of the Theatre that Sullivan & I have raised to its present position of exceptional prosperity & distinction, & point out to me that, by our agreement, I am merely a hack author employed by you to supply you with pieces on certain terms, I have no alternative but to accept the position you assign to me—during the few months that our agreement has yet to run. Henceforth I will be bound by its absolute & literal terms.

If this course of action should result in inconvenience or loss to yourself, you will do me the justice to remember that it is of your own creation.[16]

Carte now had the problem of pacifying Gilbert without conceding too much. He protested his personal regard and respect for the librettist and his grief at being misunderstood. With a flash of wistful candour, he exclaimed, 'What is my position compared with yours. I envy your position but I could never attain it. If I could be an author like you I would certainly not be a manager.'[17] Sullivan told Carte that Gilbert feared he might 'ruin the business' if left to himself. Carte admitted the possibility, but he, in turn, ran the risk of the collaborators writing a failure and thus ruining the business themselves.[18] Happily a meeting of the three at Sullivan's flat ended in reconciliation. Gilbert no doubt realized he had overstated his point or, as was his habit, taken Carte's words to their furthest conclusion. He evidently apologized to some extent, as he usually did after what he himself recognized as a burst of temper. Yet he was not *au fond* completely satisfied.

On 21 June after a round of goodbyes, Sullivan sailed for New York. On the same day Gilbert wrote him a long letter from Ramslade where he and Kitty were summering. Carte's behaviour still rankled: 'When he thought you would side with him, on the management question, he snapped his fingers at me (figuratively) and referred me to our agreement. I confess I am furious at his conduct.' In Gilbert's opinion, Carte sent out too many touring companies, had far too many irons in the fire,

---

[16] DOYC/TM.     [17] Copy, 2 June 1885: DOYC/TM.
[18] Copy, 5 June 1885, DOYC/TM.

and had 'neither the head nor the capital for so large an undertaking'. Worst of all, perhaps, when Carte succeeded, 'he shows a disposition to kick away the ladder by which he has risen': that is, Gilbert and Sullivan themselves.[19]

Gilbert did nothing further, however, nor did he realize how much Carte was a romantic who saw himself as creating and controlling great business enterprises. (In fact, Gilbert considered Helen Lenoir superior to Carte in terms of management, and he may well have been right; a year later, Carte offered her an annual salary of £1,000 and a commission of 10 per cent on net profits.)

Having got these objections off his chest, the librettist turned to the next opera, which, as it happened, would not be needed until January 1887. The difficulty of finding a new plot, he wrote, was enhanced by not knowing whether it would suit Sullivan. Unable to give up the familiar lozenge, he managed to content himself with saying he still thought it admirable and could assure his collaborator that he saw his way 'right through it, to as complete a success as we have ever achieved'. Then he suggested a plot founded on Frankenstein (Grossmith) and the Monster (Barrington), who would involve his maker in every possible inconvenience. Would that suit Sullivan? It would not; so Gilbert shifted to a travesty of melodrama in which a blameless peasant is forced to become a bad baronet upon the discovery that he is the true Sir Ruthven Murgatroyd. Although Sullivan did not realize it, the plot would be worked by the lozenge of primogeniture.

Meanwhile the composer enjoyed himself in New York and auditioned Geraldine Ulmar for the American Yum-Yum before leaving (with many stopovers) for Los Angeles. Having arrived there, he settled Fred's children, the eldest of whom was 22, under the care of an excellent housekeeper. Charlotte's unemployed husband returned to England with their baby, who soon died, which Sullivan considered a relief.

The United States now became the scene of a *Mikado*-mania almost as overpowering as *Pinafore*'s had been, although shorter-lived. John Stetson had been chosen to present the authentic version, and Carte himself arrived with an almost complete company, who travelled under assumed names. (Carte was Henry Chapman.) Two days before the opening on 19 August, Stetson, characteristically confused, told the *Advertiser* that 'The room of the Mikado is copied from the original

[19] PML.

233

house occupied by the Mikado of a little Japanese village in the suburbs of London.' But before the Savoy version could appear, Sydney Rosenfeld (whom one is inclined to call 'the boy pirate of the prairies') put on a Chicago version, took it to Milwaukee, and by adroit finagling achieved a night in New York. Then he returned to Chicago a jump ahead of the police, who gaoled him when they caught up with him.

On opening night, the 'true' *Mikado* was virtually played twice, almost every number being encored. Reviewers were complimentary even though the score was sometimes described as disappointing and inferior to the libretto. George Thorne (Ko-Ko), free of Gilbert's watchful eye, delighted audiences by turning a summersault whenever he sat down. Back from the West, Sullivan conducted a gala performance on 24 September with raised prices, free flowers, an augmented orchestra, and a new non-Gilbert verse introduced by Mr Federici as the Mikado. Afterwards, the composer made a curtain speech once more protesting American piracy, a protest which the *New York Times* (25 September) took ill. Meanwhile Carte had attempted to stop James Duff from performing the opera and had lost. Judge Wallace of the US Circuit Court denied his injunction on the grounds that publication of the words in England made the libretto public property in America and the performance of non-Sullivan orchestration made independently from the published piano score did not violate Sullivan's rights. Therefore 'every miserable thieving penniless scoundrel in the States' could produce *The Mikado* with his own orchestration, and 'there is a chorus of fiendish exultant glee in all the newspapers at our defeat,' Sullivan wrote to his secretary, Walter Smythe.[20] Fortunately, Duff's production was not doing well in New York, but an all-female (except Ko-Ko) *Mikado* sprang up, and another version satirized Queen Victoria as Vicky-Shaw, played by a man. Audiences laughed at her taste for stage whiskey.

Tired of pleasure and piracy, Sullivan and Carte sailed for home, Gilbert having already sent them the plot of the new opera. Sullivan liked it, but found the librettist absent from London when they returned. Assuming Sullivan would stay in the United States until November, the Gilberts had 'run over to Cairo' until then. Before leaving he had sent Sullivan four numbers for *Ruddygore* and suggested they revive *HMS Pinafore* after *The Mikado* closed, while its original members were still with the company.[21] That revival, however, proved unnecessary and did not take place until late 1887.

[20] 19 Sept. 1885, PML.     [21] 7 Oct. 1885: PML.

A new argument with Carte began while Gilbert was still in Paris on the way home. The manager had decided to use a curtain-raiser, *The Carp*, to precede *The Mikado*, but Gilbert wrote on 19 November that, since he had not been consulted, he formally objected. Not only that, but if Carte persisted 'all friendly relations between us are at a definite End, & no consideration whatever will induce me to set foot in the Savoy Theatre again'.[22] He would return to London next day. Why Gilbert was so ready to quarrel is difficult to say. Since he believed Carte was over-extended, perhaps he thought *The Carp* an unnecessary expense. Some objection, not even completely formulated, gnawed at the back of his mind and made him peremptory. Perhaps, too, he resented Sullivan's friendship with Carte, and resented it all the more when Carte sent Gilbert's explosive letter on to Sullivan. Carte himself believed Gilbert was simply angry at not being consulted in proper form. Or, again, what might have been merely an objection was raised to fury as the pain of gout racked Gilbert.

Carte was very angry. Yet, clenching his teeth, he wrote a reasonable reply, in fact the kind of reasonable reply which further exacerbates its recipient. He would, he said, have discussed a first piece with Gilbert had he been there rather than in Egypt. Sullivan was in London, and Sullivan agreed. Surely, 'the opinions of Sullivan and myself should have equal consideration and weight with your own'.[23] He pointed out that Gilbert had hitherto never objected to adding a short piece after the first rush of a production was over, and Carte had written to ask him what he thought about doing it now, a letter which Gilbert had not answered. *The Carp* was played, and Gilbert set foot in the Savoy again. He worked off his annoyance, however, by writing a letter to *The Times* (28 November), warning travellers against the way that his Paris hotel had treated his letters, five of which were still missing. It seems likely that Carte's letter was one of these, but that explanation never occurred to Gilbert.

The year ended more happily with a generous deed. Gilbert and Kitty had become friendly with Herbert Beerbohm Tree, his wife, and small daughter Viola. ('I like *him* very much, but I detest his art,' Gilbert told Frank Burnand.)[24] Now he was investing in house property and offered to buy a house in Rosary Gardens, which he would let to the Trees for seven years: 'You will be under no shadow of obligation to me, as I shall get 5% for my money, which is the utmost I have a right to

[22] DOYC/TM.    [23] Copy, 21 Nov. 1885: DOYC/TM.
[24] 16 May 1886: PML.

expect.'[25] The Trees agreed, and Herbert played Cheviot Hill in the 1886 revival of *Engaged*, although not to Gilbert's taste. A month later he asked a favour of Tree: he wanted to settle £400 which the actor owed him, on Viola. 'I am very fond of the little woman, & it would be a great and sincere pleasure to me to feel that I had some hand, however little, in her future prosperity.'[26]

He began 1886 with two letters to *The Times* (2 and 5 January). The first explained that no alien author had any copyright in any work published in the United States;[27] the second sprang to the defence of Emily Rigl. An excellent foreign actress, she had just been reduced to tears and unintelligibility by 'barbarous interruptions' from 'the turbulent section of the audience' on the first night of *Nadjezda*. Let people hiss at the end of acts, if they must, wrote Gilbert, but a small section of coarse fellows should not become dictators of the stage. Editors and letters from the public rushed to agree. 'If we see a man or a woman struggling with the waves we cheer him or her on. If we see a man and woman struggling with words and emotions we jeer at them and heave half a bun at them. This is brave and English,' wrote one.[28] Nevertheless, some members of the gallery continued to enjoy the fun of hooting for excitement's sake.

In February *The Mikado* began to make its way from Canada (Stetson's company) to India (quasi-amateurs); Alfred Cellier conducted it in Melbourne, and in June a Carte company with Geraldine Ulmar and Courtice Pounds made a brilliant success in Berlin, followed by other German cities and Vienna. Even Calais and Boulogne enjoyed it. Back at the Savoy its run did not end until January 1887, and even then, it 'died hard and brilliantly' before a full house.

While the librettist had spent 1886 working on *Ruddygore* (which was rumoured to be an Egyptian opera), the composer had directed the Philharmonic Concerts and written a cantata, *The Golden Legend*, for the Leeds Festival. The cantata was performed before the opera was ready and was literally a roaring success at its 16 October première.

---

[25]  12 Dec. 1885: PML.                                              [26]  4 Mar. 1886: PML.

[27]  In March 1886 Gilbert wrote to the *Era* to instance an unusual example of American fair dealing. For only the second time in sixteen years, A. M. Palmer had sent him a voluntary payment of $20 a night for a short run of *Engaged* at the Madison Square Theatre. Gilbert was especially grateful, having recently received a paltry £10 cheque from Harper and Brothers in token gratitude for their pirated edition of his librettos. He gave the money to the Victoria Hospital for Children and the rough side of his tongue to Harper's in a letter, also published in *The Times* (2 Feb. 1886) and *Era* (6 Feb. 1886). Harper's reply appeared in the *Era* (20 Mar.).

[28]  Augustus M. Moore, letter to the *Era* (16 Jan. 1886), 13.

Sullivan conducted, and the chorus pelted him with flowers. Five days later Gilbert wrote: 'I congratulate you heartily on the success of the cantata which appears . . . to be the biggest thing you've done.'[29] He was sorry not to have gone to Leeds, but they had six house guests. Yet even in the temple of Sullivan's delight, Gilbert was not totally absent. 'I can't get away from it,' the composer told Alexander Mackenzie; when his heroine sang, 'I come not here to argue but to die,' he regretted he could not let the chorus respond in true Savoy fashion, 'Why, she doesn't come here to argue, but to die.'[30]

Meanwhile Kitty had been insisting that her husband have his portrait painted, and his thoughts turned toward Frank Holl, 'the English Velasquez'. Gilbert wrote on 2 November to enquire if Holl was free to undertake the commission, and rode horseback to the artist's studio to sit for his picture in riding costume of silvery greys and browns: a muted, reflective portrait, the Gilbert of *Broken Hearts* perhaps, rather than of *The Mikado*. Holl asked to exhibit it the following March, and Gilbert agreed, asking only that it remain in his own dining-room until his guests at a dinner party had the opportunity of seeing it.[31] It cost him £525.[32]

In November, probably when he dined with the Gilberts on Guy Fawkes Day, Sullivan gave Kitty an inscribed 4-shilling copy of *The Golden Legend*. On the same evening Gilbert read him the completed libretto of *Ruddygore*, and on 22 November he read it to the assembled Savoy company. 'The play is, of course, kept a profound secret,' whispered the *Era*, identifying correctly the role of each principal. So much merriment arose in the press that on 20 December Gilbert was moved to write to the *Pall Mall Gazette* to say 'It is not customary for dramatic authors . . . to publish their plots eight weeks before the production of their pieces.' He did, however, give the cast, the setting, and the date of the plot. The name had not yet been decided upon. Still at Breakspears for Christmas, Gilbert ordered a pair of Acmé skates from a shop in the Haymarket,[33] and passers-by saw a tall, muscular gentleman with rosy cheeks flashing along the ice.

But skates were put away, and trials forgotten as January 1887 rose in a crescendo with Sullivan scoring daily and Gilbert coping with staging a complicated second act. The full dress rehearsal lasted for seven hours

[29]  21 Oct. 1886: PML.

[30]  I. Goldberg, *The Story of Gilbert and Sullivan or the 'Compleat' Savoyard* (rev. edn., New York: Crown Publishers, 1935), 336.

[31]  20 Mar. 1887: PML.          [32]  2 Jan. 1887: PML.          [33]  27 Dec. [1886]: DOYC/TM.

and, as was now usual, was attended by friends and critics. Afterwards, according to Sullivan's diary, everyone went to Rule's for a very late supper.

On the next night enthusiastic applause greeted Sullivan as he stepped before an audience magnificently dressed in maize satin, deep red and cream colour, copper silk with diamonds, moonlight blue plush, and as many other silks and satins as the *Lady's Pictorial* and her sisterhood could observe. Arrayed in pale rose satin, Mrs Gilbert shared her box with Mrs and Miss Hare. Mrs Grossmith was embroidered in pearl. Whistler, Sir John Millais, Sir Frederic Leighton, Frank Holl, Marcus Stone, the George Lewis's, Henrietta Hodson and Labouchère, Lord and Lady Randolph Churchill, the Lord Mayor and Lady Mayoress—box by box and row by row—constituted the most brilliant night the Savoy ever enjoyed. Outside, lines queuing for cheaper seats had again waited for hours, in many cases without securing a seat. They went home to write indignant letters to the papers.

Lifting his baton, Sullivan began the overture which Hamilton Clarke had just written for him.

# 15

---

# Doing and Undoing

something less replete with success
*Sporting Times* (29 Jan. 1887)

A S usual Gilbert had taken great pains with his libretto although
he wrote to Herman Merivale that it was 'quite as unintellectual'
as its predecessors.[1] Having begun with a village beauty, dandies,
officers, and a remorseful father, he immediately gave the beauty a
sailor lover and added a remorseful baronet, who has inherited remorse
with his title. A kind creature, he is nevertheless shunned by everyone
and haunted by the ghost of a dead jester.[2] The dead jester dropped out
and Harrison Ainsworth's 1834 novel *Rookwood* dropped in.

Frequently dramatized in the past and holding the provincial stage
until the 1890s, *Rookwood*, like *Ruddygore*, begins with a family curse
explained in a ballad. Sir Ranulph Rookwood murdered his wife, and
Sir Rupert Murgatroyd burned witches at the stake; consequently, the
Rookwoods are thereafter condemned to be uxoricides, while the
Ruddygores (to give Sir Rupert his title) must commit a crime a day or
die.[3] Each family has a long gallery of ancestral portraits, who, in the
opera, animate to force their latest descendant to embark on a career of
crime.

In working out this supernaturally controlled plot, both Ainsworth
and Gilbert used a pair of contrasting brothers, one of whom has lived
as a peasant while the blameless other carries on as heir. In each case
the peasant, upon assuming his title, changes to a villain and is refused

---

[1] 19 Jan. 1887; quoted by the kind permission of the Lilly Library, Indiana University,
Bloomington, Ind.

[2] WSG/BL Add. MS 49,306.

[3] The Rookwood penchant for initial 'R' (Ranulph, Ralph, Reginald) is carried on by the
Ruddygores (Rupert, Roderic, Ruthven). Some combination of 'R's had, however, long been a
villain's monogram. Gilbert had already used Sir Rockheart the Revengeful (*Fun*, 11 Nov.
1865), who kills everyone, takes all the property, and lives a long, happy life.

by the girl who loves him. In fact, Robin Oakapple's hair turns from innocent fair to guilty black when he becomes Sir Ruthven Murgatroyd.

For Mad Margaret, the best role in the opera, Gilbert drew on the volatile Madge Wildfire of Sir Walter Scott's *The Heart of Midlothian*, also repeatedly dramatized. Wandering lovelorn in dishevelled Scottish peasant dress, both sing wild snatches of song and are racked by jealousy. In a number cut before production, Margaret threatens to curse her former lover, Sir Despard, while the chorus sings:

> And the cat shall crow, and the gnat shall neigh,
> And the toad shall trot, and the bat shall bray,
> And the snake shall snore, and the worm shall wail,
> Before Mad Margaret's curse shall fail!

'Sing hey the lead in her poor thick head,' Sir Despard exclaims.[4]

Madge Wildfire sorrows for her dead illegitimate child, while Mad Margaret cries, '*I* once made an affidavit—but it died—it died—it died!' Several reviewers thought she was a travesty of Ophelia, which Jessie Bond, who created the role, denied; Gilbert's sketch for her costume, moreover, makes the Scott connection clear.

The object of Margaret's jealousy is 'sweet Rose Maybud', as she refers to herself, guided by 'a hallowed volume' of etiquette, but veering with every changing wind of vantage from suitor to suitor. One of these, Richard Dauntless, travesties the chauvinist sailor of a hundred nautical plays. In short, as Gilbert himself told the *Pall Mall Gazette*, 'The piece is a caricature of transpontine melodrama, cast in operatic form.'

Although some critics thought *Ruddygore*'s satire was merely slaying the slain, even then Henry Pettit and G. R. Sims's melodrama *The Harbour Lights*, a serious blend of squire, maiden, and tar, was still in its run of more than five hundred nights at the Adelphi. Furthermore, as *Sporting Life* declared, before *Ruddygore* melodrama had never been burlesqued 'in this mercilessly exhaustive and unapproachably original manner'.

What Gilbert did was to exchange the traditional moral labels which identified his characters, so that goodness and badness were assigned to the wrong people from a melodramatic point of view. Thus Sir Despard, the guilty baronet of Act 1, is a more generous person than the hypocritical Dick Dauntless or the demurely mercenary Rose Maybud. He

[4] DOYC/TM.

gets his necessary crime over early each morning, 'and then, ha! ha! for the rest of the day I do good—I do good—I do good!' When he kidnaps a child, he atones by building an orphanage; if he robs a bank, he endows a bishopric. When he reforms, he marries Mad Margaret, and they embark upon a career of good works, although her behaviour continues to alternate between violence and decorum. ('[A] district visitor should learn to eschew melodrama,' Despard tells his daft bride.)

The plot is brought to an end by a feat of logic, which reviewers described as 'a paltry quibble', 'an anti-climax of inanity'. Even the few who found it admirably neat agreed that it was too subtle for the stage. After the ancestral ghosts who torment him return to their frames, Sir Ruthven realizes that suicide itself is a crime. Hence each ancestor who has ultimately refused to commit his daily crime really commits the crime of suicide. By the laws of logic, paramount over physical possibility in this piece, none of the Murgatroyds should have died. They all return to life.

The cast consisted of Gilbert and Sullivan's usual team: Grossmith as Sir Ruthven; Barrington as Sir Despard; Lely as Dick Dauntless; Leonora Braham as Rose; and the universally applauded Jessie Bond as Mad Margaret. Rosina Brandram and Richard Temple played the smaller roles of Dame Hannah and the ghostly Sir Roderic. Gilbert had even taken Barrington's frequent hoarseness into consideration (as *The Times* pointed out): 'Oh why am I husky and hoarse?' he sang. 'It's the workings of conscience, of course.'

For the first-act men's chorus, military tailors reproduced one each of twenty historical uniforms, accurate to the button and identified in the programme. Gilbert himself suggested the basic costumes for the women's chorus, borrowing a French fashion plate and a high-waisted dress from George Boughton, the artist.[5] Wilhelm, the costume designer, developed these into confections of apple green, blush pink, pale primrose, and other soft colours, and so full was the theatre that Gilbert could repay Boughton with tickets only for the front of the dress circle.[6]

Almost no one liked the title ('Ugh', 'shuddery', too close to 'bloody gore' for women's lips), even though it was, as Gilbert told the *Pall Mall Gazette*, not intended to be a pretty title. Nevertheless, Act 1 went enthusiastically, and encore followed encore. Act 2 began after a more than lengthy, restless interval while the picture gallery was set. During

[5] Gilbert did not return the fashion plate; it is in WSG/BL Add. MS 49,321.

[6] Sunday [1886]: PML.

this hiatus Lord Randolph Churchill went out for a cigarette and encountered Henry Labouchère. Churchill having just resigned his posts under the Conservative Government, rumours immediately flew that Labouchère was inviting him to join the Liberals; a small but noisy demonstration therefore greeted their return and put some part of the audience in a mood for hissing.

All was well, however, until the animation scene, in which some of the pictures did not roll up smoothly, and later two came down prematurely. So did a pair of opera glasses which crashed from a box onto someone's foot in the stalls. The change from picture to ghost was accomplished in total darkness, the auditorium and stage lights both turned off, while Sullivan conducted with a baton tipped with a red electric spark. Reviewers disliked it and said so.

In contrast, the second animation of the portraits took place on an undarkened stage, perhaps to emphasize the fact that the ancestors had left picturehood to become living persons. Whatever the cause, the audience objected to the effect, and, for the first time at the Savoy, hisses sibilated from some parts of the house. Sullivan's own diary comment was 'Very enthusiastic up to the last 20 minutes—then the audience showed dissatisfaction—revivification of ghosts &c very weak.' He and Gilbert appeared as usual and were warmly greeted, although some hearers thought Gilbert had been hissed.

The next day the anxious triumvirate met hurriedly for a 'powwow' to decide on changes and cuts to mitigate the so-called failure. The title was cosmetically re-spelt *Ruddigore*; some verse was cut and much dialogue, including the passage between Hannah and Sir Roderic on the question of whether she would become a widow by marrying a ghost. There was a new patter song for Grossmith, satirizing MPs and all others who are willing to do anything to be made baronets. The ghosts, except for Sir Roderic, were not revived, Gilbert sacrificing his logic to his audience. In little more than a week the revisions were being played, but by then it was evidently too late.

Each collaborator blamed the other, but not face to face. Gilbert thought Sullivan's supernatural music too solemn and grand-operatic, 'as though one inserted fifty lines of *Paradise Lost* into a farcical comedy'.[7] He had hoped for a more humorous treatment. Sullivan objected to the artificiality of Gilbert's plot. While *The Times* critic agreed with Gilbert that Sullivan treated his spectres as if they came straight from

[7] Letter to A. E. T. Watson, 24 Jan. 1887, in A. E. T. Watson, *A Sporting and Dramatic Career* (London: Macmillan & Co., Ltd., 1918), 85.

a real charnel-house, *Life* and most critics agreed with Sullivan that Gilbert's legal paradox was 'really of too puerile a character to be presented to an intelligent audience'. So much for ingenuity! But even more, the failure was the fault of the press which had wound anticipation to such a height that *The Mikado* itself could hardly have satisfied public expectation.

Furthermore, as Gilbert and Sullivan strove to revise *Ruddygore*, a new, absurd contretemps arose in the form of an attack by T. Johnson, correspondent of the Paris *Figaro* and French in spite of his name. Infuriated by Dick Dauntless's song, 'I shipped, d'ye see', which he misunderstood as an attack on the French navy, Johnson announced that it was the collaborators' revenge because 'their trash' was not played in France. Since Dick's ballad really satirized British cowardice, English newspapers enjoyed Johnson's error. When Gilbert and Sullivan replied to *Le Figaro* (in French), enclosing a copy of the words in English, the editor printed Johnson's garbled translation instead. This went on until papers had enough of Johnson's fancied grievances and dropped him. French journalists remembered him, however, and when *The Mikado* was to be produced in Paris in 1888, they protested so loudly that the project was dropped.

Cast problems rapidly arose. George Grossmith managed to play Sir Ruthven through a week of increasing pain and then took to his bed with what was described as a disordered liver or a severe cold. Hundreds of letters and telegrams inundated his bedroom from the Prince of Wales down to the Savoyard in the street. 'Lots of people wouldn't go to Ruddigore till you returned,' Burnand wrote.[8] Yet his substitute did well enough: H. A. Henri played the role until Grossmith came back on 16 February, and earned the gift of a gold-mounted walking-stick from Gilbert. In August at Gilbert's advice, Henri took a new stage name and became Henry A. Lytton.[9] After his London performances, he played Sir Ruthven in the provinces and returned to the Savoy in the 1890s for revivals and to create new roles in non-Gilbert-and-Sullivan works. Lytton became the Grossmith of the early twentieth century.

Leonora Braham presented a larger problem in every way. The previous summer she had married the singer Duncan Young, and by now was pregnant. Her secrecy annoyed Carte, who discovered her condition

---

[8]  19 Feb. 1887: Bevan Coll.

[9]  J. M. Gordon, unpublished memoirs: LG. Gilbert suggested 'Lytton' in memory of Marie Litton who had died in 1884.

in March.[10] Even in January at least two reviewers had remarked that she looked stouter in her Regency costume than in her *Mikado* kimono; so, early in May she was replaced by Geraldine Ulmar, who had played Rose in the unsuccessful American production.

Before *Ruddigore*, no Gilbert and Sullivan opera had been successfully parodied, and *Ruddy George*, which opened 26 March at Toole's Theatre, was not completely an exception. Percy Reeve's musical effects were hampered by a silly libretto in which Gilbert, Sullivan, and Carte all appeared as family portraits. Gilbert reportedly sat smiling in a private box at a performance, amused by the absence of wit in his stage caricature and by the actor's imperfect memory. The revised *Ruddigore* itself played to full houses till May and eventually ran for nearly three hundred performances, but it was not revived during the lifetime of its creators, although the twentieth century has learned to value and play it. In spite of everything, Gilbert later said, he made £7,000 from this 'failure', for which he had written the loveliest of his Horatian lyrics, at least one of which had always graced each of his librettos, mingling happiness and sadness, an acceptance and a smiling resignation:

> Spring is hope—
> Summer's joy—
> Spring and summer never cloy,
> Autumn toil—
> Winter, rest—
> Winter after all is best—

Since a new opera would very likely be needed in the autumn, Gilbert proferred the lozenge, which he would enclose in new jam. Sullivan still did not want to take it, but arrived at 'a sort of provisional compromise': Gilbert would write part, but if it did not appeal to Sullivan or was unsatisfactory for musical situations, 'no more should be said about it'.[11] This quasi-agreement was a mistake. Gilbert assumed the composer had capitulated, and Sullivan merely put off the possible explosion with which the librettist might greet a clear-cut negative. It was, as Helen Lenoir knew, increasingly difficult for the composer to meet an unpleasant situation head on.

Believing he had at last found the right coating for his 'philosophic pill', Gilbert, within a month, had reconstructed the piece and, he assumed, met Sullivan's objections: 'if you want any further modifications, I shall be very

[10] Letter from Carte to Sullivan, copy, 5 Mar. 1887, marked '*Private*': DOYC/TM.
[11] Sullivan, Diary, 9 May 1887: B/Y.

pleased to make them,' he wrote from Breakspears.[12] But Sullivan was in the country himself. The summer went by.

September began with a meeting of the triumvirate and the decision to revive *HMS Pinafore*. Even though Carte had already given his partners their usual six months' notice to prepare a new opera, Sullivan refused to agree on a definite time. Inviting him to Breakspears, where he was spending five months, Gilbert read him the latest version of the lozenge scenario. Sullivan thought it clever but dramatically weak: 'It is impossible to feel any sympathy with a single personage,' he noted in his diary, echoing the old complaint of reviewers faced with a Gilbertian comedy and ignorant of Congreve and Wycherley. The musician would not set it, and at any rate, was soon in such poor health that he did not care.

Meanwhile Carte and Gilbert were preparing a splendidly accurate set for the revival of *Pinafore*. The rigging was copied from that of a real ship; a real mast ascended into space; the sky borders, wings, and backcloth were done away with, and a panorama of Portsmouth backed the set. Gilbert found a sailor who would knot each of the seamen's lanyards elaborately for 2 shillings apiece.[13]

Rehearsals began on 27 October just after Gilbert had heard from Carte that Sullivan was very ill. He wrote to commiserate,[14] but Sullivan was back at the Savoy by 31 October. Meanwhile, still mulling over his rejected plot, by a happy accident Gilbert saw an advertisement for the Tower Furnishings Company, showing a Beefeater, which gave him a new idea. 'Charm & clockwork', as Sullivan called them, were out, and the Tower of London was in. Much relieved, although still not completely well, Sullivan conducted the first night of the enthusiastically received *Pinafore*, afterwards going to an oyster supper at Carte's with the Gilberts and others. Then he continued being ill while Gilbert continued work on the new scenario.

Perhaps another episode of gout tweaked Gilbert into taking too-public umbrage in early December when he found himself listed on the committee for Charles Warner's testimonial benefit. He had already refused, but a hastily co-opted secretary did not notice. Gilbert therefore wrote to the *Era* to explain his views: he believed that proper benefits were a legitimate and valuable means of raising money for a distressed actor or actress, and he never refused to contribute to such a

---

[12]  14 June 1887: PML.
[13]  Letter to Carte, 15 Oct. 1887: DOYC/TM.          [14]  26 Oct. 1887: PML.

benefit. He understood, however, that Warner had, for many years, been in receipt of a very large salary, so that a benefit to put money into his pockets was simply out of place. He was astonished that his name had been used.

This letter was published on 3 December, and both the secretary and the actor answered it, the first to apologize, the second to attack Gilbert's 'offensive' tone. He had always, Warner wrote, refused to take a benefit, but this one was to express his friends' kind feelings as he left for Australia. Theatrically, Warner ended, 'Mr. Gilbert has lived a few years in this world of ours. Has he yet to learn there is something in our natures above the desire for mere filthy lucre?'

Gilbert might have replied that Warner seemed likely to have both the kind feelings and the lucre, but he did not. He had written while angry and, characteristically, did not allow for mistakes. Even so, a mere negative published in the *Era* would have sufficed, had he not (also characteristically) felt impelled to state his principle. It *was* a matter of principle for him. One of the most generous of men to those in real need, Gilbert in letters such as this increased his reputation as a tartar!

In a calmer mood on Christmas Day, he read his new plot to Sullivan and Carte. The former immediately recorded his immense pleasure: it was pretty, human, funny, but free of topsy-turvy. At last, he felt, Gilbert had given him what he was convinced he had always wanted. The readiness of both to write such a comparatively serious opera as *The Yeomen of the Guard* proved to be is implied in two letters, coincidentally written on the same day (6 January 1888). 'I do not claim any other merit for [the Savoy Operas] than that they are artistically made . . . and that they have raised the standard of taste for light stage music,' Sullivan told the tenor W. H. Cummings.[15] Gilbert, sending his *Original Plays* to a friend, Mary Leslie, insisted, 'I don't want you to judge me by the Jack Pudding nonsense with which my name is now associated.'[16]

His ambivalent attitude toward his librettos was increasing, and, while he knew and would assert their value, he also deprecated them in private correspondence. Partly, this was his lifelong tactic for disarming criticism, but more immediately it was the consciousness that he had written almost nothing serious for the past ten years, except for the one-act *Comedy and Tragedy*. He began to consider an adaptation of

---

[15] PML. Sullivan wrote to thank Cummings for defending his light operas in a recent newspaper.

[16] PML.

George Eliot's *Romola*, which attracted him by its intelligent heroine and caddish husband, while, plays aside, he decided to build a new theatre as an investment. Even before settling on the site, he offered John Hare a long lease. He had also found a new protégée: Julia Neilson.

A 20-year-old music student wanting dramatic experience for her purposed operatic career, Miss Neilson secured an introduction to Gilbert and went through the 'awful ordeal' of an audition. The playwright was kind, even when she recited Lady Macbeth's letter speech, and advised her to abandon music for drama. In fact, he offered to train her and put her on the stage.[17]

His first thought was the Savoy stage, for on 21 January Julia and her mother dined with the Gilberts, Carte, and Sullivan, for whom she sang. He was not impressed with her voice, which he described in his diary as a good, but not very sympathetic, mezzo. Nor did he like her enunciation. Then she recited some lines from *Pygmalion and Galatea* in which he thought she showed true genius and crystalline diction. He prophesied a great future for her—but not at the Savoy.

Nothing daunted, in March Gilbert put her into a benefit matinée of *Pygmalion and Galatea* as Cynisca to Mary Anderson's animated statue, and he invited Clement Scott to dinner to meet her.[18] In the event, Julia took the stage, shaking with terror and not always in control of her voice. Still, most reviewers were kind and predicted a career in serious drama for her, their estimates ranging from 'promising' to 'brilliant'. But, alas for the free dinner! Scott denied that Gilbert's discovery had enough power to portray the jealous Cynisca, although she might in time be a Galatea.

Gilbert, on the other hand, always enthusiastic about his protégées, decided Miss Neilson had played Cynisca more perfectly than anyone had ever played it before. He put her into town and country performances of his fairy plays, and by May the *Era* was devoting nearly a column to analysing the new Galatea. Even Scott complimented her smile, walk, and voice, although he added that she lacked 'the true chord of tenderness, the one touch of nature'. Visually, of course, she was a complete change of face from her predecessors, Marion Terry, Mary Anderson, and Miss Fortescue, being dark, stately, and, as Gilbert himself said, Amazonian.

Meanwhile, what Carte and Sullivan perceived as a serious threat to the Savoy had taken place. On 9 February Carte and Gilbert had

---

[17] J. Neilson, *This for Remembrance* (London: Hurst & Blackett, 1941), 32.
[18] 16 Feb. 1888: PML.

attended a supper and ball to celebrate the five-hundredth performance of B. C. Stephenson and Alfred Cellier's light opera *Dorothy*. More romantic than witty, it had already been touted as proof that English art was as good as French—almost as if Gilbert and Sullivan had never existed. Sullivan was in Monte Carlo, where Carte wrote him an excited letter four days later. The long run of *Dorothy* had greatly upset him, and, even though Gilbert had already begun to write lyrics for the next piece, Carte talked of changing theatres. He considered buying a new one and immediately letting the Savoy (to Charles Wyndham) or selling it. They could disband their present company, make a fresh start! Gilbert, he admitted, was not fully reconciled to such an upheaval. Write to him, Carte urged Sullivan. He did not want to let 'other *people get ahead*'.[19]

There was little danger that Stephenson and Cellier *would* get ahead in spite of their current triumph. The music for *Dorothy* had been written years before for a completely different libretto, and had Carte stopped to think, he would surely have realized that the dilatory Cellier was incapable of maintaining an output to rival Sullivan's.

Gilbert was not only unreconciled, he was intractable. He thought Carte simply had his own financial interests in mind, but in this he was wrong. Carte's motivation was undoubtedly a recovery of what he saw as prestige rather than money. In fact, a certain hysteria evidently swept through both Carte and Sullivan, for *Dorothy* was an emotional problem for the composer as well. He was accustomed to think of Alfred Cellier as a secondary sort of musician, the person he had gaily told to write the American overture for *Iolanthe*, his *fides Achates*, as *Musical World* put it. To have a subordinate's opera running for what would be 931 performances must have been very hard for Sullivan to accept, especially since Cellier's score was described as quaint and Early English, qualities in which Sullivan's scores had hitherto been pre-eminent.

On the other hand, Gilbert, for whom B. C. Stephenson could not possibly be a rival, wrote very sensibly,

We have the best theatre, the best company, the best composer, and (though I say it) the best librettist in England working together—we are world-known, and as much an institution as Westminster Abbey. . . . What is *Dorothy*'s success to us? It is not even the same class of piece as ours? Is no piece but ours to run 500 or 600 nights?[20]

[19] 13 Feb. 1888: PML.    [20] 19 Feb. 1888: PML.

This calmer, more practical reasoning eventually prevailed, yet Carte did not give up the idea of a larger theatre, and by late June he and Sullivan were examining plans for what would be the Royal English Opera House.

In spite of having the best company in England, the Savoy was to lose one of its most valuable actors. Rutland Barrington had taken the St James's Theatre as of the following September and intended to become an actor-manager. 'I do not think he could be possibly spared from the position he holds,' wrote the Captious Critic of the *Illustrated Sporting and Dramatic News*. 'He is the typical embodiment . . . of that British Philistinism, the pachydermatous hide of which Mr. Gilbert has so long striven to penetrate by the process of holding up its own image before it.' But the pachyderm had hired a zoo of his own.

March began bleakly as Gilbert stood bare-headed in frost-bound Brompton Cemetery for the funeral of John Clayton, the actor, who had just died suddenly. On the twentieth Anne Gilbert also died, still in the family house at 14 Pembridge Gardens. It is unlikely that Gilbert's father attended her funeral; whether or not Schwenck did is not known; it is likely that he did not mourn deeply. He and Carte had just been through a small upset, each feeling insulted by the other. Carte telegraphed to Sullivan at Marseilles, 'Serious row on with author dont really see how things are to go on you must stick to me'.[21] Almost immediately the quarrel ended, but Carte's message foreshadowed the way the triumvirate would soon divide.

When Sullivan returned to England he served as best man at Richard D'Oyly Carte's and Helen Lenoir's very private wedding on 12 April. Carte's first wife and mother of his two sons, Blanche Prowse, had been dead for three years. Invalidish and lonely, she took no part in D'Oyly's success, while Helen, quiet, shy, and supremely diplomatic, was nevertheless an extraordinarily talented businesswoman, who continued to work with him after their marriage. Both collaborators admired her, Sullivan coming to have a close personal relationship, and Gilbert, a more intellectual one perhaps. 'I don't believe there is another woman alive who could have stated so complicated a case in such a masterly manner,' he once told her.[22]

By 8 June Gilbert had given some of the lyrics their final form and sent them for a first printing. After considering 'The Tower of London', 'The Tower Warders', and 'The Beefeaters', they finally decided on the

[21] Copy of telegram, 22 Mar. 1888: DOYC/TM.     [22] 25 Nov. 1883: DOYC/TM.

inaccurate, but imposing, *The Yeomen of the Guard*. Its plot is straight-forward. In the days of Henry VIII Colonel Fairfax is about to be exe-cuted on Tower Green. He marries a blindfolded stranger, Elsie, a strolling player, to keep his estate from his dastardly cousin's hands. Aided by Sergeant Meryll and his daughter Phoebe, Fairfax escapes from his cell and disguises himself as a Tower Warder. In this guise he woos and wins Elsie, who, of course, does not recognize him. A pardon brings a happy ending for the lovers, but sadness to Meryll and Phoebe, each of whom must now marry an unwanted spouse to secure her or his silence. At Elsie's wedding, Jack Point, her erstwhile jester-companion, falls insensible from grief at losing her. Although at times *The Yeomen of the Guard* is a funny opera, it is not really happy. The tone is autum-nal; Fairfax echoes the callous Prince Florian of *Broken Hearts*, and the only truly unselfish characters are the Merylls.[23]

When Sullivan began to compose the score, Gilbert took pains to meet his requests. He even suggested the musical idea of 'I have a song to sing, O', remembered from 'Come and I will sing you', a Cornish folk-song. He was therefore astonished when Sullivan suddenly demanded some 'rather important alterations', as the musician called them in his diary, changes which would require Gilbert practically to rewrite the second act.

'You might have told me of these requirements six months ago,' Gilbert replied; 'If I can meet them, I will, but I must decline to pull the act to pieces, at this stage of the proceedings. You have had the act in your possession for several months, & if you had told me, in reason-able time, I have no doubt I could have done all you wanted.'[24]

Sullivan considered this a 'haughty letter' and wrote back a 'snorter', ending with an ultimatum: if Gilbert would not make changes, they had better stop rehearsals.[25] Gilbert immediately protested that Sullivan had said in June it was the best act he had ever been given to set. Could not a skilled musician tell at a glance if the proportion of lyrics to dialogue was not satisfactory or if the lyrics were too sombre or too lively?[26] Sullivan had never before threatened to halt rehearsals; in fact, it is almost impossible that he really would have done so, but the opening night was moved from September to 3 October.

[23] Robert A. Hall, Jun., 'The Satire of *The Yeomen of the Guard*', *Modern Language Notes*, 73 (Nov. 1958), 494.

[24] 15 Aug. 1888: PML. Gilbert was in Manchester.

[25] Copy, 16 Aug. 1888: published by permission of the Houghton Library, Harvard University: MS Eng. 1231 (3).

[26] 17 Aug. 1888: PML. Gilbert was still in Manchester.

Each felt aggrieved at the other's tone; still, Gilbert set to work and prepared a reconstruction consisting mostly of a few deletions and alterations in the order of lyrics. Surprisingly enough, he was prepared to cut Fairfax's important solo 'Free from his fetters grim' had Sullivan insisted. Sullivan, his point nominally gained, went to Ireland for five days.

In the midst of these altercations, Gilbert was building his new theatre on Charing Cross Road. It would be constructed of iron and concrete, be electrically lit, and be called the 'Garrick'. When an underground stream threatened to flood the foundations, he remarked, in an often-repeated quip, that he was in grave doubts whether to keep on building or to let the fishing rights.

As the première of *The Yeomen of the Guard* approached, Gilbert was in a tense mood—one of his worst, Sullivan said. They had 'a regular flare-up' at the full music rehearsal, Gilbert irritating his collaborator into anger as great as his own. Then they disagreed over Sergeant Meryll's song, 'A laughing boy but yesterday'. Both wanted to cut it, but Sullivan refused to be 'hectored', and it stayed in for one night only.

On 29 September *The Mikado*, which had been put on for a few months as a stopgap, ended, and Barrington bade farewell in a flurry of speeches; the company gave him a writing-desk. On 3 October he was, for the first time, a member of the audience. Backstage Gilbert was nearly beside himself with nervousness, and Jessie Bond, opening the opera alone on stage as Phoebe, had to tell him to leave. 'He gave me a final frenzied hug, and vanished'[27] to the Alhambra to distract himself, leaving his wife and father behind to enjoy the performance. Sullivan, too, was nervous until 'I have a song to sing, O' was encored three times.

The curtain rose on a solidly-built replica of the White Tower: wonderfully effective, the *Era* thought. Sir Spencer Ponsonby-Fane had furnished Gilbert with information about the Beefeaters,[28] and the stage pictures were striking. W. H. Denny took over from Barrington, and Courtice Pounds from Durward Lely. Grossmith played Jack Point; Geraldine Ulmar, Elsie; Temple, Sergeant Meryll; and Brandram, the small role of Dame Carruthers.

Reviewers commented on Gilbert's new style. 'There is a Shakesperian halo about the whole,' remarked the *Morning Post*, but others missed topsy-turvydom or noticed that the blindfold marriage

---

[27] *The Life and Reminiscences of Jessie Bond* (London: John Lane, 1930), 148–9.
[28] Letter from Gilbert to Sir Spencer Ponsonby-Fane, thanking him, 21 Sept. 1888: PML.

and escape were reminiscent of Wallace's romantic opera *Maritana* (1845). True to form, *Punch* emphasized this initial resemblance in a page-long notice, which was offensive without being funny. Even more unpleasant was *Truth*'s long, excoriating review, attacking Gilbert's ability as librettist and stage director: 'Marionettes are more natural than the Savoy puppets.' At least *Punch* and *Truth* admired Sullivan's score, which was almost universally praised, but this did not console Gilbert.

The later question of whether Jack Point, the rejected jester, dies of grief when he falls insensible had not yet arisen. Several critics commented on his pathos, but when the curtain rose again on the final tableau, Grossmith did not stand, but waggled his leg to acknowledge the applause. The tragic Point was born on 1 November in the person of George Thorne (in Carte's 'C' company at Manchester), who introduced the jester's death, a change allegedly cleared with Gilbert. Soon thereafter, Henry Lytton in 'E' company learned Thorne's business and used it ever after.[29] Since Walter Passmore in the 1897 London revival, Point's have always died: Martyn Green ostensibly of a heart attack with dropped jaw and staring eyes, John Reed in ghastly make-up, with scarcely audible voice and broken dance, destroying the balance of the scene.

Although there is no evidence, popular tradition associates Jack Point with Gilbert himself. If so, the resemblance lies in the jester's song 'Oh a private buffoon', which ends 'They don't blame you—as long as you're funny!' This bitter line suggests a man who wants to return to serious drama, but who cannot—a fact which would be demonstrated almost immediately.

With *The Yeomen of the Guard* launched for a run of 423 performances, Gilbert turned to Rutland Barrington and his St James's Theatre. In June he had been working on *Romola* and presumably decided to finish it for Barrington after *Yeomen* appeared. He stipulated moreover that Julia Neilson play the most important role. Since the first St James's production would be Grundy and Philips's *The Dean's Daughter*, Gilbert must have counted on at least three months free and clear.

[29] G. Thorne, 'The Tragic Jack Point', *Graphic* (25 Feb. 1922), 214. Henry Lytton's memoirs *The Secrets of a Savoyard*, in which he asserts he was the first to make the change, were ghost-written by A. H. Godwin. Other Thorne letters and press cuttings are quoted by G. Glynn, 'The Evidence for Thorne', *W. S. Gilbert Society Journal*, 1 (spring 1985), 9–15. J. M. Gordon's unpublished memoirs say that Gilbert intended Point to be 'a *coward*, playing on his own grievances'.

Two things upset this schedule: the Savoy opening was moved to early October, and *The Dean's Daughter* proved daring, but a failure. Consequently, Gilbert found he needed a play much sooner than he had supposed and that there was no time to finish *Romola*, even though it was already rumoured as Barrington's next production. It seems likely that the dramatist turned to a store of old, unperformed plays and chose *Brantinghame Hall*, which he could hastily modify. Perhaps he had already tinkered with it, for he tried to interest Mary Anderson in playing the heroine four years earlier.[30] Certainly, the Captious Critic began his review by saying that, had the programme not described *Brantinghame Hall* as a new play, he would 'have been inclined to think that it was a youthful effort revised'. At least two other reviewers compared the heroine's biblical diction (which Gilbert had just parodied in *Ruddigore*) to that of Dorothy Druce twelve years earlier, while the plot reads like a play of the 1860s with its passionate villain, inheritance, and mortgage. The return of Ruth's husband from the dead reminded critics of Robertson's *Caste* (1867), and in those days the innocent heroine who proclaims herself sexually guilty would have been daring and advanced.

Revising rapidly, building up Barrington's small role, and making the villain psychologically interesting and repentant, Gilbert sent his first two acts to the printer on 1 November, to be set in type for the cast's use. Act 3 was finished the next day, and he hoped to complete the fourth before rehearsals began on 5 November.[31] The Cartes now offered to buy the American rights for £1,500, Gilbert suggesting Miss Fortescue for the lead.[32]

He had himself designed Julia Neilson's costumes, including unconventional widow's weeds. 'I have my own ideas about ladies' dresses,' he told an interviewer for the *Pall Mall Gazette*; 'I abhor bustles, . . . tight lacing, and all such abominations, and think that woman's dress should fall in natural folds to the figure.' ('Mr. Gilbert . . . now adds millinery to his other accomplishments,' sneered *Truth*.) The final rehearsal went well, invited friends applauding Miss Neilson. Nevertheless, Gilbert was not quite satisfied and, to the indignation of some ticket-holders, postponed the opening for two days.

Like most of Gilbert's serious plays, *Brantinghame Hall* has its social

---

[30] M. Anderson, *A Few Memories* (London: Osgood, McIlvaine & Co., 1896), 232. Miss Anderson's memory of which play Gilbert offered her may not be accurate.

[31] Letter [to Henderson, Rait, & Spalding], 1 Nov. 1888: PML.

[32] Letter to Mrs Carte, 24 Nov. 1888: DOYC/TM.

tensions. Lord Saxmundham, for instance, would rather lose his family home than accept relief from his widowed daughter-in-law, whose father was a reformed criminal. To save him, Ruth announced mendaciously but nobly that she has no right to her husband's money: they were never married, and she forged his will. 'Keep your own,' she cries, 'and leave me to my legacy of untold shame.' Almost every critic objected to this speech as utterly inappropriate to Ruth's character. Still, with an experienced, less nervous actress, it might have been a successful *coup de théâtre* even then.

Ruth's husband, however, almost immediately returns alive from a desert island, and should have ended the play with a happy assertion that 'we will never part again!'[33] Unfortunately, during rehearsals Gilbert added a curtain line for Ruth; 'Let us pray,' she says, sinking to her knees. The audience laughed, and when Gilbert did not appear for a curtain-call, they gave Barrington rude messages for him.

It was a failure, the worst failure of Gilbert's career. Next morning he wrote to Carte, releasing him unconditionally from their agreement. Only one critic had really liked the play, although none of the others bayed against it as loudly as did Clement Scott. Under the guise of reprobating the audience, Scott left no detail of their (and his) displeasure in doubt. Nor did he spare Julia Neilson, who, Gilbert rightly supposed, was made a stalking-horse for an attack on Gilbert's stage-management.

Chivalric as usual, Gilbert leapt to her defence. He broke off all personal relations with Scott and invited Edward Lawson, a proprietor of the *Daily Telegraph*, to come and see for himself, which Lawson was scarcely prepared to do, having just praised his critic for 'perfect taste and tact'.[34] Gilbert sent a copy of this letter to Scott, who spread it about and gave an interview to the effect that the dramatist had asked Lawson to sack him, which was not true. Gilbert threatened an action for libel, but, joined in the camaraderie of the press, most periodicals censured him, making especially merry over his unfortunate statement that he was in the habit of taking criticism quietly. The *Era* commanded him to apologize to Scott; the *Entr'acte* described him as cutting a funny figure.

Poor Barrington, caught between a leading dramatist and the most powerful critic of his day, assured Scott he had never disparaged him

---

[33] LC/BL.

[34] Friday [1888]: PML. Lawson was in mourning, which gave him a good excuse for not seeing *Brantinghame Hall*.

and begged him to see *Brantinghame Hall* again,[35] now that Gilbert had deleted Ruth's final line. Scott refused although the reviewers of the *Pall Mall Gazette* and the *Athenaeum* found Miss Neilson much improved on a second visit. John Hare offered fruitlessly to mediate. It was not so much that Scott disliked the play and actress—Gilbert did not quarrel publicly with others who disliked them, and when *Truth* had been jollily vicious in its condemnation, he took it for granted that nothing better might be expected from Labouchère—it was Scott's tone which got under Gilbert's skin, a tone he disliked even before it was turned on him.[36] He thought that Scott's enmity had been increasing since June when Gilbert wrote to him that his objections to the stage direction of a *Broken Hearts* matinée were not justified by the text (and they were not).

Truth to tell, Scott was not a judicious critic. For years he had been involved in libel suits: 'In future, be as severe as you like, but keep strictly within the bounds of dramatic criticism,' James Mortimer, editor of the *London Figaro*, had written to him as early as 1872. 'This sending people to Coventry costs over £100 for each fare.'[37] Scott had tempers and carried grudges: the *Entr'acte*, for instance, wondered if he were trying to settle some score in one of his sneering reviews. Sydney Grundy, the playwright, described him as 'a weak-minded man, who allows his judgment to be swayed by his personal feelings'.[38] Nor was Scott careful about accuracy.[39] In reviewing William Archer's *English Dramatists of To-day*, for example, Scott changed facts to Archer's disadvantage. In a few years he was to accuse Pinero of plagiarism in *The Second Mrs. Tanqueray*, and when victims protested, he 'apologized' by making the same accusation again in a different way.

Moreover, even though he was something of a lecher in private life,[40] his writing always took a high moral tone, and his style generally went down well with the public, although pit and gallery booed him for his last review when he appeared at *The Dean's Daughter*. Scott's refusal to reconsider *Brantinghame Hall* because Barrington had printed an

---

[35] Monday [1888]: Scott Papers/TM.

[36] Letter to Austin Brereton, 6 Oct. 1884: in the private collection of T. Rees.

[37] 9 Feb. 1872: Scott Papers/TM.

[38] Letter to William Archer, 2 Nov. 1880: Archer Corr./BL Add. MS 45,291.

[39] [W. Mackay], *Bohemian Days in Fleet Street by a Journalist* (London: John Long Ltd., 1913), 93. At one time Mackay, Scott, and Archer all worked on the same journal—the *London Figaro*.

[40] J. Juxon, *Lewis and Lewis: The Life and Times of a Victorian Solicitor* (London: Collins, 1983), 154.

excerpt from his review next to a favourable one in his advertisement was disastrous for the actor-manager, who could not continue after two failures in a row. Although a friend had earlier given him £2,000 and Gilbert refused to accept any author's fees, the St James's closed, and Barrington was in Bankruptcy Court the following year, not to be out of debt till 1894.

In Gilbert's case, the failure of *Brantinghame Hall* had far-reaching consequences: it was instrumental in driving him exclusively into comic librettos at a time when Sullivan was determined to compose his long-deferred grand opera. 'I have written my last play,' Gilbert said in a letter of 10 December to Scott, '& I have no doubt that it will gratify you to know that you have driven me from a stage for which (in our days of friendship) you have so often declared that I was pre-eminently fitted to write.'[41]

Twelve days later, he told a correspondent that critics followed, rather than led, public taste: 'There are a few exceptions—rancorous men—disappointed dramatists—not without ability, but whose ability is warped by private & personal considerations',[42] and in a revival of *The Mikado*, he changed 'lady novelist' to 'critic-dramatist', who 'never would be missed'.

Although Julia Neilson was crushed by Scott's review, she was not defeated. Gilbert again suggested her to Sullivan the next year, and the composer temporarily thought she might do for his Romantic opera after refusing her again for the Savoy. But she had already begun a long engagement with Beerbohm Tree, and in 1893 created the role of the pretty American Hester in Wilde's *A Woman of No Importance*. Her serious speeches were very much like those she had delivered as Ruth in *Brantinghame Hall*, but now the critics did not object. Her long career was assured.

On 15 December 1888 Gilbert was present when Helen D'Oyly Carte laid the foundation stone of the Royal English Opera House.

[41] PML.

[42] Gilbert was answering an appreciative letter from an unnamed correspondent, 22 Dec. 1888: PML.

# 16

## Stringing the Lyre with a Tangled Skein

I've had a difficulty with Carte.
Gilbert to Sullivan (22 Apr. 1890)

A S January 1889 began, the *Era* did not improve Gilbert's temper by publishing a comic 'letter' from 'A Dramatic Author's Wife'. In this little burlesque, Mrs Gilbert, unnamed but obvious, attempts to conceal all the reviews of a recent play (*Brantinghame Hall*) from her husband. She shows him only the one favourable exception, but he finds the others and explodes. It was unfair to Gilbert, but amusing, and perhaps began a continuing misapprehension that Kitty pruned criticism before Gilbert saw it. He often said he did not read reviews, but letters show that this was not strictly the case, and in the nineties he admitted he read—the bad ones.

A few days later on 9 January, Sullivan undertook to explain his views of their future to Gilbert. He intended to write his long-delayed grand opera, preferably with Gilbert, but the music would have to be more important than heretofore. He wanted words which would let him develop more complex musical effects and a voice in the musical construction of the libretto.[1] Gilbert agreed, or Sullivan supposed he did. The dramatist, however, was not likely to accept the *Era's* recent pronouncement (3 November 1888) in its 'Sir Arthur Sullivan on Music'. The librettist of an opera proper, said the *Era*, must 'inspire' the composer rather than having much effect in actual performance. Gilbert was by no means ready to be the handmaid to his collaborator's muse.

How far he might go beyond the heightened seriousness of *The Yeomen of the Guard* was another matter. Probably not far, since *Yeomen's* success seemed unlikely to reach that of *The Mikado*, and he was already thinking about a plot concerning a theatrical troupe. In the

---

[1] Diary, 9 Jan. 1889: B/Y.

mean time, after a Sandringham house party, Sullivan left for Paris, writing again to Gilbert that he was determined to do a large work.

His librettist answered sympathetically, but practically:

to speak from my own selfish point of view, such an opera would afford me no chance of doing what I best do—the librettist of a grand opera is always swamped in the composer. Anybody . . . can write a good enough libretto for such a purpose—personally, I should be lost in it.

The success of *Yeomen* did not sufficiently warrant a still more serious collaboration, Gilbert wrote, and, much as he himself preferred serious plots, they obviously were a risk. 'I think we should do unwisely if we left, altogether, the path which we have trodden together so long & so successfully.' If Sullivan could write *The Martyr of Antioch* while occupied with *Patience* or *Iolanthe*, could he not write a grand opera without giving up works such as *Yeomen?* Anyhow, where would he find a grand opera soprano who could act and sing? Gilbert ended by suggesting Julian Sturgis as the best serious librettist of the day. '*My* work in that direction would be, deservedly or otherwise, generally pooh-poohed.'[2]

Perhaps Gilbert might have been more ready to accept Sullivan's proposal had he not so recently been 'pooh-poohed' by the critics. A musical version of *The Wicked World*, which Gilbert had thought of from time to time, might then have reached the stage twenty years before it appeared, with music by Edward German, as Gilbert's last libretto. The Sturgis whom he recommended instead, began as a novelist and had done little in the way of drama. In the late seventies and early eighties he published *John-a-Dreams*, *An Accomplished Gentleman* (which the *Graphic* called clever and sketchy), and *Little Comedies*, one of which he turned into a stage dialogue. The *Athenaeum*, while acknowledging its delicacy and quiet humour, thought it without dramatic interest, but, no doubt, Gilbert had in mind Sturgis's libretto for Goring Thomas's opera *Nadesha*. Still, it was a rather strange choice—until one asks what librettists there were to choose from in 1889, whatever Gilbert thought. Sullivan accepted Sturgis.

Meanwhile, Gilbert, with his usual forthrightness, had answered a letter requesting his opinion of Sunday theatre openings. He was opposed, 'not, however, on religious grounds, for I cannot believe that Commandments framed for the exceptional conditions of a tribe of semi-barbarians, wandering for forty years in a desert, were intended to

[2] 20 Feb. 1889: PML.

apply to all Englishmen of the 19th Century, except publicans'. He believed that hard workers such as actors were entitled to one day of rest in seven.[3]

At the Savoy *The Yeomen of the Guard* continued, and Gilbert whimsically answered a friendly request for seats: 'Parting with a box at the Savoy is like parting with my heart's blood—but as all my heart's blood is at your service (if you really want it) so are all the Savoy boxes. Here is one of them.' He added a PS: 'Will you have the heart's blood in a 9 gallon cask, or shall I bottle it off for you?'[4]

A day or two before this amusing note, Gilbert received an unamusing letter from Sullivan, saying he could no longer bring himself to write comic opera, to compose for type characters and for 'wildly improbable' plots without some human interest in them. (*Pinafore*, *Patience*, and *The Mikado* had, he considered, human plots.) Sullivan felt he had too long sacrificed himself to Gilbert and reiterated his desire 'to do a work . . . where words are to suggest music, not govern it, and where music will intensify and emphasize the emotional effect of the words'. Could they not find a *modus vivendi* in which his requirements were met without detriment to Gilbert's 'hearty interest in the piece?'[5] Gilbert was astonished:

If you are really under the astounding impression that you have been effacing yourself during the last twelve years—and if you are in earnest when you say that you wish to write an opera with me in which 'the music shall be the first consideration' (by which I understand an opera in which the libretto, and consequently the librettist, must occupy a subordinate place) there is most certainly no 'modus vivendi' to be found that shall be satisfactory to both of us.

You are an adept in your profession, and I am an adept in mine. If we meet, it must be as master and master—not as master and servant.[6]

Sullivan, aggrieved, worked up a new complaint ('I am a cipher in the theatre'), and wrote to Carte from Venice, with a day-long headache, to describe how Gilbert wore out the chorus by making it wait while he rehearsed dialogue and making it repeat music over and over till the 'business' was right: 'my objection is that *I* am the sufferer . . . & that my music gets cruelly murdered.'[7] He asked Carte to pass on the gist of this letter to Gilbert, whose letter of 19 March he had not yet

---

[3] Letter to W. W. Cadell, 15 Jan. 1889: PML. Public houses were allowed to open on Sunday to serve bona-fide travellers.

[4] Letter to 'My dear Mabel', 15 Mar. 1889: PML.

[5] Draft of letter, 12 Mar. 1889: PML.     [6] 19 Mar. 1889: PML.

[7] 26 Mar. 1889: DOYC/TM.

answered, but instead Carte sent the letter itself to Gilbert. As might easily have been predicted, the dramatist broke out, 'it is most monstrous & unfair & unjust & false in every detail. . . . It is of course impossible that I can ever write with Sullivan again.'[8] He invited the Cartes to dinner to discuss the future.

On 27 March Sullivan brought himself to answer Gilbert's last letter, which, he said, was so annoying that he had wanted to let it stand over a few days. Again he insisted his requests were not unreasonable and again he asked for some weight in laying out business and musical situations and for rehearsals which would not tire the voices. 'In no way do I trench upon your ground, or demand anything but what has to do directly with the music and its efficient representation,' he added. If Gilbert accepted this request, they could act together smoothly; if not, Sullivan promised to send him no more recriminations.[9]

Gilbert's reply four days later began soothingly enough. 'The requirements contained in your letter of the 27th are just and reasonable in every way. They are requirements with which I have always unhesitatingly complied, and indeed I have always felt, and fully appreciated, the value of your suggestions whenever you have thought it advisable to make any.' He pointed out, however, that Sullivan was probably not present at more than one in six rehearsals during the first two weeks when business was arranged. But—and it was a portentous but—there was Sullivan's letter to Carte which now stood between them, and which 'teems with unreasonable demands and utterly groundless accusations'. It was a 'most cruelly unjust and ungenerous letter'. He reminded the composer of business arranged and rearranged to meet his objections, and concluded:

You say that our operas are Gilbert's pieces with music added by you, and that Carte can hardly wonder that 12 years of this has a little tired you. I say that when you deliberately assert that for 12 years you, incomparably the greatest English musician of the age—a man whose genius is a proverb wherever the English tongue is spoken—a man who can deal *en prince* with operatic managers, singers, music publishers and musical societies—when you, who hold this unparalleled position, deliberately state that you have submitted silently and uncomplainingly for 12 years to be extinguished, ignored, set aside, rebuffed, and generally effaced by your librettist, you grievously reflect, not upon him, but upon yourself and the noble art of which you are so eminent a professor.[10]

---

[8] 29 Mar. 1889: DOYC/TM.     [9] PML.     [10] PML.

Gilbert was right, although he did not always give in to Sullivan's demands as easily and readily as he thought he did, both of them having forgotten the composer's ultimatum for revising *Yeomen*. But Sullivan could not plausibly cast himself for the role of a poor put-upon composer, and Gilbert's highly complimentary description of his collaborator *en prince* must have gratified him. When he returned to London in April, he was in charity with Gilbert, a charity which need not have been so strained had Carte been sensible enough to send Gilbert only Sullivan's gist, not his petulant remarks in the letter of 26 March.

The Gilberts were not there when Sullivan arrived. The dramatist had been ill (probably of a surfeit of letters!), and they were away on a cruise to Palermo, stopping in Portugal, Spain, Gibraltar, and Algiers. Gilbert's health improved as he visited ships and barracks at Malta and took part in two fancy-dress balls on board, wearing a black silk costume to the second.[11] While he was gone, the Garrick Theatre opened (24 April) with Pinero's new drama *The Profligate*. Sullivan was there, having composed an incidental song for the piece and played it from the wings; 'Very brilliant success,' he recorded.

On the same day he wrote to Gilbert, seizing on the latter's willing admission that his musical requirements were reasonable, but gliding over the rest with a general remark about differences of opinion. Sullivan now saw no reason they should not work together harmoniously, especially since he would be able to 'realize the great desire of my life'[12] without losing their collaboration, which, as he once said, was his bread and cheese.[13] Could Gilbert set to work on a Savoy libretto immediately, before the new opera house was ready? Carte also wrote on 24 April, confirming Sullivan's readiness.

Nevertheless, Gilbert had no heart to begin again. He was still wounded by Sullivan's 'cipher' letter with its *'cruelly unjust charges* [which] *have not been withdrawn or qualified in any way'*. He thought Sullivan no longer respected his work, and he lacked 'that lightness of heart which I take to be absolutely essential to success in such an undertaking'.[14] It was not only for himself that respect was important, but for the whole profession of dramatist. The stage was becoming much more intellectually respectable, but Gilbert knew and resented the fact that a composer still ranked a playwright.

[11] Gilbert's travel diary: WSG/BL Add. MS 49,345.     [12] Draft of letter: PML.
[13] 'To-day's Tittle Tattle', *Pall Mall Gazette* (6 Sept. 1889), 6.
[14] 8 May 1889: PML.

Sullivan apologized, after a fashion, on 8 May, and fearful lest Gilbert present him with a libretto about lozenges or a theatrical troupe, suggested a Venetian subject which the dramatist had mentioned to Carte. That would obviate any necessity for argument.[15] He had just been in Venice himself and was full of its musical possibilities.

The following day they met, 'shook hands & buried the hatchet', as Sullivan thankfully recorded. He invited Gilbert and Kitty to his birthday dinner the next Monday. After the tempers of rehearsing *Yeomen* and of the cipher quarrel, a new golden age seemed about to begin for the collaborators. The sketch plot, which Gilbert read to him on 8 June, delighted Sullivan, and, since Grossmith had made up his mind to leave the Savoy company, the two went that evening to see Frank Wyatt in *Paul Jones* as a possible replacement.

Irrelevant to Sullivan, Gilbert as a director of the Regency Theatre Brighton Company took part in choosing a manager (Charles Brookfield) for the as-yet unbuilt playhouse. Then a long-buried ghost rose to exasperate him.

August Van Biene and Horace Lingard (unpleasantly memorable for his connection with *The Wreck of the 'Pinafore'*) decided to tour the 1871 translation of *Les Brigands* the next autumn. William Boosey, whose company held the copyright, therefore wrote to Gilbert in June, asking if he would like to look over his old libretto first. Boosey later assumed the company would make new terms with Gilbert, although he did not say so when he wrote.[16] Very likely again in the throes of gout, Gilbert's temper led him to reply immediately and forgetfully that his *Brigands* was only a copyright translation and unfitted for the stage. He allowed himself to end his letter touchily, 'I shall retain a very vivid impression of your singular lack of courtesy in making arrangements for its production without having in any way consulted me on the subject.'[17]

As July drew to its close, Sullivan attended the house-warming party of the newly built Savoy Hotel, in which both he and Gilbert owned shares. The hotel was Carte's new enterprise, built with the profits from their operas, and Sullivan was on its board of directors. At that time it consisted of only the river block, but it was extraordinarily luxurious, with a plethora of bathrooms, room service on every floor, and Charles

---

[15] Draft of letter, 8 May 1889: PML.

[16] W. Boosey, *Fifty Years of Music* (London: Ernest Benn Ltd., 1931), 36. Boosey said that he had programmes showing Gilbert's adaptation had been performed earlier in the provinces, but this point does not appear in the long reports published by *The Times* and the *Era*.

[17] 'Boosey and the Brigands', *Era* (21 Sept. 1889), 13.

Ritz as manager before he built his own hotel. During the coming autumn, Gilbert and Sullivan would have many a 'powwow' and 'confab' beneath its rose-shaded table lamps.

George Grossmith played Jack Point for the last time on 17 August and was replaced by John Wilkinson, whom Gilbert did not like and who had been chosen without consulting him. Although Gilbert thought Grossmith was not a good actor either, he suggested that the triumvirate present him with some sort of testimonial since 'he has been very zealous & willing & good-humoured'.[18] They gave him two silver bowls, as he set out to tour the provinces alone with his piano in a one-man show. Richard Temple, too, at almost the last moment, was to decline a role in *The Gondoliers*, the next opera. Instead, he intended to produce and appear in a short-lived comedy-opera, *Gretna Green*, with Leonora Braham in the cast.

Meanwhile, *The Brigands* was rehearsing apace in order to open on 2 September in Plymouth. The house, drawn by Gilbert's name, was crammed, and the *Era*'s critic enjoyed it. But to Gilbert's dismay, Van Biene had interpolated both a song of his own and another 'ridiculous & vulgar' lyric, allegedly written by a former music-hall singer. The dramatist did nothing about the provincial performances, but when the production came to London two weeks later, he was prepared. He had secured an interim injunction so that his name could not be used unless his text were unaltered. Unfortunately, this injunction was soon dissolved.

Boosey offered to print a disclaimer in the programme, and Sullivan offered himself as mediator. Gilbert refused both and chose to appeal, which did him little good since *The Brigands* was not booked for a long London run. Reviews were mixed, and most of the cast substandard. Ironically enough, the tenor, Frank Wensley, whom the critics praised, died in December.

Gilbert's appeal was heard on 6 November and failed because the Lords Justices refused to believe his reputation had been injured. Their position was a long-held one, which dramatists before Gilbert had found intolerable and which continued to have implications in the continuing question of a dramatist's legal rights.[19] As Gilbert wrote bitterly to the *Era* on 9 November,

[18] Letter to Carte, 14 Apr. [1889]: DOYC/TM.

[19] J. Coryton, *Stageright: A Compendium of the Law Relating to Dramatic Authors, Musical Composers, and Lecturers as Regards the Public Representation of Their Works* (London: D. Nutt, 1873), *passim*.

If a grocer buys a tin of Colman's mustard, and, having adulterated it with a mustard that is not Colman's, nevertheless sells it across the counter as Colman's the majesty of the law is outraged, and the thunderbolts of the Courts of Chancery are not invoked in vain. This is a situation which the Courts of Chancery can grasp—it appeals to them as a mercantile outrage, concerning which there can be no two opinions. The Courts of Chancery have invariably shown themselves hopelessly unable to apply this simple principle to works written for the stage.

During Gilbert's embattled September, E. L. Blanchard died. Only 69, he had seemed elderly for twenty years. Like Planché, he had outlived his best days and had seen his innocent pantomimes overwhelmed by music-hall performers. As a reviewer he had long gone out of fashion, replaced by Clement Scott's more colourful style. Like a last leaf, Blanchard had clung to the Arundel Club, but Gilbert scarcely noticed his gentle fall. He was enjoying his warm creative relationship with Sullivan.

Never had he been quite so ready to offer alternatives; never had his collaborator been so pleased as with the opportunity for a long musical scene at the very beginning of the opera. Gilbert also made a brilliant suggestion for setting another number, 'In a contemplative fashion', a quartet in which each solo voice would emerge and drop back into a continuum. He wrote the pattern out for Sullivan and asked, 'Is it practicable—& if so, will it be an improvement?'[20] It was both, and, amusingly enough, when Frank Burnand wrote in delight to congratulate Sullivan, he exclaimed, 'How did you arrive at it? Whence came the suggestion of the musical treatment?'[21] Whence indeed!

On the other hand, Sullivan deleted a chorus without consulting Gilbert, who wrote to say, 'I certainly did not understand that the growling chorus was cut out.' The piece would be unintelligible without it, for the republican Venetians agree to become courtiers only if strict equality is observed:[22]

> Republicans we
> And we do not agree
> That under a monarch a man can be free.
> We grunt & we groan
> At the thought of a throne
> We prefer to be free with a will of our own.[23]

[20] 22 Sept. 1889: PML.    [21] 18 Dec. [1889]: PML.    [22] 10 Aug. 1889: PML.
[23] WSG/BL Add. MS 49,298.

Sullivan, the friend of princes, was adamant, and a comic duet, 'They all shall equal be', suffices. Also deleted were the Duchess's lines, including 'He's the only Duke I've ever met | Who every day pays every debt!' (which he doesn't), as well as references to the Duke's 'bunkum eloquent'.[24] The satire on the Duke's cowardice ('He led his regiment from behind') and on the ways in which he and the Duchess trade on their rank remained, however—a faint memory of an early Gilbert attack in *Fun*:

> In short, if you'd kindle
> The spark of a swindle,
>    Lure simpletons into your clutches—
> Or hoodwink a debtor
> You cannot do better
>    Than trot out a Duke or a Duchess!

In Act 2, Gilbert originally intended to show the impractical consequences of a monarchy tempered with equality. His chorus would sing, 'Long live the King' as long as the joint rulers did as they were told, but, if not, 'Look out for squalls! | With angry heart & voice we'll sing | Confound the King!'[25] This number was also deleted, and, except for the topsy-turvyness of kings who are literally the servants of their people and the nominal elevation of everyone to Lord High something or other, Gilbert did not pursue his first line of possibilities—it would have led him back to *Thespis*. Nevertheless, several reviewers considered the court of Barataria a parody on socialism, and Gilbert himself suggested 'socialist' might replace 'republican' in the 1909 revival.[26]

During the last fortnight of rehearsals, Gilbert was temporarily distracted by a financial debate with John Hare over the latter's lease of the Garrick Theatre. Building costs had outrun estimates, Walter Emden had been replaced by C. J. Phipps as architect, and Gilbert had already borrowed £15,000. Hare's projected annual rent therefore rose to something over £4,000, which the actor thought was too high, and said so. In answer, Gilbert wrote, 'I think you must still be under the impression that I have feathered my nest very comfortably at your expense. . . . you must see that investing 44,000 in the Garrick Theatre is not quite the same thing as investing it in Consols.' It was 'a most

[24] First prompt-book (printed galleys): DOYC/TM. Stage directions had been written for this deleted number.

[25] WSG/BL Add. MS 49,298.

[26] Rupert D'Oyly Carte, quoted by D. G. Davis, 'Socialists or Republicans', *Gilbert & Sullivan Journal*, 2 (June 1929), 89.

risky & utterly inconvertible form of security', and Gilbert had plunged into it to save Hare 'from falling into the hands of City harpies who would have made you bleed to the tune of 10%'.[27] Hare gave in, saying he knew Gilbert acted out of friendship, but thought it only business-like to have protested. Gilbert gave all his attention again to rehearsing *The Gondoliers, or The King of Barataria*, a title decided only five days before the opening.

The dress rehearsal occupied nearly seven hours before a specially invited audience, which included Julia Neilson, crimson-cloaked and feather-hatted. Sullivan worked with the orchestra for nearly an hour, pausing only to shout, 'Stop that hammering in the gallery.' Carte per-ambulated the aisles, handing out librettos to the critics. As the after-noon wore away, songs, business, even a whole scene was repeated and re-repeated. Sullivan stamped his foot at wrong tempos; Gilbert leapt from stage-box to stage, shouting, 'I don't want it to go off like a steam launch', when the gondola exited too rapidly. Frank Wyatt's cloak, which made him resemble 'a faded Velasquez', had been soaked in Worcester sauce: 'he smells like a chop!' Gilbert remarked.[28]

Over a thousand persons applied for seats for the first night.[29] 'I hope you won't be bored to death!' Gilbert wrote to a friend who had secured one.[30] Seldom has a hope been so immediately and extravagantly fulfilled. Carte wore an 'air of coming triumph', said the *Daily News*, as he greeted friends and watched the performance from various points of the theatre, including his wife's private box next to Mrs Gilbert's. Back in the fold, Rutland Barrington's first entrance as Giuseppe was greeted with a roar of welcome, while Courtice Pounds as Marco hid behind the choristers until the ovation ended.

Arthur and William were themselves again in a 'glorious' setting by Hawes Craven, who reproduced the Piazetta with a backdrop of the Grand Canal. Having come through freezing streets, inches deep in snow and mud, the audience basked delightedly in the golden warmth of the Savoy. They prolonged the performance until 11.30 by demand-ing encores, shouting '*All* over again!' at the end of 'A Regular Royal Queen'; they would have asked for a third time if the quartet had breath

---

[27] Draft of letter, 22 Nov. 1889: WSG/BL Add. MS 49,335.

[28] This description has been woven together from several newspaper accounts, including those of the *Sunday Chronicle*, the *Sunday Times*, the *Birmingham Gazette*, and the *London & Brighton*.

[29] Letter to Mr Routledge, 6 Dec. 1889: PML.

[30] Letter to 'My dear Lowndes', 7 Dec. 1889: PML.

left. '[W]e have never had such an enthusiastic house & never such a brilliant first night,' Sullivan exulted in his diary. When at last the curtain fell and he and Gilbert appeared hand in hand, the house rose at them, cheering. Carte, too, had his meed of applause at his own call.

Although by now it was often easier for the collaborators to praise each other to outsiders rather than directly, Gilbert wrote next day to thank Sullivan for his magnificent work: 'It gives one the chance of shining right through the twentieth century with a reflected light.'[31] And Sullivan answered, 'Don't talk of reflected light. In such a perfect book as *The Gondoliers* you shine with an individual brilliancy which no other writer can hope to attain.' He thanked Gilbert for accepting his suggestions with such 'patience, willingness, and unfailing good nature'.[32]

At first Gilbert had set his libretto in the fifteenth century, but its final form is essentially that of an eighteenth-century moral romance. Voltaire and his imitators had used the double switching in infancy on which the plot of *The Gondoliers* rests, while cautionary lyrics emphasize the necessity of balance. 'When every one is somebodee, | Then no one's anybody,' the Grand Inquisitor explains, while the Duke teaches necessary deportment for monarchs: 'Try to combine a pose imperious | With a demeanour nobly bland.' Joy and life, sorrow and death are gently balanced:

> Try we life-long we can never
>> Straighten out life's tangled skein,
> Why should we, in vain endeavour,
>> Guess and guess and guess again?
>
> . . . . . .
>
> Wherefore waste our elocution
> On impossible solution?
> Life's a pleasant institution,
>> Let us take it as it comes!
>
> . . . . .
>
> Life's perhaps the only riddle
>> That we shrink from giving up!

Or, as Tessa sings, 'Sorrow goes and pleasure tarries' and 'Worry is melodious mirth, | Grief is joy in masquerade'.

At the denouement when Luiz, the drummer-boy, is revealed as the long-lost king, the gondoliers, freed from monarchal responsibilities,

---

[31] 8 Dec. 1889: PML.    [32] 9 Dec. 1889: PML.

happily leave Barataria for Venice where, like Dr Johnson's Rasselas and Voltaire's Candide, they will cultivate their own Grand Canal.

Even Clement Scott admitted Gilbert was a genius, although, he repeated, a genius without imagination. (This time his review appeared in the *Illustrated London News* and still contained some of the rancours of the *Brantinghame Hall* criticism; for instance, he asked why Gilbert should 'try to bully his contemporaries into hailing him as a man of imagination' when his real mastery lay in 'disciplined extravagance?') *Truth*, too, found itself forced to acknowledge that the new libretto was 'a marvel of neatness and finish', the result of 'unflagging industry that may well be commended to the attention of younger writers'.

Yet a week later, with a perversity difficult to understand, Gilbert was thanking Alfred Austin for his congratulations, but dismissing *The Gondoliers* as 'ridiculous rubbish and . . . accordingly hailed as a masterpiece. If it had deserved one half of the encomiums passed upon it, it would have been howled off the stage.' The best piece he ever wrote, he insisted, was *Brantinghame Hall*.[33] Nevertheless, he attended a private meeting that week of librettists, composers, and publishers to form an association like the French Société des Auteurs et Compositeurs—from which, however, nothing seems to have come.

On 15 December Sullivan went to Gilbert to arrange last-minute alterations in stage business and to say goodbye to Kitty. The opera would clearly have a long run (554 performances), giving him plenty of time to work on his big opera with Julian Sturgis and giving the Gilberts time to visit India, where Kitty could view scenes familiar to her parents and grandparents. They left on 20 December, accompanied by the goodbyes of Mrs Beerbohm Tree and thirty-six members of the Savoy company, all of whom came to the railway station. Julia Neilson and other friends saw them to the ship, and they sailed from the damp, blowy weather of England into the sun of Algiers. Gilbert left behind him a collection of his short stories, *Foggerty's Fairy and Other Tales*, published for the Christmas trade.

Two weeks later, Gilbert's father died of apoplexy at his daughter Jane's home in Salisbury. He had signed his will on 29 December with an illegible scribble, leaving a quarter of his estate to each of his children, the household effects of 14 Pembridge Gardens to Florence and Maude, and his library together with three pictures to his son, who was one of the executors. For Lucy there was a £100 to buy a piece of

[33] 14 Dec. 1889: PML.

jewellery as a memorial of his affection, but it was to contain no inscription. William Gilbert also stipulated that his funeral should be simple, costing no more than £20. He was buried in the cloisters of Salisbury Cathedral, and his nephew Sutherland Edwards wrote a long obituary in the 4 January *Daily News*. Who sent the news to Gilbert, his reaction to it, all personal communications among the four children have evidently not survived, thanks again to the Gilbert habit of not keeping personal letters.

Nevertheless, the tour of India and Ceylon did Schwenck good, even though he was 'anything but enthusiastic on the subject of Indian hotels', according to the *Sunday Times* (6 April 1890). They went to Colombo, Kandy, Calcutta, Darjeeling, and Bombay, hospitably welcomed everywhere, and he collected seventy papiermâché heads representing all walks of life in case he should decide one day to write an Indian libretto. Meanwhile they decorated his library.

While Gilbert was away, Carte sent a group of English performers to join the American company of *The Gondoliers* about to open in New York. It died in thirteen weeks ('The Gone-dollars', as wags called it), even though Richard Temple was sent over to bolster the shaky cast. At home, and with Gilbert's permission, Carte re-dressed the male chorus, whose second-act costumes had been badly made. Now they shone 'magnificently gorgeous', as *England* redundantly exclaimed, in orange watered-silk, ruby velvet, turquoise-blue and silver, cloaks trimmed with the new metallic chenille, and other gauds and fancies—all in time for the Prince of Wales's third visit to his favourite opera.

When the Gilberts returned in April, however, Kitty went to a performance at the Savoy, only to find that interpolated gags were rife. She wrote an acerbic note to Barrington, evidently the chief offender, and, of course, informed her husband. He in turn complained to Carte:

The piece is, I think, quite good enough without the extraneous embellishments suggested by Mr. Barrington's brief fancy. Anyway it must be played *exactly as I wrote it*. I won't have an outside word introduced by anybody. If once a license in this direction is accorded it opens the door to any amount of tomfoolery.[34]

It was an annoying homecoming all round, exacerbated by a return to the roast beef of old England, which intensified Gilbert's gout, at its painful worst during the 1890s. A little more than a week before he wrote to Carte, the latter had told him that preliminary expenses for

---

[34] 30 Apr. 1890: DOYC/TM. Evidently Gilbert relented a little when he heard the gags.

*The Gondoliers* were £4,500, which astonished him. He asked for details and was given a résumé.

By their 1883 agreement, Gilbert, Sullivan, and Carte had formed a partnership which rented the Savoy Theatre for £4,000 from Carte as owner. After this was paid, together with 'all expenses of producing and performing the operas', such as lighting and 'repairs incidental to performance', the profits were divided equally among the three. As Carte pointed out more than once during the following months, he was charging £1,000 less than the current annual value of the theatre, and he included bar and programme advertisement profits in the sum to be divided. (The programmes themselves were free.)

What Gilbert found upon examining the résumé was a charge of more than £100 for Miss Moore's costumes, £100 for Miss Brandram's second dress, £450 for carpenters' work, etc. etc., but most surprising of all, £500 for new carpets *'for the front of the house!'*[35] He burst into Carte's office the next day to put this right.

What happened there must be pieced together from Gilbert's own account of 22 April, from Carte's brief letter to the *New York Times* (10 June), refuting a report published on 16 May, and from Helen Carte's more detailed account in her very long letter to Gilbert, written on 7 and 8 May.[36] There are also allusions to the interview in Sullivan's diary and in the correspondence of all three.

Gilbert began excitedly by insisting that he and Sullivan were being robbed right and left and that Carte did not even check his carpenters' bills. Helen Carte found his manner incomprehensible; he addressed D'Oyly 'in a way that I should not have thought you would have used to an offending menial'. Gilbert's words at this point are not recorded by anyone; more than a month later, Carte denied that Gilbert called him a blackguard. According to one of Gilbert's biographers, Hesketh Pearson, Gilbert called Carte 'a bloody sheenie', but Pearson admitted he had made the phrase up himself.[37] Unlistened to, Helen said, 'I am sure you are not thinking what you are saying, Mr. Gilbert.' She thought him strangely violent and insulting.

Then came the carpet and Gilbert's refusal to accept it as 'incidental to performance'—a contention, he wrote to Sullivan, which would justify Carte in redecorating and reupholstering the whole theatre a month before they might leave the Savoy, charging them two-thirds and keeping everything for himself. Why had they not been consulted

---

[35] Letter to 'Dear S.', 22 Apr. 1890: PML.    [36] Copy: DOYC/TM.

[37] In private conversation with the late Reginald Allen, who, in turn told it to the author.

about this purchase? Gilbert wanted to know. By now Carte had become angry and resentful in his turn and refused to answer, but when Gilbert insisted they should have a new agreement, he said that he would raise the theatre rent to £5,000. 'If so,' Gilbert riposted, 'he must get another author for the Savoy.'

'That might be practicable,' replied Carte, but Gilbert was certain that he had said, 'Then you write no more for the Savoy.' Helen, who had the coolest head of the three, was certain Carte had not, but knew Gilbert believed he had. Furious at, as he thought, being dismissed from the theatre, Gilbert hotly demanded what Carte did for his share. Again the manager refused to answer, but told Gilbert to talk to Sullivan if he were dissatisfied. With a last line (repeating his earlier image for Carte) to the effect that it was a mistake to kick down the ladder by which Carte had risen, Gilbert flung away. His passage had been like a thunderstorm, but it did not clear the air.

Sullivan answered Gilbert's letter describing the 'difficulty' next day, agreeing costs were too high but saying that he had left the ordering of costumes and scenes to Gilbert, the 'expert'. He promised to investigate.[38] Unfortunately, he must have showed this letter to Carte, who wrote to Gilbert himself that expenses were enormous because Gilbert ordered 'blind' without consulting management. The cost of the carpet, which Gilbert now put as £330, was really £140: 'a fair example of your general inaccuracy,' Carte wrote to him.[39] Meanwhile Gilbert had sent Mrs Carte a letter, saying that he had asked Hare the cost of the elaborate set for his production of *La Tosca* and had been told it was £141, as compared with £450 for *The Gondoliers*.[40]

Carte's letter arrived on 27 April, the day after a long meeting between Sullivan and Gilbert. The composer did not agree about the carpet, but undertook to arrange a meeting where all three could consider accounts. Gilbert agreed, but stipulated that no one should mention his scene with Carte,[41] a reservation which suggests he was beginning to feel ashamed of his temper, although not of his principle. His outbursts, as we have seen before, frequently yielded to reconciliation, even when reconciliation was difficult. He was probably thinking

[38] Copy, 23 Apr. 1890: PML.

[39] Copy, 26 Apr. 1890: DOYC/TM. Carte wrote a letter of corrections to this letter dated 28 Apr., saying he understood Gilbert and Sullivan were meeting that day. They met on the twenty-seventh, however, so Carte must have misdated the second letter.

[40] 25 Apr. 1890: DOYC/TM.

[41] Memorandum, 26 Apr. 1890: quoted in A. Jacobs, *Arthur Sullivan: A Victorian Musician* (Oxford: Oxford University Press, 1984), 311.

of it now, even while he still resented what he considered Carte's insults. Then the manager's letter came.

Gilbert took it to Sullivan the next morning together with tentative notes for a new agreement. Although Sullivan felt that Carte's tone was inexcusable, he still preferred to wait; he himself had been avoiding the manager lately because the latter was so irritable. He wanted to go to Newmarket for the races; so he proposed they do nothing for a week— which he thought would help smooth things over. Again Gilbert acquiesced to a delay, and Sullivan left London in the happy supposition that friendly times would soon come again.

This was a costly outing, for the hiatus gave both antagonists time to harden their positions. If Carte were irritable, he now had a week in which that irritability could feed itself. If Gilbert felt insulted, he now had time to remember and brood over each former instance when he had objected to Carte's methods of keeping accounts. Had manager, librettist, and musician met sooner, perhaps they might have at least patched up a working truce, but when Sullivan returned, Carte wrote to say he could not meet Gilbert again as if nothing had happened.[42]

Gilbert also wrote to Sullivan on 5 May, saying he was about to begin a new libretto and would have it ready in six months for Sullivan to set whenever he chose or not at all; he also reiterated the need for a new agreement.[43] Yet Sullivan continued to put it off. He was too busy to go into financial arrangements, and it would be well to settle the disputed points before beginning on *The Gondoliers'* successor, which would not be needed for months anyway. Gilbert then revoked Carte's licence to perform his librettos outside London after Christmas 1890 (an error for 1891, as Helen Carte pointed out) and his licence for London after the current opera finished its run.[44] Supposing that Sullivan intended to tell him when he could start work, he also broke off relations with his collaborator, accusing him of 'marked discourtesy', consistent hostility, and 'contemptuous indifference'.[45]

'How have I stood him so long!! I can't understand,' Sullivan exclaimed in his diary. He answered Gilbert that night: the charges were baseless and uncalled for, merely actuated by his refusal to act always 'in accordance with the impulse which seizes you'. When Sullivan chid Carte for his insult to Gilbert, he was given a very different account of the passage at arms with the librettist. He therefore

---

[42] Copy, 5 May 1890: DOYC/TM.    [43] PML.    [44] 5 May 1890: DOYC/TM.
[45] 5 May 1890: PML.

accepted the breach with 'deepest pain'[46] and became ill from kidney trouble and tension.

In spite of this supposed end of the partnership, all three combatants (for Sullivan could not hold aloof) circled warily in letter after letter. Gilbert explained that 'discourtesy' referred to Sullivan's implication that he, not Gilbert, should decide when the latter should begin to write. As for the 'imperious will' which Sullivan ascribed to him, 'In a matter in which my self-respect is involved, I must claim the right to be arbitrary.'[47] For his part, Carte asked Sullivan to give him Gilbert's letters in case anything in them affected him.[48]

At this point Gilbert immediately offered a libretto to Horace Sedger, manager of the Lyric Theatre, suggesting that he did not expect the same payment as at the Savoy, but would take 15 per cent of the gross, the entire stage-management and control of cast to be his.[49] Sedger, of course, accepted, and the librettist then co-opted Alfred Cellier to set—the lozenge plot. At last!

Back at the Savoy, a substitute whom Gilbert had not rehearsed was playing the Duchess, Rosina Brandram being ill. This brought forth repeated cries of insult from Gilbert, who asked his solicitor to discuss the possibility of arbitration with Carte[50] (who was still refusing to let Gilbert see the Savoy books).

Rumours of a separation were now beginning to spread, and Malcolm Salaman of the *Sunday Times* approached Gilbert to ask the reason. Gilbert drafted an answer to the effect that Sullivan was dedicating himself to grand opera and they thought it advisable to end their partnership with 'a marked success'.[51] He sent this for approval to Sullivan, who angrily protested that it gave the impression that he, not Gilbert, was responsible.[52] So a revised note merely told Salaman that they had agreed the public were not concerned with their reasons.[53] The public, however, heard a great deal about them during the next six months.

May also held a small annoyance for Gilbert, beginning with a request from George Bainton two years earlier for information about his method of composition, allegedly for a lecture he would give 'our

[46] Copy, 5 [6?] May 1890: PML.       [47] 8 May 1890: PML.
[48] Copy, 7 May 1890: DOYC/TM.
[49] Draft of letter, 9 May 1890: WSG/BL Add. MS 49,332.
[50] Letter to Sullivan, copy, 13 May 1890: WSG/BL Add. MS 49,333. Gilbert was probably unnecessarily touchy on this point, coming, as it did, when he expected slights from Carte.
[51] 15 May 1890: PML.       [52] Copy, 16 May 1890: PML.
[53] 16 May 1890: PML.

young people'. Gilbert replied that he believed 'a writer's style should be guided by canons analogous to those which regulate a gentleman's dress: if it attracts the attention of the non-critical reader, it is probably because it is disfigured by glaring errors in taste.' He recommended studying late Tudor and early Stuart English and believed no work could be compared with the historical books of the Bible for 'simplicity, directness & perspicuity'.[54]

Bainton, although he was presumably a clergyman, did not hesitate to publish this letter and those from many other writers without permission in *The Art of Authorship: Literary Reminiscences, Methods of Work, and Advice to Young Beginners, Personally Contributed by Leading Authors of the Day*, which appeared in 1890. 'His action appears to me to amount to a breach of faith,' Gilbert told *The Author*, which exposed Bainton's dishonesty in the first issue of its first volume. His condemnation was unusually mild compared to the objections of some of the others. He was saving his wrath for the Savoy, where another skirmish began over Carte's accusation that Gilbert was luring away Savoy singers. Of the principals, however, only Geraldine Ulmar and Frank Wyatt went to the Lyric when their engagement with Carte ended, and Gilbert accepted some chorus members who had asked him for employment. He would have liked Jessie Bond. On the whole, the Savoy company was generally on Gilbert's side.

Nevertheless, he felt himself almost alone. His public image was unsatisfactory, for although intense quarrels were by no means unique in the theatre, the triumvirate were more widely known by the general public than, for instance, was Cecil Raleigh, whose epic but unpublicized battles with his collaborators outdid the Savoy dispute.[55] Sullivan's general affability made him seem an artist caught in the toils of the overbearing Gilbert, and the press censured the latter's temper while admitting his genius. Moreover, whatever Sullivan told Gilbert, he was himself really on Carte's side: Carte had built him an opera-house and he felt closer to the impresario who addressed correspondence to him as 'Dear Arthur' while his collaborator was 'Dear Gilbert'. As a minor musician, Carte was further drawn to England's greatest composer, while Sullivan in turn felt that Carte understood him in a way that Gilbert could not. And, most of all, Gilbert represented for

---

[54] 24 Sept. 1888: PML.

[55] G. Deghy, *Paradise in the Strand* (London: Richards Press, 1958), 123. Raleigh's collaborators were Henry Hamilton and G. R. Sims.

him an aesthetic status quo, while Carte represented those 'higher' things which critics continually urged.

To make things worse, Carte allowed himself the temporary pleasure of being indiscreet in an interview published in the *Star* on 23 May. Referring to Gilbert as a very difficult man, he boasted that when he handled hundreds of thousands of pounds, a mere £140 for a carpet was nothing much. As to Gilbert's projected collaboration with Alfred Cellier, Carte said the musician was a good friend, and 'I do not think [he] would consent to do anything that we should not like.' He accused Gilbert of intending to damage *The Gondoliers* by running a new work in competition, but he himself preferred to wait till the coming production materialized before deciding whether he had any right to stop him.

This suggestion that Carte could control Cellier and perhaps Gilbert too infuriated the dramatist and surprised Sullivan, who wrote, 'I think Carte's interview deplorable. So does he.'[56] Chagrined, Carte explained in a letter to the press that the *Star* had printed inaccuracies and 'observations not intended . . . for publication'. Gilbert suffered a migraine attack and influenza, followed in early June by whooping cough!

Quarter day for distributing Savoy profits came round on 4 July, but Carte withheld them on his solicitor's advice. After waiting until 30 July, Gilbert issued a writ for his share, which he calculated at £3,000 or more. The manager sent £2,000; so, when Gilbert's solicitors told him he must move for a receivership or lose the whole, he took their advice. Snappish because Sullivan had advised paying, Carte nevertheless ended a long letter to him with an emotional, and perhaps calculated, appeal: 'if *you*—my friend of so long standing . . . are not going to back me up thoroughly in the trouble—then it *is* hard and I feel disheartened for the first time and in a way that nothing else could make me.'[57]

By now the situation had become a welter of I said—you said—he said in which simple truth grew increasingly difficult to find. The court action was adjourned twice: first to enable Sullivan to be joined as a joint defendant, then to allow Gilbert time to return from Carlsbad, where the pangs of gout had driven him. He wanted to sign a new affidavit. Carte's counsel objected to this 'cruel conduct', which might injure Carte's chances of arranging mortgages to complete the Royal English Opera House, but he bowed to a doctor's certificate. After all this, the receivership was denied because legally it could not be granted

[56] Copy, 26 May 1890: PML.     [57] Copy marked 'Private', 13 Aug. 1890: DOYC/TM.

if there were outstanding expenses. Gilbert swore there were not; Sullivan swore there were. Carte, however, was ordered to pay Gilbert £1,000 the next day and to produce the year's accounts in three weeks.

The hearing over, Gilbert wrote unexpectedly but not uncharacteristically to Helen Carte, suggesting a reconciliation. Although Carte bitterly resented Gilbert's statement that he could only conclude Carte used their money for his own private purposes, his wife met the dramatist. On hearing that his own sense of injustice was founded on a misapprehension, Gilbert gave in, but he still wanted to reopen accounts from 1883 onward.

He also wanted Sullivan to admit he was mistaken in the affidavit produced in the recent legal action. The librettist had sworn that he had authorized no legal expenses 'not yet brought into account', and he believed there were none of any significance outstanding. Sullivan, on the other hand, had sworn there *were* legal expenses still outstanding in an action Gilbert had authorized, thus implying that the latter had committed perjury. (The action to which Sullivan referred had been begun by Lillian Russell, which, as Gilbert wrote to him, was settled five years earlier. The only outstanding legal expenses were a mere £46 for matters Gilbert did not authorize.) He believed that 'deceptive representations' had been made to Sullivan, and he asked him to retract.[58] Sullivan refused and in the press of finishing *Ivanhoe* wanted no further discussion.

Since Sullivan's diary tells us that on 2 September he swore the affidavit in the office of Frank Stanley, Carte's solicitor, it seems more than likely he had been told what to say. (Stanley's attitude was that the collaborators were employed to write for the Savoy and paid by a share of the profits rather than by fees or royalties. They were therefore only entitled to information to satisfy themselves as to the amount they were paid.)[59] Just before the première of *Ivanhoe*, Gilbert tried again to make Sullivan understand his position: all he asked was that the composer should acknowledge he was mistaken when he swore the affidavit—he required no public statement, only a personal letter. Sullivan was not interested, but he hoped that his erstwhile partner would attend his grand opera (suggested by the Queen, housed in a palace of coloured marbles, double cast, and with no expense denied in its lavish produc-

[58] 14 Oct. 1890: PML.

[59] Bolton, letter to Gilbert, 14 July 1890: PML. Bolton was Gilbert's solicitor and had interviewed Stanley.

tion). After all, a few months ago Gilbert had dedicated his *Songs of a Savoyard* to Sullivan 'In just acknowledgment of the distinction his genius has conferred upon these songs during the fourteen years that we have worked together.' But now he refused to come unless Sullivan sent him the assurance that he had sworn his affidavit under a misapprehension.[60]

He did not: his answering letter foolishly asked why Gilbert should question his good faith when he had never questioned Gilbert's. He refused to admit he was wrong, even though Carte had already given up the point, but suggested that Gilbert's presence in the audience that night would be 'an intimation that you are as ready and willing as I am to think no more of what has happened and to allow nothing to disturb our old friendship'.[61] He enclosed two stalls—he would have liked to make it a box, but the Royals were coming in force.

Gilbert wrote two more letters in return, again explaining he wanted only a statement that Sullivan had been misinformed. 'If you will give me this, I will use the stalls with the utmost pleasure.' Then, more brusquely, 'You deliberately swore that the costs in Russell v. Carte were still unsettled and by so swearing you defeated me and put me to an expense of £400 in costs . . . I decline your stalls.'[62] Sullivan called this communication 'a rough and insolent refusal', unaware that his intransigence had made it so. Gilbert spent opening night at the renovated St James's Theatre. Yet he went on writing, trying to drive through the composer's *Ivanhoe*-filled head the indisputable fact that his affidavit was wrong and he was honourbound to correct his error.

Ironically enough, Gilbert and Carte had become reconciled more than a month before and had shaken hands with most of the symbolic implications of that gesture. No doubt their accord was the work of Helen Carte, whom Gilbert had never ceased to respect. He did not, however, go to the first anniversary of *The Gondoliers* to the regret of the cheering audience and the now-friendly press.

Gilbert and Sullivan were still estranged as February 1891 began. The silver cord had been broken and the golden bowl of the perfect plot had been shattered. They would eventually tie the cord together again and mend the bowl, but the knots and joins would still show. Moreover, handshake or not, from 1890 onward, Carte imagined fresh litigation in every Gilbert proposal, and Gilbert saw a possible insult in Carte's every response.

[60] 30 Jan. 1891: PML.     [61] 31 Jan. 1891: PML.
[62] Both letters 31 Jan. 1891: PML.

# 17

## The Road to Utopia

He ought himself to be the Public Exploder.
*Moonshine* (21 Oct. 1893)

DURING the throes of the quarrel, Gilbert bought a country
estate: Graemes Dyke, or, as he soon respelled it, Grim's Dyke.
Breakspears, where he and Kitty had been spending extended sum-
mers, would no longer be available, its owner Mrs Drake having died
and her heir wanting the house for himself. There was an argument
over who owned the valuable plants in the greenhouses (Kitty was a
knowledgeable gardener), and at last the new owner, Captain Alfred
Henry Tarleton, suggested they toss up for them. Amused, Gilbert
agreed, lost the toss, and perhaps 'caught it' from Kitty. She soon had
other greenhouses to fill, however, and the Tarletons became their
friends.[1]

It was, perhaps, harder for Gilbert to leave Breakspears, where he
wrote in a sunny dressing-room, than to leave Harrington Gardens with
its large study and amusing architectural idiosyncrasies. Grim's Dyke
had larger grounds, however, being set in Harrow Weald, with a farm
of its own, a mile or so from the spot where legend placed Boadicia's
suicide. The house itself was built in 1870–2 in the early Tudor style of
its architect Norman Shaw, and its first owner was the painter
Frederick Goodall. In 1882 he sold it to a banker named Henriot, who
in turn sold it to Gilbert. Henriot had added a billiard-room, and
Gilbert would add a kitchen wing with bedrooms above. He also turned
Goodall's painting-room into an enormous drawing-room with a pink
alabaster mantelpiece, ceiling high and supported by terms of satyrs,
for which he himself had roughed out the first sketch. He liked satyrs

[1] Letter from Helen Fagan to the author, 16 Aug. 1971: JWS. Helen Fagan was Captain
Tarleton's daughter.

and eventually acquired two wooden figures, formally dressed to the waist, beast beneath, which the servants called 'the devil'.

His heavy mahogany desk fitted well into his new study, together with his six-legged 'Burgomaster' chair, comfortable but requiring long thighs if one wanted to lean back. The desk-top was a clutter of brass objects, among them a statuette of a goose, pulling up the shirt of a curly-headed child. (All these are now in the London Museum.) A statue of Charles II stood in the grounds until Gilbert made an artificial lake (and developed arthritis working in the clay); after that Charles stood in the lake.[2]

This was Gilbert's home for the rest of his life, except for the January–February stays in rented London flats, always in Belgravia or Chelsea, and for the time spent travelling. At first the place was infested with rabbits, which had to be shot,[3] but apart from them no other destruction was allowed. He could not bear taking life himself—not even that of a black beetle.

Year by year he added to well-established collections of blue-and-white china, of pictures (including a van Ruisdael, a van Everdingen, a Tintoretto, and a Giorgione), and of books—ultimately some five thousand with more than four hundred in his bedroom. There was a weighing-machine in his bathroom and a suit of armour in the hall; an eighteenth-century musical clock with a scene which animated above the dial may have suggested *The Gondoliers*.[4]

Persian rugs were everywhere; Morris-tiled fireplaces, inscribed cig-arette cases, his portrait by Frank Holl; a monogrammed coffee and tea service, eighteen dessert plates with pictures from the Bab Ballads, longer and longer stretches the inventory. There were seventy towels for servants and five cottages. In 1905 Gillow's valued the contents of Grim's Dyke at £12,692. 18s.[5]

Yet 'some lurking bitter', as a trio sings in *The Yeomen of the Guard*, had already begun to poison the dramatist's relation with his new col-laborator. Alfred Cellier liked Gilbert's scenario, and they had gone through it to arrange musical situations before Cellier, who was tuber-cular, left for Australia and warmth.[6] He stipulated that the subject

---

[2] Lady Gilbert's will returned the statue to its original site in Soho Square.

[3] Draft of a letter to T. Blackwell, 19 Apr. 1891: WSG/BL Add. MS 49,332.

[4] 'A Gilbertian Clock', *The Times* (12 Apr. 1960).

[5] Waring & Gillow, Valuers, copy of inventory at Grim's Dyke, taken for the purposes of Fire Insurance, Dec. 1905.

[6] Cellier to Edward Chappell, 30 Apr. [1891]: WSG/BL Add. MS 49,332.

should not be Spanish and the characters should not be guerrillas since he had just finished setting a libretto laid in Spain. Gilbert understood his reluctance, but while Cellier was still at Portsmouth, he wrote that he had revised the plot, offering to send the new version to await the composer at Naples. Cellier telegraphed that he preferred the original, but would be glad to hear more about the revision—a serious mistake since Gilbert habitually took polite gestures as acquiesence.

At Naples, as his ship left for Port Said, Cellier learned that the opera was now laid in Sicily and its chief characters were banditti. He wrote his objections from Suez to an angry Gilbert, who had not yet heard from him and who made no allowance for the postal exigencies of travel. When Cellier arrived in Australia, he received a letter cancelling their collaboration[7] although the new opera, *The Mountebanks*, was due in Sedger's hands in September. Yet Gilbert did not find another composer: very likely he did not look. He had, after all, worked with Cellier long ago in *Topsyturvydom* and knew his music for *Dorothy* had been a great success.

Meanwhile the Royal English Opera had opened with fanfares of publicity, which not even *Aida* or *Parsifal* could live up to. Sullivan recorded that he entered to a 'Tremendous reception by a brilliant and packed house'. Nevertheless, more than one review fell short of the superlatives Carte had anticipated, and *Moonshine* (if Sullivan read that second-class comic paper) must have galled him by saying *Ivanhoe* lacked 'the spontaneous freshness and flow of the composer's comic operas'. Sturgis's adaptation and verse did not make a good impression, and G. B. Shaw in the *World* wrote that it served Sullivan right for not doing the libretto himself.

In a continuous run, *Ivanhoe* lasted for 160 performances before Carte closed the opera-house without recouping the expenses of its extravagant production. Evidently he supposed audiences would come again and again as they did at the Savoy, although as *Irish Society* pointed out, 'the public who can pay such [high] prices is practically limited'. Nor did the impresario have a second opera ready even though he had asked the composer Frederick Cowan to provide one.

Having refused Sullivan's first-night tickets, Gilbert saw a later performance and admitted he was not bored (as he usually was at operas), but made some suggestions about staging. On 6 March Carte took *The Gondoliers'* London Company to give a command performance at

---

[7] Cellier to Edward Chappell, 30 Apr. [1891]: WSG/BL Add. MS 49,332.

Windsor Castle. It was the first light opera chosen by Queen Victoria, who already knew the music. She thought the scenery pretty, Jessie Bond very clever, and Rutland Barrington very fat. After hearing a touring *Mikado* company perform for her at Balmoral six months later, the Queen decided she preferred *The Gondoliers*.[8] According to rumour, Carte hoped for a knighthood after the expensive gesture of closing the Savoy for an evening, but, whether he did or not, no knighthood came. Gilbert, of course, had no direct part in this performance.

By early April Alfred Cellier had returned to London, too ill even to write Gilbert. He dictated a letter, insisting that delays in correspondence were really delays, not discourtesy, and promised he would set the revised scenario.[9] Gilbert was notified a few days later that he had been made a Justice of the Peace for Middlesex; he took the appointment very seriously and worked hard at fulfilling his new duties.

In May, too, Carte, with auditors still going through disputed accounts, admitted 'an unintentional overcharge of nearly £1,000 in the electric lighting accounts alone'. He promised payment when *The Gondoliers* ended. 'As you will, I suppose, benefit considerably by this re-adjustment,' Gilbert wrote to Sullivan on 28 May, 'I thought it possible that you might wish to share with me the costs of the action by which it was brought about.'[10]

In June Desprez, Dance, and Solomon's *The Nautch Girl* replaced *The Gondoliers*. It was well enough, meaning not very well in spite of a cast which included Barrington, Bond, and Denny. Reviewers remarked that stage business and treatment of the chorus had been much better *sub regno Gilberti*. Also in June the Vaudeville Theatre mounted a benefit performance of *Rosencrantz and Guildenstern*, Gilbert's last contribution to *Fun*. In this staged version of a closet burlesque, Ophelia's father is Lord Chamberlain, 'reading all the rubbishing new plays'; Hamlet advises the players to eschew huge red noses and extravagant wigs, and Claudius in youth wrote an appallingly bad tragedy, for resurrecting which Hamlet is banished to the Lyceum. The next year the playlet had a run as part of a triple bill at the Court Theatre with Brandon Thomas (author of *Charley's Aunt*), Weedon Grossmith (George's brother), and Decima Moore.

[8] G. Rowell, *Queen Victoria Goes to the Theatre* (London: Paul Elek, 1978), 107–8. Gilbert was the only dramatist three of whose plays were given command performances (the third was *Sweethearts*), although both *Cavalleria Rusticana* and *Carmen* were each performed for the Court on three separate occasions.

[9] Harriet Cellier to Gilbert, 6 May [1891]: WSG/BL Add. MS 49,332.

[10] Draft, 28 May 1891: WSG/BL Add. MS 49,333.

The summer of 1891 went by. Gilbert found Horace Sedger far less pleasant to deal with than Carte and Alfred Cellier far less compatible as a collaborator than Sullivan. The librettist was ill himself; so Sedger reluctantly postponed the opening of *The Mountebanks*. He could do nothing else: Cellier had not composed the music. (Even putting health aside, he had the reputation of being a desultory worker.) That autumn, when Carte reopened the Royal English Opera House with Messager's *La Basoche*,[11] Gilbert and Sullivan were seen publicly in congenial conversation: 'this was regarded as an incident,' announced a journalist, for they had agreed to do another opera together after their present commitments elsewhere. Although they had decided to let bygones be bygones, Gilbert could not help remembering that Sullivan had sworn to an untruth, but he said nothing.

Carte sold off some Savoy properties that November, from which Gilbert selected the executioner's axe, block, and the bell from *The Yeomen of the Guard* for his billiard-room. He was also corresponding with George Grossmith, whom he had asked to compose a score for *Haste to the Wedding*, enlarged from his old success, *The Wedding March*. It seems a strange choice: Grossmith had written only comic songs, but, as he would tell an interviewer from the *Pall Mall Gazette*, he had studied harmony with Edward Solomon, read several books on orchestration, and closely observed the Savoy band. (Scarcely enough to replace Sullivan as reviewers were to agree!)

But *Haste to the Wedding* was still in the future, while *The Mountebanks* was supposedly now. Gilbert had read it to the company in August when Cellier assured him the music was 'practically finished'. Rehearsals had begun in September, at which time Cellier had composed only four quartets: music rehearsals had to be put off. Justifiably annoyed, Gilbert told Cellier that he would not begin his necessary five weeks of stage rehearsal until the cast had learnt all the music.[12] This proved unfeasible, however, for the music was never completed. The irritation at Cellier's incapacity to approximate any kind of a schedule spilled over into an interview the librettist gave the *Pall Mall Gazette* on Christmas Day. He had already moved the opening ahead—again—, had had two sleepless nights, and had not yet been able to get an overall view of the whole work. The music was very skilful, but Cellier was not used to the give and take of working collaboration.

---

[11] In spite of excellent reviews, *La Basoche* lasted only till 16 Jan. 1892, and the house was dark again.

[12] Draft, 25 Sept. 1891: WSG/BL Add. MS 49,332.

In a few days Cellier was not used to anything. He was dead. He had been at Bournemouth where the air was supposedly better for consumptives, but he came to London for the last rehearsals of his yet uncompleted score. Five days of constant fog hung over the capital, thick and smothering. People died under it, and so did Cellier on 28 December. In Paris, Sullivan heard the news by telegraph and wrote to Cellier's brother Frank with eyes full of tears and pen dipped in irony: 'I wonder what Gilbert thinks now of his kindly & generous expressions about him in his "Pall Mall" interview. Anything more selfishly egotistical or in worse taste, I cannot conceive & even *he* ought I think to feel a bit sorry now.'[13] But Gilbert had not known how close Cellier was to death; he had been seemingly more ill months before and had survived, and Gilbert did know that *The Mountebanks* had somehow to be pulled together. Exasperation and the frustration of a man who sees his work still piecemeal around him for causes he cannot control made him speak more sharply than he otherwise might have done.

Opening night was moved again—to 4 January 1892—and Gilbert tried to pick up the pieces:

I had to make rough & ready alterations to supply gaps—musical gaps—caused by poor Cellier's inability to complete his work. It follows that Act 2 stands out as a very poor piece of dramatic construction. . . . this is the worst libretto I have written. Perhaps I am growing old.[14]

A printed folder published the words to three songs Cellier had left unset; one, 'When your clothes from your hat to your socks', was revised and inserted in *The Grand Duke* four years later; another, 'If my anticipation's correct', was a complex variation on 'The Bridegroom's Song' in *A Sensation Novel* years before; while the third 'I'm an excellent Duke' was a biting comment on the nobility, ending

> His rank he may drag through the mud;
> If his life is depravity's essence,
> After all, it's the mere effervescence
> Of uncorked aërated blue blood—
> For, you see, he's a person of rank;
> If he does now and then play a prank,
> He's a dashing young fellow,
> When older he'll mellow:

[13] 29 Dec. [1891]: published by permission of Mrs Dorothy Palmer Lewis.
[14] Letter to Mrs Stephenson, 7 Jan. 1892: JWS.

> So many temptations
> Unknown to our stations
> Beset a young fellow of rank![15]

The fourth of January was frosty but fogless, enabling the audience to throng to the new Gilbert work. In the plot of *The Mountebanks*, the essential lozenge is a magic potion which all drink. According to the label,

*Man is a hypocrite, and invariably affects to be better and wiser than he really is. This liquid . . . has the effect of making every one who drinks it exactly what he pretends to be. The hypocrite becomes a man of piety; the swindler, a man of honour; the quack, a man of learning; and the braggart, a man of war.*

Burning the label produces a happy status quo ante, which ends the opera.

Gilbert, like the critics, praised the cast, in which Frank Wyatt was a brigand chief turned monk by the potion; Lionel Brough, a mountebank; Geraldine Ulmar, 'a *Village Beauty . . . in love with herself*'; and Eva Moore, a young girl whom the potion turns to an old woman. As automatons, Harry Monkhouse and Aida Jenoure proved most popular, Gilbert having particularly trained them in mechanical movements, designed Miss Jenoure's dress, and supervised her long-lashed eye make-up. He also endeared himself to the women's chorus, who, unlike the men's, had no other employment and had lost money by the postponed openings. Gilbert sent each one a week's salary, and in return they wrote gratefully that they would always remember his 'kindness and consideration' during rehearsals. They 'could wish no better than always to be in your productions, to be ever under your kind surveillance.'[16] Each girl signed it.

The *Era* was delighted with *The Mountebanks* and prophesied that it would be one of the greatest triumphs of modern comic opera; most reviewers, in fact, were complimentary to Gilbert and kind to Cellier, while admitting his music was not dramatic. Gilbert's wit, they agreed, was more caustic than ever. He described himself in a mountebank's song:

> Other clowns make you laugh till you sink,
> When they tip you a wink;
> With attitude antic,
> They render you frantic—
> I don't. I compel you to think!

---

[15] All three songs are repr. in T. Searle (ed.), *Lost Bab Ballads* (London: G. P. Putnam's Sons, 1932).  [16] 9 Jan. 1892: WSG/BL Add MS 49,332.

The hit of the show was the automatons' duet 'Put a penny in the slot' to move usurer, tax-collector, venal police constable, and the audience itself—a lozenge within a lozenge, which the listeners apparently had no trouble in swallowing. At the end, there was an enthusiastic call for Gilbert, who refused to appear alone.

Although he made improvements after the first night, he still thought the opera a poor thing. '[F]ortunately the public have not yet discovered how bad it is,' he wrote to Alfred Austin's wife, adding bitterly, 'It's good enough for *them*.'[17] He had been sceptical of British theatrical taste since his early days on *Fun*; now, after misplaced laughter and jeers had greeted *Brantinghame Hall*, he was thoroughly antagonistic. Fortunately, the public did not discover 'how bad' *The Mountebanks* was, and it ran for 229 performances, fifteen more than Grundy and Sullivan's *Haddon Hall*.[18]

Even after the opera was launched, there were rough seas for Gilbert in January 1892, for Edward McNulty, a former Bank of Ireland official, sent letters to several papers, asserting that *The Mountebanks* was essentially his and that he had sent the manuscript to Cellier six months before Gilbert's libretto was staged. Gilbert answered, via letters to editors, that the plot had originally been worked out for the Savoy seven years before and the revision had been completed by January 1891. He doubted Cellier had ever read McNulty's play, which by its author's own showing had a Pygmalion–Galatea plot.

More annoying was an exchange of letters with Sedger, who had agreed to produce Gilbert and Grossmith's *Haste to the Wedding* at the Prince of Wales's, his other theatre. First, he denied their verbal agreement, then shilly-shallyed about arrangements, and finally sold his interest in the theatre to a syndicate, subject to producing the Gilbert–Grossmith piece as the second work after their take-over—or so Sedger said. 'How am I to understand this?' Gilbert asked,[19] and looked elsewhere. At the Lyric, Sedger was trying to increase his own profit at Gilbert's expense, arguing over already-settled terms and saying he had been treated unfairly. Gilbert answered,

Your letter won't do. You have charged me, practically, with having swindled you, & I will have a distinct retraction & unqualified apology before I consent

---

[17] 11 Jan. 1892: PML.

[18] One of *The Mountebanks* touring companies broke the record for comic opera receipts at the Theatre Royal, Birmingham. Lillian Russell played in it in America, and Charles Ryley and Henry Bracy, formerly of the Savoy *Princess Ida*, were in the Australian cast.

[19] Draft, 23 Jan. 1892: WSG/BL Add. MS 49,332.

to deal with you except through the medium of solicitors. It is as well that you should learn that charges of this class are not to be made against gentlemen with impunity.[20]

Truth to tell, Sedger was not a gentleman, and Gilbert's anger, while personal, was once again emphasizing the status of a playwright.

Gilbert and Kitty then left for Cairo, where rumour erroneously reported he was working on an Egyptian libretto. They returned in time to attend the wedding of Effie Hare and George Bancroft, and for the dramatist to discover that Sedger was dismissing chorus members for the sake of 'economy' in spite of *The Mountebanks'* large profits. Appealed to, Gilbert did what he could, which was not very much, and Sedger's business manager wrote he had been misinformed. Two years later, Sedger tried the same ploy again on a larger scale and was successfully sued by one of the ousted chorus men. Gilbert was more fortunate when the manager put a touring company of the opera into the Grand Theatre, Islington, claiming it as a provincial playhouse, already included in the £500 he had paid. Armed with affidavits from prominent actors and managers attesting the Grand counted as a London theatre, Gilbert thwarted this plan and won a perpetual injunction, forbidding Sedger to play without Gilbert's approval of the cast. Having made his point, the dramatist then allowed a fortnight of performances for the sake of those who had already bought tickets.

By 24 April Gilbert had found a different manager and completed arrangements with Charles Wyndham for the production of *Haste to the Wedding* at the Criterion Theatre. Nearly twenty years before, he had begun the libretto when Sullivan intended to set it and his brother Fred to play Woodpecker Tapping. Fred's death had ended that. Now, in 1892 some, perhaps all, of the lyrics were more recent and more complex, including a song sung by

> An over-devotional,
> Super-emotional,
> Hyper-chimerical,
> Extra-hysterical,
> Wildly-aesthetical,
> Madly phrenetical,
> Highly-strung sensitive Duke!

(Gilbert evidently was drawn to dukes during the 1890s!) Yet the musical numbers scarcely go beyond duets, some accompanied by the

---

[20] Copy, 29 Jan. 1892: WSG/BL Add. MS 49,332.

chorus. Gilbert had told Grossmith he would like them set simply, which is what the comedian-composer did.

While he worked on the score, Sarah Bernhardt opened the Royal English Opera House, which had been closed since January. In spite of appearing in such roles as Cleopatra and Tosca, she did not draw as well as formerly, and Carte did not accept Gilbert's suggestion that good new productions of four Offenbach operas in repertory would be able to play for a year.[21] Instead, at the end of June he sold the freehold and building itself to a company of which Sir Augustus Harris ('Druriolanus') was managing director; it reopened in December as a variety house called the Palace Theatre. Sullivan's dream was dislimned; Carte's reach had exceeded his grasp. 'A cobbler should stick to his last,' Sullivan told the American composer Reginald deKoven.[22] His 'last' turned out to be a romantic-comic score for Sydney Grundy's *Haddon Hall*.

Sullivan had been abroad when *The Mountebanks* opened, but he went to the first performance of *Haste to the Wedding*, curious, no doubt, to see what sort of a substitute Grossmith made. His diary does not comment, however. As an actor, Grossmith habitually gave himself a shot of morphine to relieve first-night tension, and perhaps he did so now—for better or worse.[23] Gilbert, whatever he thought of the score, presented its composer with a silver-tipped ivory baton. There were, however, dissenting voices at the curtain-call, and the general consensus was that *Haste to the Wedding* lacked 'finish'—an unheard-of criticism for a Gilbert piece. Nevertheless, the cast was warmly praised, including as it did, Frank Wyatt, Lionel Brough, and George Grossmith Jun., making his acting début as Cousin Foodle. The fact that the opera appeared during the theatrical doldrums told against it, and it did not survive even until the end of August.

Gilbert returned Sullivan's visit by joining the brilliant crowd at the première of *Haddon Hall* on 1 October, and by going backstage to congratulate him and Grundy. The *Illustrated London News* explained to its readers that his presence there afforded 'living testimony' of the collaborators' intention to work together again. It also described Grundy's

[21] Letter to Mrs Carte, 17 June 1892: DOYC/TM.

[22] I. Goldberg, *The Story of Gilbert and Sullivan or the 'Compleat' Savoyard* (rev. edn., New York: Crown Publishers, 1935), 398, quoting an article on deKoven by Rennold Wolf, in the *Green Book Magazine* (Dec. 1913). deKoven proposed himself to Gilbert as a collaborator but was kindly refused. See J. W. Stedman, '"Then Hey! For the Merry Greenwood": Smith and deKoven and Robin Hood', *Journal of Popular Culture*, 12 (winter 1978), 432–45.

[23] Interview with J. C. G. George, Kintyre Pursuivant of Arms, 10 Aug. 1974.

book as 'a fairly palatable mixture' of seriousness and Gilbertianism, but it praised Sullivan's score at length. The collaboration to come was, of course, *Utopia (Limited)*,[24] for which the painful process of working out an agreement began on 31 October. Now willing to reckon the rental of the Savoy at £4,500 if Carte paid all front of the house expenses, Gilbert started with a simple proposition: continue Sullivan's current contract with Carte, give himself a third share of the profits and complete stage authority. He understood, mistakenly, that Carte would need Sullivan's permission before spending more than a moderate sum on renovations and that Sullivan would not give it if Gilbert disapproved.

The Cartes immediately rejected this proposal as impractical—it was the old agreement with its problems all over again, and Helen wrote several letters to Sullivan, telling him he must not agree to anything without consulting them first. Gilbert, she said, had 'now acquired a liking . . . for taking any possible question in dispute into a public court',[25] and they feared he was manipulating Sullivan into endless arguments and unwise concessions. That they were themselves directing Sullivan for their own purposes did not occur to them.

At times Helen's letters become repetitively importunate; she warned Sullivan that Gilbert had a prima donna in his eye for the next opera, and she warned him that one of his proposed letters to Gilbert 'would be the smell of blood to the hungry lion'.[26] Gilbert had, in fact, become wild in their eyes, to be warily approached with a chair at the ready. D'Oyly did not dare to use a whip.

Gilbert, on the other hand, amused himself by attending a mind-reading demonstration in November, during which Mr Cumberland invited him to the stage, asked him to imagine committing a forgery, and then succeeded in writing down the amount he was thinking of, the forged signature, and the country whence he intended to flee. On New Year's Eve he felt relaxed enough to thank Marion Johnson amusingly for her season's greetings: '*You* wish me every happiness in the coming year. I don't confine myself to that—*I* wish you every happiness in *all* the coming years. But that's so like me—reckless & profuse in Everything!'[27]

In contrast, as the new year began, Helen Carte was having bad dreams nightly: 'I wake up with the horrors', and the horror was always

---

[24] The parentheses were later dropped from the title.

[25] Copy, 3 Dec. 1892: DOYC/TM.          [26] Copy, 31 Dec. 1892: DOYC/TM.

[27] 31 Dec. 1892: PML. Miss Johnson, 'Johnnie', had been a member of the Savoy chorus, and was now Mrs Long.

that Gilbert had taken them to court for signing something.[28] Weary and exasperated, she wrote to Sullivan that he was too ready to soften what should be stern replies to the librettist.[29] When, at last, the agreement with Carte was signed, Gilbert was no longer a member of the triumvirate; his powers of stage-management were intact, but he settled for 11 per cent of gross receipts rather than the old equal net division. Six months later, sure he had made a miscalculation, he asked Sullivan not to let him be placed 'in a position of striking inferiority'.[30] To this plea his collaborator remained deaf, while to Gilbert's later plaint that he felt humiliated by the arrangements, he answered waspishly (as his diary for 16 December shows) 'that so long as steps were taken by which he would be absolutely prevented from going to law upon any question, it was open to him to make any other arrangements for the future.'

In January 1893 Sullivan invited Gilbert to Roqueburn near Monte Carlo where he was staying, and Gilbert read the sketch-plot of *Utopia (Limited)* to him there. Although Sullivan liked it very much, it was six months before he commenced work on it. Gilbert had feared the musician's health might keep him from finishing a score, and the month before had even sounded out the singer, composer, and teacher George Henschel.[31] In the event, he was not needed, but Gilbert evidently liked his work and asked if he would reset *Princess Toto*, the rights of which had recently reverted to the dramatist. He now thought Clay's music was 'sickly sentimentality',[32] but Henschel was not interested.

Gilbert was also engaged with the formation of the Theatrical Choristers' Association, prompted in part by Sedger's behaviour. Its aims, as reported in the *Era*, included pay for rehearsals, full salary for matinées, a fixed salary for six performances a week, and contracts for the run of the play, as well as a fixed pay scale for understudies (who often were chorus members), and better dressing-rooms. Although the choruses of the early 1890s had higher musical and social standards than those even of five years earlier, their pay had been halved.[33] Carte lent the Savoy, considered a fair-acting theatre, for their meeting, and Gilbert, who was elected president of the Association, gave them practical advice, together with a beginning donation of 20 guineas.

In spite of these calls upon his time, Gilbert busied himself with *Utopia (Limited)*, beginning Johnsonially with the Happy Valley ruled

[28] Letter to Sullivan, copy, 6 Jan. 1893: DOYC/TM.
[29] Copy, 14 Jan. 1893: DOYC/TM.          [30] 23 July 1893: PML.
[31] 12 Dec. 1892: PML.          [32] 27 Feb. 1893: PML.
[33] 'Life in the Chorus', *Era* (28 July 1894), 13.

by King Rasselas the 35th. Later he shifted the scene to a wildly Anglophilic South Pacific island whose king was first named Philarion and then Paramount. Since Utopia's subjects, who believe Great Britain is the epitome of excellence, long to copy her language, manners, and institutions, Gilbert was free to satirize whatever he chose, even including Victoria's refusal to provide refreshments at her Drawing Rooms. (At one stage, Gilbert thought of including a 'tea minuet'.) Generally, however, the satire is more tightly focused by six Flowers of Progress representative of a range of professions, whom Princess Zara brings with her when she returns from Girton.

Gilbert worked hard on rethinking and rewriting this libretto. Occasionally he recommended choristers or small-bit players to Carte, one a friend of 'ours', implying Mrs Gilbert had some voice in his suggestions (which she did). Carte rarely accepted these amateurs, although Gilbert may have been more successful in placing persons in reduced circumstances as ticket-takers or typists.

One of his jests that spring passed into legend even though it was not original with him. At a dinner-party, someone spoke of Beerbohm Tree's Hamlet. 'Funny without being vulgar,' Gilbert immediately commented to everyone's amusement. The joke was repeated so widely that Gilbert contritely wrote to Mrs Tree that he had an unfortunate tendency to speak without thinking. Tree, on the other hand, was delighted and circulated the story himself, having 'too high an opinion of my work to be hurt by it'.[34]

While Gilbert coped with *Utopia (Limited)*, Sullivan was querulously objecting to paying his share of the Savoy rental while the house was dark during the hiatuses between non-Gilbert-and-Sullivan productions. He was unhappy that *Ivanhoe* had brought him only £1,800 in royalties where Carte lost £35,000—as Helen Carte reminded him in twenty-three handwritten pages.[35] In fact, from 1893 to Sullivan's death in 1901 the Cartes were often exasperated with him. He thought the Savoy chorus was not up to the mark; he wanted a larger orchestra; he needed money and thought briefly of writing for another theatre; he continued to send important letters to Gilbert which they had not vetted, and he did not always say what he meant if he thought it would be unpleasant.[36] Yet D'Oyly and Helen stuck to him; whatever his

---

[34] Letter from Beerbohm Tree to Gilbert, 25 Mar. 1893: WSG/BL Add. MS 49,332.

[35] Copy, 7 Feb. 1893: DOYC/TM.

[36] e.g. Richard D'Oyly Carte made this point in a letter dated 9 Mar. 1894, and Helen Carte repeated it more than once.

demands, they remained friends even though they chid him from time
to time. Perhaps Carte was still suffering from 'an old standing stricture
of the uretha', which excused him from jury duty the December before;
it obliged him 'to retire at frequent intervals to pass water' so that he
had to sit, if possible, in an aisle seat in theatres and take railway carriages near lavatories.[37] This scarcely helped his composure in discussions with Sullivan—or with Gilbert, for that matter.

While Sullivan argued about money, Gilbert found himself once
more in the throes of gout. He had finished Act 1 when a violent attack
seized both feet and his right hand, making him, as he said, write like
a crab. From late April to early June he was more or less housebound,
allowed only to 'eat and drink things that I detest'.[38] Hard for a man
with a sweet tooth! Kitty was 'groggy' too, her horse having knocked
her over. In July they went to Homburg for the cure:

My right foot (which I call Labouchère) is very troublesome, and I take a
vicious pleasure (not unalloyed with pain) in cramming him into a boot which
is much too small for him. My left foot (known in Homburg as Clement Scott)
is a milder nuisance, but still tiresome, and would hurt me a good deal if he
could.[39]

Unfortunately, the regimen made him worse, not better, and he came
home for new treatment. He read his Utopian libretto on crutches to
the cast, after postponing the meeting for four days. For rehearsals
themselves he frequently appeared in a wheelchair.

The libretto had become a battleground for the collaborators, for
Sullivan objected to the proposed character of Lady Sophy, describing
her as old or middle-aged and ugly, 'seething with love and passion . . .
and other feelings not usually associated with old age'.[40] Gilbert wrote
back to him, sensibly pointing out that the composer had not objected
to the character for months, that Lady Sophy was 45 and no uglier than
the actress playing her (Rosina Brandram), and that her frenzy was 'not
of the gross or animal type at all, as you seem to imagine'.[41] In his early
scenario, Gilbert had described her as keeping in check a 'spirit of wild
& passionate devilry' beneath her cold exterior,[42] but he had already
banked her fires and evidently made no substantive changes to meet

[37] Carte to 'Dear Sirs', copy, 12 Dec. 1892: DOYC/ TM.

[38] Letter to Mrs Bancroft, 13 May 1893: PML.

[39] Quoted by H. Pearson, *Gilbert: His Life and Strife* (London: Methuen & Co. Ltd., 1957),
171.

[40] 1 July 1893: WSG/BL Add. MS 49,333.     [41] 3 July 1893: PML.

[42] PML.

Sullivan's objection. Perhaps the fact that Sullivan's mistress Mrs Ronalds was undergoing the menopause made him unusually touchy about middle-aged passion. Yet for Gilbert it was always an interesting emotion and in his plots often as important as the romance of tenor and soprano, who have sometimes fallen in love before the action opens. In *Utopia (Limited)* Paramount (played by Barrington) and Lady Sophy provide the ongoing love interest.

Another, more protracted dispute was yet to come. Mrs Carte was right in supposing that Gilbert had a soprano in mind for Princess Zara. She was an American without a 'twang', Nancy McIntosh, young, delicately blonde, naïve, and charming, who had been in London for three years. Her father accompanied her, in part to escape from memories of a disaster at home. He was a member of the hunting and fishing club whose dam had burst and allowed a river to roar down and obliterate Johnstown, Pennsylvania, beneath it. Nancy's brother Burr was still in the United States, a reporter and character actor, who was to play the Squire in D. W. Griffith's motion picture *Way Down East* and to become a radio personality.

Sullivan had heard Miss McIntosh at the farewell concert of Alice Shaw, *la belle siffleuse*, but had completely forgotten her. Since then she had sung at the Saturday and Monday Popular Concerts and those of the London Symphony, among others. Hans Richter thought well of her; *The Times* described her voice as 'a soprano of great beauty and considerable power', and *Musical News* predicted she would rank high among sopranos of the day. Some American reviewers, however, described her as a contralto or mezzo, while she herself said her compass ranged from high C to low F.[43] In England she was a soprano, even though both Gilbert and George Bernard Shaw thought Sullivan's music was often too high for her. 'I know the value of top notes in concerted music', Gilbert wrote to George Henschel, Miss McIntosh's teacher, but he intended to suggest that Sullivan might transpose her solo declamation. It would mean a snubbing from his collaborator, '*but he usually carries out my suggestions*, nevertheless'.[44] In this case Sullivan may have snubbed, but he did not give in.

Unluckily, Miss McIntosh, an utter novice as to the stage, was often nervous while performing, which caused a good deal of variation in her

[43] 'Princess Zara: A Chat with Miss Nancy McIntosh', *Sketch* (11 Oct. 1893).

[44] 15 Sept. 1893: quoted by the kind permission of the Clement D. Johnston Collection (#6693–B), Manuscripts Division, Special Collections Department, University of Virginia Library.

vocal quality. But Mrs Ronalds took an interest in a fellow American, and Mrs George Lewis told Gilbert she would be excellent for the Savoy.[45] Ultimately Sullivan, though not enthusiastic, agreed to accept her. Carte at first offered her £7 a week and then evidently raised it to £10, a good sum in the Savoy scale of salaries, but Gilbert tried unsuccessfully to raise it to £15. His partisanship seems at first to have been motivated by chivalry and Nancy's general likeness to his earlier protégées Marion Terry and May Fortescue. Then, too, he may have wanted the éclat of presenting a musical find to Sullivan. As always, opposition hardened his position.

As time went by, Nancy began to see more of the Gilberts: Kitty liked her, and Schwenck found her intelligent and receptive to coaching. She already had a clear enunciation, which he improved, while the fact that she was a good horsewoman endeared her to both. In return, she may have started a youthful crush on Gilbert: she was, after all, the youngest prima donna the Savoy had had.

Up to the last moment of rehearsals, Gilbert worked on the stage pictures and lighting. He snapped at a journalist who interrupted his reconstruction of a complicated scene, but wrote to him apologetically, explaining and inviting him to a less fraught rehearsal. He wanted more diamonds for Nancy as a princess and tighter stays: 'she has an idea that she can't sing unless her stays are quite loose. I don't advocate tight lacing, but there is a medium in all things. . . . I will get my wife to talk to her about it . . . . Don't let her have her way in any dress question—she has no idea of dressing herself.'[46]

In Act 2 the ceremonial of a Royal Drawing Room gave them all trouble, but it was finally worked out authentically and lavishly, lit by hundreds of electric bulbs shining above a specially laid parquet floor. Some nights later, the Prince of Wales assured Carte that it was very well done; yet he was 'a little exercised' over Barrington's wearing the Garter on stage (later removed).[47] As an authority on military costume, the Prince was careful about orders and decorations on theatrical

---

[45] Gilbert to Sullivan, 20 June 1893: PML.

[46] Fragment of longer letter to Carte, n.d.: PML.

[47] Helen Carte to Sullivan, copy, 18 Oct. 1893: DOYC/TM. Colin Prestige points out (in a letter to the author [9 Feb. 1993]: JWS) the falsity of the legend which says that the Prince of Wales complained because Paramount wore the Garter with a Field Marshal's uniform, a combination which he alone of living men was entitled to wear. The Duke of Cambridge, Victoria's first cousin and Commander-in-Chief (1856–95), also was a Field Marshal and a Knight of the Garter.

costumes.[48] What might he have said had he known that in an earlier draft, Paramount was allowed two indiscretions before being dynamited by the Public Exploder Tarara (surname Boomdeay until almost the last moment)—the indiscretions no doubt being a reference to the Mordaunt Divorce and the Tranby Croft scandal?

As a whole, *Utopia (Limited)*, even after some of the bitterest lines were deleted, was more politically specific than any Gilbert play since *The Happy Land*, to which Paramount refers in a fairly late version. The basis of his satire is the contrast between England as she is and England as she should be—in this case, Utopia. Yet the equation is not quite that simple. The imported Flowers of Progress introduce serious improvements never totally achieved in Great Britain, but they also jokily persuade King Paramount to accept as English such absurdities as a Cabinet Meeting *à la* Christy's Minstrels. Even the rigidly correct Lady Sophy tells Utopians in all seriousness that English girls never quarrel over a suitor: they toss for him. Zara and her Captain invent a fantastic England to keep away the amours of Scaphio and Phantis, Paramount's Wise Men, under the Rival Admirers' Clauses Consolidation Act. These shifting multiple and ironic images of lands of hope and glory made *Moonshine* exclaim that Gilbert himself should be the Public Exploder. In a private flick at Sullivan, Gilbert had Tarara make an affidavit that what the Utopians suppose is happiness is really misery: 'You know you can't help believing an affidavit.' Although *Truth* praised this line, it was deleted at Sullivan's behest.

Finally, Utopia and Great Britain coalesce in a repetition of Gilbert's old theme of the 1870s; that is, man cannot bear perfection long. So improved is the South Pacific kingdom that its natives rebel at being 'swamped by dull Prosperity' until Zara remembers what is missing:

Government by Party! Introduce that great and glorious element . . . and all will be well! No political measures will endure, because one Party will assuredly undo all that the other Party has done; and while grouse is to be shot, and foxes worried to death, the legislative action of the country will be at a standstill. Then there will be sickness in plenty, endless lawsuits, crowded jails, interminable confusion in the Army and Navy, and, in short, general and unexampled prosperity!

---

[48] For example, when John Hare played Prince Petrovsky in *Ours* in 1866, the Prince of Wales summoned him, congratulated him, and pointed out several mistakes in Hare's haphazardly chosen decorations: J. Hare, 'Reminiscences & Reflections', *Strand Magazine*, 35 (May 1908), 521.

The finale, which gave Sullivan great difficulty in setting, and was arrived at only five days into the run, again juxtaposed views of Great Britain. Zara and the King each sing a verse extolling that nation as 'the bravest of the brave' and 'a monarchy sublime', but the ensemble has the last word:

> Let us hope, for her sake,
> That she makes no mistake—
> That she's all she professes to be!

'Together again' was the keynote of the first performance. The audience cheered Gilbert and Sullivan as they shook hands at their curtain-call; called them back and cheered again; applauded the cast, especially Barrington and Brandram, who took the star curtain-call, and went home in a sentimental glow. Many of the reviewers struck the same note; Shaw and Labouchère liked the scope of the satire, the latter taking no public notice of Gilbert's anonymous allusion to his having been publicly thrashed. Others, however, hinted or spoke plainly of defects in music and libretto. It was a superb production (never had William Clarkson, the *perruquier*, made so many expensive wigs),[49] but was the dazzling Drawing Room, for instance, really necessary for the plot? Did Gilbert begin lines of minor development and then drop them? Like *Ruddigore*, *Utopia (Limited)* suffered from the great expectations of public and press.

Nancy McIntosh's performance was attractive albeit nervous, both as singer and actress. Her only solo, 'Youth is a boon', which plays with youth as a capital investment on commercial principles, was cut after first night.[50] Sullivan, who had found her 'nice, sympathetic & intelligent' in June, was now sure she would never be a singer and told Gilbert so on 16 December; she had no sympathy in her voice, he said, but he changed his mind when she sang for him again and urged her to return to the concert stage. She continued at the Savoy.

She started a series of bad throats in January 1894, which dominate her diary, missing performances and consequently losing money because of them. People were kind, though: lilies from Barrington, eggs and violets from Kitty Gilbert, and for St Valentine's Day candied fruit from Sullivan and, appropriately, Valentine's meat juice from Gilbert. Still, she was discouraged and sometimes sank into fits of crying. When

---

[49] 'Mr. Clarkson at Home', *Era* (4 Nov. 1893), 11.

[50] R. Allen (ed.), *The First Night Gilbert and Sullivan* (New York: Heritage Press, 1958), 413.

Gilbert's influence secured her the role of Dorothy in William Mollison's calling-card performances of *Dan'l Druce*, which he was directing, she had almost no voice for the first performance, although she redeemed herself at the second. The dramatist, rehearsing the cast, had even transformed himself into a half-shy, half-loving maiden to show her how to play a scene.

Whether Miss McIntosh would have a part in the next Savoy opera was now the question. Gilbert admitted he was not altogether disinterested, for, unless she earned a living elsewhere, she and her father would be on his and Kitty's hands forever. If Sullivan could procure enough concert engagements for her, he would never again mention Miss McIntosh in connection with the Savoy. But Sullivan and Carte were considering ways to get rid of 'Miss M.'; even Helen Carte wondered why such 'a really amiable and sweet girl ... should be such a wet blanket and such a damper on the performance'.[51] She thought Gilbert should attend a performance to see how badly she did.[52]

Gilbert had, so Sullivan wrote in his diary, already appealed to him:

by our old friendship, by our long & honourable collaboration, by the regard & respect that I have for you & you, I hope for me, to let me *as a favour* write a small part in the next piece for Miss McIntosh, & save her from starvation!

This was an extreme position, perhaps, but it is true that when Carte asked Nancy what salary she expected, she had answered 'enough to live on'. Sullivan wanted the weekend to think it over. 'Come, why not say so at once,' Gilbert replied and 'went away delighted'. Two months later, the composer, backed by D'Oyly and Helen, plainly and utterly rejected Nancy; he would not compose any piece with a part for her or a part suitable for her. If Carte revived *The Mikado* next (which he did not), Sullivan would not accept her as Yum-Yum.

Upon the rock of Gilbert's partisanship, the collaboration split again. He may have been impelled by Kitty, who seems to have found Nancy very congenial, but the stubbornness was his own. And, after all, he felt justified by the reviews. He turned immediately and unsuccessfully to George Henschel as a possible collaborator and went as far as proposing, but not consummating, an agreement with Sedger! A Henri III plot which he had been mulling over and had proposed to Sullivan proved abortive.

[51] Letter to Sullivan, copy, 24 Feb. 1894: DOYC/TM.
[52] Letter to Sullivan, copy, 18 Oct. 1893: DOYC/TM.

On 9 June *Utopia (Limited)* ended its run of 245 performances with a last night which the *Era* described as memorable for dash and spirit. If Gilbert felt vindictive toward his erstwhile triumvirs, he could now take pleasure in the £4,600 his 11 per cent on gross receipts had brought him. Carte's and Sullivan's profit-sharing arrangement brought each of them only £1,800.

# 18

## Other Voices—Other Tunes

I feel instinctively—superstitiously if you like—that the luck has
gone from the theatre for a time at least.

Sullivan to Helen D'Oyly Carte (24 May 1899)

IT was clear that *Utopia (Limited)* would not be a money-maker on
the old scale. Costs of production were too high, and on 3 January
1894 Carte wrote to Gilbert suggesting ways of cutting expensive corners—and more than corners—on the next opera. Why not let
Barrington go and bring in the lower-salaried Lytton? There were less
expensive sopranos and comedians to be had. Especially, Carte asked,
could not Gilbert and Sullivan write a frankly comic piece? People
wanted fun, and the less sentiment the better.[1] In fact, Carte unconsciously was repeating Gilbert's own, earlier advice to Sullivan; that is,
that the more irresponsible their approach, the larger the box-office.[2]
Yet, when Gilbert later suggested a modern farcical comedy such as
*Engaged* as the basis for a libretto, the manager was not interested.

Soon thereafter Gilbert Murray, Schwenck's cousin, reappeared
briefly in his life. Although Murray saw the Savoy Operas as they came
out, he had evidently seen little of Gilbert himself. Now he needed help
in placing his play *Carlyon Sahib*, having unsuccessfully tried his uncle
Sutherland Edwards and the actress Janet Adchurch. 'It will give me
great pleasure to introduce your work to Beerbohm Tree & to
Alexander,' Gilbert wrote to him. 'They will certainly read any MS that
I ask them to read, but I am not at all sure that either of them is likely
to express an opinion that may be relied on.' However, 'it will at least
gratify them to learn they have been complimented with the work of so
distinguished a scholar'.[3] They may have been gratified; after all,
Murray was a leading classicist, but neither wanted to stage it. Gilbert
therefore wrote to him again, apologetically, on 6 April, saying that

---

[1] Copy: PML.    [2] 20 Feb. 1889: PML.    [3] 13 Feb. 1894: Bodleian.

'there are not two actors on the English stage who are qualified to carry on an intellectual dialogue for three minutes without boring their audience. . . . If you want to make money, put anything into your play but brains & you may possibly succeed.'[4] Although *Carlyon Sahib* did not reach a stage until 1899, when it ran for twelve performances, Gilbert had more influence on Murray than he supposed, for, as has been frequently pointed out, his metrical style furnished a model for Murray's translations of Aristophanes.

At the Savoy Gilbert continued to work on a new libretto, and even jotted down a tentative cast, including Nancy McIntosh, and their salaries.[5] He was still at odds with Sullivan over Nancy, with Carte trying to smooth things over and to persuade Gilbert that the composer would arrange concert work for her or that, like Julia Neilson, she was better suited to the serious stage.[6] Gilbert was angry, and was hurt because, though the Cartes had staged *Haddon Hall* for Sullivan and a new librettist, they were unlikely to put on his own work with a new musician. Nevertheless, he ceased to invite the reluctant Henschel to collaborate. Instead the *Era* (16 June 1894) announced that Gilbert would write an opera-comedy with Dr Osmond Carr while Sullivan would set a libretto by Adrian Ross.

Sullivan did no such thing, although Ross was a skilful versifier. Instead, late in 1894 Sir Arthur turned to Frank Burnand and their old work *The Contrabandista*, enlarged and retitled *The Chieftain*. Despite Sullivan's heroic efforts, it proved how wrong Burnand was in supposing the Savoy successes might as easily and satisfactorily have been Burnand and Sullivan as Gilbert and Sullivan. In fact, he still did not understand his limitations, and his importunities became a tiresome nuisance for Helen Carte.

On the other hand, Gilbert was indeed working with Osmond Carr, using the libretto he had intended for the Savoy. He had already assembled a cast, which included Jessie Bond, George Grossmith, Rutland Barrington, and Alice Barnett, as well as Nancy McIntosh. (Grossmith now asked £70, but Gilbert hoped to go only as high as £50.) In July he added the current Savoy tenor Charles Kenningham, after a flurry of letters in which Mrs Carte could not decide whether to keep him or recall Courtice Pounds. She accused Gilbert of subverting Savoy choristers, but he took only those for whom he had room and who preferred

---

[4] Bodleian.    [5] WSG/BL Add. MS 49,289.    [6] Copy, 3 Jan. 1894: DOYC/TM.

his methods, pointing out that they were out of an engagement anyway when the Savoy closed in June.[7]

*His Excellency*, as the new opera was called, was now intended for the Lyric Theatre, where George Edwardes had replaced Horace Sedger as manager, although Sedger was still lessee. Gilbert knew Edwardes well from the days when he had been Carte's deputy business manager. A large expansive Irishman, who married Julia Gwynne (the original London Edith, Saphir, and Leila), Edwardes became famous as 'The Guv'nor' of the post-Hollingshead Gaiety.

The setting of *His Excellency* is Elsinore, whose Governor (Grossmith) and his daughters (Bond and Ellaline Terriss) have a mania for practical joking. For example, he has sent the girls' suitors letters promising them high positions at the court of Denmark. When the Prince Regent arrives, disguised as a strolling player, the Governor is struck by what he supposes is a fortuitous resemblance and hires the Regent to impersonate himself and to confer bogus honours on everyone. Christine, a ballad singer, also sees the 'player' as a double for the Prince's nearby statue, with which she has fallen in love. When the true identity of the Prince Regent is revealed, he confirms the honours he has distributed, proposes marriage to Christine, and demotes the Governor to sentry.

On opening night, 27 October 1894, the audience proved rowdy because the London County Council had just closed another Edwardes' enterprise, the Empire Theatre, a music hall, until it abolished what was virtually a prostitutes' promenade. (Six days earlier Gilbert had sent his sympathy to a protest meeting, although he did not care much for music halls or prostitutes.) At the Lyric, Edwardes quieted the gallery by an amusing speech, hoping the Council would find no reason to interfere with *His Excellency*. The crowd laughed and applauded.

It applauded the opera itself just as heartily, hailing George Grossmith loudly as he sang:

> Quixotic is his enterprise, and hopeless his adventure is,
>> Who seeks for jocularities that haven't yet been said.
> The world has joked incessantly for over fifty centuries,
>> And every joke that's possible has long ago been made.

Characteristically imperturbable as the comic—romantic Regent, Barrington was at his best, even singing in tune. ('First night nerves,'

---

[7] 21 July 1894: DOYC/TM. Gilbert wrote further letters to Mrs Carte on 6, 8, 10, and 13 Sept., reiterating he had not raided her chorus for his own.

Gilbert said.) Some of the characters seemed superfluous, however; perhaps even Nancy McIntosh's role was really unnecessary although Gilbert gave her a satiric fable to sing in which a bee earns his queen's displeasure by trying to swarm alone.

During rehearsals Grossmith had caught the proper 'undercurrent of chuckling impish malignity running through the character', but on opening night he was often too severe. (Later, there were reports that he was overacting, which Gilbert sent Kitty to investigate. She reported nothing more *outré* than a far-fetched gag, but she preferred the original words 'in which I think I agree with her', Gilbert wrote to Grossmith, 'but that may be merely a parent's prejudice in favour of his own offspring'.)[8]

As the Governor's daughters, Bond and Terriss were so delightful that reviewers forgave their malice, and one of Gilbert's most touching little scenes is their surprise when one cries a real teardrop. During rehearsals, Gilbert began a lifelong friendship with Miss Terriss, who was the daughter of William Terriss, hero of robust melodrama, who would be murdered three years later at the private entrance to the Adelphi Theatre. In 1894 she went fearfully to rehearsals, having heard that Gilbert was a blistering-tongued martinet, only to find him kind and helpful. They discovered they might be very distantly related, and he named her 'The Tuneful Nine' because 'Hicks [her married name] = Icks = IX = 9.'[9]

Funniest of all the cast was the male chorus as the King's Hussars, led by Arthur Playfair, whom the Governor forces to drill as a *corps de ballet.*

> Never was seen such tawdry trickery
> Soldiers, tough as oak or hickory,
> Turned to votaries of Terpsichore

The non-commissioned officers entered like *premières danseuses*, pirouetting and falling into each other's arms, one leg extended as John D'Auban taught them. Playfair, the dancing corporal, told a *Sketch* interviewer that his spurs kept him from doing *entrechats*; he didn't want them, 'but Mr. Gilbert says we're cavalry, and cavalry wear spurs'. Spurs and all, they were encored nightly.

Another masterpiece of drollery, was the *Era*'s opinion of *His Excellency*, although 'Monocle' of the *Sketch* suggested that Jove and

[8]  6 Jan. 1895: Bevan Coll.

[9]  E. Terriss, *Just a Little Bit of String* (London: Hutchinson & Co. Ltd., 1955), 113–14.

the audience sometimes nodded. Osmond Carr presented a greater problem to the critics. Reviews of his earlier scores for *Round the Town* and *Blue-Eyed Susan* had been mixed and scarcely prepared him to set a libretto originally intended for Sullivan. 'Pretty', 'peculiarly appropriate', 'sometimes gay, and not infrequently humorous' were some of the commendatory adjectives applied to his score, but other critics thought he tended to monotony, lacked Sullivan's humour, or was overshadowed by Gilbert's 'muscular' book. Be that as it may, musician and librettist took three curtain-calls; nevertheless, Carr did not pursue a career in light opera for long—four years later he took over the Carl Rosa Opera Company. He had not been up to the pressure of Gilbert's lyrics, nor had he been able to hold his own in a powwow, if, indeed, he and the librettist had met to argue out the final structure. 'If [*His Excellency*] had had the advantage of your expensive friend Sullivan's music, it would have been a second Mikado,' Gilbert told Mrs Carte.[10] Still, it was running admirably, and he could now turn his full attention to an annoying episode which began ten days before opening night. The Comtesse Anna de Brémont, a novelist and journalist, had asked then to interview him for *St Paul's* magazine, and with no time to spare, Gilbert put her off, he thought, by answering that his terms were £20— whereupon the Comtesse replied that 'she anticipate[d] the pleasure of writing his obituary notice for nothing'.[11]

Although later she described it as only a joke, this letter appalled Gilbert. He hated to give anyone an opening for wit at his expense, and he had certainly done so with the Comtesse; moreover, that someone wished him dead was an outrage (a word he was fond of using, although its meaning was much less forceful than it is today). He wrote to the editor of *St Paul's*, suggesting he keep a careful eye on any article the Comtesse might write about him; then he wrote to *The Times* and the *Daily Telegraph*, including copies of her note and saying she was known to him by repute. She sued him for libel.

Although Gilbert had reacted too strongly, her suit was ill-advised, for she was not a countess. A handsome American, born Anna Dunphy, she had married Dr de Brémont, often misaddressed as Comte, although he had no claim to the title. When, after his death, she turned to a literary career, she dedicated her erotic, pseudo-Rossettian *Sonnets and Love Poems* to his memory. At one time, she had been a not-very-good actress and had even auditioned for the Savoy. Allegedly friendly

[10] 4 Nov. 1894: DOYC/TM.
[11] *The Times* (23 Oct. 1894), 6. The letter was written 19 Oct.

with Lady Wilde, Anna claimed a 'mysterious soul-sympathy' with Oscar, which he did not acknowledge.[12] Mrs Bernard Beere, the actress, thought her insinuations in a theatre article were 'a little disgusting';[13] so Gilbert may have been right in warning *St Paul's*.

When the trial came before a special jury a year later, Gilbert won easily. His investigators had discovered the Comtesse's liaisons with young men in South Africa (one actor who became in middle age a pillar of the British Empire in Hollywood!). In short, Anna had no character to lose, and, watching her reputation torn to shreds in the courtroom, Gilbert could not help pitying her. He told his solicitor not to press for costs, and she wrote him a reconciliatory letter.

Meanwhile, as 1894 drew to a close, Gilbert felt himself out of touch with his own immediate world. He refused requests to contribute to periodicals, writing to one editor that 'I have sufficient modesty left to feel convinced that my personal opinion upon any point unconnected with my profession cannot be of the smallest interest to any human being',[14] and to another, 'the views that I entertain on most theatrical subjects are so diametrically opposed to accepted ideas that they would certainly damage any magazine in which they might appear'.[15] He and Kitty turned to what had become his panacea and pleasure: travel.

In mid-January 1895 they embarked on a two-month cruise to the West Indies, on a ship, the Orient Company's *Lusitania*, which advertised a string band, electric light, and 'high-class cuisine' for £283 apiece. The *Era* expected Gilbert to return with a new libretto, and, as a matter of fact, he had already begun work on what would be *The Grand Duke*, having passed two characters, A and B, through an elaborate plot-book development. More immediately, however, his third series of *Original Plays* was published in London during his voyage. The *Athenaeum* praised his extraordinary lyrics, but rather hoped he would strike out in a new line.

Upon his return, Gilbert unhappily discovered that *His Excellency*, for all its good reviews, was now in mid-March on the verge of closing. Influenza had been raging in London, which sent the box-office plummeting. Grossmith had even offered to take no salary for a fortnight,

---

[12] Anna, Comtesse de Brémont, *Oscar Wilde and His Mother: A Memoir* (London: Everett & Co. Ltd., 1911), 129.

[13] Undated letter to Clement Scott: Scott Papers/TM. In his own letter to *The Times*, published 23 Oct., Gilbert said he had been unwilling to place himself 'at the mercy of the good taste and discretion of this lady', whom he knew 'by repute'.

[14] To C. Duncan Lucas, 19 Dec. 1894: PML.      [15] To F. Hawkins, 30 Nov. 1894: PML.

and, when closing notices went up, other principals willingly accepted reduced salaries in order to keep the theatre open, but to no avail. Hearing from three persons that Grossmith was gagging, Gilbert fired off an angry letter, to which the actor replied, 'I have a goodly collection of letters of complaint from you during the last seventeen years, and after two days consideration, I have come to the conclusion, that your last has gone beyond the bounds of my endurance.' He and Barrington had occasionally engaged in 'some mild badinage', but he had never altered the lines themselves. He deserved thanks for offering to play without pay, not an irritated letter, which was not 'an incentive to a nervous actor to play your work properly'.[16] Nancy McIntosh told Gilbert of Grossmith's continued annoyance, and he wrote to explain who his informants were. He believed that 'Edwardes allowed all kinds of liberties and gags to be taken . . . during my absence,'[17] which was very likely true, although perhaps not of Grossmith. In spite of everything, when *His Excellency* closed in April, Grossmith wrote in his family book, 'I feel so sad that our lovely show has ended.'[18]

With a better score and Gilbert's continuing presence to make post-production alterations in the text, *His Excellency* would no doubt have had a longer life in spite of influenza. Yet some of the responsibility was Gilbert's own, for in his librettos of the 1890s, he relaxed his long-held principles of comic construction. More than his contemporaries, he had hitherto adhered to the unities of French drama in his librettos, a form in which other writers notoriously sprawled. His best plots are neat, ingenious, and single (or so balanced as to seem single), and are confined to two acts between which little time elapses. Although the incidents may be melodramatic, they are arranged in a framework of logical alternatives, often beginning with an absurd premise related to a seemingly simple romantic problem. This initiating problem, ostensibly solved in Act 1, gives rise to a more difficult problem for Act 2, the solution of which allows the first solution to be put into effect, as in *The Mikado*.

The post-1890 librettos, however (except for *Haste to the Wedding*), have multiple plots, often with enough incident to furnish two of Gilbert's early operas. This loosening had begun unnoticed in *The Gondoliers* with its three pairs of lovers, its dramatis personae, whom

[16] 30 Mar. 1894: WSG/BL Add. MS 49,332.

[17] To Mrs Carte, 10 Oct. 1905: DOYC/TM.

[18] The Grossmiths kept a book in which to record a comment or illustration at the end of the day; it was entitled 'Retired Tired', and is now in the possession of James Bevan.

Gilbert determined 'all shall equal be', and its long time-lapse between acts. Fortunately, the brilliance of the lyrics and score concealed the suggestion of diffuseness in the structure, but Cellier and Carr were not Sullivan.

Nevertheless, Edwardes sent out a fairly successful touring company and a less successful American one with some of the London cast. He still wanted to produce another Gilbert opera the next October, although he did not like the scenario, undoubtedly *The Grand Duke*, as much. By April, however, Gilbert and Sullivan had fallen in again, and Gilbert cancelled his contract with Edwardes. The problem of financial arrangements again arose at the Savoy, the Cartes and Gilbert continuing to be wary of each other. 'You have I fancy an idea—an altogether mistaken one—that we are always trying to get the best of you in a bargain,' Helen wrote to him. 'It would much simplify our doing business if you could once & for all put this idea out of your mind.'[19]

Gilbert could not, but at last, after much negotiation, he sold the complete rights of *The Grand Duke* to Carte for £5,000, which he intended to invest in real estate. In July Helen went to Grim's Dyke for his signature, but found him so ill he could not raise his head. He had contracted influenza, which 'turned to a sort of cholera—he has had cramps and constant diarrhoea night & day'.[20] Although he was too weak to sign the contract, they went through it clause by clause. Slowly he regained strength until by August he was able to take part in the preliminaries for the new opera.

These included hiring a soprano, in this case the Hungarian Ilka Palmay,[21] with wickedly expressive eyes and considerable dash, whom Sullivan had once stopped from playing a transvestite Nanki-Poo in Berlin. Allegedly she spoke excellent, if accented, English, but when she later appeared, Gilbert found her command of the language was by no means what he had expected. Engaging a tutor for her, he also coached her himself,[22] and luckily she improved rapidly. Her irreducible accent would be accounted for by making her an 'English' actress in Ernest Dummkopf's 'German' troupe. Audiences found this reversal hard to keep in mind.

The evolution of *The Grand Duke* was probably more complex than that of any other Gilbert libretto. At one point, the characters A and B

[19] Copy, 15 May 1895: DOYC/TM.
[20] Letter to Sullivan, copy, 10 July 1895: DOYC/TM.
[21] Erroneously but frequently called von Palmay.
[22] Letters to Mrs Carte, 7 and 10 Dec. 1895: DOYC/TM.

possessed complementary virtues and vices; at another they became Barons, and their author played with perhapes until they became professional philanthropists. Eventually, H and I, their surrogates, were involved in a duel, which consisted of drawing lots, the winner to assume the legally dead loser's responsibilities. To make this plausible, Gilbert invented a Grand Duke, whose duchy has been decimated by real duels and who dictates a less lethal form of settling differences. 'The legally dead form a body of ghosts,' Gilbert speculated,[23] and the faint form of the final libretto appears, although many plot-book pages were necessary to give it shape.

Coincidentally, Gilbert had received a letter before leaving England, enclosing an editorial, 'Dead, Yet Alive', cut from the *Keene Evening Sentinel* (New Hampshire). The writer, Bertram Ellis, thought Gilbert might use it for a plot since it dealt with the comic problems of an electrocuted criminal, pronounced legally dead, but resuscitated. His wife would be a widow; his heirs would claim his property; he would have to be christened anew and begin another life—a solution unconsciously in the style of Gilbert's own short story 'Tom Poulton's Joke' and his play *Tom Cobb*. He thanked Ellis, telling him that curiously enough, he was already working on a plot which involved legal death. It was unlikely he would incorporate any material from the editorial, but he promised to pay Ellis £50 if he did.[24] In fact, Gilbert went so far as to write out the hypotheses, but they dealt with the executed man's problems. The man who 'died' was not the person to exploit, he noted, but rather the survivor.

Until a very late stage, Gilbert intended his Grand Duke Rudolph (killed by an actor in a statutory duel) to be named Wilhelm, as an allusion to the Kaiser, Germany being unpopular in England because of its attitude toward the Boers. His duchy would be Hesse Halpfennig; he would be a pig and miserably stingy. Perhaps Sullivan, friendly with Wilhelm II, objected; so the name was altered and 'Hesse' was dropped.

This role fell to Walter Passmore, who had created the small part of Tarara in *Utopia (Limited)*; Rutland Barrington played Ludwig, leading actor of Dummkopf's troupe, who finds himself Grand Duke after drawing an ace in the duel with Rudolph. Although he is about to marry Lisa (Florence Perry), Ludwig discovers he is engaged to the penny-pinching Baroness von Krakenfeldt (Rosina Brandram); to the

---

[23] WSG/BL Add. MS 49,290.

[24] Copy, 14 Jan. 1895: WSG/BL Add. MS 49,332. The letter is really a draft rather than a clean copy.

actress Julia Jellicoe (Ilka Palmay), who claims the role of Grand Duchess as her professional right; and to the Princess of Monte Carlo (Emmie Owen), betrothed to him in childhood, who arrives with her suddenly wealthy father. (He has just invented roulette.) The tangle of obligations is finally straightened out when the actors' solicitor finds that an ace counts as the lowest, not the highest, card in a statutory duel. Rudolph regains his title, marries the Princess, and everyone returns to everyone else.[25]

Preparations for this complicated plot were progressing nicely when Sullivan began to ask for voice changes. He wanted Brandram to be a muted Julia, which would eliminate Palmay and require someone new to play the Baroness.[26] Gilbert agreed, but Helen Carte feared he would now have two grotesque women's roles. She wrote and telegraphed to Sullivan, objecting that he had once again failed to consult the Cartes before sending important letters to Gilbert and adding that they felt '*entirely disheartened*'.[27] Sullivan sensibly capitulated; whether or not he felt like rebelling against the Cartes' habit of controlling his letters is another question.

In the meantime Gilbert had a new idea for a melodrama, which he proposed to the actor Seymour Hicks. Hicks and his wife, Ellaline Terriss, just returned from the American tour of *His Excellency*, were spending a few days at Grim's Dyke, when their host read a newspaper account of the military degradation of Captain Dreyfus, after one of the most important trials of the century. 'Fancy if that man were innocent!' Gilbert exclaimed. 'What a drama! and what a wonderful scene the degradation would make! . . . why don't you write it?'[28]

---

[25] From the first, Gilbert was said by the press to have borrowed important portions of his plot from Tom Taylor's 'The Duke's Difficulties', *Blackwood's Magazine* (1853), which Taylor made into a performed but unpublished play, 'A Duke in Difficulties'. In this plot, a poverty-stricken Grand Duke cannot pay his courtiers; so they leave and are replaced by members of a theatrical company. After a good deal of romantic intrigue, the actors assist the Grand Duke to marry a princess who arrives with her brother. H. B. Farnie and Alfred Murray had turned Taylor's story into a light opera, *The Prima Donna* (1888), which was not very successful. Although Gilbert denied it, there may have been a subliminal memory at some point in the development of his libretto, but his characters, motivation, comedy, and peripeteia are very different from Taylor's. Instead, the plot of *The Grand Duke* is essentially a throwback to that of *Thespis*, in which actors replace Olympian gods and mythology provides an equivalent of Julia Jellicoe's professional right to play the Grand Duchess. Sir St Vincent Troubridge ('Another Gilbert Borrowing', *Theatre Notebook*, 10 (Oct.–Dec. 1955), 20–1) puts the case for Taylor, but Gilbert's plot-books were then unavailable for consultation.

[26] Telegram from Helen Carte to Sullivan, copy, 14 Aug. 1895: DOYC/TM.

[27] Letter from Helen Carte to Sullivan, copy, 14 Aug. 1895: DOYC/TM.

[28] *Seymour Hicks: Twenty-Four Years of an Actor's Life*. By Himself (New York: John Lane Co., 1911), 193.

With the help of George Edwardes, Hicks did. Their *One of the Best* opened at the Adelphi Theatre on 21 December 1895, with William Terriss speaking the defiant line: 'You may take my name, my honour, my life, but you cannot take my Victoria Cross!' It ran for a year, which was longer than *The Grand Duke* would. Earlier Gilbert had hoped Hicks would appear in his new opera and had invited Ellaline to play in a piece he intended to write for the actor E. S. Willard. Neither accepted; indeed, Gilbert never wrote the play although a fragment of dialogue in which a newly rich girl prepares to enter society may be a preliminary sketch of it.[29]

At the end of November Gilbert sent the final version of *The Grand Duke* to be printed for rehearsals. In the interim, the Cartes re-opened the theatre, which had been empty for nearly eight months, and revived *The Mikado*, with Temple, Bond, Barrington, and Brandram in their original roles. Contrary to his usual practice, Gilbert went to see it twice. Sullivan, on the other hand, went hopefully to Berlin on the twenty-sixth for the production of a revised *Ivanhoe*; it proved a failure—German critics preferred *The Mikado*.

Both collaborators were on edge; it had been some six years since the great success of *The Gondoliers*, and they were anxious for a new triumph, which Carte needed for economic reasons as well as prestige. Sullivan did not like the new libretto very much, and Carte may have done them a disservice by reviving *The Mikado* since it reminded audiences of the standard they themselves had set. Again Gilbert rehearsed in agonies of gout until, as Sullivan wrote to Burnand, 'Another week's rehearsal with W.S.G. & I should have gone raving mad. I had already ordered some straw for my hair.'[30]

Yet when *The Grand Duke* opened on 7 March 1896, there was not a seat to be had in the crammed theatre. Six encores were demanded, and many reviewers were complimentary, some enthusiastic while admitting occasional drawbacks. (*Truth* suggested that Gilbert might be guilty of *lèse-majesté* in Germany—so much for his deletion of 'Wilhelm'!) A storm of applause greeted Palmay's demonstration of how to play a melodramatic 'first-rate part', and 'I play that part you bet' was a far-off echo of Henrietta Hodson just as the Prince of Monte Carlo's job lot of cheap 'noblemen' was a last resurgence of the Adelphi supers Gilbert had so satirized thirty years before. Barrington's complex patter song, 'At the outset I may mention', was encored as was the satiric quintet which describes death in real duels:

[29] WSG/BL Add. MS 49,290.     [30] 12 Mar. 1896: PML.

And this barbarous transaction
Is described as 'satisfaction'!

.    .    .    .    .

Each is laid in churchyard mould—
Strange the views some people hold.

The exquisite costumes of blue, violet, mauve, grey, and grass-green and the Herald's bold red, white, and black tabard delighted the eye, while the *Troilus and Cressida* dresses in Act 2 gently mocked the current 'trendy devotion to Greek costume'.[31]

'Opera went well ... Parts of it dragged a little—dialogue too redundant but success great and genuine I think. . . . Thank God opera is finished and out,' Sullivan recorded tiredly in his diary. This time, however, there were no hurried consultations, no meetings for improvements, no rewriting: in three days he was in Paris on his way to Monte Carlo. Nor does his diary mention Gilbert during those three days, although it describes the press notices as 'splendid'.

Left to himself with an opera which obviously needed cutting, Gilbert deleted whole numbers, including, alas!, the Prince of Monte Carlo's roulette song, unnecessary but one of the best in both words and music, as well as being a good-natured allusion to Sullivan's passion for gambling. After pulling the libretto about, he wrote (9 March) to Mrs Bram Stoker, 'I have had rather a bad time of it, but now that the baby is born I shall soon recover ... I'm not at all a proud Mother, & I never want to see the ugly misshapen little brat again!'[32] And he never did, although the twentieth century has proved that *The Grand Duke* is by no means unplayable. It ran for 123 performances, not a failure by general theatrical standards of the day, but a failure for the Savoy. Late in the run Gilbert told Helen Carte that it was not their fault. Two actors, one supine, one without ability, Palmay's frequent absence from matinées, and other reasons Gilbert alluded to but did not specify had injured it, nor had his cutting helped.[33] On 11 July 1896 *The Mikado* returned with its old favourites and ran till February 1897.

The creative collaboration was over. When *The Mikado* reached its 1,037th performance, Sullivan returned to conduct, but he and Gilbert took their bows without any public gesture of friendship. At the end of the run Jessie Bond left the stage to marry: 'little fool!' was Gilbert's response, or at least that is what she remembered.[34] Although she had

[31] D. Wilson, *Gilbert Murray OM 1866–1957* (Oxford: Clarendon Press, 1987), 103.
[32] PML.          [33] 26 June 1896: DOYC/TM.
[34] *The Life and Reminiscences of Jessie Bond* (London: John Lane, 1930), 201.

been one of his favourite performers, he did not give her a wedding present until the last year of his life when he sent her a silver mentieth, engraved with all her roles as 'a Birthday present, a Wedding present, and a New Year's present. All Rolled into One!'[35]

At the end of 1896 the Gilberts were once more on their travels—this time to Burma. Before leaving, he told Mrs Carte he understood that country 'furnishes admirable unused material for dramatic purposes',[36] but in a second letter he was not so keen about using it—'at least that is my feeling just now'.[37] Surprisingly enough, he offered to help anyone else who wanted to write a Burmese libretto! Returning to London in March, however, he was more in the mood for work and once again purposed to turn *The Wicked World* into a libretto. When Carte objected to an all-female chorus, he suggested they should be sirens luring a shipload of classical warriors to their rock.[38] But to no avail; *The Yeomen of the Guard* was revived until November 1897 with Ilka Palmay miscast as Elsie and a new set for Act 2, suggested by Sullivan. When *Yeomen*'s receipts dropped, Mrs Carte considered staging a revised version of *Princess Toto*, but D'Oyly rather foolishly sent Gilbert a page of corrective comments on it, at which the librettist took umbrage. Nothing happened, nor did the increased theatrical attendance expected from Queen Victoria's Diamond Jubilee materialize in any playhouse. Carte was recurrently ill, and his wife longed for peace from Gilbert's thin skin and Sullivan's sometimes wounding desire for more money.[39]

Unable or unwilling to place a new libretto, Gilbert turned back, after nearly a decade, to serious drama. On 27 September his play of modern life, *The Fortune Hunter*, opened in Birmingham with Miss Fortescue as Diana Caverel, an independent, unconventional Australian heiress. She passionately loves and marries a Gilbertian cad, Vicomte Armand De Bréville. When she loses her fortune, however, he decides to take advantage of the 183rd Article of the French *Code Civile* in order to nullify their marriage since he was under age at the time and had not his parents' consent. Iconoclastically enough, when they learn of Armand's intention, they repudiate him and welcome Diana, who bears his child—unknown to him. In the meantime he has returned to a former love, an American Duchess with a yacht and a Yankee gal accent out of

---

[35] *The Life and Reminiscences of Jessie Bond* (London: John Lane, 1930), 226–7.
[36] 9 Nov. 1896: DOYC/TM.  [37] 28 Nov. 1896: DOYC/TM.
[38] Letter to Mrs Carte, 11 Apr. 1897: DOYC/TM.
[39] Letter from Helen Carte to Sullivan, copy, 4 Aug. 1897, *inter alia*: DOYC/TM.

*Punch*. Diana's love has turned to contempt, but she tells him that nullification will bastardize their child. Since the case is even now about to be heard he can stop it only by provoking a duel and allowing himself to be killed. Diana kisses the dying Armand at his request, but, all passion spent, it is not the kiss of love. Only the Duchess weeps for him.

In certain ways this is a very modern play. Diana frankly, with the language available to her, describes the way in which her unmistakably sexual passion has subjugated her individuality. When, after absence and humiliation, he asks for her heart again, she exclaims, 'Great heavens, have you lost your senses? To you?' She despises him. Nor did Gilbert revive him at the last moment for a pleasing reconciliation scene as Pinero had been forced to do in *The Profligate*. 'How a man of [Gilbert's] experience should have made such a mistake is a mystery,' Malcolm Watson wrote to Clement Scott.[40] And by conventional standards it was a mistake.

Nevertheless, Gilbert had six curtain-calls on the first night; at least seventeen London papers sent critics, and a number of London first-nighters came to the première. (Scott, though invited, was not among them.) Most of them were disappointed in spite of an unusual plot, careful dialogue, and Miss Fortescue's best acting in exquisite costumes, which earned a small review of their own. Critics disapproved of the duel—a trumped-up, unnecessary solution, and there was even a suggestion that the stage-management was old-fashioned. As usual, they were not pleased by another of Gilbert's variations on his recurrent theme of woman victimized by man's double standards, sexual, economic, and social, but possessing greater integrity than the man or society which judges her. Again it did not produce an acceptable long-running play.

Gilbert had no fixed intention for the future of his drama. London managers had inquired about it before production as had the actress Gertrude Kingston.[41] He decided to wait until Miss Fortescue played Edinburgh, in the mean time revising still further than the heavy cuts he had already made during rehearsal. On 4 October he took the night train to Edinburgh, where, at breakfast, one of the company told him that Birmingham business had been magnificent.[42] He then made the

[40] Tuesday, n.d. [30 Sept. 1897]: Scott Papers/TM. In 1879, the *Pall Mall Gazette* reported a real instance of a husband's using the *Code Civile* to negate his marriage to an English girl, but without a solution by duel.

[41] Gilbert to Miss Kingston, 13 Sept. 1897: Bodleian.

[42] Gilbert to 'Dearest Kits' [Lucy Gilbert], 4 Oct. 1897: WSG/BL Add. MS 49,345.

mistake of giving an interview to Isaac Donald of the *Evening Despatch*.

Characteristically, Gilbert admitted that *The Fortune Hunter* had faults, but praised the cast. Next he said he intended to retire and cease being 'a cock-shy' for critics, who treated the author of an unsuccessful play as if he were a scoundrel—a complaint he had made nine years earlier. After that, led on by Donald, Gilbert decried what he described as the habit of delivering blank verse in a monotone. Actors, he said, 'keep to one note through the sentence, and finish a semi-tone higher or a semi-tone lower as the case may be'. He preferred to counteract the 'necessary mechanical structure' of iambs by using as much variety of inflection 'as the sense of the verse admitted'.[43] Did this apply to Irving? Donald asked. To Tree? Alexander? Vezin? Others? Yes, in a general way it did, Gilbert replied, but he had not chosen the names or Vezin would not have appeared among them.

Nevertheless, the London press descended happily upon him, led by the *Era*'s editorial against his 'abnormal self-esteem', which made his life a series of unsuccessful combats to vindicate his view of the universe. It also implied that Gilbert was ungrateful to the actors who had helped make his reputation. Gilbert himself did not see the *Evening Despatch* until 19 October and, appalled, wrote to Tree, Alexander, *et al.*, explaining what he had and had not said as he remembered it. Then he sued the proprietor of the *Era* for £1,000, case to come up the next March. After this, he developed a blinding headache, an incapacitating migraine which turned him back from the railway station on his way to consult Miss Fortescue.[44]

He brought *The Fortune Hunter* no closer to London than Crouch End. Reviews continued to be bad, and the *Sketch* thought it would be Gilbert's last play, a gratuitously unpleasant remark. He could not give it up, however, and, revising and retitling it as 'Cynthia's Husband', he tried in 1906, 1907, 1908, and 1910 to find a producer for it. By then, it was far too old-fashioned in form, although perhaps not in content.

A lesser, but real irritation was the reappearance of James Hogg, erstwhile editor of *London Society* in the 1860s, who once again attempted to blackmail Gilbert. Twice before he had threatened to publish Gilbert's very early contributions to that magazine unless the dramatist

---

[43] Letter to George Alexander, 19 Oct. 1897: JWS. Gilbert told Alexander, and others, that his long discussion had been 'boiled down' and words he never said put into his mouth.

[44] Letter to Miss Fortescue, 25 Oct. 1897: PML. Gilbert also said he had been told the *Era* article was libellous.

bought back their copyright for £50. Gilbert had, of course, refused and was not at all sure that Hogg owned the copyright. Now the former editor abusively repeated this threat, adding that any attempt to set the law against him would 'make [Gilbert] rue [his] temerity'.[45] More cajolingly, a second letter suggested Gilbert might like to revise his old 'Thumbnail Sketches' and repeated that other literary gentlemen had been glad to buy back their copyrights.[46] Gilbert was not, and after being as great a nuisance as possible, Hogg dropped back out of sight.

The year ended with Routledge's publication of *The Bab Ballads with which are included Songs of a Savoyard* (dated 1898), which went through six editions in the next decade. For it, Gilbert had redrawn (or omitted) more than half the original illustrations, making the boldly grotesque originals much weaker, partly because the newer use of line block produced a blander effect than wood engraving,[47] but partly because he could not resist tinkering with what he had already perfected.

Nancy McIntosh did not spend Christmas 1897 at Grim's Dyke; she had secured an engagement in America, where she played 'a very pretty and gentle Hero' to Ada Rehan's Beatrice and Favorita in *The Circus Girl*. As O Mimosa San in Sidney Jones's *The Geisha*, the Boston *Evening Gazette* found her 'simply perfect', but once more illness intervened. Despite rumours that she would appear in a play by her brother Burr, she evidently did nothing further.

In March 1898 Gilbert directed the first *Gondoliers* revival and took the silent role of the Associate in a performance of *Trial by Jury* for the Testimonial Benefit of Nellie Farren, once long ago his flashing Mercury, now crippled by arthritis. In March, too, the Gilbert–*Era* libel trial came on. Edward Ledger's solicitors had been busily searching for evidence of Gilbert's egotism, but when they queried the critic Moy Thomas, he refused his help.[48] He could not remember if Gilbert had been angry at his unfavourable review of *Gretchen*; he thought not, but if he had, Thomas was content to scratch it off since the dramatist had often commented appreciatively on his criticism.[49] Others were not so well disposed.

---

[45] 5 Oct. 1897: WSG/BL Add. MS 49,332.

[46] 14 Oct. 1897: WSG/BL Add. MS 49,332.

[47] P. James, 'A Note on Gilbert as Illustrator', in *Selected Bab Ballads Written and Illustrated by W. S. Gilbert*, introd. H. Pearson (privately printed; Oxford: Oxford University Press, 1955), 118.

[48] John H. Mote & Son to Moy Thomas, 1 Mar. 1898: PML.

[49] Copy, 2 Mar. 1898: PML.

For his part, Gilbert asked Mrs Carte to testify if necessary that he was not 'a man in whom vanity & egotism have degenerated into a disease—that I do not desire . . . to dominate the universe—& that I am not in the habit of abusing & insulting the actors who play in my pieces'.[50] In court Isaac Donald testified that he understood Gilbert had initiated the interview to 'unburden something'. Actually, Miss Fortescue had arranged it for obvious publicity purposes, and Donald must have been very naïve if he supposed Gilbert intended or desired to bare his soul to the *Evening Despatch*. Although he insisted his report was accurate, Donald had not kept the notes he took at the time of the interview.

Edward Carson appeared for Ledger, the proprietor of the *Era*, and *The Times* reported frequent laughter as Gilbert neatly parried Carson's attempts to make him seem contentious. For instance, the barrister asked for an example of the current taste for musical comedy, and the dramatist suggested the Drury Lane pantomime. Carson: 'But that only goes on a short time in the year.' Gilbert: 'It goes on for a long time in the evening.'[51] Amusing though the give and take may have been, it did not help Gilbert's case. 'A monument of senile imbecility' (Gilbert's description of Mr Justice Day) presided, and the jury failed to agree. 'To the very last,' Gilbert wrote to Helen Carte, Day 'could not be made to understand that the action was not brought against the *Era* for publishing the interview—but for publishing the *comment* on the interview'.[52] Gilbert and Kitty left for three weeks in Naples 'to blow the "frowst" of the Law Courts out of my brain'.[53] He had fired his ringing shot and passed.

At the end of May Sullivan's *The Beauty Stone* interrupted the run of *Gondoliers* at the Savoy. Its librettists, Comyns Carr and Arthur Wing Pinero (whom the Cartes had long been absurdly eager to engage), knew nothing about writing words to be set to music and would not listen when the composer tried to tell them. Their obduracy made him mourn for the good old days of Gilbert, who wrote 'beautifully' for music, but he said nothing about reviving their association. Gilbert himself had expected to be invited to the first night and had even asked a party of friends to dine and accompany him, when he learned from

---

[50] 18 Mar. 1898: DOYC/TM.

[51] H. Pearson prints a large section of testimony in *Gilbert: His Life and Strife* (London: Methuen & Co. Ltd., 1957) 197–201. *The Times* (29 and 30 Mar. 1898) printed the testimony at length.

[52] 31 Mar. 1898: DOYC/TM.                          [53] Ibid.

Mrs Carte that Sullivan preferred his absence. Hurt and furious, he would not let Sullivan explain, and when they appeared for the twenty-first anniversary of the revived *Sorcerer*, they did not speak. *The Beauty Stone*, handicapped by a lumbered pseudo-medieval libretto and a failure to find a stylistically unified score, lasted only fifty performances. Although Gilbert did not say it, he might have pointed out that the stone was a simple kind of lozenge, which makes plain persons beautiful.

Having no new dramatic work in hand, Gilbert and Kitty once more embarked on an expedition, this time an autumnal six weeks in the Crimea and Caucasus, taking Nancy McIntosh with them. What were Gilbert's feelings when he saw the terrain over which he had hoped to fight some forty years before? Regret? Recognition? (One of his favourite books was Kinglake's *History of the Crimean War*.) Thankfulness that he had not gone to die of the terrible illnesses which killed so many there? He does not tell us.

Back at Grim's Dyke, he made another unsuccessful attempt to procure an engagement for Nancy, who did not return to the stage until 1909. Instead, she sang at church and for friends; she gave singing lessons and more and more took over the duties of a daughter of the house, although never legally adopted. (The term was merely a late Victorian way of referring to a girl who stood *in loco filiae* without a legal ceremony.) The ambition Sullivan had seen in her was unfulfilled—or replaced by what she may have thought was a higher one.

Occasionally, local people hinted that Nancy was Gilbert's mistress, but that is very unlikely. First, in the late 1890s Gilbert had both a hernia, which would make intercourse painful, and adult-onset diabetes, which would make it infrequent. Second, he was not the kind of man who brings his mistress home to live with his wife; it would offend his sense of propriety. Furthermore, Nancy was also Kitty's companion and a friend of her family, paying visits to Mrs Turner in her own right. After Gilbert died, she continued to live with his widow for twenty-five years, a daughter deferring to an ageing mother, for Kitty was accustomed to direct events her long life through. No doubt Nancy loved 'the Judge', as she called him, but it was not consciously sexual love.

Kitty, however, whether in 1898 or earlier, was the occasion of an attempt at blackmail: 'I am in possession of a secret which concerns you very nearly & which for reasons of my own I have hitherto not divulged. There are now reasons why I shall probably have to acquaint you with it; prepare therefore on this day week or thereabouts for a very startling disclosure.' This letter, unsigned, undated, was sent to Gilbert, and a second, dated only 'October 26th', went to Kitty: 'I have now given you every chance and you have exhausted my patience. Your husband has heard once from me and expects another letter with full details. This I shall supply him with unless before this day week I hear from you. Direct to *Menton—pour Mr Audran. Poste Restante.*'[54] She evidently handed this to Gilbert, who neither wrote nor paid. No evidence remains of what the secret was—the context suggests sexual—and it is a small mystery. Perhaps it was related to the fact that when Mrs Gilbert was 53, someone saw her with her husband, and, not knowing her, suggested a scandal, news of which reached Mrs Carte. Kitty retained her youthful looks well into middle age.

Eighteen ninety-nine was a gout year, even though in May Gilbert managed to direct a revival of *HMS Pinafore* at the Savoy. Richard Barker, the general stage-manager, drove him nearly mad. A bully by everyone's account, opinionated, and determined by now to conduct rehearsals without any consideration for an author, he 'interfere[s] with the stagemanagement—deliberately ignores & varies my instructions', and pre-empted the chair intended for Gilbert, who could hardly stand. Could not Mrs Carte get rid of him?[55] But she was ill herself, and Barker continued his wrong-headed way, insulting Gilbert when he remonstrated.[56]

By July Gilbert was so debilitated that he could scarcely hold a pen and was ordered to Buxton, the mineral waters of which were considered efficacious in curing gout. In autumn he had improved enough to turn down an offer for Nancy to play a boy's role[57] and to offer the Cartes 'a wonderfully good & fresh idea for a libretto',[58] embodied in a story 'The Fairy's Dilemma', which he was writing for the Christmas *Graphic*. They did not accept: D'Oyly had never really regained his health, and Helen was engaged with Sullivan's new opera, *The Rose of Persia*, which would follow the *Pinafore* revival. She offered the Gilberts a box for the première, but Sullivan's 'slight' still rankled. Gilbert preferred to see the second or third performance.

The librettist Sullivan had chosen was Captain Basil Hood, who had

<hr>

[54] WSG/BL Add. MS 49,332.

[55] Letter to Mrs Carte, 31 May 1899: DOYC/TM. Barker tried to bar both Carte and Gilbert from the stage of which he considered he was the sole director.

[56] Letter to Mrs Carte, 6 June 1899: DOYC/TM.

[57] Letter to Gatty, 14 Nov. 1899: PML.     [58] 22 Sept. 1899: DOYC/TM.

turned from the army to the stage, and whom the composer considered superior to everyone, except, of course, Gilbert. Gilbert himself liked Hood's lyrics, and well he might, for they frankly imitated his own. The only drawback to the performance was the phenomenally high soprano, Ellen Beach Yaw, whom Mrs Ronalds had pushed Sullivan into accepting. Replaced by Isabel Jay, she left the company, Mrs Carte acting as a buffer between the composer and his mistress.[59]

Now that Gilbert was fit to travel, he felt again the impetus of an itching foot, or perhaps Kitty did, for they began a second trip to India in December 1899. Before leaving, he wrote a sympathetic little note to the sister of his friend Rowland Brown, who had written a small play for charity performance. A rather gushing young woman, she thanked him effusively; so he added, 'As to my chance of being appreciated by posterity, I fancy posterity will know as much concerning me as I shall know of posterity.'[60]

[59] Letter to Mrs Ronalds, copy, 16 Dec. 1899: DOYC/TM. In a letter to Sullivan the next day, Helen explains how unjustly she feels she has been treated since the Cartes had not wanted to engage Miss Beach Yaw in the first place. Sullivan, at Mrs Ronalds's request, had made hiring her a condition of his happily writing *The Rose of Persia*.

[60] To Miss Rowland Brown, 5 Dec. 1899: Bodleian. She did her best to contradict Gilbert's supposition, for she continued writing the biography her brother had begun before his death. See S. Dark and R. Grey, *W. S. Gilbert: His Life and Letters* (London: Methuen & Co. Ltd., 1923). 'Rowland Grey' was Miss Rowland Brown's pen-name.

# 19

---

# Growing on the Sunny Side

'I've left the Stage, and haven't said "Good bye"!'
That sounds ungrateful—but to be quite plain,
I hoped I might be coming back again,

> Address by Gilbert for Miss Lydia Thompson
> on the Occasion of her Farewell to the Stage,
>
> 2 May 1899

DURING the first nine years of the new century, Gilbert spent a pleasant life at Grim's Dyke and in the luxurious flats or houses he rented in London for each three cold months. He continued to travel *en famille* to such places as Switzerland and Wiesbaden, where he took 'rotten egg baths' at the art nouveau Rose Hotel while Nancy and Kitty had treatments for their eyes.

At Grim's Dyke, he welcomed the new century by turning the water into his just-completed artificial lake, and each successive New Year's Eve was spent with a few friends, poker perhaps, perhaps the music of the orchestrelle (a kind of mechanical organ), and at midnight a far-from-innocuous milk punch. Made from a recipe later printed in *Kitty's Cookery Book* (compiled in aid of a deserving charity), it contained among other ingredients five bottles of rum. The Gilberts continued to entertain throughout the year, sometimes at large garden parties of forty or fifty guests and an Hungarian band; sometimes at dinners for sixteen or eighteen, when the table might be decorated with pink double tulips or pale yellow azaleas in silver pots. The menu, in peacock-holders, often began with *consommé Richelieu* and might end with *Petits Cygnes Glacés* or *Fleurs de Nénupher*.[1]

At other times rugs were spread on the grass for tea parties; sometimes an oriental-patterned tent was erected. Exquisite ladies drifted by: Marion Terry absent-mindedly left her boa, and Jessie Bond's

---

[1] The Gilberts' guest book: WSG/BL Add. MS 49,347A.

318

forgotten hat crowned the suit of armour beside the staircase. In comfortable wicker chairs sat men in light suits, mustachios, and straw boaters, or ladies in large hats, with an occasional long-legged girl in curls and white frock. The young playwright Captain Robert Marshall came to visit his favourite dramatist. Mrs Gilbert, hatless, shirt-waisted, and upright, presided, their images preserved by Gilbert's or Nancy's indefatigible photography. Student actresses arrived for coaching, or Gilbert went in turn to examine candidates at the Academy of Dramatic Art.

Sometimes Gilbert was photographed with one of the lemurs, who frequently escaped from their own little house to the strawberry beds. References to the youngest, Paul, the first lemur bred in England, occur almost daily in Gilbert's diary. Paul lived in the house, sat on Gilbert's shoulder as he dressed for dinner, ate the smoke from his cigars, and pulled his moustache to get what he wanted from the breakfast- or dining-table. When he died, he was buried beneath a bush in the garden, where his neat tombstone may still be seen. Visitors were taken to visit the outdoor lemurs, and the lemurs came indoors to see the visitors at dining-room breakfast, for the house was open to Gilbert's pets.

It was so free, in fact, that at mealtimes little tablecloths were spread on the floor for the dogs and cats, who ate with the family. No one seems to have found it strange that a servant should wait on a Pekinese. Perhaps it was an extension of Gilbert's belief in the wonderful mechanism of life. 'I have a constitutional objection to taking life in any form,' he once told William Archer. 'To tread on a black-beetle would be to me like crushing a watch of complex and exquisite workmanship.'[2] Or perhaps he, Kitty, and Nancy were besotted with animals and now could give full rein to their affections—Kitty continued to love her animals and spread tablecloths for them after her husband died. Or the pampered pets may have been belated compensation for childlessness—very likely a mixture of all three.

Mrs Gilbert often went riding on horseback or bicyclette to visit her mother, for whom they had taken a house nearby on Bushey Heath. Old Mrs Turner gave a hymnal and a prayer book to each of the Grim's Dyke head-gardener's daughters and had them to tea once a summer. They remembered how good her cook's gingerbread was. Gilbert stayed home to play croquet, for which two separate lawns had been laid out. Even if there were no guests, he and Nancy had a game, and he noted

[2] W. Archer, *Real Conversations* (London: William Heinemann, 1904), 108.

the winner in his diary. Sometimes host and friends walked around the grounds, past the clipped and shaped evergreens of the sundial garden to a small observatory or away from the warm brick walls, surmounted by metal Japanese cranes, to the artificial lake. Here they might take a boat or bathe. Gilbert himself swam daily from April or May through September.

In autumn the strollers could munch luscious black grapes from one of the two vineries. There was a melon house, and another greenhouse was devoted to peaches, for Gilbert was 'a glutton for fruit', as his gardener's daughter said.[3] He entered in his diary the appearance of the season's first strawberries, first melon, first asparagus, and first gooseberry tart, as well as the first chestnut leaves and first cuckoo. Sometimes he and his wife went mushroom-hunting in their own fields. He enjoyed food and did not part with his last tooth till 1905. (It was still a sweet one.)

Gilbert liked flirtation too—with intelligent women—and christened a small room 'The Flirtorium' although there is no evidence he used it à deux. An often-repeated anecdote tells how Kitty watched her husband flirting at his end of the long dinner table: 'My dear,' she called, 'this must not go on!' 'Oh, my darling,' he instantly replied, 'didn't you know I was always too good to be true.'

He prided himself on up-to-date comfort: electric lights even in the scullery, boot-room, and larder. Year by year he thought of improvements: a lengthened tennis court for his ferocious serves, a hundred orchard trees, masses of rhododendrons, an elaborately decorated Broadwood piano chosen with Nancy. He continued to devote a good deal of time to the lake, deepening it, lining it with concrete, building a new boat- and dressing-house. He even painted a scarecrow.

The Gilberts involved themself in local affairs, such as the Bushey Heath Cottage Hospital, of which he was Honorary Secretary; the choice of a Common Keeper; performances of *Rosencrantz and Guildenstern* for charity with Gilbert himself as the King. His wife arranged Christmas entertainments for the hospital (tea, magic lantern, and conjurer) and parties for the children of the large domestic and outdoor staff of Grim's Dyke. To each child at Christmas, Mrs Gilbert gave a useful present such as an umbrella or writing-case, but

[3] Mrs A. Beedie, daughter of James Fulton, Gilbert's head gardener from the end of the 19th cent. on. Information about greenhouses, parties for servants' children, and Mrs Turner's gifts in this chapter come from conversations with Mrs Beedie and her sister Mrs Hunt in spring 1971.

from each little girl she expected a curtsey. In her soft voice, she made her weight felt.

Since 1891 Gilbert had been Justice of the Peace for Middlesex, sitting on the bench for the Edgware Petty Sessions and later for the Wealdstone Petty Sessions as well. Most cases were those of small offenders: speedsters, ticket-evaders, pugnacious drunkards, and the like, but one was 'a ghastly murder . . . a little girl of 5 stabbed in 40 places with a pocket knife by a devil', which was sent for trial to a higher court.[4]

As a magistrate Gilbert was popular among court officials. He spoke little, but incisively, and drew sketches on his note sheets, which clerks rushed to snatch from the wastebasket after court closed. He was especially hard on motorists although his own cars were sometimes involved in traffic accidents. Generally he considered these were not his fault, for he constantly told his gentleman-chauffeur McHardy not to exceed the speed limit. He had bought his first car in 1900—a Locomobile Steamer, and, like his houses, subsequent cars increased in luxury (and speed). In 1906, for instance, Kitty Gilbert drove in a Cadillac and her husband in a Darracq.

What was more important was Gilbert's refusal to believe that a policeman's evidence must necessarily be right. No doubt he retained a subliminal memory of the day forty years before when he had voluntarily attended court to testify that the police had wilfully and unnecessarily manhandled a drunken prisoner, only to be told his evidence was not wanted. Nor was this almost universal assumption that a policeman *qua* policeman must be correct by any means a thing of the past. The *Sketch*, for example, in 1895 reported that George Alexander had been arrested by a constable who thought the actor's attempt to avoid an importunate beggar was evidence of *in flagrante delicto*!

As a magistrate Gilbert always asked himself, 'What chance in life has this man had?' Honesty, he considered, was simply freedom from temptation:[5] a resurgence of the 'Fagan for a father' motif of *Charity* and *Iolanthe*.

In 1902 he became a Deputy-Lieutenant of Middlesex and discovered the pleasures of clothes from Henry Poole & Co. of Savile Row by purchasing his official coatee there, heavy with silver bullion epaulettes. He expected to wear it for Edward VII's Coronation, which was, however, postponed because of the King's sudden appendectomy.

---

[4] Letter to Mrs Talbot ('My very dear Old Lady'), 2 July 1909: Talbot Corr./PML.

[5] E. A. Browne, *W. S. Gilbert* (London: John Lane, 1907), 40.

Nevertheless, so satisfactory was Poole's that Gilbert wore their clothes for the rest of his life: soft tweeds, white flannels (like a tropical colonel's, the little Maude girls thought), evening suits, a brocaded silk smoking-jacket. He paid extra for pure silk linings, but settled his bills promptly and in cash, which gave him a discount.[6] Kitty, too, preferred not to owe money; she never put on a dress till it was paid for.[7] Her jewels were good, but not opulent, although Gilbert bought her a tiara on the Rue de la Paix for £450 and exchanged her diamond necklace for a more costly one of pearls.

Certain events and friendships stand out against this relatively calm background. As the century began, Gilbert and Sullivan were still estranged. The librettist continued to direct revivals of former successes for the Savoy at £200 an opera, but he wrote rather wistfully to Mrs Carte the day before *The Pirates of Penzance* opened, 'I am sorry Sullivan won't come, but I don't think he cares to face me. He need not have minded—I wouldn't have hurt him!'[8]

He himself went back to Buxton for another fruitless attempt to cure the arthritis which had now replaced gout as his constant companion. When in October he began to rehearse *Patience*, he again used a wheelchair and had to be carried upstairs. Yet he rose to the occasion: 'Everything went as smooth as butter ... I was not tired after it.'[9] At this point, Helen Carte had a brilliantly theatrical idea: D'Oyly, Sullivan, and Gilbert were all invalids in their several ways; why not have them appear in wheelchairs for their curtain-call? Carte and Gilbert were delighted, Sullivan acquiescent, but in the event could not leave his bed: 'kidneys and throat. Pray tell Gilbert how very much I feel the disappointment. . . . Three invalid chairs would have looked *very well* from the front.'[10] The other two hobbled out to take the call alone. 'I must have looked more like a performing ape than a human being when I was called on,' Gilbert wrote to Kate Terry Lewis; 'I hope no one thought I had been drinking, but my knees shook so that I almost fell over.' He had lost sixty pounds in six weeks. 'There is Gilbertian flesh amounting to two large sirloins of beef, three turkeys & a sucking pig knocking about Buxton somewhere.'[11]

He wrote Sullivan a conciliatory letter, saying how much he had looked forward to shaking hands again, and would have come to see

[6] Henry Poole & Co., account books. Thanks are also due the helpful staff.
[7] Interview with Emily Paxton, Lady Gilbert's maid, spring 1971.
[8] 29 June 1900: DOYC/TM.        [9] Letter to Mrs Carte, 29 Oct. 1900: DOYC/TM.
[10] Letter to Mrs Carte, n.d. [Nov. 1900]: DOYC/TM.        [11] 10 Nov. 1900: PML.

him but was too unwell. He, Nancy, Kitty, and her maid were preparing to leave for Egypt where he hoped the sulphur baths at Helouan near Cairo might help. He feared, however, that he was crippled for life; he could not rise unaided from a low chair or undress himself.

On 22 November 1900 Sullivan died of heart failure. It was a week before the news reached Gilbert, who wrote at once to Bertie Sullivan, who assured his uncle's old collaborator that Sullivan had indeed felt they were reconciled. Later, when a memorial to Sullivan was erected in the Embankment Gardens, Gilbert supplied a verse, 'Is life a boon', from what both men had felt was their best opera, *The Yeomen of the Guard.*

A year of deaths followed Sullivan's: Queen Victoria died in the arms of her grandson Kaiser Wilhelm II on 22 January 1901; Richard D'Oyly Carte on 3 April. (Gilbert wrote Helen a letter of deep sympathy and affection, but took no part in a Carte memorial.)[12] Finally, at the end of the year, W. H. Seymour, long-time stage-manager at the Savoy died, as did W. H. Leon, a small-parts player. Gilbert offered 10 guineas if money were wanted.

Meanwhile Gilbert, somewhat improved, took his first Egyptian outing, a short train ride to Cairo, which proved a frightening excursion. The train left the rails, locomotive and two cars plunging down an embankment and flinging passengers about 'like parched peas in a drum'. Gilbert, who could not rise, expected to be boiled alive in steam, but Nancy intrepidly managed to pull him up and out. Then she went back for his hat and their 'traps', and walked to Cairo for a carriage. Seven people were killed in the wreck, and for years Gilbert could not forget their dying screams.[13]

After finishing the Egyptian cure in March, he found he did not have rheumatoid arthritis after all. It and gout had eloped together, he told everyone, but his change from a diet of red meat to one of fruits, fish, and vegetables no doubt assisted the flight of the gout. In 1904 and again in 1906 a mysterious hip ailment tied him to the sofa until he and Kitty discovered Dr Hokansson and his Swedish treatment, which Gilbert recommended to everyone.

In 1904 Clement Scott died after a long illness during which Gilbert contributed generously to a fund being raised for him, while still making it clear that he and Scott were not reconciled. As the critic's life ebbed away, Gilbert daily inquired after him and helped Mrs Scott by

---

12 Letter to François Cellier, 6 Aug. 1901: Dorothy Palmer Lewis.
13 Letter to Mrs Talbot ('Cousin Mary'), 18 Feb. 1901: Talbot Corr./PML.

contributing, without charge, unsigned articles for the magazine she edited. At Scott's funeral Gilbert's eyes were bright with tears[14] for the young man Scott had been, not the aging megalomaniac he had become, for the 'Kitten' of *Fun*, who had not yet learned to scratch.

Gilbert's best friends these days, aside from his neighbours Helsham Jones and the barrister–entomologist Henry Rowland Brown, were probably Mary Talbot and Mrs Henry de la Pasture. The first, whom he came to address playfully and inaccurately as 'Cousin Mary', was the invalid married daughter of the Henry Schlesingers, friends of Browning and other literary and musical figures. 'Cousin Bill' wrote frequently to Mary, discussing the serious events of his life, but almost always ending with some comic story or anecdote he had heard.[15] Perpetually lamenting that the Talbots rarely visited Grim's Dyke, he sent her a complete run of *Punch* to date, all the World's Classics volumes, and a complete set of Dickens in small, comfortably holdable volumes.

Elizabeth de la Pasture, on the other hand, was a frequent visitor, and in the winter of 1906–7 saw him almost daily in London where they lived close to each other. Witty, faintly malicious, a popular novelist, and mother of E. M. Delafield, 'The Provincial Lady', she published her best-known work *Peter's Mother* in 1905 and made it into a play in 1906. A blend of maternal self-sacrifice, feminism, patriotism, wit, and middle-aged love, it caught the temper of the time exactly. Marion Terry played the eponymous heroine; A. E. Matthews, already 37, her 18-year-old son. Gilbert saw *Peter's Mother* several times, and King Edward thought it one of the most charming pieces he had ever seen; in fact, he commanded a performance at Sandringham for Queen Alexandra's birthday.

To some extent Gilbert became a play 'doctor' for Mrs de la Pasture. Although the timing seems impossibly tight, he was involved in her next work, the 1907 farcical comedy, 'Her Grace the Reformer'. Later he wrote or contributed to the scenario of one, perhaps two, other plays, and accompanied her to inspect E. T. Reed's proposed illustrations for her amusing children's book *The Unlucky Family*.

Although Gilbert was out of sympathy with much of the Edwardian

[14] Mrs C. Scott, *Old Days in Bohemian London* (London: Hutchinson & Co., n.d.), 71–2. I have been unable to find the articles Gilbert wrote for Mrs Scott.

[15] When S. Dark and R. Grey published *W. S. Gilbert: His Life and Letters* (London: Methuen & Co. Ltd., 1923), they often deleted passages in the Talbot letters they chose to print which showed Gilbert's serious feelings, but left in the 'stories'.

drama except Pinero's, he did not completely stop writing. On 3 May 1904 he directed a new play of his own, *The Fairy's Dilemma*, 'a domestic pantomime', at the Garrick Theatre. (As a short story it had appeared in the Christmas number of the 1900 *Graphic*.) He still rehearsed by acting out the roles himself; Suzanne Graham remembered that for the tiny role of the policeman he 'walked up and down the stage exactly like a policeman. Gilbert took his gestures off completely.'[16]

With an adroit cast headed by Arthur Bourchier and his wife Violet Vanbrugh, *The Fairy's Dilemma* charmed reviewers. 'Here was the fantastic Gilbert that we knew at something very near his best,' rejoiced *The Times*. Only Gilbert 'could have handled such a theme and make the impossible seem almost possible, and, indeed, in a sort of mad way, well nigh probable,' commented the *Play Pictorial*, devoting a monthly number to this travesty of pantomime in which Fairy Rosebud unintentionally but stupidly scrambles two pairs of lovers and sends three of them to the Revolving Realms of Radiant Rehabilitation, where they become Harlequin *et al.*: 'it's not as great a change as I should have supposed!' exclaims a Judge turned into Pantaloon.

Everyone at the Garrick was very civil to Gilbert, but he found 'a sad want of method' there and 'had to put my foot down on the sad laxity that prevails'.[17] For a month or two *The Fairy's Dilemma* drew excellent houses; then audiences fell away, perhaps, as Violet Vanbrugh thought, too many of them were too young to remember the harlequinade as it was before having been reduced to a token gesture.[18] They did not understand a parody of a pantomime.

Gilbert had already decided to write no more librettos. 'A Gilbert is of no use without a Sullivan—& I can't find one,' he told Frank Cellier.[19] He insisted he would not write another libretto 'If Mozart rose from the dead & paid me the compliment of asking me to write with him.'[20] Yet in the same year (1904) he tried unsuccessfully to interest André Messager in a collaboration. Happy though he was as a country squire, he could not let go of the other life he had lived so long.

He was forced, however, to limit himself to directing the 1906–7 and 1908–9 London repertory seasons of the old operas, the first of which

---

[16] Suzanne Graham in a telephone conversation, 4 Aug. 1974. She understudied Mrs Crumbles in the touring company of *The Fairy's Dilemma* and remembered Gilbert as an ordinary nice man with 'no side to him'.

[17] Letter to Mrs Talbot ('Cousin Mary'), 24 Mar. 1904: Talbot Corr./PML.

[18] Letter to Rowland Grey, n.d.: Sands/BL Add. MS 57,317.

[19] 19 Nov. 1903: DOYC/TM.          [20] Letter to Mrs Bram Stoker, 16 Sept. 1904: PML.

by no means contented him. He had fruitlessly suggested Nancy for the role of Elsie in the opening *Yeomen*, together with as many old Savoyards as possible. What he got was a cast chosen by Mrs Carte 'shamefully on the cheap'.[21] The old company was scattered: retired—in America—engaged elsewhere. Reviewers did not find their substitutes generally 'up to the mark', but audiences overwhelmed Gilbert with applause. He did not like the productions; indeed, *The Gondoliers* so exasperated him that he wrote to *The Times* to disclaim everything but the 'ordinary duties of a stage manager'. In letter after letter, he objected to the 'indignity' Mrs Carte had inflicted on him. He objected to the *Patience* costumes and asked Ruby Gray, a small-parts player, if her combination of black eyebrows and yellow hair were natural. Yes. 'Well, I don't like 'em. Block 'em out!' he gruffed.[22] He also rehearsed *Trial by Jury* for the Ellen Terry Benefit held in June 1906, again playing the silent role of the Associate, although he felt that Miss Terry's salary was far too high for 'an object of charity'.[23]

In 1907 the Lord Chamberlain banned *The Mikado* lest it offend Prince Fushimi, paying an official visit to England. Gilbert was furious. 'It is so easy to be tactful when the cost has to be borne by somebody else,' he wrote bitterly to Cousin Mary.[24] Mrs Carte, who now had to pull the opera out of her London Repertory Season allegedly wept for two hours in the Lord Chamberlain's office, as well she might. She did give one illicit performance with the touring company at Sheffield, which did not go unnoticed. Luckily the ban was lifted after some six weeks (too late for the season and without compensation), but Gilbert never forgot it. In his prose version of *The Mikado* for children, published posthumously, he alluded satirically to the 'great and wise' British Government's fear of the Japanese.

Fortunately for Gilbert's temper, the second London season, running eleven months from 28 April 1908, was a great improvement on the first. *The Mikado* was back in place, and Mrs Carte had engaged Rutland Barrington, Richard Temple, and Henry Lytton as well as finding a good soprano. The tenor alone was 'too awful for words'.[25] Gilbert himself felt healthier too—tests showed no sugar in his urine—

[21] Letter to Mrs Lewis, 25 Dec. 1906: PML. Mrs Carte had married again and was now Mrs Boulter; she continued to use 'Carte' professionally.

[22] Telephone conversation with Ruby Gray (Mrs Gough), 26 July 1971, who confused *Patience* with *Fallen Fairies* and misremembered the costume.

[23] Letter to Mrs Talbot ('Cousin Mary'), 13 June 1906: Talbot Corr./PML.

[24] Letter to Mrs Talbot ('Cousin Mary'), 30 Apr. 1907: Talbot Corr./PML.

[25] Gilbert to Mrs Carte, 22 Apr. 1908: DOYC/TM.

so his diabetes was well under control, aided by his daily three-mile walks.

During this first decade of the century, Gilbert found two new protégées. The first, Regina Repton, had temporarily been a member of the Savoy chorus and had played a bit part in *The Fortune Hunter*. Now Gilbert cast her as Cynisca in Janet Steer's production of *Pygmalion and Galatea*. Steer, who was by no means a great actress, disliked Repton and made rehearsals so vexatious that Gilbert went home ill, probably with migraine. On opening night Steer deviated from her rehearsed business and the letter of Gilbert's text in Repton's most important scene, engrossing the audience and distracting her rival. Gilbert wrote icily to her, explicitly to the newspapers and applied for an injunction, which the judge refused to grant, even though Pinero and Bancroft appeared as witnesses for Gilbert. Steer dismissed Repton, who nevertheless continued her career, and remained a friend of the Gilberts.

Gilbert's second protégée was the delicate, fair-haired, bad-tempered novice Maud Cressall, who played Zeolide in a 1905 revival of *The Palace of Truth* and the small role of Pauline in *Comedy and Tragedy*. Her beauty was reputedly so extraordinary that she later alleged Gilbert commissioned John Singer Sargent to paint her portrait;[26] since there is no mention of this in Gilbert's diary, which records lesser events, it seems unlikely. He recommended her to managers and to William Archer, as well as getting her an engagement for the next autumn, but she proved to be 'an ungrateful little cat & looks upon all that I have done for her as quite in the natural order of things'.[27] After the successful première of *The Palace of Truth*, for example, she left without speaking a word to her mentor, who was being heartily applauded.

[26] In 1948 Maud Cressall told an *Evening News* reporter that Gilbert asked Sargent to paint her, that she hated the stuffy studio, and, having had a row with Gilbert before the picture was finished, never returned to Sargent. In 1926, however, she told a reporter that the portrait had been finished, although she had not seen it. Both 1907 and 1911 have been advanced as possible dates for the actual painting, although a reproduction published in the *Graphic* (9 Jan. 1926) suggests an older face and figure than Miss Cressall would have had at either time. Both dates are later than her association with Gilbert. Shown in the Sargent exhibition at the Royal Academy in 1926, the year after the painter's death, the portrait was 'believed to have been sent abroad soon after it had been painted', according to the *Graphic*, and had 'only recently been re-discovered in London'. At some time it had been found in a warehouse by a collector and dealer. He kept it in his home, which was blitzed in W.W.II. Gilbert may have introduced Miss Cressall to Sargent, but there is no evidence that he paid for a full-length portrait such as this was, nor does it appear in the inventory of pictures at Grim's Dyke.

[27] Letter to Mrs Talbot ('Cousin Mary'), 3 June 1905: Talbot Corr./PML.

Maud was evidently quarrelsome; when she fell out with her brother, Gilbert advised her 'to put your pride in your pocket (provided, that is, that you possess a pocket capacious enough to hold it) and write to him in a conciliatory spirit'.[28] She also quarrelled with Gilbert for reasons he did not understand, until he lost interest in her career, though she continued it without him. Mary Weigall, Jane Morris Weigall's daughter, a beginning actress, was more appreciative of her uncle's interest and advice. (Jane herself died in July 1906.)

Honours came to Gilbert. At long last in 1906 he was specially elected to the Garrick Club, which had blackballed him by mistake so long ago. Now that it offered immediate membership 'on account of my public distinction' he saw no reason to hold off. (Burnand's was one of the supporting signatures!) The OP Club of theatre aficionados gave him a banquet, where, sitting between its president and his future biographer, Sidney Dark and Mrs Dark, he looked out over 450 guests, nearly forty of whom were old or present Savoyards. They ate their way through an elaborate menu, including *mazarine de foie gras, faisan rôti au cresson*, and *bombe glacée*, after which 'any amount of melted butter [was] poured (figuratively) down my back'.[29] After making a witty speech he drove home, spent a sleepless night, and developed a headache so blinding that he put off a coaching session with Brandon Thomas's daughter Amy.[30]

He had already been sounded out to see if he would accept a knighthood, and in the King's Birthday List for 1907, that honour was thrust upon him—rather like 'a commuted old-age pension', he said.[31] As he wrote to Henry Arthur Jones, he accepted the title because he thought it 'a good thing that the King should, at last, have turned his attention towards dramatic authorship as a profession worthy of recognition.' After all, no one had been knighted for writing plays before. 'The honour is conferred upon me by the melancholy virtue of my seniority'.[32]

On 15 July he went to Buckingham Palace in full levee uniform '& was duly tapped with a sword on both shoulders by Teddy VII & then kissed hands'. He was now Sir William but was annoyed because he had been officially described as a 'playwright' rather than a 'dramatist', but the latter 'is not applied to us until we are dead & then we become

---

[28] 8 July 1905: in the private collection of Peter Joslin.

[29] Letter to Mrs Talbot ('My very dear Cousin'), 13 Jan. 1907: Talbot Corr./PML.

[30] 31 Dec. 1906: in the private collection of T. Rees.

[31] Speech at a celebratory dinner, 2 Feb. 1908, *The Times* (3 Feb. 1908). He used almost the same or identical words in several letters.

[32] 10 July 1907: PML.

dramatists as oxen & sheep & pigs are transfigured into beef, mutton & pork after their demise'.[33] He continued to growl over 'playwright', which he said made his work, by analogy, like that of a shipwright, a millwright, a wainwright. Still, he was pleased although he continued outwardly to disparage his new title. William Archer wrote him that it should have been a baronetcy, and Bertie Sullivan that it should have been a dukedom. Altogether Gilbert received almost four hundred letters of congratulation and a celebratory dinner at which he dilated on Sullivan's 'Promethean fire' and, misquoting William Morris, called himself 'the idle singer of an idle day'.

A short biography by Edith A. Browne was published that year as the third in the series 'Stars of the Stage'. Gilbert gave her at least three interviews, talking freely, if not always accurately. Although she evidently prided herself on being a modern young woman and recognized Gilbert as an exponent of the Drama of Ideas, Miss Browne seems rather humourless. Certainly, she completely misunderstood *The Wicked World* when she chid the dramatist for not realizing his theme was really 'the mystic love of the gods matching its strength against the magic flame that burns in the heart of the demi-god Man'.[34] Gilbert returned the proofs she sent him with some candid comments on the cocksureness with which she treated him as a neophyte and herself as an authority. If his verse plays were as bad as she thought, why write his biography? 'I can hardly believe that I owe the compliment to the easy trivialities of the Savoy *libretti*.'[35] To this she returned a soft answer, which turned away at least his outward wrath.

Gilbert could still be tart, however, occasionally for no reason, but often with a cause. He wrote an unnecessarily gruff note to the eager young costume designer Herbert Norris, who had sent him some examples of his work: 'You are not justified in sending me a parcel of your sketches without my permission. I return them.'[36] On the other hand, he wrote to *The Times* (20 July 1908), when a thief hit him in the mouth and snatched at his watch as Gilbert entered a cab after the theatre. Gilbert returned the blow heartily (and retained his watch),

[33] Letter to Mrs Talbot ('My very dear Cousin Mary'), 16 July 1907: Talbot Corr./PML. This analogy he also re-used; in the 16 July letter he attributed 'playwright' to 'Court Flunkeydom': 'the atmosphere of royal palaces reeks with the stink of flunkeydom—no wonder that typhoid breaks out in them from time to time!'

[34] Browne, *W. S. Gilbert*, 48.

[35] 10 Mar. 1907, tipped into copy of *W. S. Gilbert*: BL C132.g.72.

[36] Letter from Lillian Everett to the author, 28 July 1974: JWS.

but criticized the police: 'this kind of outrage ought to be impossible within 50 yards of the chief metropolitan police station Bow Street'.

Most protracted of his annoyances was his quarrel with the Reverend J. Pullein Thompson, Vicar of Christ Church, Chelsea, and Honorary Secretary of the National Blind Relief Society. In response to the said plight of the Griffin Sisters, publicized by Thompson, Gilbert sent a contribution and followed it up to make sure they had received it—only to find that the clergyman had taken it for his general fund. Although slovenly about times and sums, the Vicar high-handedly brooked no interference—no question even—until Gilbert challenged him. His auditor was an amateur. Gilbert's hackles rose, especially after his appeal to the Bishop of London was dismissed as 'suspicion run mad'. He set a law case in motion, which, however, did not go to court, but, on his solicitor's advice, he printed a pamphlet, *My Case Against the Rev. J. Pullein Thompson* 'For the information of the Charity Organization Society'. Upon learning that the Misses Griffin did not always tell the exact truth, Gilbert decided that Pullein Thompson 'est probable assez honnete mais il parait etre faible, faineant, et stupide'.[37] Thompson's daughter, later in life, described him as exactly like Mr Barrett in the play *The Barretts of Wimpole Street*,[38] but many of his parishioners continued to love him.[39] They had not read Gilbert's pamphlet. Nevertheless, when Gilbert's attack was over, the Vicar went abroad to calm himself.

At roughly the same time, Gilbert became involved in his fellow dramatists' attempt to abolish stage censorship or at least to establish an independent board of appeal—the alternative he preferred. Although there was a meeting on 12 November to make plans for a petition to be drawn up by Gilbert Murray, it was not until the following 25 February that their deputation was received by Herbert Gladstone, standing in for the Prime Minister, who was ill. Then 'we tumbled through . . . somehow or other', Pinero wrote to William Archer. He had spoken second; Barrie began, and Gilbert was last, telling an anecdote 'about his own dealings with the Censor, almost Georgian in their remoteness from the present day'.[40] A newspaper picture of the elderly dramatist—

---

[37] Diary, 30 Nov. 1907: WSG/BL Add. MS 49,325.

[38] Interview with John Gardner, 11 July 1974.

[39] Letter from Christine Popescu (née Pullein-Thompson) to the author, 23 Apr. 1974: JWS.

[40] *The Collected Letters of Sir Arthur Pinero*, ed. J. P. Wearing (Minneapolis: University of Minnesota Press, 1974), 211.

top hat, rolled umbrella, long white moustache—shows a man still vigorous and upright, with a pugnacious stance and brows bent.

Even though nothing happened immediately, on 29 July a Joint Select Committee began meetings to investigate the Censorship. The Lord Chamberlain did not attend, however, and, in spite of testimony from many important dramatists and writers of fiction, censorship was not abolished, and the Committee's recommendations for some improvement were never put into force.[41] Gilbert, when testifying, had enunciated 'a very wide distinction between what is read and what is seen'. One might read, 'Eliza stripped off her dressing-gown and stepped into her bath', but on stage 'it would be very shocking.'[42] Referring to his own clash with the Lord Chamberlain in 1873, he said, surprisingly, that the censor had been right!—a strange touch of conservatism in his old age. Nevertheless, in 1910 he signed a letter to *The Times* (3 October) urging that the Lord Chamberlain's judgment 'should be made subject to appeal'. The seventeen other signatories included Conan Doyle, Somerset Maugham, and Israel Zangwill.[43]

Gilbert himself had done little writing during this decade; apart from *The Fairy's Dilemma*, his chief work up to 1909 was turning *HMS Pinafore* and *The Mikado* into narratives for children. At first he intended to illustrate them himself, but his hand proved too stiff; so George Bell & Sons, his publishers, chose Alice Woodward instead. Gilbert was dissatisfied: he thought her pictures lacked humour (which they do, charming though they are).[44] Ernest Bell, on the other hand, was dissatisfied with sales, only 5,000 copies in the first year, which a friend told Gilbert was good for a children's book. After all, the advertising had been minimal, and *The Pinafore Picture Book* was competing with Queen Victoria's very popular snapshot book.[45] After a wrangle over contracts, Bell & Sons paid him the agreed-on advance of £750, but did not bring out *The Story of the Mikado* (for which he consented to £500) until after the First World War.

Nevertheless, in his last years Gilbert was again trying to find a composer for his long-unplaced opera based on *The Wicked World*. After

---

[41] R. Findlater, *Banned! A Review of Theatrical Censorship in Britain* (London: MacGibbon & Kee Ltd., 1967), 104–13.

[42] J. Palmer, *The Censor and the Theatre* (New York: Mitchell Kennerley, 1913),181–2.

[43] Laurence Housman's play *Pains and Penalties* had been rejected by the censor without any reason given; when the Lord Chamberlain was forced to explain, his reason was ridiculous. Findlater, *Banned!*, 117–18.

[44] Letter to Ernest Bell, 2 Jan. 1909: PML.

[45] Letters from Gilbert to Ernest Bell, 23 and 28 Dec. 1908: PML.

failing to interest several musicians, he offered it to Edward German on 21 December 1908, noting, however, that 'the chorus *must all be ladies.* You will be able to judge whether this would be a delightful novelty or an insuperable difficulty.'[46] In 1888 the young German had written the music for a song Julia Neilson sang in *Broken Hearts*; now he agreed to collaborate on 'Selene' (Gilbert's provisional title). German, the *World* said (21 December 1909), carried on Sullivan's tradition without copying Sullivan; in fact, he had completed the score of Sullivan's last, uncompleted opera *The Emerald Isle*, and had set *Merrie England* (1902) and *A Princess of Kensington* (1903) for the Savoy.

Immediately Gilbert began to revise the libretto he had worked out several years earlier, finishing at noon on 28 February 1909. 'I had some difficulty in getting the rusty, creaky old machine to work again—but after a few essays I found the harness sit well enough on me.'[47] Mrs Carte's London repertory season would finish at the end of March; after that the company did not return till 1919, contenting itself perforce with touring. Although both Seymour Hicks and J. A. E. Malone were interested in producing *Fallen Fairies* (the final title), Gilbert chose C. Herbert Workman, who had played Grossmith roles for more than a decade and who in May put together a syndicate which would back him for a season at the Savoy. He would play Lutin, and Gilbert wanted Nancy McIntosh for the Fairy Queen. 'She is very keen to play the part,' Gilbert wrote to German.[48] Since Nancy was now in her early forties and had not acted professionally for more than ten years, it is more likely that the keenness was Gilbert's, although he and Kitty would be sorry to lose her company during what he supposed would be a long run.

The contract, as drawn up by Gilbert, stipulated 10 per cent of gross receipts for him (5 for writing, 5 for directing), 5 per cent for German; he would have absolute control over staging and German over music; the approval of both would be necessary for cast, chorus, designer, and dressmaker, while no changes could be made in dialogue or musical numbers without their express sanction.[49] In short, it was a typical Gilbert and Sullivan contract except for the division of the spoils. Workman would produce it as the second work of his Savoy season.

Unhappily, he waited till October to give a definite yes. Gilbert in the meantime had been taking a course of pine inhalations at Wiesbaden.

[46] PML.
[47] To Mrs Talbot ('My dearest Cousin Mary'), 7 Feb. 1909: Talbot Corr./PML.
[48] 21 Mar. 1909: PML.     [49] Typed agreement, copy, 6 July 1909: PML.

('I never enjoy any place to which I am obliged to go,' he wrote to Mrs Talbot on 9 October; 'I shall not enjoy heaven unless it is left optional whether I go there or not.'). The syndicate, it now appeared, wanted Gilbert to read the piece and German to play the music to them before deciding if they would produce it. 'I decline altogether to recognize the existence of the syndicate—who are merely his bankers,' was Gilbert's position.[50] Meanwhile he was increasingly delighted with German's score, 'its high technical qualities, its fund of delicate melody, & its great variety'.[51] But he did ask for slower tempos in two numbers so that the words might be heard and the singer have more chance to act.[52]

The single set was designed by Joseph Harker, whose uncle John O'Connor had designed the original scene for *The Wicked World*. Harker and Gilbert had a rousing quarrel just before the opera opened, when, Harker wrote much later, Gilbert demanded changes in the set.[53] Gilbert said publicly that he objected to the scene but that his wishes were ignored. Reviews were divided: the *Daily Mirror* thought everyone else was pleased with its art nouveau blossoms and writhings, but for 'Rooty-Tooty' of the *Sporting Times*, the effect was too red and garish. *The Times* described it as a gaudy transformation scene. The costumes, however, were delightful. Designed by Percy Anderson, whom Gilbert said surpassed himself, the fairies' headdresses suggested orchids and dragonflies; Nancy wore pale blue, a diamond coronet, and downy wings. Other dresses were spangled with silver or appliquéd with iridescent beetle-wing embroidery; great eyes of reddish-purple were painted on the wings of a blue-purple costume.

*Fallen Fairies* opened on 15 December 1909. Early-comers sang Gilbert and Sullivan songs while waiting to encore Gilbert and German. But though the audience was almost hysterically enthusiastic, critics were by no means unanimous: 'rather cruel,' Gilbert called them.[54] True, the *Pall Mall Gazette* praised the opera highly, but the *Yorkshire News* correspondent remarked that 'the public does not associate homilies with a libretto by Sir William Gilbert, but such are freely provided in the closing scene'. The *Observer* missed topsy-turvydom: 'It is a strange compound of trifling and tragedy, of gossamer and gnashings of teeth. . . . the effect is a little like that of an act of "Othello" pieced into "The Merry Wives of Windsor".' And saddest of all, the

[50] Letter to German, 16 Oct. 1909: PML.
[51] Letter to German, 24 Oct. 1909: PML.      [52] 28 Nov. and 2 Dec. 1909: PML.
[53] J. Harker, *Studio and Stage* (London: Nisbet & Co. Ltd., 1924), 85–7.
[54] Letter to German, 21 Dec. 1909: PML.

*Daily Express*, after praising the performance, continued, 'But with it all "Fallen Fairies" belongs to yesterday.'

Like most of the numbers, Nancy's had been encored; her enunciation and that of the entire cast had been praised; her singing was described as fresh, her silvery speaking voice reminiscent of Ellen Terry's, yet several critics commented on her lack of sonority or vocal strength. Sixteen years before, the press had perceived her as an ice-maiden, a girl made of moonlight; now, cast as a fairy queen driven to fury by faithless human love, she found sexuality not in her sphere.

At the end of the performance, Workman literally dragged Gilbert on stage to make a curtain speech. He had been at the Beefsteak Club and then in Nancy's dressing-room for the second act. On the last of his operatic nights, he told the audience, 'There is life in the old dog yet.' He was cheered—and booed. Had *Fallen Fairies* been a success, he would have adapted *The Palace of Truth* as a libretto, but he was soon forced to recognize that the new opera was a failure. 'The press are always howling for something better than "musical comedy" & when they get it, they won't have it,' he wrote sadly to Cousin Mary.[55]

Nor would the syndicate have it. On 22 December a letter from Workman told Gilbert that he intended to remove Nancy and had names of a replacement ready to show Gilbert and German. The librettist took the next train to town, but he could not shake Workman's (and the syndicate's) decision. Not until three days later did he tell Nancy, who received the news 'avec beaucoup de courage'.[56]

According to Workman he had to replace Nancy because her singing was so out of tune that groups of people would leave the theatre, or not come at all. This infuriated Gilbert, who protested she was incapable of singing out of tune. Appealed to, German answered tactfully that they could find no more 'artistic' exponent, but her voice seemed less full than when he had first heard it, which he ascribed to nervousness or overwork. He professed himself terribly upset;[57] after all, he, too, had a heavy stake in *Fallen Fairies*. Sir William, incapable of reading the nuances of a tactful letter, took this for absolute agreement: 'there are wheels within wheels,' he wrote darkly. The syndicate, he believed, intended to bring in their own candidate, Amy Evans, a concert artist with no stage experience.[58] They did, although there is no reason to believe their interest was anything but professional.

[55] 16 Dec. 1909: Talbot Corr./PML.

[56] Diary, 24 Dec. 1909: WSG/BL Add. MS 49,326.    [57] 22 Dec. 1909: PML.

[58] Letter to German, 23 Dec. 1909: PML.

Perhaps the tacit but real reason, syndicate machinations aside, for removing Nancy McIntosh from the role of Selene lay in her incapacity to project sexuality. Her Fairy Queen was too much a tragedy queen, a reviewer said, and Rolanda Ronald, a young chorus member, described her many years later as lacking any 'star' quality, a spinster who would never attract a man.[59] Although Gilbert immediately thought of obtaining an injunction against the change of role, and asked German to join him in making an affidavit, Nancy told him she could not play Selene again. Her 'infamous treatment', as he described it, had 'sadly affected' her.[60] He accepted her decision, but suspicions and injunctions continued to run in his mind. The last Gilbert libretto ended its run on 29 January 1910.

[59] Letter to the author, 17 Oct. 1969: JWS.  [60] Letter to German, 28 Dec. 1909: PML.

# 20

---

# Quick Curtain

Yet one would pray to live/Another moon!

*The Yeomen of the Guard*

AFTER a tumultuous December, *Fallen Fairies* continued to be a battleground in the new year. When Workman offered to keep it going past 29 January if German and Gilbert would make up any deficit, the librettist exploded, 'I will most certainly not guarantee that Syndicate of rogues & fools against loss.'[1] He wished the piece were withdrawn and applied for an injunction to stop Selene's solo, 'Oh, love that rulest in our land', from being sung at the Savoy.[2] It had been cut earlier because he thought it redundant; now it was put back for Miss Evans. Gilbert's legal action was the more annoying because 'Oh, love' was now the most popular number in the opera.[3]

Dutifully German tried to stop the song, but asked if Gilbert would not reconsider. First, Gilbert shot off an intense no, but on consideration—particularly of eighty people who would suddenly be out of work if the opera closed—he agreed to let it be sung if Workman apologized, put a notice into the bills that the song was performed through Gilbert's 'courtesy & consideration', and paid the attorney's costs of the injunction.[4] Workman did, but his acquiescence did not prolong the run of *Fallen Fairies*. Nor did it keep Gilbert and Nancy McIntosh from suing him for recovery of fees and breach of contract. The librettist's 10 per cent royalties were not paid after 1 January, while German had agreed to reduce his 5 per cent by half.

As arctic weather enveloped London, Gilbert's resolve hardened, and German found himself in a debate by post over their contract. Was it

[1] Letter to German, 30 Jan. 1910: PML.

[2] Mr Justice Neville granted a week's injunction; 'News from All Parts', *Pall Mall Gazette* (15 Jan. 1910), 3.

[3] Letter from Hamish MacCunn to German, 13 Jan. 1910: PML.

[4] 16 Jan. 1910: PML. The injunction was discharged on 18 Jan.

with Workman or the syndicate? The question of Nancy's voice continued since Gilbert was still furious that she had been replaced: 'you said
to me "Miss McIntosh sang magnificently on the first night," ' he
wrote.[5] 'So far as I remember it was *you* who used the word,' German
answered.[6]

During February Gilbert continued to see his solicitor about 'l'affaire
Workman', but by the end of March he gave up. Nancy was too upset at
the prospect of appearing in court; so, bowing to nerves which had
proved so detrimental to her professional career, Gilbert stopped his suit
on condition that Workman and the syndicate pay the costs: 'that is
rather consolatory,' he wrote to German, who had at last received royalties.[7] Gilbert had not. Nancy, relieved, went to Vienna 'under contract'—to whom, Gilbert did not specify.

While 'l'affaire Workman' was going on, and Edward German was
very likely wishing he had never been given the honour of collaboration, Gilbert was busy in other directions. He was trying to find a producer for *Ruddigore*, which Helen D'Oyly Carte had not revived. In
early January he proposed it to Ellaline Terriss and Seymour Hicks. He
invited them to lunch where Nancy could play the music, and to
enhance his offer, Gilbert assured Hicks that the role of Robin
Oakapple would suit him exactly. For Ellaline Gilbert suggested Mad
Margaret, 'the best acting part I have ever written'. It would be delightful, for (forgetting the Kendals, Marion Terry, and Mary Anderson) 'I
have never had an actor & actress of your value in any piece of mine
before.' They could reduce expenses by leaving out the costly uniforms,
and Gilbert had marked an eight-minute cut of 'the most dismal music
that I have ever heard', though, as he added hastily, no doubt it was
admirable from a technical standpoint.[8] He had disliked Sullivan's
ghost music for nearly twenty-five years! But the cut was unnecessary.
The Hickses did not come to lunch. Nor did a meeting with Arthur
Bourchier yield a production.

Meanwhile he continued to write affectionately to Mary Talbot, to
examine students at the Academy of Dramatic Art, and to lunch with
old Savoyards. Although still in Eaton Square, he recorded the depth of
water in his lake at Grim's Dyke, noting on 1 March, 'Le lac est plein.'

A possible new work interested him temporarily when Sir Frederick
Macmillan suggested he write his memoirs. Gilbert answered on 22
March, 'I have only to say that the more tempting [the terms] are—the

[5] 11 Jan. 1910: PML.     [6] 12 Jan. 1910: PML.     [7] 13 May 1910: PML.
[8] 7 Jan. 1910: PML.

more likely am I to be spurred on to the necessary exertion.' But he quickly added that he was not attempting to 'put on the screw'.[9] Macmillan offered 25 per cent royalties for England and 15 per cent for New York; so Gilbert began a 'trial trip' on 31 March and again on 13 April. Yet nothing more came of it, rightly so perhaps, for judging from the few pages he wrote for the *Theatre* years before, autobiography was not Gilbert's forte. He wrote clearly but not distinctively about his public self.

Returning to the country at the end of March, the Gilbert household was plunged into the excitement of catching a thief in the late afternoon of 6 April. Frank Burgess had time only to take a purse containing 9½d. before Gilbert's Pekinese barked at him. Escaping unluckily into the arms of the butler and footman, Burgess was subdued with the help of the gardener just coming in with Gilbert's white rose buttonhole. Sir William appeared, called for a rope, tied up the housebreaker and notified the police, who took him to Wealdstone in Gilbert's own Cadillac! Burgess, who had been imprisoned before and who had stolen from other houses, went off with a true melodramatic flourish, threatening to 'do for' everyone when he came out. 'Happily', Gilbert wrote to Mary Talbot, 'I am not likely to be alive then—so *I'm* all right.'[10]

Having played croquet while Edward VII was dying, Gilbert went to London for a not very good view of his funeral cortège. On 11 May he signed his will, and on 17 May had the first gooseberry tart of the season. Since Nancy was in Vienna, Sir William took Kitty for a cruise. Accompanied by the Messels, they visited Lisbon, Gibraltar, Tangiers, the Canary Islands, Madeira, and Vigo. He was elected president of the ship's sports committee, but was glad to get home on 13 June. He had never seen 'such super-human hideousness as was presented by some of the party. I seemed to have been born into a world of Pantomime masks.'[11]

The rest of the summer of 1910 was quiet except for a frosty refusal to allow Workman to buy the performing rights to the Savoy Operas when Mrs Carte's five-year contract expired. She renewed it for another five years for £5,000, although the librettist said her recent productions had devalued the pieces. Gilbert continued his work as a magistrate, bought two du Maurier sketches in an exhibition, and watched the moon through the telescope he had recently set up. He swam daily in

---

[9] Macmillan Papers/BL Add. MS 54,999.  [10] 11 Dec. 1910: Talbot Corr./PML.
[11] Letter to Mrs Talbot ('My dearest Cousin Mary'), 14 June 1910: Talbot Corr./PML.

his lake after the curator of Kew Gardens told him how to clear out the encroaching weeds.[12]

Then, on a train to London, Gilbert ran into his friend Sir Charles Mathews, Director of Public Prosecutions. The Bow Street committal hearings for Crippen and Le Neve had just begun, and Sir Charles promised Gilbert a ticket for the following Tuesday. A sensational but likeable murderer, about whom books are still written, Dr Hawley Harvey Crippen had given hyoscine to his wife, a minor music-hall performer, dismembered her, and buried her torso in their cellar. *En route* to America with his mistress Ethel Le Neve in boy's clothing, Crippen was identified by the captain of the vessel, who used the recently invented wireless telegraphy to inform London. Thanks to a faster ship, Inspector Dew was on hand to help arrest Crippen and Le Neve when they reached Canada.

The unusual drug and the use of the new marconigram added to the interest in the crime, and England was agog over the details. Even Kitty's mother, Herbertina Turner, 95 years old, made her little 'tweeny' read each day's news aloud.[13] On 6 September Gilbert used Mathews's ticket and found himself seated as a spectator on the Bench, looking rather grim. He went again on 8, 14, 16, and 21 September, Nancy accompanying him on the fourteenth; on the twenty-first Crippen and Le Neve were committed for trial. But before that trial began on 18 October—with writers and stage figures packing the court, Gilbert had left England.[14]

'You will know me by my wearing a speckled brown & white suit with a purple & yellow tie,' he wrote to Philip Hogg,[15] with whom he was going to travel to Constantinople. Kitty, worried about her mother's poor health, would go only as far as Bath, with Nancy.

His trip began badly with a French railway strike, which forced Gilbert and Hogg to take an unintended route to Paris and then to spend sixteen hours on a train, with only a sandwich, before reaching Marseilles.[16] There was cholera at Naples; so they went to Villebranche,

---

[12] Letter from George E. Bean, son of curator W. J. Bean, to the author, 22 July 1974: JWS.

[13] Mrs Brien, telephone interview with the author, 27 July 1974.

[14] This fact, of course, demolishes Pett Ridge's circumstantial account of seeing Gilbert on the day the verdict was announced, in a fever of excitement until the news that Crippen was guilty was brought to the club: *A Story Teller: Forty Years in London* (London: Hodder and Stoughton Ltd., n.d.), 26. Hesketh Pearson copied this untrue story in his first *Gilbert and Sullivan* but modified it (still inaccurately) in the later *Gilbert: His Life and Strife* (London: Methuen & Co. Ltd., 1957).

[15] 11 Oct. 1910: PML.     [16] Diary, 12 Oct. 1910: WSG/BL Add. MS 49,328.

with a side trip to Monte Carlo, where Gilbert won 15 francs—the only luck so far on the trip. Both of them had forgotten their passports, which meant visits to consulates in Messina, Piraeus, and Athens. At Messina the stench of dead bodies from a recent earthquake was 'quite perceptible', to say the least.[17] At Smyrna the bazaar was dirty and ugly, but the weather at Athens was glorious and Gilbert took three dozen photographs. He had a new toy: a stereoscopic camera. Hogg had proved to be a considerate travelling companion, but few other passengers were interesting; they, in turn, voted Gilbert 'unsociable', and once more he was glad to return. He bought a new lemur.

The last month of 1910 was tranquilly spent at Grim's Dyke, with frequent excursions to London where Sir William bought pears, honey, and Camembert.

The Crutchleys came for Christmas, and Sybil went with Gilbert to the Christmas Eve rehearsal of the Drury Lane pantomime. As usual they sat behind the conductor. Ordinarily Gilbert enjoyed the children's voices, the *mise-en-scène*, and most of the comedy, but his last pantomime was a 'poor affair'. They left after the first act.[18]

When Gilbert received his 1911 diary, he wrote to Mary Talbot that looking through its blank pages 'set me thinking. At my time of life . . . the future becomes a serious consideration & one can't help wondering what miseries[,] sorrows, calamities, deaths & other horrors will have to be set down before it is finished—if ever it *is* finished, which seems unlikely.' But this was 'rather morbid', and Gilbert changed the subject.[19] He had five months and nine days to live.

Perhaps this mood returned in early January, for his diary records that he was destroying papers on the fourth, rather haphazardly, judging from what survives. On the sixth he went to examine candidates at the Academy of Dramatic Art in spite of having diarrhoea, but then he had to spend the evening lying on the sofa. He was well the next day. For a man in his seventy-fifth year, Gilbert had remarkable powers of recuperation. He no longer rode, but he was a great walker except on an occasional gouty day or when he had a cold. No doubt his continued active life controlled what his doctor called a tendency to (adult-onset) diabetes. His heart was not what it had been, but walking was good for that too.

Although Gilbert continued to coach would-be actresses and

[17] Letter to Kitty, 19 Oct. 1910: WSG/BL Add. MS 49,345.
[18] Diary, 24 Dec. 1910: WSG/BL Add. MS 49,328.
[19] 20 Dec. 1910: Talbot Corr./PML.

rehearsed an abortive production of *Creatures of Impulse* for Richard Temple, the greatest interest of his last winter was his new drama *The Hooligan*, which he wrote specially for the Coliseum. Theoretically, plays could not be produced in music halls, which were not under the Lord Chamberlain's jurisdiction, but Oswald Stoll of the Coliseum continually challenged this prohibition, until the Theatre Managers' Association agreed that plays of thirty minutes and not more than six speaking characters might be performed. (Even so, in practice music-hall plays often ran over the half-hour.)

No important dramatist, however, had risked his theatrical purity by writing for the halls. But Stoll, with visions of George Bernard Shaw dancing through his head, was persuaded that a work by Gilbert would bring other playwrights to his stage.[20] Gilbert promised to think it over, taking James Welch, the current Coliseum star, to lunch at the Junior Carlton Club just before Christmas 1910 and proposing an idea to him. Full of the club's excellent cuisine, Welch readily agreed. Thinking about Crippen, although in no sense using him as a model, Gilbert had decided to write a play about a murderer.

In January after moving back to town, he began work. Obtaining Home Office permission, he visited Pentonville Prison and questioned its governor about the condemned cell routine. On the foggy morning of 16 January he began to write *The Hooligan*, reconnoitring the ground that evening by taking Kitty, Nancy, and Helsham Jones to the Coliseum. By 2 February the one-act play was finished; by 3 February he had read it to Welch and sent it to his typist (Ethel Dickens, Charles's granddaughter, whom Gilbert probably met through her aunt Kate Perugini). Ten days later, dramatist, actor, producer, and scene-painter went to Pentonville to interview the chief warder. Welch was surprised at the picture of the Crucifixion in the condemned cell. ' "I see," he said. "They show the poor wretch how they used to do it." '[21]

Since Welch was a notorious ad-libber and since Gilbert was directing his own play, there were bound to be clashes. They got through two rehearsals; Gilbert missed a third because he lost his voice; and then the dramatist walked out—to the Garrick Club, whence he despatched an immediate note. He was stopping the production. By gagging, Welch had not carried out his contract; Gilbert was not accustomed to actors altering his lines. Welch immediately wrote an amusing apology, and

[20] S. Blow, *Through Stage Doors* (Edinburgh: W. & R. Chambers, Ltd., 1958), 202–5.
[21] Ibid. 206.

altering his lines. Welch immediately wrote an amusing apology, and Gilbert, mollified, returned next day, walking from Eaton Square to the Coliseum as usual.[22]

Stoll himself was by no means sure of *The Hooligan*. His policy was unusually puritanical—no coarseness or vulgarity on stage[23]—which may have influenced Gilbert's willingness to write for a music hall. Still, *The Hooligan* was grim, a *tranche de vie* unlike the usual programmes he presented. Nevertheless, Gilbert's 'Character Sketch' opened at the Coliseum on 27 February, as the last number before an interval during which the band played selections from *The Gondoliers*. The second half of the programme ended with the Bioscope and included a mimed play of violence and sexuality, *Sumurûn*, by Max Reinhardt's Deutsche Theatre company from Berlin. Evidently the absence of words satisfied Stoll's conscience.

As usual Gilbert kept away from the first night, leaving Kitty and two friends at the Coliseum, but going to the Beefsteak Club himself until he joined them at 10.15. The play was an instant success. Its plot is very simple, but its implications are far-reaching. Solly, a coster-boy with a weak mind and a weak heart, is going to be hanged on the day the play takes place. He has killed his former girl, whose new boy called Solly 'a 'eap o' tea-leaves'. Solly alternates between terror, fury at the judge, and a desire to be brave, while the warders try to hearten him. At last the prison governor, chaplain, doctor, and others enter, sending Solly into paroxysms of fear, but the governor announces that his death sentence has just been commuted to penal servitude for life, which means twenty years with good behaviour. Asking dazedly, 'I'm to live?', the hooligan falls dead of heart failure.

The enormous Coliseum stage was draped in black to reduce it to the size of a cell.[24] Welch, a colourless little man, accomplished in cockney dialect and capable of both comedy and pathos, believed that all farce is based on tragedy.[25] He had been the original Lickcheese of Shaw's

---

[22] Blow, *Through Stage Doors*, 206–7. The actor may have made one addition to his lines in spite of the dramatist, for Richard Hugget quotes Solly as saying to a warder, 'Take your bloody hands off me.' *The Truth about 'Pygmalion'* (London: William Heinemann Ltd., 1969), 50–1. This 'bloody' was not licensed, nor did it appear in the typescript of the play. The text printed in the *Century Magazine* included 'Gawd split yer! Take yer hands off!' Stoll's notorious objection to 'strong language' makes it unlikely that Welch regularly interpolated the adjective.

[23] F. Barker, *The House that Stoll Built* (London: Frederick Muller Ltd., 1957), 70.

[24] Letter from Ruby Miller to Rolanda Ronald for transmission to the author, 31 July 1969: JWS.

[25] Blow, *Through Stage Doors*, 117.

demned boy was described by the *Pall Mall Gazette* as a triumph of morbid realism. He was called four times, and cheered, although there were also hisses from thoughtless spectators angry at Gilbert's 'hideous piece of realism'. Thought was what Gilbert hoped for. He told 'The Clubman' of the *Sketch* (7 June) he intended to point out 'that the punishment of a man who never had been given a chance to rise out of the gutter should not be the same as the punishment of a man who had thrown away his chances'. In short, *The Hooligan* was Gilbert's last statement of a lifelong theme. Solly himself, child and friend of thieves, cries, 'Am I to be judged like a bloke wots been brought up fair and strite, and taught a tride, and can look on a ticker wiv 'is hooks safe in 'is trowsers pockets?' He is, in fact, a younger brother of Ruth Tredgett from *Charity* long ago, and, as in Strephon's deleted song, he has had Fagin for a father. He is the murderer whose trial *Fun*'s Own Correspondent attended still longer ago in 1866. Solly's 'gruesome' life and death 'will certainly provoke discussion as to the present method of dealing with capital cases,' thought the *Sketch*. The *Illustrated London News* announced that 'the successor of Robertson, the apostle of fantasy, suddenly elects to rival the newest school of our dramatists on their own ground!' Galsworthy had shown the isolation cell in *Justice*, but Gilbert had shown the condemned cell itself!

Yet at times there are also ironic flashes from the comic Gilbert. The amusing psychology of the Nightmare Song in *Iolanthe* becomes the serious psychology of Solly's recurrent dream of an enormous court with a long-armed judge, who squeezes the hooligan's throat while everyone else nods.[26] Solly says he only intended to hurt his girl a little, 'But I never cut a gal before . . . and my 'and slipped on account of youth and inexperience. . . . is a bloke to be 'ung becos 'e never cut a gal afore?' Or he refuses to 'own up' to the chaplain: 'I 'ave howned up. . . . Why, I howned up to the Judge! "Not guilty," says I, strite out.'

Altogether, this mixture of irony, of social theme, and of grubby realism suggests that Gilbert was beginning a new career; he had, however, no evident inclination to pursue it. Someone called to suggest translating *The Hooligan* for the Grand Guignol which performed grim, socially conscious playlets as well as sensational ones, but nothing came

---

[26] Perhaps this dream is a reminiscence of Irving's great success *The Bells* (1871), in which Mathias dreams he is being tried in a court of justice for the long-ago murder of the Polish Jew and dies of an imaginary hanging. Solly's dream was originally much longer and included a variation in which the court was so small that the judge, jury, and barristers breathed into Solly's face and stared into his eyes: WSG/BL Add. MS 49,305.

of it. Nor was he interested when on 11 March Herr Spontelli and a Mrs Fitzgerald asked him to write a pantomime.

Instead, he enjoyed the last of their formal dinner parties on 14 March, when, at a table decorated with yellow azaleas and freesias, the Hares, Sir Charles Mathews, Lady Coleridge, and eleven others joined the Gilberts and Nancy to drink consommé Richelieu and to eat their way through quail soufflé, chicken *à la diable*, asparagus, *roses pompadour*, and Viennese sandwiches, to say nothing of turbot with lobster sauce, lamb, and green beans.

On 29 March *The Hooligan* closed when Welch's contract ended, but the little actor offered £200 for two years' acting rights. Gilbert had indeed shown other dramatists the path to the music halls although they took it slowly and not to the Coliseum. Shaw capitulated the next December and let the Palace stage *How He Lied to Her Husband*, while Barrie's *The Twelve Pound Look* had a Hippodrome revival in 1912.

In early April the Gilberts and Nancy left Eaton Square and were soon enjoying Grim's Dyke strawberries. The gazelle Gilbert had ordered in town was delivered and strolled about with him; a fawn named Florian joined the menagerie. Sir William still wrote an occasional angry letter—to Julia Neilson, who, he thought, had slighted his correspondence, and to G. W. Smalley for an unpleasant remark about *Patience*. (He later apologized to Smalley, who had written a 'soft answer'.)[27]

But generally in these last months, Gilbert was happy: the happiest man in London, he said.[28] '[M]y experience is that old age is the happiest time in a man's life,' he told Sydney Grundy. 'The worst of it is, there's so little of it.'[29] He would have been glad of twenty years more.[30]

He spent a few days turning his old 'Actors, Authors, and Audiences' into a playlet for possible use by the Academy of Dramatic Art, and he was correcting proofs of *Princess Toto* for the fourth volume of his *Original Plays*. Surrounded thus by the past, he wondered if one or two of the operas might be staged for the Coronation season.

On 24 May Gilbert spoke at a P & O dinner, emphasizing the universality of drama and the difficulty of its being read by amateurs. To make an ample living, he said, re-using his favourite gastronomic

---

[27] Pearson, *Gilbert: His Life and Strife*, 241.

[28] Letter from G. S. Mersey to Lady Gilbert, 3 June 1911: WSG/BL Add. MS 49,342.

[29] Quoted by the *Daily Chronicle* (1 June 1911), quoting the *Westminster* (31 May 1911).

[30] Letter from T. Douglas Murray to Lady Gilbert, n.d. [May 1911]: WSG/BL Add. MS 49,342.

figure, one should aim at a kind of rumpsteak and oyster sauce play, a medium between the quails' breasts of the stalls and the baked sheeps' heads of the gallery, a comparison he had already used in an 1888 speech for the Green Room Club. He took a last fling at Shakespeare and the actors who cut his lines and rearranged his scenes to suit their own egos and to give themselves greater opportunities. It was not a particularly new speech, but it was an amusing and a practical one from an old professional.

The last week was a busy one. Gilbert lunched at the Dramatists' Club, of which he was a founding member, saying as he rose to leave, 'I don't know whether you fellows are aware of it, but we have been thirteen at table. However, as I am the first to go, the rest of you are all right.'[31] He attended a dinner for Thackeray's centenary and a reception for the dancers Pavlova and Mordkin (whose name he remembered as 'Nordkin').

Except when the water was colder than 58° F, Gilbert swam daily; that was the border between pleasure and a possible touch of lumbago. Otherwise he thought his daily plunges kept him from catching cold.[32] He was teaching Isabel Emery, Winifred Emery's niece,[33] to swim and tried to persuade a little Parisienne guest to join him—until she objected that cold water was not good for her heart and that 'I did not want to give him an emotion and obliged [sic] him to save me!'[34] Gilbert laughed, although his own doctor had insisted he should not enter the water suddenly. In fact, Kitty, who did not like the lake,[35] had taken to hiding her husband's bathing-suit to try to keep him on shore.[36]

Gilbert's last diary entry, for 28 May, records superb weather. He played croquet, interrupted by friends who came for lunch and later chatted in his elegant Egyptian tent. Of course, they had a swim— Gilbert's twenty-third of the year. Nancy sang after tea; more guests arrived, and when they left the lemurs were let loose. The first melon was ripe enough for dinner.

[31] A. Sutro, *Celebrities and Simple Souls* (London: Duckworth, 1933), 176.

[32] Letter from Gilbert to Mrs Talbot ('My dearest Cousin'), 10 Sept. 1910: Talbot Corr./PML.

[33] Although she is referred to in accounts of Gilbert's death as 'Winifred' Emery, Miss Emery signed her letter to Lady Gilbert as 'Isabel'. 'Winifred' was her middle name.

[34] Letter from Therese Wittmaury [Wittmaning?] to Lady Gilbert, 'Thursday' [May 1911]: WSG/BL Add. MS 49,343.

[35] Letter from Sybil Carlisle to Lady Gilbert, 30 May 1911: WSG/BL Add. MS 49,341. See also letter from Harold L. Turner to Lady Gilbert (his aunt), 1 June 1911.

[36] Mrs Brien, telephone interview with the author, 27 July 1974.

On Monday, 29 May, Sir William went to London again to watch, as always, the Royal Hospital's parade and inspection with Lady Sybil and Sir Charles Crutchley, the lieutenant-governor. Then he lunched at the Junior Carlton Club, where he surprised his old enemy W. H. Kendal by joining him and talking pleasantly of the past.[37] In the early afternoon Gilbert visited Miss Fortescue, ill in a darkened room after a riding accident. 'I won't ask what you think of her appearance, for you can scarcely see her,' her mother told him. 'Her appearance matters nothing. It is her disappearance we could not stand,' Gilbert replied.[38]

By four in the afternoon, he had picked up Isabel Emery and her 16-year-old pupil Ruby Preece at Harrow Station and brought them to Grim's Dyke. They entered the water while Sir William was looking for his bathing-suit (long-legged, blue-striped).[39] As he left the little changing hut, Ruby, the better swimmer, went further out, lost the bottom, and panicked. Shrieking, 'Oh, Miss Emery, I am drowning!', she floundered about. Gilbert called to her, dived in, and swam out rapidly, saying, 'Put your hands on my shoulders and don't struggle'.[40] As she did, he sank and they both went under. Ruby resurfaced immediately, but Gilbert had died instantly of the heart attack his doctor feared. He had rushed to save what he thought was a drowning adolescent, and the water was surprisingly cold for such a warm day. His body lay 6 feet deep at the bottom of his lake.

Crying for help, the girls splashed about until Ruby reached the bank and roused the gardener. He took out the boat in which Gilbert and Nancy had rowed about, and with menservants dragged the lake. Crushing the blue forget-me-nots at the edge as they beached, they carried Gilbert's body toward the house. When Herbertina Turner, in nearby Bushey, learned there had been a death at Grim's Dyke, she cried, with the tremulous voice of old age, 'Oh, it's not Lucy? It's not Lucy, is it?'[41]

'No death could have been more free from suffering than his was,' Gilbert's doctor, William Shackleton, wrote to his widow.[42] The inquest was held on 31 May in the billiard-room where photographs of Savoyards and drawings by Bab looked down upon the scene. Azaleas

[37] S. Dark and R. Grey, *W. S. Gilbert: His Life and Letters* (London: Methuen & Co. Ltd., 1923), 221.

[38] Ibid. 222.    [39] P. Maude, *Worlds Away* (London: John Baker, 1964), 133.

[40] Dark and Grey, *W. S. Gilbert: His Life and Letters*, 222.

[41] Mrs Brien, telephone interview with the author, 27 July 1974.

[42] 3 June 1911: WSG/BL Add. MS 49,343.

crowded against the windows. Ruby Preece was necessarily there, very pale, and the foreman of the jury asked if her name might be suppressed. The coroner refused, saying, 'I cannot interfere with the Press at all.'[43] Dressed in deep mourning, Isabel Emery, too, gave evidence and then sat in a corner, sobbing quietly. 'I cannot tell you how terribly—terribly sorry I am. . . . I feel you can never forgive [me],' she wrote to Lady Gilbert; '. . . had [it] not been for me it would never have happened.'[44]

In the coroner's words, Gilbert's death was 'a very honourable end to a great and distinguished career'. Yet it was a totally unnecessary death. Accounts immediately published, even before the inquest, were generally inaccurate and gave rise to errors still repeated.[45] In some, Gilbert was said to be alone in the water, the girls on shore. Sometimes the ladies were identified as Lucy and Nancy; sometimes he had asked 'lady friends' to watch how well he could swim; sometimes instead of women, there were two children. And many times he was said to have drowned. The confusion of these reports would have annoyed him, but Lucy was not in a mood to care about these mistakes.

The question of her husband's burial had been immediately thrust upon her, for he had once said he would like to be buried in the churchyard of St John the Evangelist at Stanmore. Although Gilbert was neither a regular churchgoer nor a parishioner of St John's, he found its vicar pleasant and the quiet place attractive. But that vicar, S. F. L. Bernays, proved unavoidably obstinate. His congregation did not want their churchyard crowded with strangers, however distinguished. Regretfully he refused to bury Sir William unless he were cremated. Ashes need not take up much space, and the vicar urged Lady Gilbert to accept his suggestion.[46] She did.

On 2 June at ten in the morning, Gilbert's body was cremated at Golder's Green and his ashes in a small oak casket taken to Stanmore for burial. Nancy had lined the grave with white flowers,[47] and Kitty's lilacs were also white. The American ambassador sent a chaplet of laurel, orchids, and fern; George Grossmith, a red and white floral anchor; Mrs D'Oyly Carte, a large floral harp of orchids and lilies. Wreaths

[43] *Nottingham Guardian* (1 June 1911).

[44] n.d. [30 May 1911]: WSG/BL Add. MS 49,341.

[45] In the 1970s I heard from two separate sources that Gilbert died during a nude bathing party!

[46] Letter from S. F. L. Bernays to Lady Gilbert, 30 May 1911: WSG/BL Add. MS 49,341.

[47] Lucy Gilbert, unsigned note in pencil, replying to condolences from 'you and Gordon': WSG/BL Add. MS 49,341.

came from Lady Macmillan, the Critchetts, Celliers, Terrys, and hundreds more, some as obscure as the Misses Griffen or 'little Columbine', the Mlle Rosa (Montrose) to whom Gilbert had been Harlequin in that long-ago pantomime.

The O. P. Club, the staff of the Academy of Dramatic Art, the First Nighters' Club were all represented. Characteristically, Burnand wrote to the vicar next day to say his wreath was not mentioned in the *Daily Telegraph*. Would he inform the newspaper if it had arrived?[48] The Burnands did not attend the funeral although a special train from Euston brought Rutland Barrington, Stanley Weigall, Jessie Bond, Birkett, Pinero, Hare, Alexander, Kate Perugini, and Richard Temple among many others. The Bancrofts were there, of course; Sir Squire never missed a theatrical funeral, but Marie was too old to be able to weep for Gilbert as she had for Robertson forty years before.

A boys' choir sang the Ninetieth Psalm and the hymn 'Jesus lives!' Bertie Sullivan and Rowland Brown took the oak box to the grave, and the boys' voices rose again in 'O God, our help in ages past'. Afterwards, a Roman Catholic priest, presumably accompanying Bertie, blessed Gilbert's grave, where in a quarter-century Lucy would join him, and where after more years Nancy too would be buried.

Condolences had already begun to pour in: from Burr McIntosh in America; from Georgina Hogarth; Martin Harvey; Charles Wyndham; from Mary Talbot too ill to attend the funeral; from Mrs Brandon Thomas, whose daughter Amy had begun her professional career with Gilbert's help. At the Wealdstone Petty Sessions, Gilbert's colleagues passed a resolution of sympathy. The Theatrical Ladies' Guild sent theirs. Miss Fortescue was too ill to be told. In Switzerland, Sir Bruce Seton, a close friend since the 1870s, broke down completely on reading the news. The Mother Superior of Nazareth House wrote to say that the Sisters prayed daily for Sir William, 'a good Benefactor to our poor'. Over and over again, letters stressed Gilbert's kindness, children's love for him, and his hidden charities. During the first fortnight Nancy and Lucy wrote more than two hundred letters in addition to four hundred printed letters of thanks: 'alas! our eyes get so tired,' Nancy told Mary Talbot.[49]

The obituary notices in the press swung wildly from 'he had no subtlety, and not always as much taste as he might' to 'he had . . . a fastidious taste and an infinite capacity for taking pains';[50] from 'his criticism

---

[48] 3 June 1911: WSG/BL Add. MS 49,341.     [49] 28 June [1911]: Talbot Corr./PML.
[50] *Truth* (31 May 1911), 1387.

is often ungenial and negative and his irony stings and hurts'[51] to '[he set up] a mild but, on the whole, truthful criticism of life'.[52] Gilbert was compared to Molière on the one hand and to Shaw, Sudermann, and Ibsen on the other. 'His natural bias was towards the ethical criticism of life,' was the *Manchester Guardian*'s summary, while a dispatch in *The Times of India* (31 May) described his combination of humour and fancy as 'a kind of knavish sprightliness'.

The *Frankfurter Zeitung*, the *Berliner Lokal-Anzeiger*, and the *Journal des Débats* all carried articles, and the *Pall Mall Gazette* (30 May) suggested a festival of Gilbert's non-Sullivan works. All the old enemies were falling in line—even *Truth*, mellowed by Labouchère's retirement to Florence, said of Gilbert (7 June): 'He took a despised art, an art overshadowed and smothered by that of the composer, and he made it so great an art that he almost dominated the composer.' Gilbert was, wrote the *Daily Telegraph* on 30 May, 'the Bayard of latter-day writers for the stage, at once irreproachable and fearless'.

A month later, on the advice of Rowland Brown and Sir Frederick Macmillan, Lady Gilbert sold the publication rights of *The Hooligan* and 'Trying a Dramatist' to the *Century*, an illustrated American monthly, which featured the first play in November, the second in December.

On 9 August Gilbert's will was probated: its value amounted to £118,028. 2s. 0d., double that of Sullivan's. Almost everything was left to Lucy, including the Garrick Theatre, which at her death would go to Nancy, and after that to the Actors' Benevolent Fund. Relatives, both Weigalls and Turners, were remembered, as were friends, servants, and such charities as the Bushey Heath Cottage Hospital and the Royal General Theatrical Fund.

At the end of November Sir Squire Bancroft wrote to George Bernard Shaw, inviting him to take Gilbert's place on the Council of the Academy of Dramatic Art. Shaw immediately accepted.

Lucy put up a memorial to her husband in All Saints' Church, Harrow Weald, where she regularly attended services and where Nancy often sang. Under Gilbert's marble profile there is a quotation chosen by Rowland Brown, thinking perhaps of Gilbert as a magistrate: 'The tongue of the Just is as Choice Silver.' Now Lucy began her long widow-hood with Nancy as companion. She cut down staff, but she was good to her maids. Dignified and determined, she kept the library just as it was

---

[51] *Aberdeen Free Press* (3 June 1911).     [52] *The Nation* (2 June 1911).

when her husband died. She, too, liked fruit and insisted on having it sent when she went on holiday. 'Oh, those peaches again!' exclaimed her gardener. At first, flowers were taken to Gilbert's grave in Stanmore every Sunday; later, on the anniversaries of his birth and death; and finally an elderly Nancy visited it every three months. Rowland Brown said of Lucy that she was like a Daudet character—the widow of a great man.[53]

In 1912 the question of a London memorial to Gilbert began to be mooted, although final mounting had to wait until after the First World War. An imposing committee of writers, painters, actors, and actresses, assembled by Rowland Brown, commissioned George Frampton's bronze medallion, still in place on the Thames Embankment near the Savoy Hotel. Again there is Gilbert's bust in profile with Comedy and Tragedy beside him. Small emblematic figures from his librettos cluster in Comedy's sleeve, and her right hand holds the Mikado. Although Rowland Brown suggested a line from *Pygmalion and Galatea* as the accompanying legend, the words finally chosen were Anthony Hope Hawkins's, arranged as verse to summarize the mind and life of W. S. Gilbert:

> His foe was folly, and his weapon wit.

Not a bad exit line.

---

[53] Conversations with Mollie Sands, who, in childhood, knew Rowland Brown well. His sister Lilian (Rowland Grey) was afraid he might marry Lady Gilbert.

# SELECT BIBLIOGRAPHY

## WORKS BY W. S. GILBERT

### Bibliographies

ALLEN, REGINALD, *W. S. Gilbert: An Anniversary Survey and Exhibition Checklist* (Charlottesville, Va.: Bibliographical Society of the University of Virginia, 1963).

DILLARD, PHILIP H., *How Quaint the Ways of Paradox! An Annotated Gilbert & Sullivan Bibliography* (Metchuen, NJ: Scarecrow Press Inc., 1991).

DuBOIS, ARTHUR E., 'Additions to the Bibliography of W. S. Gilbert's Contributions to Magazines', *Modern Language Notes*, 47 (May 1932), 308–14.

JONES, JOHN BUSH, 'W. S. Gilbert's Contributions to *Fun*, 1865–1874', *Bulletin of the New York Public Library*, 73 (April 1969), 253–66.

SEARLE, TOWNLEY, *Sir William Schwenck Gilbert: A Topsy-turvy Adventure*, introd. R. E. Swartwout (London: Alexander-Ouseley Ltd., 1931).

### Collections

*Foggerty's Fairy and Other Tales* (London: George Routledge and Sons, 1890).

*Original Plays* (London: Chatto & Windus, 1876).

*Original Plays*, 1st series (London: Chatto & Windus, 1881).

*Original Plays*, 2nd series (London: Chatto & Windus, 1881).

*Original Plays*, 3rd series (London: Chatto & Windus, 1895).

*Original Plays*, 4th series (London: Chatto & Windus, 1911).

*The Savoy Operas* (London: Oxford University Press, 1962). 2 vols.

ALLEN, REGINALD (ed.), *The First Night Gilbert and Sullivan containing Complete Librettos of the Fourteen Operas, Exactly as presented at their Première Performances: Together with Facsimiles of the First-Night Programmes* (New York: Heritage Press, 1958).

*The 'Bab' Ballads: Much Sound and Little Sense* (London: John Camden Hotten, 1869).

BRADLEY, IAN (ed.), *The Annotated Gilbert and Sullivan* (Harmondsworth: Penguin Books Ltd., 1982), 2 vols.

ELLIS, JAMES (ed.), *The Bab Ballads* (Cambridge, Mass.: Harvard University Press, 1970).

GOLDBERG, ISAAC (ed.), *New and Original Extravaganzas by W. S. Gilbert, Esq.* (Boston: John W. Luce & Co., 1931).

HAINING, PETER (ed.), *The Lost Stories of W. S. Gilbert* (London: Robson Books Ltd., 1982). [NB One of these stories, 'The Poisoned Postage Stamp', is by Tom Hood, not by Gilbert.]

ROWELL, GEORGE (ed.), *Plays by W. S. Gilbert* (Cambridge: Cambridge University Press, 1982). [*The Palace of Truth, Sweethearts, Princess Toto, Engaged, Rosencrantz and Guildenstern*]

SEARLE, TOWNLEY (ed.), *The Lost Bab Ballads* (London: G. P. Putnam's Sons Ltd., 1932).

STEDMAN, JANE W. (ed.), *Gilbert before Sullivan: Six Comic Plays* (Chicago: University of Chicago Press, 1967; London: Routledge & Kegan Paul, 1969). [*No Cards, Ages Ago, Our Island Home, Happy Arcadia, A Sensation Novel, Eyes and No Eyes*]

—— 'Three New Gilbert Lyrics', *Bulletin of the New York Public Library*, 74 (December 1970), 629–33.

### Single Works

Works collected in any of the above are not included separately.

*An Algerian Monkey versus British Apes: A Satirical, Political, Poetical Squib* by 'The Spectre', with twenty-six illustrations by W. Schwenck Gilbert (London: Chapman & Hall, 1864).

'Allow Me to Explain'. Typescript made from the licence copy in BL.

'An Appeal to the Press', *Era Almanack and Annual* (1878), 85–6.

'The Astounding Adventure of Wheeler J. Calamity, related by himself', *Fun* (Christmas number 1865), 17–18.

'An Autobiography', *Theatre*, NS 1 (April 1883), 217–34.

'The Blue-Legged Lady', text in Jane W. Stedman, 'A New Absurdity from Tomline: W. S. Gilbert's "Dramatic Sell"', *Nineteenth Century Theatre Research*, 3 (spring 1975), 1–21.

*The Brigands: An Opera Bouffe in Three Acts*, music by Jacques Offenbach, English version by W. S. Gilbert (London: Boosey & Co., n.d.).

*The Brigands: An Opera Bouffe in Three Acts*, French Libretto by Meilhac and Halévy, English trans. W. S. Gilbert, rev. and adapted Arthur Charlton (London: Boosey & Co. Ltd., 1914).

*A Colossal Idea*, introd. Townley Searle (London: G. P. Putnam's Sons Ltd., 1932).

'Committed for Trial', typescript made from the licence copy in BL.

'Great Expectations', typescript made from the licence copy in BL.

*The Happy Land: A Burlesque Version of 'The Wicked World'*, with Gilbert à Beckett (London: J. W. Last & Co., 1873).

*Harlequin-Cock Robin and Jenny Wren; or, Fortunatus and the Water of Life, The Three Bears, The Three Gifts, The Three Wishes, and The Little Man Who Woo'd the Little Maid* (London: Music Publishing Co., 1867).

'Highly Improbable' An Original Impossibility, typescript made from the licence copy in BL.

'A Hornpipe in Fetters', *Era Almanack* (1879), 91–2.

*A Letter Addressed to the Members of the Dramatic Profession in Reply to Miss Henrietta Hodson's Pamphlet* (privately printed [1877]).

'A Medical Man', in *Drawing-Room Plays and Parlour Pantomimes*, collected by Clement Scott (London: Stanley Rivers & Co., 1870).

*The Mountebanks* (London: Chappell & Co., 1891); annotated: 'Lionel Brough's Copy. Signed, With Many Alterations and Elisions Including Several Lyrics Not Performed and which Probably Exist Only in this Copy.'

*My Case Against the Rev. J. Pullein Thompson* (printed privately, for the Information of the Charity Organization Society).

'My Pantomime', *Era Almanack* (1884), 77–9.

*The Ne'er-Do-Weel* (privately printed, n.d. [1878]).

*On Bail* (London: Samuel French, n.d.); a revision of 'Committed for Trial'.

*An Old Score* (London: T. H. Lacy, n.d. [1869]).

*On Guard* (London: Samuel French, n.d.).

'Ought We to Visit Her?' (London: Samuel French, n.d. [1874]); printed as MS.

*The Pinafore Picture Book* (London: George Bell & Sons, 1908).

'A Proposal for Elevating the Position of the Modern Drama', *Era Almanack* (1875).

'Quits!', Pre-production title of *An Old Score*; also later title.

*The Realm of Joy*, ed. with introd. by Terence Rees (London: privately printed, 1969).

*Robinson Crusoe* (London: *Fun* Office, 1867).

'Ruy Blas', *Warne's Christmas Annual* [1866], 50–6.

*A Stage Play*, ed. William Archer in *Papers on Playmaking*, 3rd ser. (New York: Dramatic Museum of Columbia University, 1913).

*The Story of the Mikado* (London: Daniel O'Connor, 1921).

*Thespis: A Gilbert & Sullivan Enigma* by Terence Rees, with reconstruction of the original text (London: Dillon's University Bookshop, 1964).

*Topsyturvydom* (Privately printed for Charles Plumptree Johnson. Oxford: Oxford University Press, 1931).

*Uncle Baby*, ed. with introd. by Terence Rees (privately printed, 1968).

*The Vagabond*; a revision of *The Ne'er-Do-Weel*.

*The Wedding March*. An Eccentricity (London: Samuel French, n.d.).

## OTHER WORKS

### A Note on Periodicals

I have worked my way issue by issue through the Victorian periodicals in the following list, beginning in the 1860s, or if they began later, taking them from their beginning until the 1890s or 1900 if they continued to publish till then. I have worked through the entire runs (thus far) of the twentieth-century periodicals.

*Academy, Athenaeum, Broadway, Dramatic Notes, Entr'acte, Era, Fun, Gilbert & Sullivan Journal, Graphic, Illustrated Times, Judy, Moonshine, Pall Mall Gazette, Punch, Savoyard, Theatre, Theatre Notebook, Tomahawk, Under the Clock,* and *W. S. Gilbert Society Journal.* I have consulted *The Times, Illustrated London News,* and others at relevant dates, and have read what is available of *Mrs Brown's Budget, The Hornet,* and comparable ephemera. I have also traced Gilbert's father through *Good Words, Good Words for the Young, Argosy,* etc.

### Books and Articles

À BECKETT, ARTHUR WILLIAM, *Green-Room Recollections* (Bristol: J. W. Arrowsmith, [1896]).

ALLEN, REGINALD, and D'LUHY, GALE, *Sir Arthur Sullivan: Composer & Personage* (New York: Pierpont Morgan Library, 1975).

ANDERSON, MARY, *A Few Memories* (London: Osgood, McIlvaine & Co., 1896).

ARCHER, WILLIAM, *English Dramatists of To-Day* (London: Sampson Low, Marston & Co., Ltd., 1882).

—— *The Old Drama and the New* (Boston: Small, Maynard & Co., 1923).

—— *Real Conversations* (London: William Heinemann, 1904).

—— *The Theatrical 'World' for 1893* (London: Walter Scott Ltd., [1894]).

—— *The Theatrical 'World' of 1894* (London: Walter Scott Ltd., 1895).

—— *The Theatrical 'World' of 1895* (London: Walter Scott, Ltd., 1896).

—— *The Theatrical 'World' of 1896* (London: Walter Scott Ltd., 1897).

BAILY, LESLIE, *The Gilbert and Sullivan Book* (revd edn., London: Spring Books, 1966).

BANCROFT, MR and MRS, *Mr. & Mrs. Bancroft On and Off the Stage: Written by Themselves* (3rd edn., London: Richard Bentley & Son, 1888), 2 vols.

BARHAM, RICHARD HARRIS, *The Ingoldsby Legends: or Mirth and Marvels,* ed. with introd. by D. C. Browning (London: J. M. Dent & Sons Ltd., 1960).

BARRETT, DANIEL, 'The Dramatic Authors' Society (1833–1883) and the Payment of English Dramatists', *Essays in Theatre,* 7 (Nov. 1988), 19–33.

BARRINGTON, RUTLAND, *Rutland Barrington by Himself,* pref. by W. S. Gilbert (London: Grant Richards, 1908).

BEERBOHM, MAX, *A Note on 'Patience'* (London, 1918, unpaginated pamphlet).

—— *Around Theatres* (New York: Simon & Schuster, 1954).

BLANCHARD, E. L., *The Life and Reminiscences of E. L. Blanchard, with Notes from the Diary of Wm. Blanchard*, ed. Clement Scott and Cecil Howard (London: Hutchinson & Co., 1891), 2 vols.

BLOW, SYDNEY, *Through Stage Doors* (Edinburgh: W. & R. Chambers Ltd., 1958).

BOAS, GUY, *The Garrick Club 1831–1947* (London: Garrick Club, 1948).

Bond, Jessie, *The Life and Reminiscences of Jessie Bond | The Old Savoyard | As Told by Herself to Ethel MacGeorge* (London: John Lane, 1930).

—— *et al.*, 'New Stories of Gilbert and Sullivan', *Strand Magazine*, 70 (Dec. 1925), 645–32.

BOOSEY, WILLIAM, *Fifty Years of Music* (London: Ernest Benn Ltd., 1931).

BROWNE, EDITH A., *W. S. Gilbert*, Stars of the Stage Series (London: John Lane, 1907).

BUCHANAN, ROBERT, *A Look Round Literature* (London: Ward & Downey, 1887).

BURNAND, SIR FRANCIS C., *Records and Reminiscences Personal and General* (London: Methuen & Co., 1904), 2 vols.

COOK, DUTTON, *Nights at the Play: A View of the English Stage* (London: Chatto & Windus, 1883), 2 vols.

CORYTON, JOHN, *Stageright: A Compendium of the Law Relating to Dramatic Authors, Musical Composers, and Lecturers As Regards the Public Representation of Their Works* (London: D. Nutt, 1873).

COX-IFE, WILLIAM, *How to Sing Both Gilbert and Sullivan* (London: Chappell & Co. Ltd., 1961).

CRANE, WALTER, *An Artist's Reminiscences* (New York: Macmillan Co., 1907).

DALY, JOSEPH FRANCIS, *The Life of Augustin Daly* (New York: Macmillan, 1917).

DARK, SIDNEY, and GREY, ROWLAND, *W. S. Gilbert: His Life and Letters* (London: Methuen & Co. Ltd., 1923).

DE BRÉMONT, ANNA, *Oscar Wilde and His Mother: A Memoir* (London: Everett & Co. Ltd., 1911).

DE LA PASTURE, MRS HENRY, *Peter's Mother: A Comedy in Three Acts* (London: Samuel French Ltd., n.d.).

ELLIS, TED. R. III, 'The Dramatist and the Comic Journal in England, 1830–1870', *Victorian Periodicals Review* 14 (1971), 29–31.

—— 'Burlesque Dramas in the Victorian Comic Magazines', *Victorian Periodicals Review* (winter 1982), 138–43.

FATOUT, PAUL, *Ambrose Bierce: The Devil's Lexicographer* (Norman: University of Oklahoma Press, 1951).

FILON, AUGUSTIN, *The English Stage: Being an Account of the Victorian Drama*, trans. Frederic Whyte, introd. Henry Arthur Jones (London: John Milne, 1897).

# Select Bibliography

FINDLATER, RICHARD, *Banned! A Review of Theatrical Censorship in Britain* (London: MacGibbon & Kee Ltd., 1967).

FITZGERALD, PERCY, *The Savoy Opera and the Savoyards* (1894; London: Chatto & Windus, 1899).

FORSYTH, GERALD, 'Wilhelm: A Noted Victorian Theatrical Designer', *Theatre Notebook*, 11 (Jan.–Mar. 1957), 55–8.

FURNISS, HARRY, *Some Victorian Women: Good, Bad, and Indifferent* (London: John Lane, 1923).

GIELGUD, KATE TERRY, *Kate Terry Gielgud: An Autobiography*, foreword by Sir John Gielgud (London: Max Reinhardt, 1953).

GILBERT, WILLIAM, *Shirley Hall Asylum; or, The Memoirs of a Monomaniac* (London: William Freeman, 1863).

GOLDBERG, ISAAC, *The Story of Gilbert and Sullivan or the 'Compleat' Savoyard* (rev. edn., New York: Crown Publishers, 1935).

GONCOURT, EDMOND, *Paris under Siege, 1870–1871: From the Goncourt Journal*, ed. and transl. George J. Becker (Ithaca, NY: Cornell University Press, 1969).

GOODMAN, ANDREW, *Gilbert and Sullivan's London* (Tunbridge Wells: Spellmount Ltd., 1988).

GROSSMITH, GEORGE, 'Recollections of Sir W. S. Gilbert', *Bookman*, 40 (July 1911), 162–5.

—— *A Society Clown: Reminiscences* (Bristol: J. W. Arrowsmith, 1888).

HALL, ROBERT A. Jun., 'The Satire of *The Yeomen of the Guard*', *Modern Language Notes*, 73 (Nov. 1958), 292–7.

HARKER, JOSEPH, *Studio and Stage* (London: Nisbet & Co. Ltd., 1924).

HAY, CECIL, *The Club and the Drawing-Room: Being Pictures of Modern Life: Social, Political, and Professional* (London: Robert Hardwicke, 1870), 2 vols.

HELYAR, JAMES (ed.), *Gilbert and Sullivan: Papers Presented at the International Conference Held at the University of Kansas in May 1970* (Lawrence, Kan.: University of Kansas Publications, Library Series, 37; 1971).

HICKS, SEYMOUR, *Me and My Missus: Fifty Years on the Stage* (London: Cassell & Co. Ltd., 1939).

HINDLE, E. B., 'W. S. Gilbert, Playwright and Humorist', *Manchester Quarterly: A Journal of Literature and Art*, 4 (Jan. 1885), 55–85.

HODSON, HENRIETTA, *A Letter from Miss Henrietta Hodson, An Actress, to the Members of the Dramatic Profession, Being a Relation of the Persecutions which She has Suffered from Mr. William Schwenck Gilbert, A Dramatic Author* (privately printed).

HOLLINGSHEAD, JOHN, *My Lifetime* (London: Sampson Low, Marston & Co. Ltd., 1895), 2 vols.

—— *'Good Old Gaiety'* (London: Gaiety Theatre Co. Ltd., 1903).

How, Harry, *Illustrated Interviews* (London: George Newnes, Ltd, 1893).

Irving, H. B. (ed.), *Trial of the Wainwrights* (Edinburgh: William Hodge & Co. Ltd., 1920; Notable English Trials Series).

Irving, Laurence, *Henry Irving: The Actor and his World* (New York: Macmillan, 1952).

Jacobs, Arthur, *Arthur Sullivan: A Victorian Musician* (Oxford: Oxford University Press, 1984).

James, Philip, 'A Note on Gilbert as Illustrator', in *Selected Bab Ballads Written and Illustrated by W. S. Gilbert, introd. Hesketh Pearson* (privately printed; Oxford: Oxford University Press, 1955).

Jay, Harriet, *Robert Buchanan: Some Account of his Life, his Life's Work and his Literary Friendships* (London: T. Fisher Unwin, 1903).

Jones, John Bush, *W. S. Gilbert: A Century of Scholarship and Commentary* (New York: New York University Press, 1970).

Joseph, Tony, *George Grossmith: Biography of a Savoyard* (Bristol: published by the author, 1982).

Juxon, John, *Lewis and Lewis: The Life and Times of a Victorian Solicitor* (London: Collins, 1983).

Kendal, Madge, *Dame Madge Kendal by Herself* (London: John Murray, 1933).

Knight, Joseph, *The Stage in the Year 1900: A Souvenir being a Collection of Photogravure Plates Portraying the Leading Players and Playwrights of the Day and a History of the Stage during the Victorian Era* (London: Spottiswoode & Co. Ltd., 1901).

—— *Theatrical Notes* (London: Lawrence & Bullen, 1893).

Lauterbach, Charles E., 'Taking Gilbert's Measure', *Huntington Library Quarterly*, 19 (Feb. 1956), 207–15.

Lauterbach, Edward S., *'Fun and its Contributors: The Literary History of a Victorian Humor Magazine'*, Ph.D. diss., Urbana, Ill.: Univ. of Illinois, 1961.

Lawrence, Elwood P., ' "The Happy Land": W. S. Gilbert as Political Satirist', *Victorian Studies*, 15 (Dec. 1971), 164–72.

Layard, George Somes, *A Great 'Punch' Editor: Being the Life, Letters and Diaries of Shirley Brooks* (London: Sir Isaac Pitman & Sons, Ltd., 1907).

McElroy, George C., 'Whose *Zoo*; or, When Did the *Trial* Begin?' *Nineteenth-Century Theatre Research*, 12 (Dec. 1984), 40–54.

McIntosh, Nancy, 'Sir William Gilbert's Lemurs by a Member of the Household', *Strand Magazine*, 38 (Nov. 1909), 604–9.

[Mackay, William], *Bohemian Days in Fleet Street by a Journalist* (London: John Long Ltd., 1913).

McMullen, Roy, *Victorian Outsider: A Biography of J. A. M. Whistler* (New York: E. P. Dutton & Co. Inc., 1973).

Martin-Harvey, Sir John, *The Autobiography of Sir John Martin-Harvey* (London: Sampson Low, Marston & Co. Ltd., n.d.).

MAUDE, CYRIL, *Behind the Scenes with Cyril Maude by Himself* (London: John Murray, 1927).

MAYO, ISABELLA FYVIE, *Recollections of Fifty Years* (London: John Murray, 1910).

MIDWINTER, ERIC, 'W. S. Gilbert: Victorian Entertainer', *New Theatre Quarterly*, 11 (Aug. 1987), 237–9.

MURRAY, GILBERT, *Gilbert Murray: An Unfinished Autobiography*, with contributions by his friends, ed. Jean Smith and Arnold Toynbee (London: George Allen & Unwin Ltd., 1960).

NATHAN, ARCHIE, *Costumes by Nathan* (London: Newnes, 1960).

NEILSON, JULIA, *This for Remembrance* (London: Hurst & Blackett, 1941).

PALMER, JOHN, *The Censor and the Theatres* (New York: Mitchell Kennerley, 1913).

PEARSON, HESKETH, *Gilbert: His Life and Strife* (London: Methuen & Co. Ltd., 1957).

PEMBERTON, T. EDGAR, *John Hare Comedian 1865–1895* (London: George Routledge and Sons Ltd., 1895).

—— *The Kendals: A Biography* (London: C. Arthur Pearson Ltd., 1900).

—— *Sir Charles Wyndham* (London: Hutchinson and Co., 1904).

—— *A Memoir of Edward Askew Sothern* (London: Richard Bentley & Son, 1889).

PHYSICK, JOHN, and DARBY, MICHAEL, *'Marble Halls': Drawings and Models for Victorian Secular Buildings* (London: Victoria & Albert Museum, 1973).

PINERO, SIR ARTHUR, *The Collected Letters of Sir Arthur Pinero*, ed. J. P. Wearing (Minneapolis: University of Minnesota Press).

PLANCHÉ, JAMES ROBINSON, *The Extravaganzas of J. R. Planché, Esq., (Somerset Herald) 1825–1871*, ed. T. F. Croker and Stephen Tucker (testimonial edn. London: Samuel French, 1879), 5 vols.

—— *The Recollections and Reflections of J. R. Planché, A Professional Autobiography* (London: Tinsley Brothers, 1872), 2 vols.

PRICE, R. G., *A History of Punch* (London: Collins, 1957).

REYNOLDS, A. M., *The Life and Work of Frank Holl* (London: Methuen & Co. Ltd., 1912).

REES, TERENCE, *Theatre Lighting in the Age of Gas* (London: Society for Theatre Research, 1978).

RIGHTON, EDWARD, 'A Suppressed Burlesque—*The Happy Land'. Theatre*, 28 (1 Aug. 1896), 63–6.

ROLLINS, CYRIL, and WITTS, JOHN, *The D'Oyly Carte Company in Gilbert and Sullivan Operas: A Record of Productions 1875–1961* (London: Michael Joseph, 1962).

*The Romance of a Famous London Theatre: The Old Savoy Theatre and the New* (London: Curwen Press, n.d.).

ST JOHN-BRENON, EDWARD, 'Mr W. S. Gilbert's Original Comedy, "Pygmalion and Galatea"', *Grand Magazine*, 1 (Apr. 1905), 484–91.

—— 'Mr W. S. Gilbert's Original Plays', *Grand Magazine* 1 (Mar. 1905), 309–16.

SCOTT, MRS CLEMENT [MARGARET], *Old Days in Bohemian London* (London: Hutchinson & Co., n.d.).

SCOTT, WILLIAM HERBERT, *Edward German: An Intimate Biography* (London: Cecil Palmer, 1932).

SEELEY, PAUL, 'The Japanese March in "The Mikado"'. *Musical Times* (Aug. 1985), 455–6.

SHAW, GEORGE BERNARD, *Music in London 1890–1894* (London: Constable & Co. Ltd., 1932), 3 vols.

SMITH, GEORGE MURRAY, 'The Recollections of a Long and Busy Life', typescript in NLS, 2 vols.

STEDMAN, JANE W. 'Come, Substantial Damages!', in Kristine Otteson Garrigan (ed.), *Victorian Scandals* (Athens, Oh.: Ohio University Press, 1992).

—— 'From Dame to Woman: W. S. Gilbert and Theatrical Transvestism', in Martha Vicinus (ed.), *Suffer and Be Still: Women in the Victorian Age* (Bloomington, Ind.: Indiana University Press, 1972).

—— 'General Utility: Victorian Author-Actors from Knowles to Pinero', *Educational Theatre Journal*, 24 (Oct. 1972), 289–301.

STEPHENS, JOHN RUSSELL, *The Censorship of English Drama 1824–1901* (Cambridge: Cambridge University Press, 1980).

—— *The Profession of the Playwright: British Theatre 1800–1900* (Cambridge: Cambridge University Press, 1992).

SUTRO, ALFRED, *Celebrities and Simple Souls* (London: Duckworth, 1933).

SWINBURNE, ALGERNON CHARLES, *The Swinburne Letters*, ed. Cecil Y. Lang (New Haven: Yale University Press, 1959–62), 6 vols.

TERRISS, ELLALINE, *Just a Little Bit of String* (London: Hutchinson & Co. Ltd., 1955).

THORNE, GEORGE, *Jots* (Bristol: J. W. Arrowsmith, [1884]).

TINSLEY, WILLIAM, *Random Recollections of an Old Publisher* (London: Simpkin, Marshall, Hamilton, Kent & Co. Ltd., 1900).

TREWIN, J. C., 'Gilbert and Sullivan Then and Now', *Far and Wide* (Sept. 1949), 30–5; includes costume sketch of Mad Margaret.

TWEEDIE, MRS ALEC, *Me and Mine* (London: Hutchinson & Co. Ltd., 1932).

—— *My Table-Cloths: A Few Reminiscences* (London: Hutchinson & Co., 1916).

'Two Victorian Humorists: Burnand and the Mask of Gilbert', *Times Literary Supplement* (21 Nov. 1936), 936.

VALENTINE, E. S., 'Sir W. S. Gilbert as an Artist; Illustrated by Early Sketches of Character and from Originals in the Artist's Possession', *Strand Magazine*, 37 (Feb. 1909), 139–44.

WATSON, ALFRED E. T., *A Sporting and Dramatic Career* (London: Macmillan & Co. Ltd., 1918).

WEARING, J. P., *American and British Theatrical Biography* (Metuchen, NJ: The Scarecrow Press Inc., 1979).

WEST, FRANCIS, *Gilbert Murray: A Life* (London: Croom Helm, 1984).

WILSON, DUNCAN, *Gilbert Murray OM 1866–1957* (Oxford: Clarendon Press, 1987).

WILSON, GWENDOLINE, *Murray of Yarralumla* (Melbourne: Oxford University Press, 1968).

WINTER, WILLIAM, *The Stage Life of Mary Anderson* (New York: George J. Coombes, 1886).

WOLFSON, JOHN, *Final Curtain: The Last Gilbert and Sullivan Operas.* (London: Chappell & Co. Ltd., 1976); includes hitherto unpublished rehearsal copies.

YOUNG, EDITH, 'Song Writers Dear to Girls', *Girl's Realm* (Dec. 1900), 123–31.

# INDEX

Titles in *italics* indicate works that have been produced on stage; titles in quotation
marks denote works that have not been either published or performed

361

# Index

# Index

# Index

# Index

# Index

# Index

# Index

# Index

# Index

374